Curriculum Models and Early Childhood Education
Appraising the Relationship

Second Edition

Stacie G. Goffin
National Association for the Education of Young Children

Catherine Wilson
Park University

Merrill
Prentice Hall

Upper Saddle River, New Jersey
Columbus, Ohio

Library of Congress Cataloging in Publication Data

Goffin, Stacie G.
   Curriculum models and early childhood education: appraising the relationship / Stacie
G. Goffin, Catherine Wilson.—2nd ed.
      p. cm.
   Includes bibliographical references and index.
   ISBN 0-13-087821-9
      1. Early childhood education—United States—Curricula. 2. Curriculum
   planning—United States. I. Wilson, Catherine (Catherine S.) II. Title.
   LB 1139.4 .G64 2001
   372.19'0973—dc21

                                                                              00-037353

Vice President and Publisher: Jeffery W. Johnston
Executive Editor: Ann Castel Davis
Editorial Assistant: Pat Grogg
Production Editor: Sheryl Glicker Langner
Production Management: Cindy Miller, Clarinda Publication Services
Design Coordinator: Diane C. Lorenzo
Photo Coordinator: Nancy Harre Ritz
Cover Designer: Rod Harris
Cover art: Stephen Schildbach
Production Manager: Laura Messerly
Director of Marketing: Kevin Flanagan.
Marketing Manager: Amy June
Marketing Services Manager: Krista Groshong

This book was set in Palatino by The Clarinda Company. It was printed and bound by R. R. Donnelley & Sons
Company. The cover was printed by Phoenix Color Corp.

Photo Credits: pp. 10, 36, 96, 170, 220 by Scott Cunningham/Merrill; p. 64 by Todd Yarrington/Merrill; p. 126 by
Anne Vega/Merrill; p. 194 by Ken Karp/PH College.

The opinions expressed in this book are the authors and should not be attributed to their institutional affiliations.
The first author worked at the Ewing Marion Kauffman Foundation while writing the second edition. She joined
the National Association for the Education of Young Children in April 2000.

10 9 8 7 6 5 4 3
ISBN: 0-13-087821-9

To those in the field who grapple with these issues on a daily basis

Discover the Companion Website Accompanying This Book

The Prentice Hall Companion Website: A Virtual Learning Environment

Technology is a constantly growing and changing aspect of our field that is creating a need for content and resources. To address this emerging need, Prentice Hall has developed an online learning environment for students and professors alike—Companion Websites—to support our textbooks.

In creating a Companion Website, our goal is to build on and enhance what the textbook already offers. For this reason, the content for each user-friendly website is organized by topic and provides the professor and student with a variety of meaningful resources. Common features of a Companion Website include:

For the Professor—

Every Companion Website integrates **Syllabus Manager**™, an online syllabus creation and management utility.

- **Syllabus Manager**™ provides you, the instructor, with an easy, step-by-step process to create and revise syllabi, with direct links into Companion Website and other online content without having to learn HTML.
- Students may logon to your syllabus during any study session. All they need to know is the web address for the Companion Website and the password you've assigned to your syllabus.
- After you have created a syllabus using **Syllabus Manager**™, students may enter the syllabus for their course section from any point in the Companion Website.
- Class dates are highlighted in white and assignment due dates appear in blue. Clicking on a date, the student is shown the list of activities for the assignment. The activities for each assignment are linked directly to actual content, saving time for students.
- Adding assignments consists of clicking on the desired due date, then filling in the details of the assignment—name of the assignment, instructions, and whether or not it is a one-time or repeating assignment.
- In addition, links to other activities can be created easily. If the activity is online, a URL can be entered in the space provided, and it will be linked automatically in the final syllabus.
- Your completed syllabus is hosted on our servers, allowing convenient updates from any computer on the Internet. Changes you make to your syllabus are immediately available to your students at their next logon.

For the Student—

- **Topic Overviews** – outline key concepts in topic areas
- **Electronic Blue Book** – send homework or essays directly to your instructor's email with this paperless form
- **Message Board** – serves as a virtual bulletin board to post-or respond to-questions or comments to/from a national audience
- **Web Destinations** – links to www sites that relate to each topic area
- **Professional Organizations** – links to organizations that relate to topic areas
- **Additional Resources** – access to topic-specific content that enhances material found in the text

To take advantage of these and other resources, please visit the *Curriculum Models and Early Childhood Education* Companion Website at

www.prenhall.com/goffin

Contents

Part III   **An Examination of the Underpinnings of Curriculum Models in Early Childhood Education,   169**

Chapter 6   In Pursuit of Answers: Comparative Evaluations of Early Childhood Curriculum Models,   171

Chapter 7   Identifying the Source of Early Childhood Curriculum,   195

Chapter 8   Curriculum Models and Early Childhood Education: A Quandary,   221

Part I

Early Childhood Curriculum Models in Context

*P*art I is comprised of a prologue and the book's first chapter. The prologue presents a personal context for the investigation of enduring early childhood curriculum models. It describes the interpretative framework that shaped the first edition's overarching questions and presents an overview of the book's organization and content. The first chapter provides a historical context and explores the circumstances that have supported the systematic promotion and development of curriculum models, first in the 1960s and then again in the 1990s.

Setting the Stage

✐ A VERY PERSONAL INTRODUCTION

When I (Stacie Goffin, author of the book's first edition) first proposed writing this book in 1991, I wanted to create a textbook for my graduate course on early childhood curriculum models. I had taught this course at least once a year for almost a decade, but had been struggling for several years to find an up-to-date text. Frankly, I kept waiting for Ellis Evans to write an updated, third edition of his classic text *Contemporary Influences in Early Childhood Education* (1975). When that expectation never materialized, I confidently proposed to write the needed text myself! I realize what follows risks exposing my intellectual naivete; yet sharing some of the pathways I traveled during the 3 years of my journey toward the book's completion in its first iteration provides insight into the struggles that shaped the book and defined its objectives.

My original intention was to write the survey text Evans had not. The second edition of Evans's text provided not only a comprehensive overview of prominent curriculum models but also situated their descriptions within the theoretical context (usually developmental theory) that supplied a conceptual basis for the model. His chapter describing behaviorally based programs, for example, first explained behavioral theory and then described several curriculum models derived from the same theoretical foundation.

Evans's presentation of various theoretical contexts enabled readers to appreciate how early childhood curriculum models have been constructed from diverse conceptual frameworks. His approach also highlighted how architects of models selected different aspects of the same theory as the focal point of their program design. The text prospectus for the book's first edition promised a similar format.

I was accepting, of course, the idea that curriculum models provided a sound framework for organizing teaching and curriculum in early childhood education. But, even then, I already was conscious that developmental theories provided a shaky knowledge base for curriculum development because their meaning for curriculum design was open to multiple interpretations. But, when students kept prodding for the source of educational goals for early childhood curricula derived from behavioral theory (and not for other theoretical foundations), I also became cognizant of the fact that, despite the supposed objectivity of theoretical descriptions of children's development, desired end points for their growth were implicit within each theory. With this new insight, I began to think more critically about the various sources of early childhood curricula.

At this point, however, I simply considered this attribute of developmental theory to be an imperfection problematic to model building. Nor was this characteristic yet a potential challenge to curriculum models as a framework for curriculum development. In fact, I incorporated these theoretical variations as a critical component of my curriculum models course. Following a fairly factual description of models that had emerged from a particular theory, students and I would analyze and compare models in terms of the various interpretations they had made of their shared theoretical base.

Curriculum models are idealized descriptions of programs that can be copied or emulated in practice across settings (Spodek, 1973). As a referent, models are frameworks for decision making about educational priorities, administrative policies, curriculum content, instructional methods, and evaluation. Through classroom discussions that scrutinized models in terms of these purposes, I found myself becoming increasingly dissatisfied with existing curriculum models. (In other words, no model quite addressed all the educational priorities that mattered to me or did so as I would have!) And then, the curricular content of models began to appear dated, either because it failed to address educational and/or developmental concerns that had arisen since its initial construction or because it described developmental events in ways that differed from prevailing understandings or failed to describe them at all. Although these dissatisfactions also were classified under the heading of imperfections, they prodded me more deeply into study and reflection. By this time, however, I was beginning to question more than the ability of curriculum models to incorporate current content. I was finding it difficult to classify my concerns as interesting ambiguities; they were becoming more troublesome, and, in the process, so was the idea of curriculum models.

What finally undermined my trusting acceptance of curriculum models was a mounting disgruntlement with the role of developmental theory, rather than educational purpose, as a primary determinant of what was educationally worthwhile. At this point in my intellectual evolution, I was questioning not only the content of curriculum models but also their structural limitations.

My response was to propose an enlarged conceptualization for models, one that I hoped would rectify these limitations. I created a programmatic distinction between curriculum models and program models. In contrast to curriculum models, program models had multiple informants. Curriculum decisions were determined by purpose (versus developmental theory) and informed by understandings of child development, family dynamics, and the impact of different environmental circumstances. I thought the focus on program purpose, such as early intervention or family support, versus a specific theoretical framework, such as Piagetian theory, also would provide program models the flexibility to incorporate new knowledge. For a short while, this more encompassing configuration of models quelled my discontent.

Ultimately, however, my concept of a program model was too general to be useful. Probably more significant to my intellectual evolution, however, was an ever-increasing puzzlement regarding the purpose of curriculum models. As I continued to delve deeper and deeper into this investigation, the very idea of curriculum models became enigmatic; by now, my questioning extended beyond the source and currency of their content. I had begun to ponder their purpose and function within early childhood education. This question eventually became a constant companion habit. Ultimately, it shaped my examination of individual curriculum models and my contemplation of curriculum models as a theoretical construct.

My interest in understanding the purpose and function of curriculum models, in general, and their impact on early childhood education in particular, expanded my initial intention for this book. In addition to being a contemporary examination of prominent early childhood curriculum models, it also became an investigation of the role of early childhood curriculum models within the context of current, as well as historical, issues and concerns. This investigation revealed the extent to which, as a theoretical construct, curriculum models have influenced the early childhood profession, and the extent to which their influence might yet be felt.

ᑯ PROBING THE IDEA OF CURRICULUM MODELS: WHY NOW?

Whereas my questions regarding the purpose, function, and impact of early childhood curriculum models could accompany me throughout the process of writing this book, the question of their relevance could not. After all, my initial intention in writing the book had been to provide a contemporary discussion and comparison of curriculum models. Once their usefulness came into question, however, I was plagued by self-doubts. Why bother to spend endless hours researching and describing various early childhood curriculum models if I was uncertain about their merit? Without an answer to this question, my commitment and enthusiasm to the arduous task of writing a textbook repeatedly waxed and waned.

But my reading and thinking about the questions I was raising for myself did not cease, and eventually, I came to better understand my concerns. I finally was able to resolve my struggle by thinking *beyond* curriculum models and considering these questions in terms of their relevance to issues of curriculum development and professionalism that confront early childhood education. The irony of my intellectual saga is that this text resumed its professional importance when I finally began to understand that these questions, in and of themselves, were of importance.

When I finally disentangled these concerns, I recognized more clearly that I had been struggling with questions revolving around *how* early childhood curriculum is determined and by *whom.* I had journeyed from dissatisfaction with the content of early childhood curriculum models to deliberating their structure and finally to recognizing that both of these concerns were part of a larger question regarding the purpose and function of curriculum models. It was when I recognized my questions as meaningful beyond curriculum models *per se* that the puzzle pieces in my thoughts began to interlock.

◌ AN OUTLINE OF WHAT FOLLOWS

Schubert (1986) defined a synoptic curriculum text as one that summarizes the state of the art of curriculum studies for the purpose of reflection on issues, problems, ideas, and procedures. He noted that any text that brings knowledge together from diverse sources provides interpretations that lean in one direction or the other and thus provides new ways of viewing the curriculum field. "Every book is an interpretation. . . . As authors study a topic or phenomenon, they interact with it; their writing about it portrays both themselves and the phenomenon under study" (p. 3).

Following Schubert's definition, this book can be considered a synoptic text of curriculum models in early childhood education. This very personal introduction, which served as Chapter 1 in the book's first edition, is an open acknowledgment of the interpretative framework that informed development of the first edition and also frames this second edition. Its inquiry into the purpose, function, and impact of curriculum models within early childhood education distinguishes this book from other synoptic texts. This text does not focus on presenting an extensive array of curriculum models for informational purposes (see Roopnarine & Johnson, 1999), nor does it attempt to evaluate one model against another (see Day, 1977; DeVries & Kohlberg, 1987; Mayer, 1971 for comparative analyses). Further, the chapters are not structured for the purpose of translation into practice.

The focus of this inquiry has been different and, to our knowledge, remains unique. In addition to a comprehensive, historically situated examination of a prominent set of curriculum models, this text ponders the purpose and function of curriculum models in early childhood education. It accomplishes this objective by investigating the life course of each model, in the process contemplating their impact, individually and collectively, on early childhood education.

Curriculum Models and Early Childhood Education: Appraising the Relationship is organized into three parts. Each chapter concludes with Further Reading recommendations. A textbook can hope only to highlight selected ideas and issues. The possibilities suggested for additional reading are presented to encourage readers to study and discuss issues in more depth.

This part's first chapter places early childhood curriculum models in a historical context. It examines the circumstances that supported the promotion and development of curriculum models in the 1960s and again in the 1990s. It also identifies the changed circumstances that provide a different context for their continued development and implementation.

Knowledge of this context is of more than historical interest. Both past and present support for curriculum models in early childhood education stems from societal expectations for early childhood education, expectations that surface from the intersection of particular historical events. Chapter 1 shares important information for understanding the conditions that have nurtured the growth and development of curriculum models in early childhood education.

Part II, which includes Chapters 2 through 5, examines enduring curriculum models: the Montessori method (Chapter 2), the Developmental-Interaction approach (Chapter 3); and models derived from behavioral (the Direct Instruction model; Chapter 4) and Piagetian theory (the Kamii-DeVries approach and High/Scope Curriculum model; Chapter 5). These have been identified as enduring models because they have, in fact, endured into the present. Clearly, many other curriculum models could have been selected, but these five models are well known within the early childhood profession; have remained popular choices for those who "shop" for curriculum models; are accompanied by an extensive literature describing their educational objectives, content and structure, and assessment procedures; and continue to be targets of longitudinal research. In addition, they provide contrasting examples of conceptual frameworks for interpreting the character of learning and development during early childhood. Further, these curriculum models have endured long enough to have histories of their own. Thus, they are particularly informative examples for an exploration of the purpose, function, and impact of curriculum models within early childhood education.

Each of these five curriculum models initially was developed for preschoolers (3- and 4- and often 5-year-olds) in out-of-home settings. With the advent of Project Follow Through, several of the curriculum models were restructured to extend into the primary grades (see Chapter 1). Others, specifically the Montessori method and the Developmental-Interaction approach, already had curricula extending into the primary grades. Each of these five curriculum models now encompasses curriculum for children preschool through third grade. Although infant and toddler programs fit into the professional definition of early childhood education, curriculum models specific to this age group are not part of this exploration. This decision was made because infant and toddler programs necessitate investigation of very different developmental and educational issues (Bredekamp, 1987; Lally, Mangione, Honig, & Wittner, 1988; National Association for the Education of Young Children & National Association of Early Childhood Specialists in State Departments of Education, 1991).

Because, by definition, curriculum models are conceptual frameworks, discussion and comparison rely on written materials that detail their assumptions and premises. To be as fair and accurate as possible, only books and articles written by the primary architects are used in describing individual models. For the same reasons, as well as to better convey the flavor of individual curriculum models, the text relies heavily on the use of quotes. Curriculum analysis, however, draws on multiple perspectives, including my own and those of Catherine Wilson, who joins me in authoring this second edition.

Throughout the second part, curriculum models are interpreted as creating unique learning environments or cultures for learning. Descriptions and discussion consider not only the learning objectives of various models, but also the nature of a model in terms of socializing children to understand themselves, their environment, and others in their world. It is assumed that teachers are being socialized, as well, to understand children and their growth and the teaching profession in particular ways.

Presentation and discussion of each model is embedded within its particular social and historical context. This frame of reference highlights the extent to which each curriculum model is a product of its time, a finding accentuated by the fact that the extent to which a particular model is accepted, lionized, and/or rejected largely has been determined by its alignment with larger societal issues.

The historical factor also informed the sequence in which the curriculum models are presented. The Montessori method, described in Chapter 2, is the oldest enduring curriculum model, whereas the models derived from behavioral and Piagetian theory are among the newest. Readers are encouraged to read the chapters in the order presented. The chapters' sequence highlights the history of curriculum models in early childhood education, enables readers to better appreciate interactions among proponents, and fosters understanding of the purpose, function, and impact of curriculum models within early childhood education. Each chapter, as it examines the life course of an individual curriculum model, brings further clarification to this overarching interest. As one reviewer concluded, "Each of these chapters—and the models discussed in each one—are really stories of how the field gets pushed along at various stages, and the book as a whole is a story of how we ended up where we are today."

The book's last part moves beyond examination of individual models to investigate curriculum models in early childhood education from the perspectives of program evaluation and curriculum development. Specifically, Chapter 6 reviews findings from comparative evaluations of early childhood curriculum models and the effect these findings have had on the perpetuation of curriculum models and public polices related to early childhood education. The discussion in this chapter highlights issues that have been of particular interest to researchers, educational decision makers, and policy makers regarding early childhood programs. It also raises questions regarding the capacity of curriculum models to be responsive to differences in children, teachers, and program sites.

Chapter 7 reviews, with broad strokes, significant shifts in thinking that have occurred within child development theory and research since the mid-1960s. Research on and deliberations about teacher effects, which have experienced a similar upheaval, also are examined. This latter body of research is pertinent to this discussion because it challenges conventional thinking about the role of teachers in relation to curriculum development and implementation. In particular, it challenges the notion of teachers as curricular technicians, as practitioners who primarily are expected to implement the knowledge of others. New understandings about child development, reassessment regarding the relationship between child development knowledge and early childhood curriculum, and research on teaching are considered in terms of the challenges they elicit for early childhood curriculum models as educational tools.

The overarching question of this book "What is the purpose, function, and impact of curriculum models in early childhood education?" is addressed directly in Chapter 8. Understandings that emerged from investigating individual curriculum models and contemporary thinking in program evaluation, developmental psychology, and research on teaching are considered in light of current expectations for early childhood education.

Chapter 9 extends this conversation through an examination of the Reggio Emilia approach. Based in Reggio Emilia, Italy, this approach to early childhood education—which burst on the U.S. scene after publication of this text's first edition—exemplifies an approach to teaching and learning that is steadfastly dynamic and emergent. It portrays an alternative conceptualization to teachers as curricular technicians. The approach also is embedded in an alternative conceptualization of children and the purpose for their early education. As a result, it illuminates in striking ways the issues raised throughout the text regarding the purpose, function, and impact of early childhood curriculum models.

This book should not be misconstrued, however, as providing a definitive answer to the question of the usefulness or appropriateness of early childhood curriculum models, not only because such an answer would be premature, but also because such a conclusion would be contrary to the book's intent. Curriculum models have potential for instigating both positive and negative consequences for children as well as the early childhood profession. And, as we hope readers will anticipate, this ambiguity derives from contemporary characteristics of early childhood education and their intersection with current societal concerns and expectations.

This book was written for graduate students, teachers and teacher educators, and instructional leaders and administrators. It is especially relevant for readers who are interested in analyzing early childhood curriculum and in contemplating the educational and professional implications of bounding curriculum and pedagogy within the confines of a curriculum model.

Writing this book provoked us to think very deeply about issues of early childhood curriculum and practice. We hope our journey provides stimulus for thoughtful and provocative discussion by others.

Curriculum Models and Early Childhood Education
A Historical Framework

*A*ttention to early childhood education has been growing in intensity since the mid-1980s. While stretched over a more extended period of time, this attention recalls the explosion of interest during the 1960s that launched Head Start, a national program for disadvantaged preschoolers. Once again, expansion of early childhood education is being driven by social, political, and economic circumstances and by faith in the capacity of early childhood education to effect dramatic change. Once again, early childhood education is being promoted as a solution for many of society's social and economic problems. And, once again, there is interest in finding—and defining—the most effective early childhood programs for achieving these ends.

In explaining the onset of interest in early childhood curricular issues in the mid-1980s, Powell (1987a) identified three contributors: (a) questions being raised about the education of 4-year-olds in public schools, (b) the successful efforts of national professional associations in promoting appropriate educational practices for young children, and (c) the results of longitudinal research that challenged earlier conclusions that differences among curriculum models were nonexistent. According to Powell, "The question of *which curriculum* to use in educating young children has regained its prominence in public and professional interest in early schooling" (p. 192, emphasis added). Although interest ebbed in the late 1980s, momentum has been sustained by at least four factors:

1. the galvanizing power of Goals 2000 and its first education goal that all children will enter school ready to learn,
2. heightened concern with the low academic achievement of children from low-income families,
3. the response of state policy makers to findings from neuroscience on early brain development, and
4. widespread evidence documenting the overall low quality of center-based and family child care.

✍ EARLY CHILDHOOD PROGRAMS AND PUBLIC POLICY

The coupling of social and political concerns with interest in early childhood education, in the 1960s and again in the 1990s, reveals a vital connection between public policy and early childhood issues. Connections between social and political concerns and children's issues have existed throughout the history of governmental policies benefiting children (Pizzo, 1983). But analysis of this relationship has increased significantly since introduction in the mid-1960s of "The Great Society," a time during which the federal government initiated a series of policies designed to help eradicate poverty and social inequality (see, for example, Grubb & Lazerson, 1988; Steiner, 1981; Zigler, Kagan, & Klugman, 1983).

Policies made by the federal government, in state capitals, and in city halls may seem far removed from the lives of children and early childhood educators. The issues decision makers address, however, are the problems children and early educators are living, and the solutions they devise become the programs and practices early educators are asked to implement (Goffin & Lombardi, 1988).

Public policies are government-proposed solutions to societal concerns. They help define the social and economic circumstances that organize for parents, early childhood educators, and others a range of choices that can be selected on behalf of children. Hence, public policies are part of the cultural context influencing children's development (Bronfenbrenner & Weiss, 1983).

Low-income parents' options for their children's early education, for example, are expanded because of the existence of Head Start, a federally supported early education program for disadvantaged preschoolers. Yet, access to Head Start is restricted because federal appropriations limit the number of children who can participate.

Further, the absence of consistent standards for child care quality engenders a wide range of health and safety regulations across states, which, in turn, affects children's daily experiences, the range of choices available to parents, and the working conditions of child care teachers. In addition, the absence of sufficient and stable financial support for early childhood programs influences the overall quality and stability of early childhood education.

Historically, government involvement with children's issues has been crisis oriented, available only for narrowly defined problems and targeted groups of individuals (Goffin, 1983; Takanishi, 1977). The onset of federally funded early intervention programs in the 1960s, which provided the impetus for curriculum model development, was prompted by such a crisis. The crisis was America's "discovery" of rampant poverty. The problem was poor children's lack of school success. Low-income preschoolers and their families were the targeted population, and preschool education was the proposed solution. Based on psychological premises regarding environmental impact and the concept of critical periods (which justified targeting early childhood), preschool programs were expected to ameliorate the effects of disadvantaged circumstances, thus enabling poor preschoolers to enter school as well prepared as their middle-class counterparts.

Changing societal circumstances again are providing a rationale for advocating government-sponsored policies on behalf of children and families. Concerns about growing numbers of impoverished children at risk for school failure, employed parents requiring child care for their children, and the competitive abilities of the nation's future workforce have coalesced to generate a new sense of national need. Public policy proposals in response to these concerns repeatedly include early childhood education as a means for addressing these issues.

Interest in early childhood education as a means for resolving these societal concerns acknowledges the success of preschool intervention programs initiated during the 1960s, longitudinal findings from experimental curriculum models (Kagan, 1987), and research documenting the developmental contributions of quality child care (Carolina Abecedarian Project, 2000; Peisner-Feinberg et al., 1999). These successes have been particularly effective in positioning early childhood education as a necessary component of school reform efforts (Carnegie Corporation of New York, 1996; Committee for Economic Development, 1987, 1993; U.S. Department of Education, 1991).

The larger issues swirling around early childhood programs are pertinent because they affect public interest and support (including financial resources) for early childhood education. They also shape public expectations regarding what early childhood programs should achieve. As succinctly stated by Bettye Caldwell, a prominent early childhood researcher and advocate: "It has consistently been economic and social needs that provided the force to move the field forward. This is just as true today as it was 200 years ago" (1989, p. x).

Still, in contrast to the 1960s, current attention to early childhood education comes primarily from the state, rather than federal, level. Driven by studies documenting the positive impact of preschool education and a desire to boost student academic achievement, 42 states now sponsor some form of prekindergarten education (Mitchell, Ripple, & Chanana, 1998; Schulman, Blank, & Ewen, 1999). State motivation parallels federal motives during the 1960s, however: concern for children's school readiness. State interest has been bolstered by the first of the nation's education goals: "by the year 2000 every child should enter school ready to learn"[1] (U.S. Department of Education, 1991).

In the mid-1960s and through the 1980s, preschool education most often was advocated as a stand-alone solution capable of providing poor children educational and economic parity with their middle-class peers. As the 1990s progressed and demands escalated for higher academic achievement, publicly

---

[1]The nation's eight education goals set targets for student achievement, safe and drug-free schools, adult literacy, teacher quality, parent involvement, and young children's readiness to learn. The strategy designated to achieve "readiness to learn" has three components: quality early care and education programs, preventive health care, and parent education and support. President George Bush and the nation's governors set the first six goals in September 1989 as an outgrowth of a National Governors Association education summit in Charlottesville, Virginia. Congress added two more goals—on teacher quality and parent involvement—when it passed President Bill Clinton's Goals 2000: Educate America Act in 1994.

funded prekindergarten programs for children from low-income families, most often for 4-year-olds, but sometimes for 3-year-olds as well, were targeted as a necessary component of comprehensive school reform efforts geared toward increasing student achievement. This shift recognized the need for more comprehensive and sustained approaches to effecting change; yet the aim is more focused. School and child outcomes, rather than broader societal reform, are now targeted.

Since the 1960s, there also have been changes in the character of early childhood education. Our understanding of child development and curriculum have undergone significant change. As a result, a more current framework for analyzing early childhood curriculum models is needed.

More than a decade ago, when interest in early childhood curriculum models first reemerged, Powell (1987a) posed a central question: *Should curriculum models be returned to the prominent position they held during the 1960s?* With the dramatic expansion of early childhood programs during the past decade, Powell's central question requires alteration.

The idea of curriculum models now is woven securely into the fabric of early childhood education. Public demands for program results and child outcomes (see, for example, Kagan & Cohen, 1997; Kagan, Rosenkoetter, & Cohen, 1997), in concert with the prevalence of poor-quality child care (see, for example, Cost, Quality and Child Outcomes Study Team, 1995; Galinsky, Howes, Kontos, & Shinn, 1994), have set up a different question: *Should curriculum models be the vehicles designated for improving the consistency and quality of early childhood programs?* Investigation of this question begins with an exploration of the circumstances that supported the creation and dramatic growth of curriculum models during the late 1960s and early 1970s.

ɔ A U.S. HISTORY OF CURRICULUM MODELS IN EARLY CHILDHOOD EDUCATION

The Early Childhood Context

Prior to the onset of experimental preschool intervention programs in the late 1950s, *systematic* variation of early childhood programs was minimal. Differences that did exist primarily were a result of differences among sponsoring agencies rather than curriculum distinctions generated by different goals and theoretical orientations (Spodek, 1973; White & Buka, 1987).

This had not always been the case, however. The history of early childhood education in the United States in the late 1800s was dominated by the growth of kindergartens that were informed largely by the work of Friedrich Froebel, who opened his early childhood program in Germany in 1837 and is credited with the creation of kindergarten education. At the beginning of the 20th century, some early childhood educators began to question Froebel's philosophy and practice, initiating an intensive, 10-year public debate (1903–1913) within the International

Kindergarten Union between those, such as Susan Blow and Elizabeth Peabody (prominent leaders of kindergarten education in the United States), who argued the continued validity of Froebelian tenets, and educators who contended his curriculum was too structured, rigid, and unscientific (see Weber, 1969, for a description of this debate; also Harris et al., 1907).

Eventually, the ideas put forth by progressive early childhood educators, such as Patty Smith Hill, a colleague of philosopher John Dewey and learning theorist Edward Thorndike, won the day. The culmination of their deliberations was reported in *The Kindergarten* (Committee of Nineteen, 1913). To a large extent, the early childhood curriculum that emerged from this debate dominated early childhood practice (with the exception of day nurseries/child care) until the 1960s.

Current interest in early childhood curriculum models surfaces some of the same issues confronted by the Committee of Nineteen in its deliberations. Do curriculum models need to remain faithful forevermore to their original tenets? Should they? Must curriculum models remain self-contained or can they accommodate to changing educational understandings and expectations? If curriculum models are responsive to changing conceptualizations of children and education, can they still legitimately be defined as curriculum models?

According to Froebel's proponents in the early 1900s, the answer to these questions was "no." His advocates argued that Froebel had designed the ideal play materials for young children. "True, these leaders recognized that in the hands of some kindergartners[2] Froebel's program had become excessively formal, but the cure for these adverse tendencies was to be found in a greater understanding of the spirit and philosophy behind Froebel's educational principles. Deviation from Froebel's program was not to be countenanced" (Weber, 1969, pp. vii–viii).

A closer examination of the term *model* supports their conclusion. By definition, models are "a standard or example for imitation or comparison, a representation to show the structure or serve as a copy of something" (*Random House College Dictionary*, 1988, p. 857).[3] The term *curriculum model* refers to a conceptual framework for decision making about educational priorities, administrative policies, instructional methods, and evaluation criteria (Evans, 1982). Curriculum models identify the essential, idealized elements of a program and serve as a referent or standard from which to judge the extent to which a program, as implemented, approximates the ideal (Spodek, 1973). They organize philosophies and/or theories of child development and learning into conceptual frameworks that define program purpose and practice.[4] According to Evans (1982),

---

[2] "Kindergartner" was a term applied to kindergarten teachers and those training kindergarten teachers.
[3] More current dictionaries (e.g., *The Oxford Dictionary and Thesaurus*, abridged ed., 1996) provide a similar definition.
[4] The High/Scope Foundation recently created a looser definition of curriculum models (Epstein, Schweinhart, & McAdoo, 1996). The definition set forth here is the one created when systematic variation in curriculum models was being formulated.

A curriculum model provides an ideal representation of the essential philosophical, administrative, and pedagogical components of a grand education plan. It constitutes a coherent, internally consistent description of the theoretical premises, administrative policies and instructional procedures presumed valid for achieving preferential education outcomes. (p. 107)

In early childhood education, theories of child development have served as the dominant foundation for curriculum model development (Day, 1977; Spodek, 1988; Weber, 1984; White & Buka, 1987). Early childhood curriculum has been largely informed by the belief that early childhood education should be directly derived from child development research and theory (Caldwell, 1984; Elkind, 1989; Sigel, 1972; Weber, 1969; White & Buka, 1987). Chapter titles in Part II of this book reflect the acceptance accorded this belief in curriculum model development.

Variations among curriculum models reflect differences in value commitments concerning what is more or less important for young children to learn as well as the process by which children learn and develop—though these value commitments frequently are not made explicit. Curriculum models in early childhood education also have varied in terms of the flexibility that they grant teachers to interpret a model's conceptual framework. According to Mayer (1971), regardless of these variations,

All curriculum models have been conceived so as to yield interactions among teachers, children, and materials in a way that is believed to facilitate the objectives of the design . . . the type of interaction(s) stressed by a program are logically related to the high priority objectives of that program and to theoretical notions about how children learn best what the program considers most important. (p. 291)

Thus, investigations of curriculum models should contemplate the consequences of relying on a template (regardless of how elastic) for determining curriculum, and teacher–child, child–child interactions.

Curriculum models also attempt to foster a conviction that one approach is better than an alternative view (Nuthall & Snook, 1973). This conviction is reinforced by definition of a curriculum model as an *ideal representation.* Comparing models in terms of their effectiveness in achieving *similar* outcomes supplies a competitive factor to curriculum model development (Evans, 1982).

The models approach to developing early childhood curriculum became prevalent during the 1960s with the advent of early intervention programs, including the initiation of Head Start, and the infusion of federal funds into their research and development (Clarke-Stewart & Fein, 1983; Evans, 1975; Osborn, 1980; Powell, 1987a). As a result, the onset of early childhood curriculum models is tightly interwoven with the history of early intervention programs, especially Head Start and Project Follow Through.

The Emergence of Systematic Variation

Prior to the onset of Head Start in 1965 (a national, federally funded preschool program for children considered at risk for school failure), early childhood education was characterized by its three discrete branches: kindergarten, day nurseries (now called child care), and nursery school.

At the time, kindergarten was considered to be a child's first experience with formal education. Even though most public schools did not yet offer kindergarten, it was considered an extension of public school education (Day, 1983).

Kindergarten history, especially since the mid-1920s, has responded to changing conceptualizations of school readiness, but prior to the onset of Head Start, kindergarten was oriented primarily toward nurturing social-emotional development (Spodek, 1986). This focus reflected not only a programmatic emphasis, but also the prevailing consensus that intellectual development was not amenable to environmental influence.

Day nurseries and nursery schools served preschoolers. Day nurseries (some of which served children younger than 2 years) began their history in the United States in the late 1800s and were full-day programs for children whose mothers were employed outside the home. Although their purpose underwent several changes during their early history, day nurseries provided primarily custodial care and were created in response to the necessity of maternal employment. By the early 1930s, due to less positive societal attitudes toward maternal employment, mothers were discouraged from working outside the home. Day nurseries developed primarily to serve low-income mothers who *had* to work and were influenced mostly by the social work, rather than education, profession (Cahan, 1989; Michel, 1999).

In contrast, nursery schools, which began to flourish in this country at the start of the 1920s, were half-day programs, mostly attended by children from middle-class families, and designed primarily to provide child-rearing advice and social-emotional enrichment to a child's home life. The expertise surrounding nursery schools came largely from university-based child development researchers (Beatty, 1995; Cahan, 1989). "Nursery schools were established for educational experimentation, for demonstration of methodology, or for purposes of research, but not for the relief of working mothers or neglected children" (National Association for the Education of Young Children [NAEYC] Organizational History and Archives Committee, 1976, p. 463). According to Abigail Eliot, a pioneer in the development of nursery schools, the major difference between nursery schools and day nurseries, aside from parental choice versus parental necessity, was program. "In the new nursery school, the children were active . . . alive . . . choosing . . . gay, busy, happy. *That* was the difference" (as cited in Hymes, 1978, p. 16).

These characteristics made nursery schools most popular among child psychologists, educators, and middle-class families (Beatty, 1995; Cahan, 1989). As a result, nursery schools remained limited in scope and influence.

Kindergartens, day nurseries, and nursery schools, therefore, experienced separate histories prior to the 1960s, served different populations of children, and developed distinctive purposes. Their curricular focus, although primarily centered on social and emotional nurturance (a focus that was reinforced as the ideas of Freudian psychology were assimilated into early childhood practice in the 1930s) ranged from custodial to enrichment to school readiness.

These programmatic distinctions coexisted when Head Start exploded onto the scene in 1965. It might be argued that the absence of a unified view of early childhood education was a factor that supported the emergence of early childhood curriculum models. As a result of the field's conceptual stratification it could be inferred that no curriculum existed for half-day "educational" programs for economically disadvantaged preschoolers. Hence, it was a niche easily perceived as wide open for educational experimentation.

It took three decades (1890–1920) of passionate debate for progressive educators to topple Froebel's dominance of kindergarten education (see Weber, 1969). If curriculum models had entered a setting where broad agreement regarding acceptable early childhood goals and practices preexisted, the proliferation of new models for preschool education might have met greater resistance.

Furthermore, in the 1960s, unlike the early 20th century, no single arena or organization existed for debating issues and developing new consensus. In contrast to the unifying role played by the International Kindergarten Union, which organized in 1892, early childhood leadership in the 1960s was divided among the National Association for the Education of Young Children (NAEYC, which was reorganized as such in 1964; until then, it was called the National Association for Nursery Education or NANE, which officially organized in 1929), the Association for Childhood Education International (ACEI, which was an outgrowth of the International Kindergarten Union), and a former department within the National Education Association (NEA) (Weber, 1969).

The curriculum upheaval in early childhood education during the early 20th century restructured early childhood curriculum and practice. It set the field's direction for most of the next 50 years. In contrast to the professional consensus forged by the Committee of Nineteen, the curriculum upheaval of the 1960s fragmented the field and left it without a mandate regarding appropriate curriculum and practice for young children.

The Political Setting

Head Start and other early intervention programs were created as centerpieces for the War on Poverty, which was part of President Lyndon Johnson's "Great Society." As part of the nation's belief in its ability to eradicate poverty and minimize social inequality, early childhood programs became the means for helping young children gain needed skills so they could take better advantage of the public school system, and thus escape poverty. The first summer of Head Start, 652,000 children participated in 2,500 centers employing 41,000 teachers (when first initiated in 1965, Head Start was organized as a 6-week summer program) (Osborn, 1980, p. 149). Head Start and related early intervention programs dramatically increased the number of preschoolers who experienced early childhood education (both in overall numbers and program [educational versus custodial] focus).

This summary of events fails, however, to convey the intense sense of purpose, optimism, and excitement that this initiative generated. Faith in the ability of early childhood education to achieve such dramatic outcomes was based on two critical and interrelated assumptions regarding the significance of childhood and its contribution to later development:

1. that the first 5 years of life were a critical period in a child's development and
2. that the character of children's early experiences was predictive of later capabilities.

A presumption accompanying these beliefs was that the experiences of children from low-income families were "inadequate" and that providing enrichment could compensate for disadvantaged home environments (Evans, 1975; Horowitz & Paden, 1973; Zigler & Anderson, 1979). Hence, early childhood programs developed for this purpose frequently were labeled compensatory education.

Program interventions were designed to bring recipients closer to "normal" functioning. In this instance, "normality" usually referred to social and academic behaviors consistent with middle-class norms (Horowitz & Paden, 1973; Sigel, 1990). It seemed logical to target the solution for eradicating future poverty toward its youngest victims. It also was politically acceptable. "In an effort to eradicate poverty while preserving the structure of the American economic system, economic deprivation was construed as cultural deprivation. The early experience paradigm was embraced by policy makers" (Ramey, Bryant, & Suarez, 1985, p. 248).

The significance of political acceptability should not be underestimated. As part of the War on Poverty, Head Start was viewed not only as a program of educational intervention, but also as a catalyst to help poor people become actively involved in advocating for their own needs. Based on this reasoning, Head Start originally was housed in the Office of Economic Opportunity and viewed as a community action program. In *The Devil Has Slippery Shoes* (1969/1990b), Polly Greenberg vividly described the dramatic political reaction to the first Head Start program in Mississippi when it acted more like a community action program than a straightforward program for early education. White and Buka (1987) have suggested that Head Start's eventual treatment by the federal government as primarily an educational program (what they called a "tacit political simplification of the program," p. 74) might have been what saved it from the terminal fate accorded other poverty programs that were enacted at the same time.

The Influence of Shifting Psychological Insights

Conclusions regarding the importance of children's early lives were informed, in part, by Hunt's (1961) and Bloom's (1964) extensive analyses of the empirical evidence on the environment's role (versus heredity) in stimulating mental development. Especially pertinent to the onset of early intervention programs were their arguments that intellectual development was particularly receptive to environmental stimulation during early childhood. According to Zigler and Anderson (1979), Bloom's (1964) conclusion that the first 5 years of life were a critical period of intellectual growth quickly became "gospel among the popular press" (p. 7).

The notion that human intelligence could be modified was a new idea in the 1960s (White & Buka, 1987). Hunt's and Bloom's conclusions were cited repeatedly in support of preschool intervention programs. Their work provided scientific justification for the federal government's political and financial support of Head Start (White & Buka, 1987). Departure from the long-standing belief that intelligence was determined by one's heredity generated optimistic anticipation for the possibilities environmental intervention might trigger. It also set the stage for a reexamination of early childhood curriculum.

This "marshalling of scientific data" (Evans, 1975, p. 2) and popular support helped legitimize public attention to early childhood education. A focus on classrooms was assisted by the 1954 desegregation ruling, *Brown v. The Board of Education of Topeka,* which directed attention toward low-income, African American children (Ramey & Ramey, in press), and the launching of Sputnik in 1957, which fostered a national self-consciousness about falling behind in the "race to conquer the frontiers of space. . . . Almost overnight, a curriculum revolution penetrated all levels of American schooling" (Weinberg, 1979, p. 912).

Research on the effects of educational programs for young children became a means for examining the plasticity of intellectual development. In fact, the possibilities of environmental intervention already were being explored by a small number of experimental preschool intervention programs that had been initiated 5 to 10 years earlier, in the mid- to late 1950s. (These research-oriented programs were to assume critical importance during the mid-1970s when the existence of Head Start became jeopardized; see Chapter 6.) The advent of Head Start propelled this examination to a national—and highly public—scale.

Developmental psychologists were interested in exploring the limits of Hunt's and Bloom's findings (Clarke-Stewart & Fein, 1983; Day, 1983). Their interest was intensified by Skeels's (1966) timely publication of the longitudinal findings from his early intervention study, which had been initiated in the late 1930s (Gray, Ramsey, & Klaus, 1982; Horowitz & Paden, 1973). Skeels and his colleagues transferred a small group of children, all of whom were judged to have mental disabilities, from an orphanage to an institution for persons with mental disabilities, where the children were cared for by residents and staff. In contrast to the relative neglect these children had experienced in the orphanage, they now were the recipients of extensive affection and stimulation. Skeels's first follow-up study, about 2.5 years following the end of the experimental period, found significant gains in these children's IQs (Skeels & Dye, 1939). These initial findings, however, were largely ignored, in part because of the strength of existing belief in the immutability of the IQ (Cravens, 1993; Gray et al., 1982; Zigler & Anderson, 1979).

Reconnecting with his subjects 20 years later, Skeels (1966) found that as adults, all 13 children from the experimental group were self-supporting and independent. In contrast, members of the comparison group, who remained in the orphanage, had a median education of less than third grade and were institutionalized, unemployed, or employed at menial jobs.

The research of Skeels and his colleagues demonstrated that, when provided an enriched environment, a group of initially retarded infants could function at normal levels as adults. Horowitz and Paden (1973) pointed out that, in contrast,

Arnold Gesell's maturational approach, which represented prevailing beliefs, recommended that retardation be diagnosed during infancy, at which point parents should be helped to understand that their child would never be normal. Gray et al. (1982), whose Early Training Project, initiated in 1959, was one of the first formal early intervention programs, described the impact of Skeels's 1966 monograph as "electric" (p. 9). Its timing was certainly fortuitous.

Given changing ideas regarding environmental impact and intellectual plasticity, Head Start and related early intervention programs provided developmental and educational psychologists the opportunity to learn whether early childhood was, in fact, a critical period for intellectual development and whether early childhood education could compensate for disadvantaged environments (Clarke-Stewart, 1988).

The dominant involvement of developmental psychologists in creating these new early childhood programs, rather than early childhood educators, perhaps can be explained, at least partially, by the historical relationship between nursery schools and developmental psychology. During the 1920s and 1930s, the Laura Spelman Rockefeller Memorial Foundation awarded significant sums of money to establish child study institutes at universities and colleges. Nursery schools were an integral part of these institutes, providing an enrichment program for preschoolers and a research site for developmental psychologists (Cahan, 1989; Cravens, 1993; Hymes, 1978; White & Buka, 1987).

An important mission of these institutes was translation of child development research for use in parent education programs. "The institutes would study children, maintain exemplary forms of preschool education, and serve as a vehicle for the transmission of the fruits of such study to parents" (Siegel & White, 1982, p. 276).

Consequently, when national concern with the ravages of poverty focused on early childhood, many developmental psychologists shifted their agenda. They needed merely to shift their research focus from middle- and upper-income children in preschool settings to children from low-income families.[5] Significantly, however, their involvement during the era of curriculum models extended beyond child development research to include curriculum development.

The social agenda of the early 1960s, in conjunction with new ideas about the environment's impact on intellectual growth, motivated the change in focus and attracted the interests of educational and developmental psychologists (Lavatelli, 1971). The diversity of experimental curricula devised by psychologists reflected intense theoretical debates occurring within the field of psychology. These debates, in turn, became a source of controversy within the early

---

[5]Additional evidence for this conclusion comes from George Stoddard's opinion that the National Association for Nursery Education (NANE, the forerunner of NAEYC) helped unite the efforts of the new child study centers "on behalf of this great movement to secure a better educational environment and a better educational experience" (p. 465, as cited in NAEYC Organizational History and Archives Committee, 1976; Stoddard was NANE president from 1931 to 1933).

childhood field regarding appropriate early childhood curriculum. As the thinking of developmental and educational psychologists came to dominate early childhood curriculum development, many nursery educators questioned why their substantial knowledge regarding early childhood education was being largely ignored (Biber, 1977; Biber & Franklin, 1967; Dowley, 1971; Greenberg, 1987; White & Buka, 1987). The political dynamics surrounding their questions were especially important to the evolution of Bank Street's Developmental-Interaction approach (see Chapter 3), which represented prevailing nursery school practice.

Development of Curriculum Models

With the advent of Head Start in 1965, the benefits of nursery education no longer were confined to middle-class preschoolers. As a result, the population of children that had been separately served by different streams of early childhood education began to commingle. The prevailing wisdom of established nursery school programs, especially as communicated by the Bank Street College of Education, was designated the official Head Start orientation toward preschool education. The idea of curriculum models as an intentional strategy would not emerge for yet another 2 years.

Basic assumptions of the prevailing child development approach included responsibility for developing the "whole child" and creating an environment conducive to exploring, manipulating, constructing, thinking, symbolizing, and talking (Biber, 1979a). According to Biber, a major figure in American nursery education and primary architect of the Developmental-Interaction approach, "Those of us who crossed the lines between private preschool education and day-care programs in our professional lives welcomed Head Start as a fulfilled wish—the chance to provide the best for the children who need it most" (p. 155). Eventually, this initial approach toward providing compensatory education came to be labeled the "traditional model" (Miller, 1979).[6]

The development of new curriculum approaches for early childhood programs was fueled by an evolving consensus, most often promulgated by psychologists, that a "traditional" middle-class nursery school curriculum could not effectively help children from low-income families to develop needed competencies (Miller, 1979; Powell, 1987a). Especially being challenged was the nursery school's emphasis on social-emotional development. The new belief in intellectual malleability and programmatic emphasis on school readiness propelled psychologists to focus

---

[6]Biber's (1984) reaction to this label is worth noting. "We could not imagine that what to us was a steady course of experimentation directed toward basic change in the philosophy of early education would come to be designated as 'traditional.' The ideological fundamentals that we assumed would gradually gain general acceptance came upon hard times in the 1960s when a narrow scholasticism dominated experimental programs in search of single-trace solutions to the pervasive damage of poverty in early childhood" (p. 25).

early childhood curriculum on cognitive and academic development. According to Day (1983), psychologists "had an important influence on early education because they dared to suggest that children under the age of six should have special academic training" (p. 61).

With support from federal and private agencies during the late 1960s and early 1970s, psychologists and others created a wide variety of experimental preschool programs. A survey commissioned for the U.S. Office of Child Development in 1972 reviewed approximately 40 preschool models and another 200 in various stages of development, the majority of which were used in Head Start programs (Miller, 1979).

New programs were constructed primarily from theories of development and learning. Reflecting the lack of consensus within psychological theory, differing and often opposing theoretical interpretations of child development and learning became the basis for program development. Researchers hoped to discover which programs could best encourage cognitive development (Clarke-Stewart, 1988; Miller, 1979; Powell, 1987a).

Early childhood curriculum models varied around this cognitive focus. The belief that developing school readiness was primarily a cognitive undertaking was an implicit assumption. To remain competitive, traditional preschool programs drew on new theoretical ideas, such as those of Jean Piaget, to justify the contributions of play and creative endeavors to cognitive development. They also searched for ways to use the medium of play to develop cognitive concepts (Lavatelli, 1971).

When Project Follow Through was established in 1967, a search for the curriculum best able to advance cognitive and academic development became directly associated with specific curriculum models. Project Follow Through, a federally sponsored educational project, was designed for children in kindergarten through grade 3 in hopes of extending the benefits of Head Start.

The Westinghouse Ohio study, an early follow-up study of children enrolled in Head Start programs, found that initial gains in children's school achievement began fading after children's entry into public schools (Cicirelli, 1969). Based on the possibility that schools were at fault for the erosion of children's gains, Follow Through was instituted as a vertical extension of Head Start into kindergarten and the primary grades (Bissell, 1973).

The program was administered by the U.S. Office of Education (USOE). Local communities were invited to design, carry out, and evaluate various approaches to early education (kindergarten through third grade). To evaluate which approaches were most effective, Project Follow Through was organized as a study of planned variation (Hodges et al., 1980; Rivlin & Timpane, 1975). It was launched using 13 different curriculum models at 80 different school sites across the country.

Models of early childhood education were chosen by USOE. Developers of these models became Follow Through model sponsors. Most models were sponsored by universities and educational laboratories. By 1971, 22 models were operational in 173 local projects. At Project Follow Through's peak in the early 1970s, 84,000 children and their parents were being served in 4,000 classrooms in every state of the nation. As of 1980, there were 19 model sponsors;

Figure 1-1   **Participating Models: Project Follow Through**

1. Bank Street College of Education Model, Bank Street College, New York
2. Behavior Analysis Model, University of Kansas, Lawrence
3. Bilingual/Bicultural model, Southwest Educational Development Laboratory, Austin, TX
4. High/Scope Cognitively Oriented Curriculum Model, High/Scope Educational Research Foundation, Ypsilanti, MI
5. Cultural Linguistic approach, Northeastern Illinois University, Chicago
6. Culturally Democratic Learning Environmental Model, University of California at Santa Cruz
7. Direct Instruction Model, University of Oregon, Eugene
8. EDC Open Education Program, Educational Development Center, Newton, MA
9. Florida Parent Education Model, University of Florida, Gainesville
10. Home-School Partnership Model, Clark College, Atlanta, GA
11. Individualized Early Learning Program, University of Pittsburgh, Pittsburgh
12. Interdependent Learning Model, Fordham University, Bronx, NY
13. Mathemagenic Activities Program, University of Georgia, Athens
14. New School Approach, University of North Dakota, Grand Forks
15. Nongraded Model, Hampton Institute, Hampton, VA
16. Parent Supported Diagnostic Model, Georgia State University, Atlanta
17. Prentice Hall Personalized Learning Model, Prentice Hall Developmental Learning Centers, Inc., West Paterson, NJ
18. Responsive Education Program, Far West Laboratory, San Francisco
19. Tucson Early Education Model, University of Arizona, Tucson

the number of local projects per sponsor ranged from 1 to 19 (Hodges et al., 1980) (see Figure 1-1).

Shortly after initiation of Project Follow Through, a similar research effort involving 12 curriculum models was launched within Head Start (Rivlin & Timpane, 1975) (see Figure 1-2). According to Miller (1979), a prominent researcher involved in evaluating the differential effectiveness of curriculum models, experimental programs varied in their assumptions about education, interpretations of the developmental process, and beliefs about the effects of culture, especially poverty, on a child's cognitive development. Curriculum models ranged in focus from didactic, drill-oriented programs of instruction in school-specific content to programs emphasizing child discovery and enrichment. Model development was heavily influenced by a developer's beliefs regarding poverty's impact on cognitive development and the type of environment that would ameliorate its effects.

The growth and evaluation of early childhood curriculum models, therefore, accompanied the federal government's investment in Head Start. Head Start was, and continues to be, one of the federal government's most significant, continuous, and direct investments in early childhood education. In the late 1960s, the federal government's support of curriculum models was, in part, a search for the best way to structure its investment. The assumption was made that there would, in

Figure 1-2   **Participating Models: Head Start Planned Variation**

1. Bank Street College of Education Approach, Bank Street College, New York
2. Behavior Analysis Model, University of Kansas, Lawrence
3. EDC Open Education Program, Educational Development Center, Newton, MA
4. The Enabler Model, U.S. Office of Human Development, Office of Child Development
5. Englemann-Becker Model, University of Oregon, Eugene
6. Florida Parent Education Model, University of Florida, Gainesville
7. High/Scope Cognitively Oriented Model, High/Scope Educational Research Foundation, Ypsilanti, MI
8. Individualized Early Learning Program, University of Pittsburgh, Pittsburgh
9. Interdependent Learning Model, Fordham University, Bronx, NY
10. Responsive Educational Program, Far West Laboratory, San Francisco
11. Responsive Environments Corporation Early Childhood Model, Englewood Cliffs, NJ
12. Tucson Early Education Model, University of Arizona, Tucson

fact, be one best approach. According to Weikart (1983), the primary architect of the High/Scope Curriculum model and a participant in both Project Follow Through and Head Start Planned Variation, the quest for a superior curriculum was consistent with the American search for "best" solutions.

Given the high stakes involved, this competitive environment spawned not only innovation but also discord. Controversy was especially intense between programs that emphasized children's social-emotional development and those that structured learning environments to advance cognitive development (Osborn, 1980; see, for example, Biber, 1969, 1979b; Moore, 1977). In assessing the impact on the early childhood field, Butler (1976) lamented, "On the one hand, the effect on the field has been positive inasmuch as new programs have been created and rethinking of all programs has been stimulated; however, the lack of agreement among professionals has created a certain amount of divisiveness when unity of purpose might be a definite asset" (p. 6).

The Ending of an Era

Intense interest in developing and comparing diverse curriculum models for preschool and primary education continued for approximately a decade. Interest declined during the late 1970s and early 1980s, and attention transferred to other early childhood issues. The disappointing findings of the Westinghouse Ohio study on the effects of Head Start helped shift debate from a question of which type of program was most effective to whether early childhood education programs were beneficial for economically disadvantaged children. Failure to find significant differences in program effects for children who participated in distinctive programs, the difficulty in designing and implementing large-scale comparison studies, and decline in federal support for such efforts contributed to the decreased investigation of early childhood curriculum models. Finally, dramatic increases in maternal employment and numbers of children in child care, which still bore its custodial, welfare label and value-laden association with maternal employment, shifted concern toward study of the impact of full-day care (Clarke-Stewart, 1988; Clarke-Stewart & Fein, 1983; Powell, 1987a).

Perhaps because child care was associated with a different purpose and still carried its custodial label, curriculum models, with their educational emphasis, had little if any impact on this fastest growing segment of early childhood education. As middle-class women entered the workforce and the number of child care programs grew in response to demand, the first wave of child care research, reflective of child care's distinctive history, focused not on its educative value but on whether child care was harmful to children's development (Belsky, 1984; Clarke-Stewart, 1987a).

Yet, even as interest was declining in curriculum models, a group of investigators who had implemented some of the first experimental preschool intervention programs was assessing the school success of program participants, who by then were in upper elementary grades and high school. Their endeavor was a collaborative attempt to justify public faith—and public investment—in the power of early intervention. The results of their efforts, collectively and individually (which began to be published in the late 1970s), demonstrated positive effects for children who experienced early childhood education (Berrueta-Clement, Schweinhart, Barnett, Epstein, & Weikart, 1984; Consortium for Longitudinal Studies, 1983; Gray et al., 1982). These findings (which are reviewed in Chapter 6) restored public optimism, rejuvenated public support for early intervention programs, and generated renewed interest in early childhood curriculum models.

The following quote, taken from a chapter written by Spodek and Walberg in 1977, captures the emotional roller coaster that must have been experienced by those who shared in the excitement of the 1960s and the letdown of the 1970s:

> The mid-1960s and just beyond seemed to represent an era of plenty in the field of early childhood education. It was characterized by unparalleled activity. Programs were provided for children not served in the past. New curriculum models were developed and evaluated. There was research relating to the characteristics of early childhood and to the impact of environmental variables on achievement and development based on naive notions concerning the power of early childhood experience and the ability of educational programs to right social wrongs. The range of goals ascribed to the programs was broader than the goals conceived earlier.
>
> The era of abundance seems to have ended, and we face the years of scarcity. Resources that sustained earlier activities have evaporated. Service programs still in operation have been cut back by the effects of inflation. There seems to be an absence of support for the type of research and development activities that characterized the earlier period, and the optimism of that period seems also to have waned. (pp. 1–2)

Spodek and Walberg's words highlight that development of curriculum models occurred during a unique time in the histories of the United States and early childhood education. Their development was bolstered by considerable financial support and a sense of larger purpose. Some participants have argued that the effects of early intervention programs during the 1960s, including well-researched curriculum models, should not be attributed solely to the benefits of early childhood education. They caution that much of the success of early intervention programs belongs to the hopeful, optimistic times of which they were a part (Gray et al., 1982; Woodhead, 1988).

℘ CONTEMPORARY BACKDROP FOR EARLY CHILDHOOD CURRICULUM MODELS

As findings regarding the long-term effects of preschool intervention programs became available to educators and policy makers in the late 1970s and early 1980s, interest in early childhood education and curriculum models reemerged. Renewed interest was fueled not only by the positive findings of longitudinal research on early childhood programs, but by studies indicating the differential effectiveness of curriculum models (for example, DeVries & Goncu, 1987; DeVries, Haney, & Zan, 1991; DeVries, Reese-Learned, & Morgan, 1991; Schweinhart & Weikart, 1997; Schweinhart, Weikart, & Larner, 1986; see Chapter 6) and to arguments for the contribution of early childhood education to school reform (Council of Chief State School Officers, 1988; Mitchell, Seligson, & Marx, 1989; U.S. Department of Education, 1991; Warger, 1988; see also Kagan & Zigler, 1987).

As the 1990s progressed, increasing concern with the academic underachievement of students from low-income families, expansion of state-based prekindergarten programs, and growing demands for public accountability helped sustain interest in early childhood education, including its curriculum models, as a powerful intervention strategy. The interplay among these factors has spawned a lucrative market for early childhood curricula and aggressive claims regarding their effectiveness.

Recent national focus on results and public accountability has led many states that fund prekindergarten programs to emphasize the use of research-based curricula. Two states, Georgia and Missouri, require that state-funded prekindergarten programs use a preapproved curriculum model (Schulman et al., 1999). Interest has begun to extend beyond specific curriculum models, however, to include attention to subject matter. Early literacy development, in particular, has become a topic of great interest (see, for example, National Research Council, 1999), propelled in part by new requirements for Head Start programs that mandate specific literacy outcomes. With the growth of formal links with public schools—and in contrast to the mid-1960s—the purpose of school readiness is being presented more in terms of future academic achievement and job readiness and less in terms of eradicating poverty and achieving social equality.

Researchers assessing different approaches to early childhood education also have redefined their task. They have determined the need to go beyond questions that ask "What works best?" Research on the effects of varied curricula moved beyond global questions of effectiveness during the mid- to late 1980s to questioning effectiveness for whom and under what conditions (Clarke-Stewart, 1988; Miller, Bugbee, & Hybertson, 1985; Powell, 1987a). A third wave of research effort launched in the early 1990s examined the intersection of program effects and children's family circumstances. Now, with the expansion and diversity of early intervention programs, attention increasingly is directed toward identifying and evaluating program characteristics, such as duration, intensity. and program components (versus a specific curriculum) that are associated with effective early intervention (Ramey & Ramey, 1998; St. Pierre & Layzer, 1998).

Following the wave of studies in the early 1970s and late 1980s, evaluators attempted to address the differential impact of diverse curriculum models on individual children. But the limitations of examining program effects in isolation from other, simultaneous aspects of children's lives became apparent. So researchers extended their investigations to include the impact of early childhood programs (including curriculum models) in conjunction with other significant contributors (such as parenting) to children's educational and developmental outcomes. Researchers asked questions that tried to disentangle the various elements of early childhood programs, and how, individually and in association with each other, these elements interacted with and affected children who bring different characteristics and family circumstances to programs (Clarke-Stewart, 1987a, 1988; Miller et al., 1985; Powell, 1987a; Ramey & Ramey, 1998).

Further, as a result of accumulated experiences gained from attempts to change the educational trajectory of large numbers of children from low-income families, the issue of differential program effectiveness has extended to elementary education. Federal funding through Title I, which is available to public schools serving children from low-income families, has been restructured to support research-based instructional programs. Reminiscent of Project Follow Through and Head Start Planned Variation, program designers are striving to establish the criteria that define effectiveness and to demonstrate the potency of their own models (see, for example, Fashola & Slavin, 1998; Pogrow, 1998).

The work of these program designers acknowledges the learning of Project Follow Through and Head Start Planned Variation from undertaking large-scale, multisite program implementations. The issues of "going to scale" or "scaling up"—of extending the benefits of "proven" programs to large numbers of children—is central to their work. As articulated by Pogrow (1996), "The best chance for real reform in the vast majority of schools lies in adapting those few 'precrafted' programs that work" (p. 40).

This argument is not limited to program designers concerned with the academic success of elementary school students, however. The argument extends, as well, to the replication of effective early childhood programs; hence, the central question of this text: Should curriculum models be the vehicles designated for improving the consistency and quality of early childhood programs?

Rekindled interest in early childhood curriculum models as vehicles for ensuring program results is confronted by more than reformulated research questions and implementation issues, however. They reemerge to different social circumstances, a shifting focus within, and away from, developmental psychology as a primary determinant of curriculum, and the field of early childhood education in transition. Equally notable, interest in early childhood curriculum models reappears at a time when the notion of packaging curriculum is under scrutiny. These changed circumstances create a developmental context for early childhood curriculum models that differs from the one that existed in the 1960s and mid-1980s. Each of these issues is discussed briefly below in order to provide a framework for the chapters that follow. These issues will surface yet again in the last four chapters.

Changing Societal Context

In the 1960s, public interest in early childhood education united around concern for the economically disadvantaged, an issue embedded within the civil rights movement. Interest in early childhood education during the 1990s reflected demographic, social, and economic circumstances specific to the decade. Intensified interest at the close of the 1990s anticipated the challenges of a new century.

During the 1990s, preoccupation with early childhood education reflected the increasing numbers of mothers with young children who were in the workforce, the national spotlight on school reform, and the need for a competitive workforce. Concerns regarding low student achievement were accentuated by frustration with the social cost of school failures.

Unlike the 1960s, when interest in early childhood education revolved primarily around promoting school readiness as a means for creating equal opportunity for economically disadvantaged children, attention to early childhood education activated since the 1980s has coalesced around the diverse issues just listed. As a result, a larger group of young children is being targeted, and interested stakeholders have expanded to include state and local government officials and business and civic leaders. Receptivity to early childhood education as a policy issue can be attributed to the effective promotion of findings on the positive, long-term effects of early childhood education (see Barnett, 1995, 1998; Karoly et al., 1998).

Increasingly, early childhood education is seen as critical in helping to minimize the ill effects of poverty and also as essential to school reform efforts. Public schools are recognizing that their success in educating children is tied in important ways to children's well-being when they begin formal schooling (see, for example, Council of Chief State School Officers, 1999). And prominent business groups, such as the Committee for Economic Development (1987, 1991, 1993), have targeted early childhood education, especially for children placed at risk for school failure, as a strategy for addressing their concerns regarding business productivity. The broadened constituency concerned with early childhood programs also includes the large population of parents employed outside the home who depend on the availability of child care. This expansion of interest, while certainly not universal, has increased public expectations for early childhood education.

Changing Configuration of Early Childhood Education

Since the 1960s, the number of young children served by early childhood programs has increased tremendously. In 1965, approximately 47% of 5-year-olds were enrolled in kindergartens; by 1986, 90% of 5-year-olds attended kindergarten, which had become almost universally available in public schools (Spodek,

1986). From its inception in 1965, Head Start had expanded to serve approximately 40% of eligible children in 1997, for a total of 793,809 children (as cited in Ripple, Gilliam, Chanana, & Zigler, 1999). One in three preschool-age children whose mothers are *not* in the labor force also attend some form of early childhood education (National Center for Education Statistics, 1996).

Yet the most dramatic growth in early childhood education has occurred in full-day early childhood programs or child care. In 1975, 39% of mothers with children under the age of 6 were in the workforce; by 1998, that percent had grown to 65% (U.S. Department of Labor, 1999).

Political interest in child care programs was heightened by passage of The Family Support Act in 1988 and the Personal Responsibility and Work Opportunity Reconciliation Act in 1996. Based on the growing conviction that low-income parents should work and be independent of government cash assistance, these two pieces of federal legislation have pushed increasing numbers of low-income women into the labor force. A significant portion of demand for child care also comes from middle-class mothers' entry into the workforce. Yet response to this demand rarely is considered in the context of school reform, thereby perpetuating the image of child care as custodial and continuing a two-tiered response by policy makers.

Increased attendance in early childhood programs of all types has sparked less fragmented conceptualization of early childhood education. Recall that at the onset of the Great Society in the early 1960s, nursery school, kindergarten, and child care were distinctive in purpose and clientele. Now the early childhood field asserts that the care and education of young children, regardless of program sponsorship, are inseparable. Early childhood advocates try to capture this emergent integration between the care and education of young children by using the phrase "early childhood care and education."

Kagan (1989) attributed coalition building among early childhood education's various strands (nursery education, kindergarten, child care, and most recently Head Start and publicly funded prekindergarten programs) to the success of the National Association for the Education of Young Children's first position statement on developmentally appropriate practice (Bredekamp, 1987). This document (which has been updated, see Bredekamp & Copple, 1997) identifies pedagogical characteristics of developmentally appropriate early childhood programs, regardless of sponsorship. It has functioned as a consensus document, presenting a description of early care and education practices around which the field can coalesce (see Chapter 4). Although still in its infancy, this emerging sense of professional cohesion contrasts with the separateness that marked nursery school, kindergarten, and child care during the 1960s.

Early childhood programs at the dawn of the 21st century are organized for diverse purposes, serve children and families in a variety of ways, and confront different internal and external challenges. They are provided by various sponsors: community and government agencies, for-profit groups, employers, churches and synagogues, public schools, private institutions, and individual providers. The daunting task of constructing and financing a cohesive system of early childhood care and education is propelling the field to deliberate issues that transcend age of child served, length of program day, program sponsorship, or program type.

Further, early childhood programs serve an increasingly ethnically and economically diverse population of children, many of whom are placed educationally at risk because of inadequate health care, family instability, and insufficient economic resources (Kagan & Garcia, 1991; National Commission on Children, 1991; Washington & Andrews, 1998)—issues rarely addressed by curriculum models. As a result, many early childhood advocates work to link early care and education programs for children from low-income families with support services for them and their families (Committee for Economic Development 1991; Schulman et al., 1999; Silver Ribbon Panel, 1990; Schorr, 1997).

Thus, early childhood education during the 1990s provided a different setting for the ongoing development and implementation of early childhood curriculum models. The first decade of the new century promises to bring continued change. But it is a changing knowledge base that supplies the catalyst for reassessing the content of enduring early childhood curriculum models.

Changing Knowledge Base

The knowledge base undergirding education in general, and early childhood education in particular, has expanded and shifted in focus since the 1960s. Studies of human development since the 1960s, which, of course, include child development, have generated new understandings of and assumptions about the developmental process. In general, these new understandings are based on much more complex, context-bound explanations of development and education (see Chapter 7).

The changing child development knowledge base has been influenced by research on early childhood program effects. Expansion of publicly supported early childhood education after the launch of Head Start in 1965 and the increasing numbers of children in child care since the 1970s has generated considerable research on the impact of early childhood programs on child growth.

These studies helped to spawn criteria for program quality (for example, Weikart, 1989, 1995). When comparative evaluations initially failed to find significant differences among curriculum models, attention turned to delineating the characteristics associated with program quality (such as group size, teacher–child ratio, and the existence of a well-developed curriculum), independent of a particular program type or curriculum approach (see, for example, Frede, 1995). This change in focus has reflected attempts to understand the effect of early childhood programs in terms of structural and programmatic characteristics associated with quality, rather than in terms of the differential effectiveness of curriculum models. As the need became apparent for improving the overall quality of early childhood programs and the effectiveness of early interventions, this distinction assumed increasing importance.

Still, early findings from program evaluations that focused on child outcomes specific to different early childhood curricula highlighted the complexity of child development, disputed simplistic interpretations of environmental impact on children's development, and spotlighted challenges associated with consistent implementation of early childhood curriculum models.

These findings, in combination with recent understandings about child development and interest in taking effective programs "to scale," spark new questions about the content and implementation of curriculum models. Interest in these questions is elevated by debates regarding the extent to which theories of development and learning should prescribe what to teach (Goffin, 1996; Silin, 1995) and the extent to which effective teaching is dependent on research-based models (Pogrow, 1996; Epstein et al., 1996). This debate is enriched by recent conceptualizations of teaching as dynamic and uncertain and classroom teachers as reflective practitioners (see, for example, Cochran-Smith & Lytle, 1993, 1999; New, 1994a; Zeichner & Liston, 1996; see Chapter 7). Consideration of these perspectives uncovers assumptions that undergird early childhood curriculum models and structure their purpose and function.

☞ CONCLUSION

Early childhood education is at a critical juncture in its evolution. Demand for early childhood programs for children from birth through age 5 has escalated. The number of new and expanded programs serving 3- and 4-year-old children identified as educationally at risk has increased dramatically. Early childhood education prior to kindergarten and first grade increasingly is recognized as children's first encounter with formal schooling. At the same time, elevated public financing of early childhood education, though still inadequate to the need, is placing pressure on early childhood programs to be results oriented.

The preparation of early childhood personnel has not kept pace with demand, however, not only because predictions of demand went unheeded, but more importantly, because caring for young children has not been perceived by the general public as an educational and/or professional enterprise. Professional preparation of early childhood educators primarily has served those in public school settings, where professional certification is required—though even this preparation is not always informed by an early childhood knowledge base or uniformly required of teachers who work with 3-, 4-, and 5-year-olds.

As expectations for quality have begun to accompany demands for program availability, competition for qualified early childhood personnel has intensified. Preparing and keeping qualified personnel, however, is undermined by the inferior compensation offered early childhood educators (Center for the Child Care Workforce, 1998). This quandary is confounded further by the profession's inability to define the prerequisite knowledge base for entering the profession (see, for example, Bredekamp & Willer, 1993).

David Weikart, a primary architect and proponent of the High/Scope Curriculum model, has proposed a solution to this quandary (1992, 1995). He recommends wide dissemination of early childhood curriculum models as a vehicle for ensuring early childhood program quality. His recommendation advances curriculum models as a strategy for justifying public investments in early childhood education and increasing its quality and consistency.

Thus, as we enter a new century, the early care and education field confronts contradictory demands and expectations. Public expectation that investment in early childhood education produce tangible results coexists with a field attempting to move toward a cohesive system for providing early childhood programs and supporting a well-compensated workforce. Increasing public demand for quality early childhood programs coexists with inadequate financial support.

Renewed interest in early childhood curriculum models has materialized, in part, because of demand for consistent program quality and accountability. Still unresolved from the upheaval of the 1960s, however, are issues surrounding early childhood curriculum and its development. Simultaneously, educators are debating the source and characteristics of professionalism in teaching. This debate and these issues place an investigation of early childhood curriculum models within a unique sociohistorical framework and locate it at the intersection of a critical juncture in early childhood education.

☞ FOR FURTHER READING

Beatty, B. (1995). *Preschool education in America: The culture of young children from the Colonial era to the present.* New Haven, CT: Yale University Press.

> This historical account of the preschool movement details the evolution of preschools in the United States and questions why the United States lacks universal access to publicly funded preschool education.

Cahan, E. D. (1989). *Past caring: A history of U.S. preschool care and education for the poor, 1820–1965.* New York: National Center for Children in Poverty, Columbia University.

> This very readable, short but thorough examination of the dual histories of child care and nursery schools documents the creation of a two-tiered system of care and education for America's preschoolers.

Evans, E. D. (1975). *Contemporary influences in early childhood education* (2nd ed.). New York: Holt, Rinehart & Winston.

> This classic textbook provides a review and analysis of curriculum models during a time of intense support for early childhood curriculum models. Extensive research findings and bibliographies relevant to various models are provided. Consistent with its date of publication, emphasis is given to half-day early childhood programs designed for economically disadvantaged preschoolers.

Weber, E. (1969). *The kindergarten: Its encounter with educational thought in America.* New York: Teachers College Press.

> Weber provides a detailed examination of the growth of kindergarten education from its beginnings in the United States until the mid-1960s. Much is also said about the growth of nursery schools. Weber's reliance on historical primary

sources and detailed analysis makes this an especially informative review of early childhood education's formative years in the United States.

White, S. H., & Buka, S. L. (1987). Early education: Programs, traditions, and policies. In E. Z. Rothkopf (Ed.), *Review of research in education* (Vol. 14, pp. 43–91). Washington, DC: American Educational Research Association.

This scholarly review documents the diverse influences on early childhood education during its 200-year history. White, a Harvard psychologist who helped shape Head Start policy, incorporates tidbits of history from the perspective of an insider.

Early Childhood Curriculum Models
A Contemporary Review

*P*art II comprises Chapters 2 through 5. These chapters examine five enduring early childhood curriculum models: the Montessori method, the
Developmental-Interaction approach, the Direct Instruction model, the
Kamii-DeVries approach, and the High/Scope Curriculum model. The description of each curriculum model is embedded within its particular social and historical context. Because historical factors influenced the sequence in which the five
curriculum models are presented, readers are encouraged to read the chapters in
the order in which they are introduced.

Chapter Two

The Montessori Method

For man, who has formed a new world through scientific process, must himself be prepared and developed through a new pedagogy.

Maria Montessori, *The Montessori Method,* 1912/1964

From minds thus set in order, . . . come sudden emotions and mental feats which recall the Biblical story of Creation. The child has in his mind . . . the first flowers of affection of gentleness, of spontaneous love for righteousness which perfumes the souls of such children and give promise of the "fruits of the spirit" of St Paul.

Maria Montessori, *The Secret of Childhood,* 1937/1966

*C*redit for being the first architect of an early childhood curriculum model belongs to the German educator, Frederick Froebel. His method of kindergarten education involved precise procedures and specially developed materials that could be replicated in other settings. According to Weber (1969), Froebel's ideas found easy acceptance in the United States in the mid-1800s because their idealistic base was consistent with the philosophy of a number of U.S. educational leaders. In addition, many German immigrants living in United States had been directly trained in Froebel's educational methods and were available to explain and demonstrate his procedures.

Froebel's ideas dominated kindergarten education in the United States until they were challenged by progressive educators in the early 1900s. The Montessori method entered the U.S. scene at just this time, when there was considerable disenchantment with Froebel's approach to early education, and early childhood educators in the United States were deliberating approaches to early education that were less philosophic in their orientation and more in line with new scientific thinking.

The Montessori method, which is the second curriculum model created expressly for early childhood education, was first implemented in Rome, Italy, in 1907. It is the oldest enduring model. In contrast to Froebel's experience, Montessori's approach to early education has withstood the passage of time despite challenges to its basic assumptions and practices.

As a result, examination of the Montessori method and its 90 years of U.S. history provides a unique opportunity to explore professional and public reactions to a specific curriculum model in relation to changing historical and societal circumstances and shifting educational thought. It also permits consideration of the circumstances that support a model's continuation over time.

Since its first introduction to the United States early in the 20th century, the Montessori method has undergone two documented revivals, in the mid-1960s and again in the late 1970s–early 1980s, attesting not only to its enduring allure, but also to the power of timely matches between educational models and societal needs and expectations. Montessori's commitment, and that of her son following her death, to retaining the purity and integrity of her methods also juxtaposes the tension of sustaining a model's "purity" and consistency alongside a changing society and professional knowledge base.

Montessori made a full-time commitment, at the age of 40, to disseminating her ideas and training teachers in her method. Although Montessori follows Froebel in a chronology of curriculum models, her method appears to be the first curriculum model carefully and intentionally mass-marketed for dissemination and replication. Furthermore, of the curriculum models to be reviewed in this text, the Montessori method is the only one in which a single individual is responsible for developing both the conceptual framework *and* the template for its implementation.

The designers of other enduring curriculum models have relied on the ideas of others, primarily developmental theorists, for their conceptual frameworks. Although each of these program designers has worked to retain the integrity of his or her model, Montessori's "ownership" of both the conceptual framework and program design, plus the program's implementation, perhaps helps explain her undiminished attempts to retain total control over the method's dissemination and the use of her didactic materials. She devoted herself to this work from 1916 until her death in 1952.

When Montessori began advocating her method full time in 1916, she gave up her other roles as physician, university professor, and classroom teacher. E. M. Standing, Montessori's official biographer, wrote in a passage Montessori herself approved, "Her mission in life had crystallized. . . . She felt the duty of going forth as an apostle on behalf of all the children in the world, born and as yet unborn, to preach for their rights and their liberation" (as cited in Kramer, 1976/1988, p. 156).

This quote begins to reveal the challenge of explaining and understanding the Montessori method. Montessori was a physician, anthropologist, educator, and mystic. She claimed to be both a scientific educator and a missionary. These last two roles, in particular, conjure up seemingly contradictory characteristics, contradictions that also imbue her writings. Yet, it is these apparent contradictions that help explain the model's endurance: Montessori's method embraces the prestige and presumed validity of a scientific approach to early education plus the emotional fervor that accompanies what Kramer (1976/1988) and Cohen (1969) labeled cultist.

❧ THE MONTESSORI METHOD: THE U.S. CHRONOLOGY

In the Beginning

Mention of Maria Montessori and her method almost always is accompanied by a statement that she was the first Italian female physician, a feat of courage and perseverance that can only be imagined. (Some of what her experiences must have been like is described by biographer Rita Kramer, 1976/1988.) Montessori also was a feminist and a crusader for children's rights. She was especially determined to liberate children from the rigidity of early 20th century Italian public education "where the children are repressed in the spontaneous expression of their personality till they are almost like dead beings" (Montessori, 1912/1964, p. 14). She believed that her approach to early education could revolutionize society by producing a new generation of children prepared for, and capable of, creating a better world.

Fifteen years prior to the opening of the first Casa dei Bambini ("Children's House"), Montessori served as an assistant doctor at the psychiatric clinic at the University of Rome and visited insane asylums to study the sick. This work led to her interest in "idiot" children (children whom we would today identify as mentally retarded and perhaps developmentally delayed) who were, at that time, housed in general insane asylums. Her conclusion that the needs of these children were pedagogical rather than medical led to the creation of the State Orthophrenic School.

At the State Orthophrenic School, Montessori was able to try out her pedagogical ideas, which largely were based on the work of Jean-Marc-Gaspard Itard (known for his attempts to educate the "wild boy of Aveyron") and Edward Sequin, who had developed a specialized method and didactic materials (instructive, self-correcting apparatus) for working with "deficient" children. For 2 years Montessori directed this program, which served children for the full length of the day. During these 2 years (1898–1900), she prepared teachers for a method of observation and education targeted to children with special learning needs. Eventually, Montessori herself worked directly with the children from 8:00 a.m. until 7:00 p.m. During this time, Montessori modified Sequin's materials and began to produce her own. She also drafted the beginnings of her method of reading and writing that would be a source of great excitement to educators and others around the world.

Montessori considered her method more rational than others currently in use. She became convinced that if her method could succeed in enabling "an inferior mentality" to grow and develop, it would "set free (the) personality" of normal children (Montessori, 1912/1964, p. 33).

The opportunity to apply her method to "normal" children came in 1906. In part, this opportunity presented itself because of her successful 2-year tenure at the State Orthophrenic School. Her method for working with children with mental retardation had succeeded so well that the children under her care successfully passed the public school examination alongside their typical peers, an event that generated considerable public attention and excitement (Montessori, 1912/1964).

The opportunity to try her techniques with typically developing children also emerged because of changing social circumstances throughout Italy. An awareness of these circumstances highlights not only the context of Montessori's achievement, but also illuminates the missionary zeal she felt for her work. Montessori was a multifaceted individual. She was obviously an amazing educational innovator, but she also was a feminist and an impassioned social reformer.

Because of economic distress, the late 1890s was a period of widespread social disorder throughout Italy. In 1903, a new prime minister initiated a series of social, economic, and financial reforms. These initiatives, especially in housing and education, were at their height in 1906 (Kramer, 1976/1988; Montessori, 1912/1964) and set the stage for the first Casa dei Bambini, which opened in 1907.

Rome was a city that had undergone a dramatic population increase, especially of immigrants from the countryside. This population growth fueled a tremendous building fever. This construction boom, however, was essentially an economic venture for Roman banks; no standards of health and safety guided the construction of new apartment buildings. When the economy shifted, uncompleted and rundown apartment houses dotted the city landscape. Abandoned structures quickly became occupied by beggars, criminals, and the homeless (Kramer, 1976/1988; Montessori, 1912/1964).

One such tenement was the Quarter of San Lorenzo, which became the first site where Montessori applied her innovative educational ideas with typically developing children. "With no sanitation and no policing, (the Quarter of San Lorenzo) became a hellhole of infection and prostitution, an abode of the dead as well as the living" (Kramer, 1976/1988, p. 109).

Eventually, a group of wealthy bankers decided to undertake an urban renewal scheme that could reap both public good and financial profit. They began their venture with the renovation of apartments in the Quarter of San Lorenzo and chose employed, married couples, many of whom had children, as tenants. When parents left in the morning for work, however, their children who were under school age were left unattended and began defacing building walls and stairs. Following on her success at the State Orthophrenic School, Montessori was invited by the Roman Good Building Institute, which administered the remodeled tenements, to develop an infant school for children 3 to 7 years of age. The invitation was extended in hopes that such a program would reduce the vandalism and protect the bankers' investment (Kramer, 1976/1988; Montessori, 1912/1964).

Montessori, however, saw larger possibilities. The Roman "Good Building" Institute owned more than 400 tenements in Rome, and each apartment house was to have its own school. Montessori envisioned the Children's Houses as having both social and pedagogical significance. "From the very first I perceived, in all its immensity, the social and pedagogical importance of such institutions, and while at that time my visions of a triumphant future seemed exaggerated, today many are beginning to understand that what I saw before was indeed the truth" (Montessori, 1912/1964, p. 48).

In the early 20th century (as well as 93 years later!), the Children's House was an amazingly progressive idea that served not only the needs of children and their parents, but the community and its business interests as well. As initially envisioned by Montessori, the Children's House was the core of what we might today call a family resource center. It provided not only comprehensive child care services that addressed children's nutritional and health care needs as part of the educational program (which she contrasted with the custodial care provided in the insane asylums), but also public baths, hospitals, and a "house-infirmary" for children who were ill.

Montessori saw the Children's Houses as realizing the educational ideal of linking family and school around educational aims. Although her frame of reference for low-income families was more judgmental than many of us might wish, her ideas demonstrated sensitivity to the need for families and educators to work together closely if children were to truly benefit. Montessori recognized the advantages to be derived from the Children's House being inside the tenement, thus making it available to parents for observation at any time. She also felt that parents' financial support of the program via their rent promoted a sense of parent ownership. The teacher even lived in the same tenement building as did the children and their families, enabling her to be accessible to parents (Montessori, 1912/1964).

Parents, however, had accompanying obligations. Mothers were obliged to send their children to the Children's House clean and to cooperate with the teacher in the educational work. The regulations (see Figure 2-1) required mothers

Figure 2-1   **Rules and Regulation of the "Children's Houses"**

The Roman Association of Good Building hereby establishes within its tenement house number _____, a "Children's House," in which may be gathered together all children under common school age, belonging to the families of the tenants.

The chief aim of the "Children's House" is to offer, free of charge, to the children of those parents who are obliged to absent themselves for their work, the personal care which the parents are not able to give.

In the "Children's House" attention is given to the education, the health, the physical and moral development of the children. This work is carried on in a way suited to the age of the children.

There shall be connected with the "Children's House" a Directress, a Physician, and a Caretaker.

The programme and hours of the "Children's House" shall be fixed by the Directress.

There may be admitted to the "Children's House" all the children in the tenement between the ages of three and seven.

The parents who wish to avail themselves of the advantages of the "Children's House" pay nothing. They must, however, assume these binding obligations:

(a) To send their children to the "Children's House" at the appointed time, clean in body and clothing, and provided with a suitable apron.

(b) To show the greatest respect and deference toward the Directress and toward all persons connected with the "Children's House," and to co-operate with the Directress herself in the education of the children. Once a week, at least, the mothers may talk with the Directress, giving her information concerning the home life of the child, and receiving helpful advice from her.

There shall be expelled from the "Children's House":

(a) Those children who present themselves unwashed, or in soiled clothing.

(b) Those who show themselves to be incorrigible.

(c) Those whose parents fail in respect to the persons connected with the "Children's House," or who destroy through bad conduct the educational work of the institution.

From Montessori, M. (1964). *The Montessori Method* (pp. 70–71). New York: Schocken. (Originally published in 1912) to meet with the teacher at least once a week to learn of their children's progress and accept helpful advice. If children came to school unclean or unruly, they were sent home.

The first Children's House opened under Montessori's guidance and direction on January 6, 1907. A second opened in the same quarter on April 7, followed by a third in Milan in the fall of 1908. In November 1908, a house was opened for middle-class children in an affluent section of Rome. By 1916, the Montessori method was an international phenomenon.

Almost from the very beginning, then, despite its initial target population, the Montessori method served both children from poor and middle-class families, and in so doing, the comprehensiveness of its initial approach to early childhood education began to wane. When the method was implemented with children from more affluent families, many of the health, nutrition and family support components were omitted.

The shift from a comprehensive program to one with a more narrow curricular focus was reinforced further by the emphasis of Montessori's followers on her methods and materials, rather than on her insightful understandings about children and families. As pointed out by Kramer (1976/1988), patenting the Montessori method via its materials promoted, and helped institutionalize, the idea that they, rather than Montessori's principles, were the central focus of the method.

One could also speculate that this shift was facilitated by the complexities associated with program replication and different community contexts. In the mid-1960s, when the Montessori method was resurrected in the United States as an early intervention program for economically disadvantaged preschoolers, the model was characterized by the visible artifacts of the method: the prepared environment, didactic materials, and prescribed teacher-child interactions. The sense of community created by locating a program within a tenement complex and the linkages initially fostered among child, family, and schooling had paled behind an emphasis on academic preparation. This academic thrust was propelled by the method's cognitive emphasis and its success in teaching children behavioral self-control and reading and writing prior to first grade, accomplishments that aligned easily with the focus of most early intervention programs of preparing children for formal schooling.

When the first Children's House opened in Rome in 1907, Montessori was 37 years old. She was an established professional and a distinguished scientist and academic; she was highly regarded by her colleagues and Roman civic and social leaders. Montessori was also a charismatic and inspirational figure and a dynamic speaker (Cohen, 1969; Kramer, 1976/1988). The strength of her personality and convictions, plus the dramatic growth in printed mass media and international communication (Kliebard, 1986; Kramer, 1976/1988), helped ensure the rapid interest in, and transmission of, her ideas—not only to educators, but to the general public. Within the United States, the explosion of print materials also helped increase public consciousness of the changes being wrought in U.S. society by urbanization and industrialization (Kliebard, 1986).

From Italy to the United States

Montessori made her first trip to the United States in December 1913. When she arrived, she was at the peak of her career, one of the most famous women in the world. Her arrival shared headlines with the activities of Pancho Villa in Mexico and President Wilson's refusal to make a public statement on the question of women's suffrage (Kramer, 1976/1988). The beginning of World War I was only a year away. There were an unprecedented number of affluent residents and poor immigrants in the United States. The affluent were interested in education as a means for assimilating new immigrants and enriching the lives of their own children. According to Kramer (1976/1988),

> The Montessori system offered a program of reform to a reform-minded age. Through a new kind of educational institution—which seemed to have proved itself beyond anyone's wildest expectations . . . it would be possible to mold a new generation of children—independent, productive members of society—and at the same time solve many of the problems of the day, social inequities of class and sex among them. (p. 154)

Shifts toward an industrialized, urban economy and concerns with the "hordes" of immigrants created a receptive climate for Montessori's visit among the socially minded in the United States. Changing views about early childhood education furnished a less positive reception from early childhood leaders, however. The year of Montessori's arrival in the United States, 1913, was also the year the Committee of Nineteen[1] was preparing to publish its final report. Their report culminated a decade of professional, often acrimonious, debate between Frobelian and progressive educators regarding the proper nature of early childhood education. This report presented the new wave of thinking regarding early childhood curriculum. The Montessori method quickly was determined to be out of step with the new zeitgeist.

The first discussion of Montessori's work in a U.S. publication was in a series of articles by Jenny Merrill in *The Kindergarten-Primary Magazine,* beginning in December 1909. Reports of visits to Montessori schools and discussions of the method, its philosophy, and implications for U.S. kindergartens (nursery schools did not begin to flourish in the United States until the 1920s) appeared in newspapers and popular and professional magazines. Early visitors to the Casa dei Bambini included professional luminaries such as William Heard Kilpatrick of Columbia University (and a disciple of John Dewey); G. Stanley Hall of Clark University, who pioneered the child study movement; prominent child psychologists Arnold and Beatrice Gesell; and Jane Addams, the pioneer of settlement houses. But the U.S. visitors who really made a difference for Montessori were not scholarly professionals but influential individuals such as S. S. McClure, one of the most powerful

---

[1]Recall from Chapter 1 that this committee was convened by the International Kindergarten Union to resolve the conflict between advocates of Frobelian education and those wishing to develop early education programs aligned with new scientific thinking.

journalists of his time. McClure's magazine published a series of articles on Montessori in 1911 and 1912, and Mary Hubbard Bell, the wife of Alexander Graham Bell, set up a Montessori classroom for her two grandchildren in the spring of 1912 (Hunt, 1964; Kramer, 1976/1988).

Anne George, the first U.S. Montessori-trained teacher, opened the first Montessori school in the United States in the fall of 1911 with 12 children from upper-middle-class families in Tarrytown, New York. By the end of 1911, arrangements had been completed with a U.S. company for the manufacture and sale of Montessori's didactic materials. A U.S. edition of her book, *The Montessori Method,* translated by Anne George, was published in 1912. The first edition of 5,000 copies sold out in 4 days (Kramer, 1976/1988).

Popular enthusiasm for Montessori's work, however, was not duplicated within the early childhood profession. Early childhood educators expressed concern for the method's lack of interest in children's creative self-expression, the formality of activities, the exact way in which children had to use the didactic materials, and the curriculum's narrow scope (Weber, 1969), concerns that some early childhood educators continue to express. The fact that the Montessori method was mostly compared to the U.S. Frobelian kindergarten rather than more progressive programs was prophetic. According to Weber (1969), kindergarten teachers were just beginning to free themselves from "the curricular domination of one set of materials" and were less than eager to substitute a new set (p. 79).

Educators philosophically allied with progressive education especially rejected the method's failure to promote children's initiative to create and solve problems of their own making, and its lack of attention to children's social and emotional lives. Also problematic was the passive teacher role prescribed by the Montessori method. The limited role of the teacher, in sharp contrast with the "center-stage" role enacted by Frobelian educators, simply was not acceptable to many teachers. Montessori herself noted this contrast, though in her case the contrast was with conventional Italian public school educators (Hunt, 1964; Kramer, 1976/1988; Montessori, 1912/1964; Weber, 1969). Plus, according to White and Buka (1987), Montessori's ideas entered discussions in the United States at a time when the U.S. public was eager to reduce its reliance on European ideas and influence.

The death knell, however, was sounded by William Heard Kilpatrick, a disciple of John Dewey and one of the country's most influential progressive educators (Hunt, 1964; Kramer, 1976/1988; Weber, 1969). Kilpatrick (1914) contended that Montessori's ideas were tied to an outmoded theory. He wrote:

> We conclude . . . that Madame Montessori's doctrine of sense-training is based on an outworn and cast-off psychological theory; that the didactic apparatus devised to carry this theory into effect is in so far worthless; that what little value remains to the apparatus could be better got from the sense-experience incidental to properly directed play with wisely chosen, but less expensive and more childlike playthings. (p. 52)

Within 5 years of her 1913 visit to the United States, Montessori was all but forgotten by the U.S. public. Montessori continued disseminating her method throughout Europe and other parts of the world, but U.S. early childhood professionals returned to the issue that had been the focus of their attention before being diverted by the "new kid on the block"—developing a new, U.S. approach to early childhood education (Cohen, 1969; Kramer, 1976/1988; Weber, 1969).

Montessori's rapid descent was further assisted by her unwillingness to permit anyone other than herself to prepare Montessori teachers and by her insistence that her system be bought as a whole package, or not at all, thus blocking its sustenance from within the early childhood profession. For similar reasons, her popular support waned as well (Cohen, 1969; Kramer, 1976/1988).

The commercialism involved in patenting an educational method also was greeted with skepticism (Kramer, 1976/1988). Only one company in the United States was given the right to sell and distribute her didactic materials. To further ensure only authorized dissemination of her ideas, Montessori created the Association Montessori Internationale (AMI) in 1929 to supervise the training of teachers and to oversee the activities of Montessori schools and societies around the world.[2]

Montessori justified these decisions based on concern that her ideas would be distorted if not practiced exactly as she had translated them for classroom practice, and to protect her name and method from exploitation. Yet the motive for her focus on these concerns is open to speculation. In the process of giving up her other professional roles and creating a following outside the framework of any existing institution, Montessori eliminated a consistent stream of financial support. Thus, she became financially dependent on students' fees, and royalties from books and materials for her livelihood (Kramer, 1976/1988).

The Resurrection

J. McVicker Hunt, in his influential introduction to a new U.S. edition of The Montessori Method issued in 1964, attributed Montessori's decline to the fact that her ideas were too dissonant from those emerging in the early 1900s. Hunt's introduction not only placed the dissonance in historical perspective but also espoused that Montessori's moment in history had at last materialized. Accompanying the dominance of developmental and educational psychologists in early childhood education in the mid-1960s, changing psychological understandings (versus educational ones) provided justification for Montessori's reemergence as a viable model for early childhood education, even though early educators, such as Pitcher

---

[2]The AMI, which is located in Amsterdam, has 170 affiliated schools in the United States and 17 training programs. (American Montessori Society, 1999). The North American Montessori Teachers Association is affiliated with the AMI.

The American Montessori Society was formed in 1960 by Nancy Rambusch and has 900 public and private affiliated schools throughout the United States and 23 countries, and 49 affiliated teacher education programs (Baxter, 1999). Because Mrs. Rambusch attempted to Americanize the method, the AMI removed its seal of approval in 1963. According to an interview with Mario Montessori, "Nancy's grasp exceeded her reach; she thought she knew better than Dr. Montessori" (Cohen, 1969, p. 324).

(1966), expressed concern with the evangelical nature of advocates and with the program's academic focus.

Hunt identified four psychological precepts that minimized acceptance of Montessori's ideas when first introduced. First was the notion that school experience for 3- and 4-year-olds could be important for later development. Prior to the 1960s, children's development was believed to be predetermined by heredity. Adherence to this belief was aided by the fact that, to many, educating very young children outside the home was considered an infringement on the functions and rights of families.

A second deterring opinion was belief in fixed intelligence. Montessori's conception of mental retardation as amenable to pedagogical intervention contradicted this opinion. Her focus on cognitive development, including her encouragement of children learning to read, write, and count, also differed from the emphasis of the times on social development. Based on acceptance of predetermined, normative development, teaching of reading, writing, and counting to children before they were about 8 years was seen as a waste of time, and potentially harmful.

Third, the belief that all behavior was motivated by instincts or by painful stimuli, sex, or the need to achieve homeostasis (an internal balance) could not accommodate Montessori's belief that education should be based on children's spontaneous motivation for learning. Fourth, the behavioral emphasis in the early 1900s was on the response side of learning and its variations in different settings. This emphasis made Montessori's contention that generalizable knowledge could be abstracted from sensory training appear out-of-step with current psychological thinking. This was the referent for Kilpatrick's (1914; see above) contention that the Montessori method was based on "an outworn and cast-off psychological theory."

Hunt argued that revised thinking about each of these four ideas made the Montessori method appropriate for early childhood education in the mid-1960s. His analysis not only validated many of Montessori's ideas (in terms of 1960s thinking) but demonstrated just how revolutionary her thinking 57 years earlier had been.

Furthermore, Hunt's (1961) synthesis of the then-current empirical data, along with Bloom's work (1964), had recently provided scientific validation for the contributing role of environment (versus heredity) to intellectual development and argued the special receptiveness of intellectual development to environmental stimulation during the early years of a child's life. Consequently, Hunt's enthusiastic introduction to the reissue of *The Montessori Method* and his suggestion that the method provided a potential solution to the "problem of the match" (an optimum discrepancy between what an individual already knows and what is being learned) were significant.

His endorsement provided not only the aura of his prestige but also reinforced Montessori's contention that her method was based on scientific pedagogy. As expressed by McDermott in his introduction to the reissue of Montessori's

Spontaneous Activity in Education (1917/1965), "It is Montessori, above all others, who holds to entwining of empirical method, scientific data, and human aspiration as the irreducible elements in any theory of education" (p. xv). Interest in the Montessori method in the mid-1960s coincided with the U.S. search for a scientific approach to early childhood education.

Renewed enthusiasm for the Montessori method also was fostered by the fact that the Children's House had been organized for "the culturally deprived" of the Quarter of San Lorenzo. "From the observations of Americans who visited Montessori's Houses of Children, one gathers they were successful at precisely this business of counteracting the effects of cultural deprivation on those symbolic skills required for success in school and in an increasingly technological culture" (Hunt, 1964, p. xxvi).

Intense interest in early childhood curriculum models, including the Montessori method, diminished during the late 1970s and early 1980s, however, as federal support for diverse approaches to early education waned, program evaluations disappointed, and new social needs surfaced (see Chapter 1 for further discussion). Individuals who continued to use the Montessori method practiced primarily in private early childhood programs. So, it is perhaps somewhat unexpected that the most recent surge of interest in the Montessori method comes from the public schools (Chattin-McNichols, 1992b; Weiss, 1992) and publicly funded charter schools.

According to Weiss (1992), national director of the American Montessori Society, the first public school Montessori program was established in the late 1960s, but public school programs began to multiply with development of the magnet school concept in the mid-1970s, and in the 1990s with the creation of charter schools. Magnet schools often were created to help school districts comply with federal desegregation requirements, and to draw white, often middle-class families, into city public schools. Charter schools use public funds and operate under contracts or "charters" with local school boards or states to provide educational alternatives to public schools. In 2000, there were 245 public schools with Montessori programs (North American Montessori Teacher Association, 2000) and approximately 50 charter schools (D. Shapiro, personal communication, January 11, 2000). According to Chattin-McNichols (1992b), the increase in Montessori programs demonstrates that the Montessori method has proven its "salability" (p. 208) to parents.

☞ MONTESSORI'S METHOD

The review of Montessori's method is organized into two parts: an examination of her essential pedagogical premises and a descriptive overview of the program and its practices. This organizational framework was selected so emphasis would be placed on the ideas that explain Montessori's thinking. It also is an attempt to portray the relationship between Montessori's philosophical framework and her method. Isolating the specifics of her method from their philosophical underpinnings diminishes not only an understanding of her intent but also decreases appreciation of the coherence in her thinking.

Montessori's method and her writings about it, however, are very detailed. Not only was she concerned with every aspect of a child's life, but because her method was based on scientific pedagogy, she was obligated to specify every particular in order to ensure accurate replication. Consequently, it is not possible for a single chapter to provide a thorough overview. Readers are encouraged, therefore, to read at least one of Montessori's publications directly, especially those noted in "For Further Reading."

We rely on Montessori's own writings for descriptions of her method. Chattin-McNichols (1992b) has challenged this decision when made by other authors because he feels reliance on Montessori's original publications ignores changes that have occurred over the years. Yet, by his own admission, additions have been "small changes and adjustments" (p. 21), primarily modifications to sequence or content, not reformation of any of the basic premises that define the Montessori method. Thus, in an attempt to present Montessori to others most accurately, it still seems valid to minimize the number of interpretations between the original Montessori and the reader.

Because of the redundancy found in her publications, it can be assumed that the ideas discussed here can be found throughout her writings, unless otherwise indicated. Words and phrases placed in quotes unaccompanied by a citation reflect wording consistently used by Montessori. By frequent use of her own words, we have attempted to better represent her thinking and also to corroborate our interpretations.

It should be pointed out that Montessori wrote only five of the many books that bear her name as author. Four of these works were written and translated into English prior to 1920: *The Montessori Method,* which was published in English in 1912; *Pedagogical Anthropology,* published in English in 1913; and *The Advanced Montessori Method: Spontaneous Activity in Education,* Volume 1, and *The Advanced Montessori Method: The Montessori Elementary Material,* both published in English in 1917. Montessori was directly responsible for the content of these books and supervised their translations from Italian into English. The fifth work, *Dr. Montessori's Own Handbook,* appeared originally in English and was published in 1914 after her return from the United States. These five publications, which describe her method and didactic materials, contain most of what is essential and original in Montessori's thinking, a fact also noticed by reviewers of her later writings (Kramer, 1976/1988).

Other works by Montessori, such as *The Absorbent Mind* (1949/1963), *The Discovery of the Child* (1948), and *The Secret of Childhood* (1937/1966), are published translations of her many lectures and did not directly involve Montessori (although Montessori did rewrite *The Absorbent Mind* into Italian after its initial publication, which, in turn was retranslated into English). These publications are problematic because Montessori always delivered her presentations in Italian, which, in turn were translated by an interpreter, recorded by listeners, and *then* retranslated into the language of publication. Furthermore, Montessori always spoke extemporaneously and never used notes; thus, there is no way of checking the various translations against an original (Bentley, 1964).

Essential Conceptual Elements

Montessori's writings are dominated by five recurring, interlocking beliefs:

1. her method represents a scientific approach to education;
2. the "secret of childhood" resides in the fact that through their spontaneous activity, children labor to "make themselves into men";
3. mental development, similar to physical growth, is the result of a natural, internally regulated force;
4. liberty is the imperative ingredient that enables education to assist the "complete unfolding of (a child's) life";
5. order, most especially within the child, but also in the child's environment, is prerequisite to the child becoming an independent, autonomous, and rational individual. (See Montessori, 1912/1964, 1917/1964, 1936/1970, 1937/1966, 1949/1963.)

These beliefs were embedded in Montessori's conviction that her method would revolutionize society by creating an educational environment that responded to children's innate nature and nurtured the child's complete spiritual and psychic actualization. This anticipated outcome, in turn, defined the purpose of education. Montessori's method was directed to the development of the individual child and to the purposeful and useful contributions made by individuals to the social collective, thus contributing to society's enhanced functioning.

The Montessori Method as Scientific Pedagogy. The original title of the Italian version of *The Montessori Method* was *The Method of Scientific Pedagogy Applied to Child Education in the Children's Houses.* Montessori emphasized repeatedly that her method was an approach for putting new principles of science into practice. "My method is scientific, both in its substance and in its aim. It makes for the attainment of a more advanced stage of progress . . ." (Montessori, 1917/1965, p. 8).

Montessori drew directly from the experimental psychology, pedagogical anthropology, and medicine of her time. She advocated the potential of a scientific approach to pedagogy by describing the progress medicine had made since becoming scientific in dramatically improving the physical well-being of individuals. Similarly, scientific pedagogy would ensure the spiritual and intellectual well-being of children and, in so doing, transform the future of civilization. Scientific pedagogy was a means toward "the science of forming man" (Montessori, 1912/1964, p. 2).

Montessori credited Guiseppe Sergi, her teacher from medical school, for proposing the idea that the scientific principles of anthropology could be applied to studying pupils (Montessori, 1913, 1912/1964). In the early 1900s, which also marked the beginning of the scientific movement in psychology and education, the methods of anthropology involved measurements of human features to determine ideal racial characteristics and physical anomalies. Although Montessori did, in fact, regularly measure children's physical characteristics, the significance of pedagogical anthropology for her came from the shift it facilitated toward directly observing and learning from children. Children and their actions, rather than general principles or abstract philosophical ideas, became the basis of pedagogy (Montessori, 1912/1964, 1913).

Naturalistic observations of individual children led to an understanding of children based on their common characteristics, which, Montessori emphasized, were not those of adults reduced to a diminutive scale. "This is precisely the new development of pedagogy that goes under the name of *scientific*; in order to educate, it is essential to know those who are to be educated . . . because we cannot educate anyone until we know him thoroughly" (Montessori, 1913, p. 17).

According to Montessori, it was the naturalistic observation of children within a carefully prepared environment, and the teacher's new role as objective observer, that characterized her method as scientific. It was also this aspect that required specialized teacher training, so that teachers could learn "to divest (themselves) of personality in order to become instruments of investigation" (Montessori, 1913, p. 24). Scientific preparation of the teacher was joined with preparation of the spirit: "But let us seek to implant in the soul the self-sacrificing spirit of the scientist with the reverent love of the disciple of Christ, and we shall have prepared the *spirit* of the teacher" (Montessori, 1912/1964, p. 13).

Scientific pedagogy emerged from her experimentation (Montessori, 1912/1964). The prepared environment was initially a classroom organized for the careful observations that "determine experimentally, with . . . a precision not hitherto attained, what is the mental attitude of the child at various ages, and hence, if the fitting material for development be offered, what will be the average level of intellectual development according to age" (Montessori, 1917/1965, pp. 80–81). Once Montessori concluded her 2-year experiment, the prepared environment, determined by the findings from her experiment, became the scientifically arranged context that precisely nurtured children's development.

The liberty of the child, the freedom to develop spontaneously, also possessed scientific importance. Liberty was synonymous with an environment free of unnatural inhibitors to the child's growth and the teacher's observations. Montessori's emphasis, however, was on knowing the child as a member of the species, not as a unique, multifaceted individual. This frame of reference permitted her to assume that her findings could uniformly apply to all children.

The Secret of Childhood: Spontaneous Activity. Montessori discovered the "secret" of childhood from her careful observations of children at the Children's House, where children's spontaneous activity emerged and took shape unhampered by adult intervention and imposition. The secret Montessori tried to share with the world was her finding that children were psychic (psychological and spiritual), as well as biological, "creatures" and were endowed with a plan of organic development, which was expressed through their spontaneous activity. The formative outcomes of children's spontaneous activity, however, could be fully realized only in a carefully prepared and orderly environment that freed children's natural evolution from external obstructions.

Montessori contended that children's spontaneous activity was especially critical between 3 and 6 years. During these sensitive years, children are intrinsically motivated to bring their chaotic inner world as expressed through spontaneous activity into an orderly coherence, a prerequisite to the development of rational, intellectual thought. Once the sensitive period passes, special proclivity toward the needed developmental activity disappears. In her later writings, Montessori expressed the belief that the first 2 years of life are the formative years that influence the entire construct of the child's personality (see, for example, *The Absorbent Mind*, 1949/1963; *The Child in the Family*, 1936/1970).

Although Montessori, unlike most of her contemporaries, believed that the environment was critical in its ability to help or hinder a child's development, she also strongly believed that the environment could never create. The prepared environment, with its emphasis on liberty, provided an environment where a child could respond to his or her inner forces of growth without being stifled.

This relationship between the child and the prepared environment occurred by organizing for each child "the means necessary for his internal nourishment" (Montessori, 1917/1965, p. 70). These means, which were informed by Montessori's experiments, facilitated a congruence between a child's inner needs and the environment's ability to fulfill those needs. "In order to expand, the child, left at liberty to exercise his activities, ought to find in his surroundings something organized in direct relation to his internal organization which is developing itself by natural laws" (Montessori, 1917/1965, pp. 69–70).

Equally important, in order to be educative, the environment needs to focus the child's activity toward the essential task of self-formation in accordance with the inherited plan. "And the spirit, organized in this manner under the guidance of an order which corresponds to its natural order, becomes fortified, grows vigorously, and manifests itself in the equilibrium, the serenity, the self-control which produce the wonderful discipline characteristic of the behavior of our children" (Montessori, 1914/1964, p. 82).

Montessori's emphasis on children's self-creation in conjunction with liberty necessitated that the well-prepared environment contain the means for self-education. Consistent with Montessori's views regarding scientific pedagogy, however, the process of auto-education was not random. The activities for auto-education had to correspond to the child's emerging inner life, which, in turn, could be determined only by careful study of the child. Montessori created her well-known didactic materials for this purpose. Once Montessori completed *her* direct study of children, however, teachers' child study occurred in reference to what already was documented about children. The intent of careful observation of children no longer was to learn about children and their unique interests or ways of knowing about the world but rather to ensure the appropriate correspondence between child and material.

Independence was a necessary behavioral accompaniment to Montessori's concern for liberty and auto-education. The meaning of independence referred not only to "freedom to" but "freedom from," freedom *to* take care of one's own needs, and freedom *from* dependency on others. Montessori described the child at birth as helpless, and "circumscribed by bonds which limit his activity" because of social dependency on others. Freedom from these bonds defines individual liberty.

The first phase of Montessori's curriculum, the exercises for practical life, is organized to overcome these limitations and facilitate a child's independence. The resultant independence enables a child to care for herself and nourish her self-formation through auto-education. Consistent with Montessori's philosophy, the exercises of practical life (described below) are carefully structured to ensure that the child's independent movements and actions become increasingly coordinated and orderly.

Montessori's definition of child respect was demonstrated in her intense interest in the child's natural development and her utmost care to avoid intrusions into the child's activity. Respect for the child's spontaneous activity, however, should not be confused with a laissez-faire approach. Montessori prepared the environment to ensure that the environmental liberty provided to children promoted, rather than diminished, their developmental "ascent." When properly prepared, the environment offers children the external means needed for self-perfection—which, according to Montessori, could not be found in a chaotic, unruly environment.

At a more tangible level, the limits of individual liberty are set by the collective interest, represented by "what we universally call good breeding" (Montessori, 1912/1964, p. 87). Montessori discouraged ill-bred acts and annoying and offending behaviors. Teachers' suppression of inappropriate behaviors also is important in helping children come to know the difference between good and evil. Thus Montessori's interpretation of liberty was not synonymous with permitting children to do whatever they pleased.

Teachers' observations of children are critical to securing the method's success. Teachers' careful observations ensure that lessons never provoke "unnatural effort" on the part of the child. Provoking unnatural effort not only alters the child's natural, developmental ascent but also obstructs the teachers' ability to know the spontaneous activity of a child.

Knowledge of a child's spontaneous activity is critical to enabling teachers to determine when individual children are ready for the next step in their formation and for ensuring that the environment provides the needed "nourishment." In this subtle fashion, the teacher structures the alignment between the child and the environment (recall Hunt's conclusion that the Montessori method solved the problem of the match) and shapes the formative sprouts of children's emergent psychic and physiological development in the directions they are predisposed to grow.

This conceptualization of teaching, plus Montessori's negativity toward existing, rigid teaching practices in Italy, led her to name her teachers *directresses.* The directress does not directly teach children; instead she ensures that the environment provides what individual children need for their own inner construction.

Because Montessori conceived of children's behaviors as innately driven, extrinsic rewards and external punishment are considered not only unnecessary but also harmful, because of their potential to disturb a child's natural development. Children's disruptive behaviors are interpreted as indicators that their innate predisposition for orderly development is being thwarted. Relying on similar reasoning, Montessori interpreted fantasy and imaginative behaviors as characteristic of immature, disorderly minds.

The Child's Labor. The child, according to Montessori, is born in a state of physical and psychological chaos. The primary outcome of positive psychic and physiological development is growth from disorder to order, which, in turn, leads the child toward more adaptive behavior. Disorder is synonymous with confusion and awkwardness; order is associated with purposefulness, rationality, achievement, and self-satisfaction. Consequently, work, defined as purposeful and ordered activity toward a determined end, is highly valued. Play, defined as its antithesis, is not. The ". . . achievement of psychic order . . . is the beginning of progressive evolution in the inner life" (Montessori, 1917/1965, p. 90).

Psychic order is created as a by-product of the child's innate ability to become totally absorbed in an activity. This attentive fixation promotes psychic formation by bringing order to internal chaos,

> as if in a saturated solution, a point of crystallization had formed, round which the whole chaotic and fluctuating mass united, producing a crystal of wonderful forms. Thus, when the phenomenon of the polarisation of attention had taken place, all that was disorderly and fluctuating in the consciousness of the child seemed to be organizing itself into a spiritual creation, the surprising characteristics of which are reproduced in every individual. (Montessori, 1917/1965, p. 68)

Internal chaos is behaviorally characterized not only by unfocused/disorderly behavior but also by lack of sensory differentiation (which also is disorderly). Montessori specifically designed her didactic materials to bring order to the child's perceptions of the environment. Intimately related to her concern for order, orderly development of the senses was also important because education of the senses was considered the basis of intelligence. The more differentiated (ordered) children's perceptions of stimuli, the more intelligent their behavior.

The ultimate manifestation of internal order is the child's increasing ability to discipline him- or herself toward the accomplishment of a goal, either self-determined or set by someone else. The development of self-discipline indicates the growing presence of will, which is exhibited in focused, self-directed, purposeful actions.

The conclusive sign of active self-discipline, the evidence of mature autonomy, is reflected in a child's ability to so discipline herself that she can submit her spontaneous activity to the will of a higher authority. This achievement requires that a child learn not only to impose self-restraint, but also to actively coordinate her chaotic movements and thoughts and direct them toward a useful purpose.

Montessori's ideas about obedience frequently are challenged. But the meaning of obedience, as discussed by Montessori, is imbued with meaning that extends beyond passively conforming to someone else's expectations. To the contrary, the true meaning of obedience for Montessori resided in an individual willingly, actively, even joyfully, submitting herself to someone else's will. To those who criticize Montessori's views on obedience for fostering conformity, Chattin-McNichols (1992b) responded:

> This notion of obedience is one in which the spiritual side of Montessori and her world view are clearly seen. People who deny the existence of God, feel that it is impossible to enter into a personal relationship with God, or feel that such discussions have no bearing on child development or early education will have trouble understanding Montessori's view on this matter. Such people will not understand how people, including children, can find freedom in obedience to a higher authority. (p. 165)

Once Montessori's interpretations of will, of discipline, of liberty, and of order are situated within her spiritual/metaphysical framework, the seeming contradictions among these concepts, and between her dual roles of scientist and mystic, dissipate. Montessori's pedagogy was predicated on her beliefs in the existence of a superior being. The first 6 years of a child's life, similar to the beginning of creation, produce order out of chaos. The directress represents an all-knowing, benevolent power. Through creation of the prepared environment, she nourishes children's inherent destiny and determines the future:

> When the teacher shall have touched in this way, soul for soul, each one of her pupils, awakening and inspiring the life within them as if she were an invisible spirit, she will then possess each soul, and a sign, a single word from her shall suffice; for each one will feel her in a living and vital way, will recognize her and will listen to her. . . . They will look toward her who had made them live, and will hope and desire to receive from her, new life. (Montessori, 1912/1964, p. 116)

Nor did Montessori's belief in scientific, "rational" thinking challenge her framework. For Montessori, science provided a means for verifying her metaphysical constructs. She conceptualized science, as she did her method, as a carefully sequenced technique, not an ongoing process of discovery. Science, like her method, could create order out of disorder and produce absolute truth.

The Montessori Program

Based on her experiments in the Children's Houses, Montessori believed that she had created a scientific and rational method for facilitating the child's "inner work of psychical adaptation." The method was not amenable to child or teacher modification because, in line with Montessori's thinking, any modification would annul its scientific validity. The method and its materials were deliberately devised and were to be precisely used.

In addition to the physical environment of the Children's House, which includes the actions of the directress, Montessori outlined three components to her method for 3- to 7-year-olds who work together in multiaged groupings: motor education, sensory education, and language education.

Children's care of the classroom environment provides a primary means for motor education. The didactic materials provide for sensory and language education. Montessori described the accomplishments of this formative developmental period as preparation for life: children emerged adaptive and self-disciplined, their personality ordered and equipped for higher order learning. The elementary curriculum builds on the academic skills already possessed by Montessori preschool graduates and is extraordinarily detailed and highly sequenced. The elementary curriculum encompasses the teaching of Italian grammar, reading, arithmetic, geometry and metrics, and drawing and music (Montessori, 1917/1964).

The Prepared Environment. The learning environment, which could vary if resources were limited, included several rooms plus direct access to a real garden that could be tended by the children. The principal room was the space for "intellectual work," referring to the work with the didactic materials that are described below. Other proposed rooms included a sitting room or parlor for children's casual interactions and a dining room with low, accessible cupboards for dinner and silverware so children could set the tables and return utensils to their place.

The plates were real china and the tumblers glass so children could learn to take care of fragile items and directly understand the consequences of their being treated carelessly. The dressing room contained shelves for each child and wash basins of child height, so children could learn and practice proper hygiene.

Although Montessori apparently cannot be credited for originating the use of child-sized furniture (see Hewes, 1983), the frequency with which child-sized furniture is suggested as a Montessori innovation suggests that she must have helped to popularize its use. Perhaps what is unique to Montessori is her emphasis on the classroom design of furniture and its adaptation to children as critical to the child's healthy development. Now, of course, child-sized furniture and learning materials specially designed for children's intellectual development is an accepted part of early childhood classrooms; Montessori's ideas on this subject now seem commonplace. But Montessori reasoned that without these adjustments, children cannot learn to socially adapt to their environments; nor can they learn to function independently and responsibly.

The furniture, child-sized tables, chairs, and sofas, was light in weight so it could be moved by children and light in color so children could easily wash it. Montessori also emphasized that the working room had to contain a long, low cupboard with large doors to store the didactic materials. The height of the cupboard helped make the materials easily accessible, thus fostering independence. A second indispensable piece of furniture was a chest of drawers containing several columns of little drawers, each with a bright handle and a small card with a name on it. Each child had his or her own drawer for personal belongings. The room was decorated with pictures hung at children's eye level, and there were ornamental and flowering plants. Montessori believed beauty promoted concentration and refreshed the spirit. Again, it might be hard to read this information with appreciation because today such furnishings are commonplace; but a child-centered environment was quite innovative in the early 20th century.

Motor Education.   Motor education describes a series of exercises that aid the normal development of physiological movements, such as walking, breathing, and speech, and enable children to care for their own practical needs of dressing and undressing. Montessori divided motor education into two parts: free gymnastics and educational gymnastics. Free gymnastics did not involve apparatus; it incorporated required and directed exercises, such as marching, to facilitate self-control and poise, and free games with balls, hoops, and kites.

The aim of educational gymnastics was to foster independence and to "give order to (a child's) movements, leading him to those actions which his efforts are actually tending" (Montessori, 1917/1965, pp. 20–21). Educational gymnastics included caring for plants and animals and the practical life exercises. These exercises embraced not only the development of what we would today call self-help skills, but also care for the Children's House, rhythmic movements, gardening, and manual work, which had as its aim production of socially useful objects, such as clay pots.

To teach children self-help skills, Montessori created a collection of wooden frames to which different materials were attached that could be buttoned, hooked, tied together, and so forth. Montessori's description of how the directress should model their use illustrates the way in which she promoted, in careful sequence, the orderly development of children's movements. The teacher, sitting beside a child, "performs the necessary movements of the fingers very slowly and deliberately, separating the movements themselves into their different parts, and letting them be seen clearly and minutely" (Montessori, 1917/1965, p. 22).

As with all the materials, the directress silently demonstrates their appropriate use. Montessori felt words should be kept to a minimum because they distract children from focusing on what they are to learn. Children are taught all movements in this way, including how to sit, rise from one's seat, take up and lay down objects, and offer them to others; wash their faces, polish their shoes, wash the furniture, and set the table. Each exercise is broken down into its component parts and carefully sequenced and analyzed in order to promote the larger purpose of these exercises: the child's coordinated, proficient, and self-restrained movements, all of which are directed toward a useful outcome increasingly under the child's personal control.

Inasmuch as preparing the environment is analogous to a scientist's preparation of instruments, motor education is comparable to the scientist's preparation of subjects. In this instance, preparation of the child primes him

> to exercise himself and to form himself as a man. It is not movement for its own sake that he will derive from these exercises, but a powerful co-efficient in the complex formation of his personality. . . . From his consciousness of this development . . . the child derives the impulse to persist in these tasks, the industry to perform them, the intelligent joy he shows in their completion. (Montessori, 1917/1965, pp. 151–152)

Sensory Education. The Montessori method emphasizes methodical education of the senses based on Montessori's belief that education of the senses is the basis of intellectual development. Montessori aimed to refine the differential perception of stimuli by means of repeated exercise. The didactic materials, which are the vehicles for sensory development (see Figure 2-2 for a listing of Montessori's didactic materials), were developed so children could exercise (versus educate) their senses. The didactic materials are probably the Montessori method's best known attribute. Their use, though, only comprised 1 hour of her proposed daily schedule (see Figure 2-3), which, it will be recalled, initially corresponded to parents' working hours (Montessori, 1912/1964).

The didactic materials were designed to develop a child's increasingly refined ability to differentiate qualities of color, form, size, texture, temperature, and weight. They are carefully sequenced/graded so that as a child moves from one material to another, distinctions in size, texture, and so forth are finer and finer.

The didactic materials are auto-educative. They are structured to allow only one correct response. This characteristic makes them self-correcting and allows children to proceed at their own pace, independent of the directress, once a lesson

Figure 2-2   **Montessori Didactic Materials**

Didactic Materials for the Education of the Senses
3 sets of solid insets
3 sets of solids in graduated sizes: pink cubes, brown prisms, and colored rods
Geometric solids (e.g., prism, pyramid, sphere)
Rectangular tablets with rough and smooth surfaces
Collection of various stuffs (e.g., velvets, satins, woolens)
Small wooden tablets of different weights
2 boxes, each containing 64 colored tablets
Chest of drawers containing plane insets
3 series of cards on which are pasted geometrical forms in paper
Collection of cylindrical closed boxes (sounds)
Double series of musical bells, wooden boards on which are painted the lines used in music, small wooden discs for the notes
Didactic Materials for the Preparation for Writing and Arithmetic
2 sloping desks and various iron insets
Cards on which are pasted sandpaper letters
2 alphabets of colored cardboard in different sizes
Cards on which are pasted sandpaper numerals
A series of large cards bearing the same figures in smooth paper for the enumeration of numbers above ten
2 boxes with small sticks for counting
Drawings belonging to the method and colored pencils
Frames for lacing, buttoning, and so forth

From Montessori, M. (1964). *Dr. Montessori's Own Handbook* (pp. 18–21). New York: Robert Bentley, Inc. (Original work published in 1914)

Figure 2-3   **Schedule of a Child's Day**

Opening at Nine O'clock—Closing at Four O'clock
- 9–10. Entrance. Greeting. Inspection as to personal cleanliness. Exercises of practical life; helping one another to take off and put on the aprons. Going over the room to see that everything is dusted and in order. Language: Conversation period: Children give an account of the events of the day before. Religious exercises.
- 10–11. Intellectual exercises. Objective lessons interrupted by short rest periods. Nomenclature, Sense exercises.
- 11–11:30. Simple gymnastics: Ordinary movements done gracefully, normal position of the body, walking, marching in line, salutations, movements for attention, placing of objects gracefully.
- 11:30–12. Luncheon: Short prayer.
- 12–1. Free games.
- 1–2. Directed games, if possible, in the open air. During this period the older children in turn go through with the exercises of practical life, cleaning the room, dusting, putting the material in order. General inspection for cleanliness: Conversation.
- 2–3. Manual work. Clay modelling, design, etc.
- 3–4. Collective gymnastics and songs, if possible in the open air. Exercises to develop forethought: Visiting, and caring for, the plants and animals.

From Montessori, M. (1964). *The Montessori Method* (pp. 119–120). New York: Schocken Books. (Original work published in 1912)

has been received. Children's repetitive use of the same didactic material was evidence, according to Montessori, of the child's work toward self-formation; in turn, it is the activity of self-formation that is the child's work.

The didactic materials represent the primary means by which the environment is prepared, that is, individualized, for each child. A child's progressive use of the didactic materials corresponds to his or her schedule of psychical development. The self-correcting component ensures a child's inner development is being appropriately directed. A child's eventual disregard for the material reveals mastery of the perceptual differentiation inherent in the material.

A child's increasing perceptual sophistication, in turn, epitomizes the child's increasingly orderly representation of the environment. Sequential mastery of the didactic materials forms the foundation of the child's intellectual development by enabling him or her to more accurately gather information through the senses and learn from the environment.

> The didactic material, in fact, does not offer to the child the "content" of the mind, but the order for that "content." It causes him to distinguish identities from differences, extreme differences from fine gradations, and to classify, under conceptions of quality and of quantity, the most varying sensations appertaining to surfaces, colors, dimensions, forms and sounds. The mind has formed itself by a special exercise of attention, observing, comparing, and classifying. (Montessori, 1914/1964, pp. 82–83)

Language Education. The language component of the Montessori method has two parts: the association of language with sensory perceptions, and reading and writing. Language education occurs at the same time as sensory education. It fixes, by the use of exact words, the ideas that the mind has acquired.

Writing, reading, and arithmetic are considered later developments that naturally follow education of the senses, emerging around 4 years of age. Sensory education, in addition to its other contributions to children's development, prepares their minds and hands for writing, and for the ideas of quantity, identity, differences, and gradation. Thus, Montessori writes of children's "explosion into writing," which precedes reading as a natural next-step in a child's intellectual development.

The directress plays a more direct role in this process through presentation of three-step lessons that accompany the child's use of the didactic materials. These lessons are presented as simply as possible, to avoid placing any obstacles between the child and the experience and to minimize any interference with the child's spontaneous activity. During the first step or period, the directress presents the name of the focal characteristic, for example, "This is red." In the second period, the child is tested on her recognition of the object corresponding to the name: "Give me the red." In the third and final period, the child is asked to identify the name of the object: "What is this?" This sequence, according to Montessori, brings order to children's experience and leads a child from sensations to ideas, from the concrete to the abstract.

Absence of an appropriate response from a child during any of these lessons is interpreted as indication of his lack of readiness for the psychic association that the directress is attempting to promote. In such circumstances, the directress is expected to retreat quietly and to try again another time. Under no circumstances should the directress try to correct the child. To do so could lead the child to make an unnatural effort to learn the desired response and thus confound his spontaneous activity.

Montessori presented learning to write and read as extensions of sensory education. The preparatory exercises for writing and reading are embedded within the practical life exercises and sensory education. These program components develop the motoric and perceptual skills needed for writing and reading.

Learning to write and read also is directed by specialized didactic materials. The specially developed didactic materials for writing have children trace outlines and insides of geometric figures with colored pencils, trace sandpaper letters using the fingers and motions associated with writing (which fixes the visual image of letters in muscular memory), and construct words from movable alphabet letters. As the child traces various letters, the directress gives the appropriate letter sound. The child sees a letter, feels it, and hears its sound. Finally, when children begin to construct words, they also learn to sound them out.

As noted previously, Montessori felt children's "explosion into writing" precedes their learning to read. Didactic materials for the lessons in reading consist of cards on which are written words and phrases well known to the children. Children already know from their previous work how to sound out words phonetically. The next step in the sequence involves understanding the sense of the word—giving meaning to the sounds—which the method provokes by giving children opportunities to associate the written word with its representation, for example, the word *ball* with the actual object. Children repeatedly sound out the word written on the card until "finally the word bursts upon his consciousness" (Montessori, 1912/1964, p. 298; it should be noted that Italian grammar and phonology suffer from few of the exceptions that characterize English). The exercise is concluded by having the child place the word read with the corresponding object.

Montessori found that most children learned to write and read by the age of 5. The ability to make use of written language to express ideas is viewed as an indication that children have achieved the mental maturity to begin elementary work, during which the process initiated in the Children's House is continued albeit with a subject matter focus (Montessori, 1917/1964).

ஐ THE IMPORTANCE OF TIMING

Initial interest in the Montessori method in the United States, as well as revival of interest after its "dismissal" in 1916, reinforces the significance of historical timing. It also suggests the extent to which preferences for particular educational ideas are linked to cultural, economic, and societal interests and beliefs.

Montessori's arrival in the United States in 1913 found a fertile environment in terms of popular interest and societal need. However, early childhood educators had just completed a stressful reexamination of their practices, thus, perhaps, making them less willing to open themselves to further debate. Furthermore, despite overlapping beliefs in science as a basis for early education and appreciation for a child-centered approach, Montessori's educational assumptions and method differed in ways that the thinking of the times would not accommodate.

This disjunction probably was exacerbated by the fact that Montessori thought of her method as complete. Her method was based on scientific pedagogy, which, in her thinking, led to the discovery of absolute truth (Montessori, 1912/1964). Even though her results were based on only 2 years of "experimentation" in the Children's Houses, she did not view her techniques as arbitrary or open to further experimentation (Kramer, 1976/1988; Montessori, 1917/1965). Montessori (1912/1964) rationalized this short experimental period by proclaiming it the culmination of years of effort that began with the work of Itard and then Sequin.

In the mid-1960s, however, Montessori's ideas found not only popular interest, but also new psychological assumptions regarding child development that brought with them scholarly support of her thinking. Even more important, her ideas corresponded with societal needs and interest, and found policy support at the highest levels for reexamining and expanding early childhood education, especially for poor children. In the mid-1960s, the Montessori method found its historical, societal, and educational "match."

With the apparent interest from public schools, the Montessori method is aligned once again at a powerful intersection of societal and educational need (academic success for a diverse student population). In the 1960s as well as the present, interest in the Montessori method has swelled in response to the model's capacity, at least rhetorically, to respond to larger societal concerns. It is noteworthy that at no time in its U.S. history has the Montessori method been touted by mainstream early childhood education. However, as the National Association for the Education of Young Children responds to challenges to enlarge the conceptualization of "developmentally appropriate" teaching practices, the Montessori method is being reexamined for its contribution in terms of what constitutes "appropriate" practices (Humphryes, 1998).

Montessori's ardent, longtime followers also deserve credit for sustaining the Montessori method, including internalization of Montessori's messianic zeal and fervor. Almost from the beginning of her work, Montessori surrounded herself with a small group of women who devoted their lives to her. On November 10, 1910, this group, along with Montessori, even met in a Roman chapel to dedicate their lives to the cause (Cohen, 1969; Kramer, 1976/1988).

On her death in 1952, Montessori's ideas and methods continued to be tightly controlled by her adherents. Her efforts were sustained by her son, Mario, who served as president of the Association Montessori Internationale until his death in 1981. Then her grandson, Dr. Mario Montessori, Jr., fulfilled this role, although he has been less involved in the AMI's activities (Chattin-McNichols, 1992b).

These efforts to sustain and control the integrity of the Montessori method have not been without negative consequence, however. In addition to sustaining the continuation of the Montessori method, they have helped ensure isolation of the method from mainstream educational thought and limited intellectual growth of the model (Kramer, 1976/1988), a characteristic further strengthened by the dominance of Montessori's writings in Montessori teacher-training programs (Simons & Simons, 1986).

As acknowledged by Chattin-McNichols (1992b), an advocate of the Montessori method and a Montessori teacher educator and supervisor, many Montessorians feel that their training (which takes about 12 months and on successful completion results in certification as a Montessori teacher) has taught them everything they need to know about children and teaching. Consequently, many feel they have no need to remain current with developments in the fields of child development and early childhood education. According to Chattin-McNichols, there is almost no communication between Montessorians and other educators.

This discussion helps explain Kramer's conclusion that Montessori's ideas "became enshrined in a movement that took on more and more of the character of a special cult rather than becoming part of the mainstream of educational theory and practice" (1976/1988, p. 16). In terms of our investigation of curriculum models, these factors reveal the interplay between the personalities of individuals and their models of curriculum.

This discussion also raises questions regarding the viability of static approaches to education. Based on their review of Montessori's ideas and methods, Simons and Simons (1986) concluded "that Montessori education, as practiced today, is misguided in its attempt to keep alive a system of education that may have been effective and appropriate in the past, but which, being fossilized, is inappropriate for the children of today" (p. 218). In attempting to protect the purity of her method, Montessori helped guarantee that it would be challenged as intellectually out of date.

These insights, which benefit from historical hindsight, need not be limited to discussion of the Montessori method. Ideally, hindsight might provoke foresight. Perhaps the Montessori experience illuminates a tension inherent to all curriculum models. If such is the case, the Montessori method, rather than being an anomaly, might function as one of the clearest illustrations of the potentially restraining character of curriculum models.

ℐ FOR FURTHER READING

Kramer, R. (1976/1988). *Maria Montessori: A biography.* Reading, MA: Addison-Wesley.

Kramer's biography of Montessori places her work within both a historical and personal context. Her conclusions help support the linkages between teaching and autobiography.

Loeffler, M. G. (Ed.). (1992). *Montessori in contemporary American culture.* Portsmouth, NH: Heinemann.

This edited text is based on a series of papers presented at a 3-day symposium held in 1990 and sponsored by the American Montessori Society (AMS). As the book's title suggests, the readings examine Montessori's legacy and contemporary application. Of particular interest is Nancy McCormick Rambusch's chapter, which describes some of the tension between AMS and its European counterpart, AMI, and Lilian Katz's chapter, and the accompanying set of replies, which detail her questions about the Montessori method.

Montessori, M. (1964). *The Montessori Method* (A. E. George, Trans.). New York: Schocken. (Original work published in English in 1912)

Montessori, M. (1964). *Dr. Montessori's own handbook.* Cambridge, MA: Robert Bentley. (Original work published 1914)

Montessori, M. (1965). *Spontaneous activity in education* (F. Simmonds, Trans.). New York: Schocken Books. (Original work published in English in 1917)

These three books comprehensively describe and explain Montessori's method for 3- to 7-year-olds. Readers interested in her elementary methods should refer to her book on advanced methods, but its content is linked to Italian grammar and phonology, which limits its direct usefulness. *The Montessori Method* is the most detailed and also includes considerable history. *Spontaneous Activity in Education* primarily describes Montessori's philosophical rationale, whereas *Dr. Montessori's Own Handbook* details the prepared environment and the use of the didactic materials. The handbook is the most readable of these three books, perhaps because it was written originally in English.

Chapter Three

The Developmental-Interaction Approach

There is a central thesis governing the choice of techniques for advancing cognitive proficiency within the developmental-interaction point of view. . . . [T] his thesis maintains, first, that in a coherent system, techniques selected in the interest of a particular educational target should be justified in terms of a comprehensive concept of an optimal learning environment. Second, there needs to be constant weighing of the impact of any given technique on any other established goals for the development of the child.

Barbara Biber, *Early Education and Psychological Development*, 1984

We thought we were the wave of the future. We could not have imagined the important place that behavior modification as applied to preschool education would attain in the 1960s and thereafter as part of government planning in particular and in academic circles in general. We also could not imagine how much the past would be forgotten or misread, as though "thinking," because it was not called cognition, had no place in the earlier educational designs. We could not imagine that what to us was a steady course of experimentation directed toward basic change in the philosophy of early education would come to be designated as "traditional."

Barbara Biber, *Early Education and Psychological Development*, 1984

An inquiry into the Developmental-Interaction approach (also known as the Bank Street approach) depicts far more than a particular approach to early education. It also reveals a significant historical slice of early childhood education; the subtle effects of status accorded theory versus practice, researcher versus teacher, and cognition versus affect; and the extent to which a profession and its practice can be influenced by external circumstances. Once again, the pivotal impact of an educational viewpoint colliding with an unsympathetic, historical moment is exposed.

Although the name "developmental-interaction approach" was not officially assigned until the early 1970s (Shapiro & Biber, 1972), the beginnings of this approach to early education can be traced to the early 1900s and the advent of Progressivism and progressive education.[1] In contrast to the curriculum models discussed in the next two chapters, the Developmental-Interaction approach evolved from the daily practice of nursery school practitioners (and pioneers), especially Harriet Johnson, Lucy Sprague Mitchell, and Caroline Pratt. Rather than a preferred theory determining the direction of practice, practice within a specified value framework was linked with ongoing research and eventually a theoretical framework.

Yet contrary to the Montessori method, which similarly grew from the experiences of a practitioner, the details of practice never became prescribed. Until its formalization as an approach to early childhood education in the early 1970s, much of what teachers knew and understood about children, child development, and education was personal and individual, even though informed by, and an informant to, practice, research, and theory.

The Developmental-Interaction approach originated with the progressive, experimental, New York City nursery schools of Harriet Johnson and Caroline Pratt, and their collaborative relationship with Lucy Sprague Mitchell, who was a dynamic and influential feminist. Mitchell wanted to foster the development of emotionally secure and healthy children because "'whole' children were the best guarantors of a progressive, humanistic society" (Antler, 1987, p. xviii). In 1916, with the financial support of a relative, Mitchell formed the Bureau of Educational Experiments (BEE), which created a supportive, organizational structure for the evolution of an approach to early education and teacher education that rapidly assumed national status (Antler, 1982, 1987). When the bureau moved its location to 69 Bank Street in 1930 (still in New York City), its approach to early childhood education and teacher education assumed the name "the Bank Street approach," even though the bureau did not officially bear the name Bank Street College of Education until 1950.

In the late 1950s, Bank Street staff became interested in placing their cumulative, practical knowledge base within a theoretical framework (spurred in part, perhaps, by the aging of their living informants such as Lucy Sprague Mitchell who retired from her work at Bank Street in 1956). Although various Bank Street faculty members helped conceptualize and describe the Developmental-Interaction approach, Barbara Biber, who joined the Bureau of Educational Experiments in

---

[1]The Developmental-Interaction approach, of course, is only one example of an educational approach whose roots extend to the progressive education movement. It would seem remiss, therefore, not to note the British Infant Schools. The British experience of the 1960s and 1970s remains unique in its successful adaptation of progressive ideas on a large scale. As exemplified by the British Infant Schools, which served 4- through 7-year-olds, the British philosophy represented a fusion of many sources, including progressive experiments in Europe and the United States in the late 19th and early 20th centuries; the ideas of Froebel, Montessori, Margaret Macmillan, Abigail Eliot, and Caroline Pratt; plus the educational philosophy of Dewey and developmental theory of Piaget. The Infant Schools were characterized by their respect for the child as a unique individual, family groupings, the use of open classrooms, unstructured days, integrated learning through play and projects, children as agents in their own learning, and concrete, first-hand experiences. In the United States, these ideas were most frequently associated with the open approach to education. For further information, the reader is referred to Rogers (1970).

1928, is credited with shaping its developmental interaction theory (Antler, 1987; Shapiro & Mitchell, 1992; Zimiles, 1987). She also was its most prolific spokesperson. According to Biber (1977b),

> By 1959, it seemed fruitful to examine critically the rationale—the basic assumptions about learning—that was the foundation for the educational practices presumed to attain the stated values and goals. Knowledge of the growing field of child development and psychology of learning had indeed influenced these assumptions, but they had been primarily derived from the direct experience of observing and teaching children in school. . . . To what extent would formulations and viewpoints in the field of psychology, arrived at independently of the field of education, corroborate these assumptions and thus provide a firmer theoretical base for the practices? (p. 425)

The advent of Head Start in 1965 served as a catalyst for continued pursuit of a more highly developed theoretical rationale for preschool education. At this time Bank Street refined its previous conceptualization and more clearly delineated the distinctions between psychological concepts and their implications for the teacher's role (see, for example, Biber, 1967b).

By the early 1970s, the Bank Street approach had been formally renamed the Developmental-Interaction approach. This name change occurred, according to Biber (1977b), because "it is time to be signified by (our) essential theoretical characteristics rather than by a bit of fortuitous geography" (p. 423).[2] This accounting, however, would seem to provide only a partial explanation. The renaming and expanded conceptualization of the Bank Street approach coincides with the 1967 creation of Project Follow Through and the influx of federal dollars for experimental early childhood programs. In contrast to the dynamic character of experimental programs in the early 1900s (see, for example, Winsor, 1973), experimental early childhood programs in the 1960s were derivatives of preconceived curriculum models.

Project Follow Through, and eventually a segment of Head Start, was structured to differentiate the effectiveness of early childhood curriculum models. Bank Street's participation in Project Follow Through necessitated the formulation of its practice into a curriculum model. Examination of the Developmental-Interaction approach, therefore, presents a singular opportunity to ponder the aftereffects of exchanging evolving, dynamic, individualistic practice for practice ordained in terms of a formal theoretical framework.

Current scholarly arguments about the activity of teaching emphasize its emergent nature and the importance of framing teaching in terms of its dynamic qualities (see Chapter 7). Current deliberations regarding teaching provide ad hoc

---

[2]Shapiro adds that although the approach had been identified with the Bank Street College of Education, its new name was, in part, an attempt to acknowledge the fact that the approach was not limited to the institution. According to Shapiro, "It would be, and would have been, presumptuous, to say the least, to act as if Bank Street was the only source of this way of conceptualizing early childhood education" (personal communication). Even so, Bank Street takes credit for having "a uniquely long-term experience" with putting the theory into practice (Shapiro & Biber, 1972, p. 55; Shapiro & Mitchell, 1992, p. 15).

validation for the experimental frame of reference that originally characterized the Bank Street approach. But the experimental tone of the 1960s was not organized around practice; it was organized around the implementation of systematized curriculum models. In the mid-1960s and early 1970s, experimentation occurred at the level of program conceptualization—not teacher practice.

With the advent of Project Follow Through, adherents of the Bank Street approach needed to direct their attention to assembling the essential components of what became labeled the Developmental-Interaction approach. Rather than an evolutionary educational approach seeking continuous input and undergoing incessant self-assessment, with the onset on curriculum models the Bank Street approach unexpectedly became designated a program option. In addition, because the Bank Street approach exemplified existing thinking about early childhood education, advocates were compelled to defend the superiority of this approach relative to the new curriculum possibilities suddenly available for young children (see, for example, Biber, 1988; Franklin & Biber, 1977).

But more than the opportunity to participate in Project Follow Through seems to have been at stake. On the one hand, based on the defensive, sometimes exasperated tone of their writings in the 1970s, one suspects that Bank Street's participation in Project Follow Through was actually an attempt to place the Bank Street approach "on the playing field," to ensure that it was, in fact, a program option, and to legitimate and validate its long-standing approach to early childhood education.[3] (The Developmental-Interaction approach contended that although the specifics of practice might change when working with children from low-income families, programmatic principles did not.)

---

[3]Greenberg (1987), in an apparent outburst of frustration with the lack of recognition given these early childhood educators, suggests their ideas were ignored because they were women:

> Have we accepted the traditional cultural assumption that child care is "women's work," and is therefore low status, so what's so great about those old nursery school teachers anyway? Are we saying that our field, because a woman's field regardless of the many warm and wonderful men in it, did not count until the male psychologists entered it in the 60s? . . . To progressive educators, harsh discipline was anathema, interpersonal interaction was of prime importance, and emotional expressiveness through play and the arts were highly prized. Lack of discipline is soft. Love and friendship are soft. The arts (unlike sciences) are soft. Emotional expressiveness is soft. Children are soft. Little children are softer still. And women are softest of all, as are the areas of work historically allocated to them. . . . Our cultural ideal, on the other hand, is tough, hard, and masculine. "Hard" science, for example, is far more highly esteemed than a "soft" field such as "domestic science." Is it coincidental that when, in the 60s, the leadership of our field for the first time became suddenly male, psychosocial went out of fashion and cognitive, learning objectives, scientific terminology, and statistical research swooped in? We have managed to overlook the progressives' extensive scientific research not because it wasn't done primarily by males, but because, far worse, it wasn't even done in the male mode—distanced, termed "objective," wreathed in statistics. The progressives "just" observed, recorded, hypothesized, experimented, and did the other things scientists do. (p. 83)

Greenberg's retort takes on additional interest when one realizes that women's choice of careers in such "female" fields as child development and preschool education during the early 1900s reflected their eagerness to participate in the era's social reform efforts. Many of these women, including Lucy Mitchell, were members of the first generation of college-educated women (Antler, 1987).

In addition, to the extent that the Developmental-Interaction approach synthesized multiple theoretical perspectives, its formalization reaffirmed the historical and contemporary importance of the "whole child." It can be argued, therefore, that Bank Street's efforts represented an attempt to reestablish a cohesive framework for a field unexpectedly fragmented by diverse and often contradictory approaches to early education (the "evidence" stitched together relative to this last point can be found in Biber, 1979a; Franklin, 1981; Shapiro & Biber, 1972; Weber, 1984).

According to Zimiles (1987), a long-term Bank Street faculty member, Bank Street faculty realized their approach had to be explicated and their method codified in order for it to be disseminated and made more accessible and universal.[4] The Bank Street approach had evolved from the practice and intellect of a handful of people. Its experimental, evolutionary character was well suited to its intimate setting, and given the relatively small dimensions of nursery education in the United States until the mid-1960s, no pressure existed to do otherwise. But, with the initiation of Head Start, not only did the number of children attending preschool programs swell, but so did the unanticipated demand for teachers, the majority of whom were hired without formal preparation as early childhood educators.[5] Thus, the push for codification was not just a theoretical issue; it also was a response to an unprecedented demand for early childhood programming.

∽ EVOLUTION FROM EXPERIMENTAL NURSERY PROGRAM TO THE DEVELOPMENTAL-INTERACTION APPROACH

The history of the Developmental-Interaction approach is a chronology of significant events and shifts in thinking that influenced the evolution of a multifaceted program toward a cognitive-affective position. The Developmental-Interaction approach is the only U.S. approach/model under consideration that is informed by multiple theoretical perspectives assembled in terms of their congruity with preferred values and practice (although in Chapter 9 readers will reencounter this use of *multiple* theoretical perspectives in the approach of teachers in Reggio Emilia, Italy). When officially labeled the Developmental-Interaction approach in the early 1970s, the program's conceptual framework reflected six decades of on-

---

[4]In response to my argument, Shapiro contended that there was another goal (personal communication, 1993).

"Partly because the writings were scattered and dealt with one issue or another, partly because the teacher's role is extremely demanding, and perhaps also because many people prefer simplicity to complexity, there were many who dismissed the Bank Street approach as a "mystique." The writing of the 1971 pamphlet (Promoting Cognitive Growth) and 1972 paper (referring to her paper written with Barbara Biber) were strongly motivated by the desire to "demystify"; the goal was not to codify but to clarify."

More recently, Shapiro acknowledged how the influx of federal dollars influenced the formal articulation of the Developmental-Interaction approach (Nager & Shapiro, 2000).

[5]This factor eventually led to the creation of the Child Development Associate credential with which Biber was actively involved.

going involvement and leadership in early childhood classrooms and the field of early childhood education. This fact led Biber (1977a) to comment, "To experienced educators many newly structured programs appeared unseasoned in quality and restricted in scope because most psychologists were newcomers to the world of early education . . ." (p. 41).

The history of the Developmental-Interaction approach is linked with the histories of progressive education and the nursery school movement. To understand the subtleties that define the Developmental-Interaction approach and its evolution, it is necessary to appreciate the intersection of these three histories. Group, out-of-home care that focused on the "educational" versus "custodial" needs of young children was rare in the early 1900s. Despite its dramatic growth through the 1920s, nursery schools remained sparse until the advent of Head Start in 1965. Today, we take the proliferation of preschool programs for granted, but in 1920, only 3 nursery schools were in existence; in 1924, there are records of 25 programs, and by 1928, with the expansion of university-based programs, 89 nursery schools were recorded (Goodykoontz, Davis, & Gabbard, 1948).

These nursery schools, even though few in number and mostly for white, urban, middle- and upper-class children,[6] were diverse in approach. The Developmental-Interaction approach represents an example of this diversity. Its evolution can be chronicled in three loosely configured phases: its experimental, progressive beginnings, from 1916, with the creation of the Bureau of Educational Experiments, through the 1920s; its alignment with psychodynamic theory beginning in the 1930s and continuing through the 1950s; and the period of its formalization as an approach to early childhood education after the advent of Head Start in 1965.

During the first phase, the organizational supports for the Developmental-Interaction approach were instituted, its enduring focus and interests articulated, and its leadership role in early childhood teacher education initiated. During the second phase, the psychological basis for the approach solidified. In the last phase, the Developmental-Interaction approach formally articulated and advocated its educational philosophy and preferred practices, delineated itself as a specific approach to early childhood education, and attempted to combat the "misreading of history" (Biber, 1977a, p. 48) by psychologists newly interested in early childhood education.

By the 1960s, Bank Street's approach, along with those of other progressive experimental programs, was considered mainstream nursery education. When the shift occurred in thinking regarding the significance of the early years for intellectual development, and concern for young, disadvantaged children erupted, Bank Street's approach to early education represented the status quo. Evans's 1975 classic examination of early childhood curriculum models reviewed the Developmental-Interaction approach in six pages, as part of a chapter entitled "The Mainstream of Early Childhood Education."

---

[6]According to Cahan (1989), there is some evidence of the existence, separate from those for whites, of a child development movement—including vigorous efforts to create nursery schools and kindergartens—among African Americans during these years.

Despite its experimental character, the Bank Street approach was labeled traditional, and cited as outmoded and resistive to change. When nursery education finally was recognized as an appropriate beginning for young children's formal education and extended to preschoolers from low-income families, the political context, theoretical representations, and educational expectations had shifted. (Chapter 1 discussed this shift in greater detail.) After almost 50 years of leading the way for others, the Bank Street approach was placed on the defensive, especially with respect to its emphasis on social-emotional development and its ideas regarding how best to promote children's intellectual abilities.

The Beginning: The Bureau of Educational Experiments

The beginning of the Developmental-Interaction approach took root in the early 1900s and was closely intertwined with the progressive education movement, especially the views espoused by John Dewey. Progressive education, in turn, was part of the Progressive movement, which sought political and social reforms in response to societal changes wrought by industrialism. Progressive education attempted to improve society through the reform of public education.

According to Cremin (1961/1964), progressivism in education meant broadening the program and function of schools to include concern for health, jobs, and family and community life; applying pedagogical principles derived from new scientific research in psychology and the social sciences; and tailoring instruction to the different kinds and classes of children that were increasingly becoming part of the public schools (pp. viii–ix). Cremin explains that, especially in the beginning of the progressive education movement, there was an inextricable relationship between social reform, reform through education, and the reform of education.

Progressive ideas affected the direction of early childhood education in at least two significant ways: the "overthrow" of Froebelian kindergartens and the establishment of experimental nursery schools. In reference to the dominant kindergarten ideology of the late 1800s and early 1900s, the ideas associated with progressive education provoked confrontation between adherents to Froebelian-inspired curriculum, which was founded on philosophical idealism, and those who advocated a more progressive, scientifically informed approach to kindergarten education. As discussed in Chapters 1 and 2, the more progressive-minded kindergarten educators emerged victorious.

About the same time and beyond, kindergarten advocates were seeking to establish kindergartens in public schools in order to establish a secure financial base. Attempts to institutionalize kindergartens in public schools were accompanied by efforts to increase teachers' professional status through increased training, alliance with other professionals, and reliance on "scientific" practice (Bloch, 1987; Cremin, 1961/1964; Weber, 1969). These aspirations helped frame kindergarten education's particular, and separate, historical course. Bloch (1987) has suggested that the kindergarten's alignment with the age-graded school system helped pave the way for nursery schools to forge a separate and autonomous movement.

The nursery movement, which began to flourish after 1920, actually encompassed different type programs. Each type program had different principles, practices, and underlying goals (Biber, 1984; Greenberg, 1987; White & Buka, 1987). Experimental nursery schools provided one of the distinctive strands within the nursery school movement, even though they, in turn, varied from each other (Antler, 1982; Biber, 1984; Greenberg, 1987). According to Biber (1984), the experimental preschools shared a common commitment to an experimental approach to early childhood education, rebellion against the rigid methods dominating education, new concepts of childhood and the learning process, and a dedication to recording and analyzing their educational experiments.

Experimental nursery schools, in contrast to research-based programs sponsored by universities and colleges, were linked with the progressive education movement and its mission to alter the practices that dominated public schools. Experimental nursery schools argued that they were a suitable beginning for children's education *and* a lever for basic change in education, "a way of making a breakthrough toward a whole new philosophy of education. This conception of nursery school education was a built-in component of the progressive education movement with a common body of basic principles and purposes" (Biber, 1984, p. 14). In her 1919 chairman's report, Mitchell stated, "We think of all our work ultimately in relation to public education" (as cited in Antler, 1987, p. 285).

Progressive nursery schools saw their experimental efforts as generating a knowledge base about practice that would help operationalize this new philosophy of education. When these experimental and research-based programs began, existing knowledge regarding developmental information about young children and conventional practice in early childhood education was, for the most part, nonexistent. It is their knowledge and experiences that form the core of our current expectations for early childhood education.

The nursery school of Harriet Johnson, which cared for children from 14 months to 3 years of age (later the Harriet Johnson Nursery School and then the Bank Street School for Children, which serves as a laboratory and demonstration center for the Bank Street College of Education and encompasses preschool through eighth grades), and Caroline Pratt's Play School, attended by children 3 years of age through elementary school (later renamed the City and Country School and, according to Greenberg [1987], probably one of the first nursery schools in the United States reflecting what we now call developmentally appropriate practice), became the bureau's sites for gathering scientific data concerning children's growth and studying educational factors in a school environment. These two programs eventually were relocated to the same building and served as the bureau's laboratory site. The practice of teachers in these two programs, in collaboration with bureau researchers, shaped the beginning of the Developmental-Interaction approach (Antler, 1982; Biber, 1977a).

The research focus of Lucy Sprague Mitchell and her colleagues differed from that of university-sponsored child development lab schools. University lab schools were research centers focused on the scientific application of developmental theory to classroom settings for the purpose of enhancing child development or supplying content for parent education. The BEE's primary purpose was to create a functional relationship between research and schooling that would inform planning within the school environment (Antler, 1982, 1987).

Their mission was embedded within the humanistic and reformist ideals of progressive education: more fully developed individuals would be more capable of being caring, productive citizens who could create a force for effecting social change. And, consistent with the tenor of progressive education (and in contrast to the behavioristic tendencies informing the habit training curriculum of kindergartens during the 1920s), interest in finding ways to stimulate intellectual development was holistically integrated with physical, emotional, and social development (Antler, 1982; Biber, 1977a, 1984; Cremin, 1964; NAEYC Organizational History and Archives Committee, 1976; Weber, 1969).

In contrast to other progressive experiments, the bureau placed a strong emphasis on scientific measurement to assist teachers in planning the learning environment for children (Antler, 1982). The new science of psychology and scientific orientation to education was generating interest in observing and documenting children's behaviors, but the BEE's interest was not in understanding children *per se*. They used their data to inform practice. "We are working on a curriculum, checking it by our growth records; and working on how to record growth, evaluating our records by the children's reactions to our planned environment" (1919 Bureau Annual Report, as cited in Antler, 1982, p. 571).

The major programmatic thrust during this early period, according to Biber (1977a, 1977b, 1981), came from John Dewey's image of schooling as a world where young children could be active questioners and experimenters and thus free to develop their thinking and reasoning powers more fully:

> If we were to free the child's intellectual capacity, we had to make learning an active, self-generating, searching experience; if we were to be responsive to the goal of educating the whole child, we had not only to stimulate independent thinking and reasoning processes but to open avenues toward creative reorganization of experience as intrinsic to the learning process; if education was ultimately to effect social change, we had to bring the reality of how the world functions into the classroom curriculum; if we expected children to become awakened to the advantages of a democratic society, we had to provide the experience of living democratically in the social setting of the schoolroom, of being part of a cooperative structure characterized by egalitarian interpersonal relations. (Biber, 1984, p. 309)

Thus, the bureau's educational and experimental emphasis was on developing the "whole child," nurturing children's individual knowledge of themselves and their world through a curriculum of experiences (a new notion at that time), and providing a variety of ways, most especially play, for children to express and represent the experiences they encountered. Given their long-standing commitment to intellectual development, it is easy to appreciate Biber's consternation over charges launched during the 1960s and 1970s that the Developmental-Interaction approach was devoid of intellectual fiber.

Mitchell and her colleagues were unique in seeing the bidirectional relationship between research and practice. They were atypical in emphasizing the importance of "observing (children's) natural behavior in situations planned for children's development" (Mitchell, 1925, as cited in Antler, 1982, p. 575) at a time when their colleagues in university lab schools were more involved in learning about children by testing them.

Both as an essential program premise and a distinctive characteristic, this broader conceptualization of measurement was significant. Almost 40 years later, it resurfaced as a divisive issue when advocates of the Developmental-Interaction approach protested the assessment of early childhood curriculum models, especially their own, based on narrow measurements of intellectual ability (see Chapter 6 for further discussion on this point; see also Gilkeson et al., 1981; Zimiles, 1977).

During the last half of the 1920s, Mitchell reassessed the bureau's priorities, in particular the relationship between its educational and research functions. Questions arose regarding the usefulness of the bureau's research efforts in terms of informing educational practice. According to Antler (1982), by the end of the 1920s,

> the Bureau was ready to abandon its faith that quantitative measurement could provide the functional indices of children's growth that could guide educational planning. . . . Moreover, Mitchell came to fear that the very formulation of exact standards of normal growth might in fact distort individual variation in development and lead to the promulgation of mechanistic, uniform norms, which if applied as educational guides could deaden rather than enhance children's impulses to learn. (p. 581)

This issue reasserted itself again after Bank Street's formalization as an approach to early childhood education, though this time, relative to the loss of individuality within theories of development; see Shapiro & Wallace, 1981.)

Although an emphasis on research was maintained, it became addressed in a separate division under the leadership of Barbara Biber, who had joined the bureau in 1928. Then, in 1931, the bureau, at the request of numerous experimental schools sharing a similar philosophy and in need of teachers who could teach in their experimental programs, established the Cooperative School for Student Teachers (later called the Cooperative School for Teachers) to train nursery, primary, and elementary school teachers for work in schools with a progressive emphasis (Antler, 1982). At this point, the program for teacher education became the bureau's primary thrust, and its thinking about the way children learned was extended to teacher education. As expressed by Mitchell in the first school catalog:

> Our aim is to help students develop a scientific attitude towards their work and towards life. To use this means an attitude of eager, alert observations; a constant questioning of old procedures in the light of new observations; a use of the world as well as of books as source material; an experimental open-mindedness. . . . We are not interested in perpetuating any special "school of thought." Rather, we are interested in imbuing teachers with an experimental, critical and ardent approach to their work. (as cited in Antler, 1982, p. 583)

By the beginning of the 1930s, the outlines of the Developmental-Interaction approach had been drawn: its child-centered approach; its attention to the nature of the learning environment; a focus on individual development as a conduit for social reform; a complex conceptualization of the teaching role; and an experimental, experiential approach to education.

The early history of the Developmental-Interaction approach highlights that, from the very beginning, its architects carved an approach to early childhood education that was distinctive from its contemporaries by uniquely mingling the critical intellectual thinking of the era. The holistic, process-oriented approach to early childhood and teacher education that emerged during these formative years eventually became problematic, however. During the 1960s and 1970s, when competitive assessment of curriculum models turned precise program implementation and outcome-based evaluations into focal points, a dynamic conceptualization of teaching and learning became a liability because it impeded rapid dissemination and resisted conventional program evaluations.

Emotions as a Prominent Theme: The Influence of Psychodynamic Theory

According to Cremin (1961/1964), when World War I ended in 1918, the progressive education movement became disassociated from its original, political concept of social reform. Rather than a more radical notion of schools as vehicles for societal change, the notion of social reform became refashioned around the belief that each individual has uniquely creative potential and that a school attentive to helping children develop their potential is the best guarantee of a society truly devoted to human worth and excellence. Following this shift, two major intellectual streams of thought converged to form the two prongs of child-centered pedagogy: expressionism (which centered on the importance of the arts and the significance of multiple modes of imaginative self-expression) and Freudianism (Cremin, 1961/1964).

The educational efforts of the BEE reflected this shift toward a focus on individual potential and a child-centered pedagogy vitally interested in children's self-expression. Interest in self-expression, however, was embedded within the context of psychodynamic theory, which provided the Developmental-Interaction approach with its first *theoretical* strand (as opposed to its previous reliance on value statements, research, and practice). Although the primary source was Freudian theory, according to Biber (1977a), the nursery school world moved more toward neo-Freudianism, giving more attention to the impact of sociocultural influences and placing less emphasis on determinism:

> New sensitivity to the undersurfaces of behavior, to the depth and power of emotional responsiveness became part of educational thinking. . . . There was increased understanding of the inner struggles of growing up: the management of overwhelming emotion; feelings of ambivalence, conflict, and guilt in relationships with loved figures; the pull between impulse and adaptation, between the lingering comfort of dependence and the siren call of independence. (Biber, 1977a, pp. 47-48)

Previously, and consistent with their progressive leanings, curriculum concerns had centered on providing a learning environment "rich in possibilities for direct contact and interaction with things, people, and ideas—one in which emerging symbolic skills would gain salience by being tested, tried out, and enjoyed in natural functional contexts" (Biber, 1977a, p. 43). Teachers were challenged to create experiences in which children were engaged with thinking and questioning in order to operationalize Dewey's vision of creating a thinking person as a means for effecting social change.

Concern with emotional processes and personality development added a new dimension to the BEE's interest in the "whole child"; attention to how emotions condition the ways children interpret their school experiences now became a primary concern. In addition, the perceived value of free play was expanded beyond its contributions as a mode of thinking and a vehicle for symbolic representation to include an appreciation for its role in supporting children's expression of diverse emotions, for synthesizing the subjective and objective aspects of experience, and providing a vehicle for symbolically resolving personal conflicts that could not be faced directly (Biber, 1981).

This second phase moved beyond the initial perspective of the early progressive school movement toward a cognitive-affective position. This evolution was informed by concepts from psychodynamic psychology of changing drives, energies, and conflicts at different stages of development (especially as informed by the writings of Susan Issacs (1930/1966) who was attempting similar work [Biber, 1981]); increased knowledge from developmental psychologists such as Piaget[7] and Werner about cognitive development, plus parallel effort by educators "who chose to continue and develop the ethos of the progressive school movement" (Biber, 1981, p. 18). According to Biber (1981), "What seems to have come together . . . is the earlier ideal image of a curious, creative, problem-solving, socially sensitive individual and the contemporary interest in the life of feeling, the condition of the self, the inner processes and opportunity for personal integration of meanings and purposes in both spheres" (p. 22).

This conceptual extension created a natural alignment with the mental health movement, which assumed national importance during the 1950s and 1960s. The mental health movement investigated ways to prevent mental illness by concep-

---

[7]Given the dominant influence that Piagetian theory exerted on early childhood curriculum in the 1960s when interest in cognitive development erupted, digressing to the reactions of Mitchell and others to Piaget's theory in the 1930s effectively highlights the significance of timing relative to professional acceptance of new ideas. Mitchell, who earned considerable fame for her children's books, criticized Piaget's assumption that the exclusive function of children's language development was the expression of logical thought and communication, to the exclusion of its function as an "art form" (Antler, 1987). Susan Issacs, whose practice and reflection were important informants to the Bank Street approach during this time, challenged Piaget for his total lack of reference to the contribution of children's psychological experiences to intellectual development, his lack of awareness of children's reasoning ability expressed within the context of their everyday experiences, and the absence of attention to the developmental effect of continuous experiences (Issacs, 1930/1966). And, according to Margaret Pollitzer, cofounder of the Walden School (a pre-1920 progressive school), "Piaget didn't say anything about creating cooperative children to be citizens in a democracy; that was a big part of our focus as progressive nursery and primary educators. . . . Piaget examined how children absorb and process information from the external world—but we knew that—we all had lab schools going long before he wrote. . . . Piaget wasn't at all interested in one of our biggest excitements—the wealth of creativity within a young child that is shaped by feeling and imagination, and bursts out in marvelous language and art. . . . Piaget was investigating mental mechanics. Progressives were concerned with developing 'the whole child' [another of Lucy Mitchell's terms]. Our goal was to create great people" (as cited in Greenberg, 1987, p. 75).

tualizing a healthy course of individual development and learning how to make social institutions, such as schools, more supportive (Biber, 1979b). Not surprisingly, during this time Biber did considerable writing about the Bank Street approach using the lens of mental health.

Although a unique opportunity to spread Bank Street's views, the relationship with mental health deepened professional perceptions that the Bank Street approach was a program concerned solely with social-emotional development. A critical error of the 1960s, according to Biber (1984),

> was the misperception of the highly developed discipline of early childhood education as being a socialization-mental health model, seriously neglectful of cognitive stimulation, with more serious consequences for the disadvantaged than for the middle class child. . . . Educators identified with these purposes and programs at Bank Street and elsewhere, felt seriously misunderstood by the critics from academe. (p. 97)

The Explosion of Preschool Education: The Bank Street Approach as Defender of "Traditional" Early Childhood Education Ideals

When Head Start was announced in 1965, it took the Bank Street approach as its prototype (Biber, 1979a, 1984; Greenberg, 1987). To some extent, this decision was influenced by economic considerations. There was concern that fewer children could be served by the cognitive-based research programs being promoted by developmental psychologists (Greenberg, 1990a). In addition, there apparently was initial resistance to "model program clones being mechanically planted in widely diverse settings" (Greenberg, 1990a, p. 45). But according to Greenberg (1987), a member of the government staff who helped formulate the Head Start program during the summer of 1964, the selection primarily reflected the staff's curriculum preference:

> The words "The basic Head Start classroom should work like a Bank Street College elementary classroom for nursery/kindergarten" are in the earliest staff-written concept paper in the Head Start historical files.
>
> It is interesting to note that neither Montessorian nor Piagetian philosophies were prominent in the minds of national staff people designing the Head Start educational component at headquarters. . . . Office of Economic Opportunity staff had collected information about the research being done by people newly interested in enrichment for "disadvantaged" young children: Susan Gray at Peabody, Cynthia and Martin Deutsch at the Institute for Developmental Studies, David Weikart at the Perry

---

[8]Williams (1977) suggests a different scenario. Based on her acquaintance with members of the original research and demonstration staff at DARCEE (Susan Gray's program at Peabody and one of the early experimental compensatory programs), Williams contends that it had been the original intent of Project Head Start planners to derive Head Start's educational program from the early experimental, research programs. This plan was not carried out, however, because some educators denounced the behavioral orientation of the demonstration projects and successfully lobbied for use of the "traditional" nursery school approach. "The advocates of reduced structure won their point, and the original Head Start adopted nursery school strategies and content" (p. 62).

Preschool Project which he had begun in 1962, and so on. But the "ideal" was Bank Street style.[8] (Greenberg, 1987, p. 76)

A question that naturally arises at this point is why the Bank Street approach was viewed as "the ideal." One possibility could simply be the fact that Bank Street's approach represented the existing prototype for nursery education and was simply the obvious choice. This possibility is supported by the fact that many graduates and admirers of the Bank Street approach, including Edward Zigler (who is recognized as a key architect of Head Start), were involved with Head Start's development. But a stronger explanation can be advanced by taking note of the philosophy and values shared by Head Start and Bank Street.

To begin with, there was compatibility between Head Start's emphasis on health care and social services and Bank Street's advocacy, originating from its progressive roots, for an expanded conceptualization of education. Further, Bank Street had experiences preparing volunteers to work with children in WPA programs (programs initiated during the Depression by the federal government), at which time it imagined nursery schools as community centers for young children and their families, offering a comprehensive set of health, social, and educational services (Biber, 1984). But an even more vital bond between Head Start and the Bank Street approach resided in their mutual belief that preschool education could provide a means to reform society.

Head Start was created as the centerpiece for the War on Poverty. It relied on the optimistic belief that early education could help eradicate the poverty of individuals and minimize inequality by enhancing children's success with public school expectations. Its initial placement in the Office of Economic Opportunity was based on the belief that Head Start was more than "just" an educational intervention for poor children. It also was a community action program with the intent of helping poor people improve their lives through the availability of new resources and technical assistance (Greenberg, 1990a). Head Start's mission was clearly harmonious with the progressive history, affiliations, and values of Bank Street.

According to Biber (1984),

Head Start represented revolutionary change in the dominant concepts of learning in early childhood and in the relation of school to family and community—revolutionary meaning here that knowledge and principles that had been developed in a sector of society with a small voice were to be applied in the encompassing public sphere. There were conflicting ideal images. Was the Headstart experience to be the most efficient route for children of poverty toward adaptation to the expectation and ideology of the existing public educational system? Or, was Headstart, as it developed as a movement, to be a stimulant toward incorporating new concepts of learning and socializing experience into the public school system? The challenge was social as well as educational. (p. 27)

It was more than politically significant, therefore, when Head Start's community action component was minimized, and the program redefined as primarily an educational intervention. Although this "tacit political simplification of the program" (White & Buka, 1987, p. 74) may have helped save Head Start from the terminal fate experienced by other poverty programs during the early 1970s, in narrowing its political definition to an educational program with the mission of preparing children for existing school practices, Head Start became disassociated from its reformist beginnings and emerged as an appropriate arena for educational manipulation by psychologists eager to apply their theories regarding effective early intervention.

With the heightened interest in cognitive development, newfound optimism regarding intellectual malleability, and the diversity of theoretical perspectives, psychologists were eager to test their theories. The Bank Street approach was challenged not only because of its "conventional" thinking, but also because, from the perspective of interested psychologists, its social-emotional emphasis failed to address cognitive development adequately. Furthermore, the fact that the program had historically served white, middle-class children of mostly professional parents led psychologists to contend that the Bank Street approach was a mismatch for the unique intellectual needs of economically disadvantaged children (Miller, 1979).

This interpretation probably was fueled further by negative attitudes toward progressive education. According to Cremin (1961/1964), 1957 marked the end of the progressive education era.

> What was already apparent in 1952, and what became ever more apparent as the decade progressed, was the presence of a large and articulate public ready for educational reform of a nonprogressive variety. . . . When the Russians launched the first space satellite in the autumn of 1957, a shocked and humbled nation embarked on a bitter orgy of pedagogical soul-searching. (Cremin, 1961/1964, pp. 343, 347)

As expressed by Admiral Hyman G. Rickover (1959),[9] "Parents are no longer satisfied with life-adjustment schools. Parental objectives no longer coincide with those professed by the progressive educationists. I doubt we can again be silenced" (pp. 189–190). And, thus was the stage set for the back-to-basics movement and more "scientific" approaches to education.

Bank Street's emphasis on social-emotional development as the most appropriate context for nurturing the whole child collided not only with psychologists' focused attention on cognitive development, but also society's new frame of mind. As lamented by Biber (1984), "The ideological fundamentals that we assumed would gradually gain general acceptance came on hard times in the 1960s when a narrow scholasticism dominated experimental programs in search of single-track solutions to the pervasive damage of poverty in early childhood" (Biber, 1984, p. 25). The backlash against progressive education, combined with Head Start's retreat from its community action agenda, further estranged the values and perspective of the Developmental-Interaction approach from those of its contemporaries.

During the expansive 1960s and early 1970s, therefore, proponents of the Developmental-Interaction approach were placed on the defensive. Through their

---

[9]Admiral Rickover's status as the principal architect of the U.S. Navy's nuclear-powered fleet added enhanced credibility to this conclusion.

participation as one of the Follow Through curriculum models and their ongoing promotion of Head Start's original intent, they became the standard bearers for educating "the whole child," resisting a constricted focus on children's cognitive development, regardless of a child's socioeconomic status, and preservers of progressive education's legacy.

☞ THE DEVELOPMENTAL-INTERACTION APPROACH

The Psychological Rationale

Their self-appropriated name, *Developmental-Interaction approach*, reflects Bank Street's historic concern with the whole child and the complexity such a comprehensive approach entails. Concern with the whole child entails appreciation of the child as both an intellectual and emotional being. Respect for the complexity of development implies sensitivity to the complex, external interactions between the child and her environment and the complicated, internal interactions between cognition and affect. As defined by Shapiro and Biber (1972) (and continually restated in later writings without revision):

> Developmental refers to the emphasis on identifiable patterns of growth and modes of perceiving and responding which are characterized by increasing differentiation and progressive integration as a function of chronological age. Interaction refers, first, to the emphasis on the child's interaction with the environment—adults, other children, and the material world—and second, to the interaction between cognitive and affective spheres of development. The developmental-interaction formulation stresses the nature of the environment as much as it does the patterns of the responding child. (Shapiro & Biber, 1972, pp. 59-60)

Discussions of the Developmental-Interaction viewpoint consistently identify it as an "approach" to early childhood curriculum rather than a model. Avoidance of the term *model* carries semantic importance because it conveys the strong and continuing belief that, despite the formalization of a conceptual framework, the daily practice of education should retain its experimental character. For example, in describing the contribution of the Bank Street School for Children to off-site Follow Through personnel, Biber (1977b) wrote, "It is utilized not only as a live image of a learning environment based on given principles, but also as an example of the 'goal in sight' and as evidence that the 'ideal' and the 'optimal' in all educational designs are matters of continuous study and trial, under any circumstance" (p. 453).

Their belief that education is an experimental, versus applied, undertaking is an important premise to understand because it directly informs the way in which the approach is explained to others, the scope of the teacher role, and the conceptualization of teacher–child interactions. Because the Developmental-Interaction approach has such a personalized interpretation of individual change and views the educational process as dynamic exchanges between the child and every facet of her environment, it cannot, by definition, present a predetermined curriculum and description of teacher strategies and still remain conceptually consistent. One of the side effects of such a conceptualization, however, is greater reliance on a teacher's knowledge and her ability to recognize and skillfully respond to the individuality of each child and his or her interests, which "is not readily come by" (Franklin & Biber, 1977, p. 26) and requires a special kind of teacher preparation.

This level of teacher sophistication was, in fact, clearly envisioned by those who developed the Developmental-Interaction approach (see, for example, Biber, Gilkeson, & Winsor, 1959; Biber & Snyder, 1948). But the result is an approach more vulnerable to the personal abilities of individual teachers.

> Stated simply, the teacher we are asking for is aware of the complexities of the interaction between intellectual development and affective experience in the developing years. Further, the ideal teacher is aware of the differences in the social codes and styles of interaction among young children from widely different cultural groups. Finally, we are looking for a teacher who can maintain healthy, cohesive group functioning which is so flexibly enacted that individual needs can be sensed, understood and met, with suitable adjustment. (Biber, 1988, p. 46)

The lack of programmatic precision contrasts with the specificity found in the Montessori method described in Chapter 2 and that of behavioral methodology to be described in Chapter 4. This contrast results not only from their stance toward the practice of early childhood education but also from the fact that the Developmental-Interaction approach conceptualizes research and theory as informants to early childhood education, rather than as determinants of educational goals and/or educational practice. Developmental theory, according to Biber, is not synonymous with educational theory. Developmental theory can provide a rationale for educational practice but not its justification. (This interpretation contrasts most strongly with the Kamii-DeVries approach, which is discussed in Chapter 5, and also the general viewpoint of the existing care and education field; see Chapter 7.)

The dynamic quality of the Developmental-Interaction approach is intensified further by its bond with psychodynamic theory. Psychodynamic theory characterizes individual development as highly dynamic and personalized. An experience can be understood only in terms of the intellectual and emotional interpretation/reaction an individual provides it.

The Developmental-Interaction approach's strong identification with psychological processes is a distinctive and distinguishing characteristic. No other curriculum model presented in this book claims an allegiance to psychodynamic principles or heavily relies on psychological constructs to rationalize its interest in social-emotional variables, even when such interest exists.

But it is important not to overestimate the interest in promoting healthy personality development because the Developmental-Interaction approach also distinguishes itself from early education programs wholly aligned with psychodynamic theory (Biber, 1984; Franklin & Biber, 1977). Progressive-based programs such as the Walden School, which based its educational efforts on psychoanalytic theory, believed that progressive ideals could best be achieved through resolution of the largely unconscious problems intrinsic to the maturational process; these programs adapted the teacher–child relationship to respond to these unconscious events

(Biber, 1984). Biber and others, however, considered a wholly psychodynamic viewpoint to be as restrictive as an overly cognitive emphasis (Franklin & Biber, 1977).

In contrast, the Developmental-Interaction approach stresses the importance of the "whole child"; it recognizes and appreciates the continuous engagement of the cognitive and social-affective parts of development. "It can be suggested that the 'whole child' is not only a guiding concept in this approach but a powerful image, an almost concrete embodiment of ideas and sentiments that serves a central generative function in elaborating theory and thinking about practice in the context of a value system" (Franklin, 1981, p. 71).

Reflecting these assumptions, formal presentations of the Developmental-Interaction approach usually begin with a statement of its progressive values, followed by a delineation of six theoretical principles acquired from psychodynamic and developmental theory. General educational goals and teaching strategies are then derived from these principles. Educational goals and teaching strategies, in turn, provide the parameters for the inclusion and promotion of possible learning experiences (see, for example, Biber, 1977b; Biber & Franklin, 1967; Shapiro & Biber, 1972).

Thus, explanation of the Developmental-Interaction approach proceeds deductively from encompassing principles to specific practices. However, specific practices can be understood only in light of the overarching principles and only as these principles, which exist independently in written form only, are being experienced by a particular child during a particular circumstance. "A competent teacher needs to know why, not only what and how. That is the only guarantee that she can make sound adaptations to differing situations" (Biber, 1979a, p. 157). Figuratively, the Developmental-Interaction approach can be visualized as a nested design, with each superordinate component setting the conceptual boundaries for the next element. Architects of the Developmental-Interaction approach intentionally kept their conceptualization complex in order for it to better match their perception of development. As a result, it is a model whose implementation is dependent on conceptual understanding rather than skillful replication.

The ultimate conceptualization of the Developmental-Interaction approach evolved from diverse sources during its first 60 years of operation. In their efforts to integrate methods and understandings about the learning process into a new educational paradigm, adherents strived to create a comprehensive and internally coherent educational approach. They concluded that their concern with the whole child necessitated the integration of multiple theories in order to comprehensively reflect the complexity of development and to support its totality (Biber, 1977b, 1984; Franklin, 1981).

> It is a basic tenet of the developmental-interaction approach that the growth of cognitive functions— acquiring and ordering information, judging, reasoning, problem solving, using systems of symbols—cannot be separated from the growth of personal and interpersonal processes—the development of self-esteem and a sense of identity, internalization of impulse control, capacity for autonomous responses, relatedness to other people. (Shapiro & Biber, 1972, p. 61)

This reasoning helps explain why Biber and her colleagues, despite numerous commonalities with cognitive-developmental approaches (see Chapter 5), rejected the various, derivative curriculum models from Piagetian theory. They denounced the preponderant emphasis on developing cognitive structures (versus intellectual processes), the separation of cognitive and affective development, and insufficient attention to intuitive processes, feelings, and fantasy "as they reflect and feed into the child's aesthetic as well as his inter- and intrapersonal development" (Franklin & Biber, 1977, p. 16; see also Biber, 1984, 1988). The Developmental-Interaction approach values nonrational and intuitive understandings as well as the more rational, logically oriented ones promoted by cognitive-developmental models.

The concept of a "family of theories," as proposed by Reese and Overton (1970), was found to be particularly useful in articulating the notion of theoretical variation built on a shared, common base (Biber, 1984, 1988; Franklin, 1981). The concept of a family of theories proposes that theories can be grouped according to shared assumptions, with members of a given family differing in certain respects but sharing a set of views that is clearly distinct, and often opposed to, the shared assumptions of other groupings. This concept provided those describing the Developmental-Interaction approach a supportive rationale for relying on multiple theoretical perspectives, as long as each new "family member" added to the comprehensiveness and coherence of their psychological rationale.

Articulating the relationships between practice and multiple theoretical perspectives within an integrated conceptual framework evolved over a period of several years. Careful consideration was given to relationships between practice and theory. A desire existed for internal consistency among values, learning-teaching practices, and psychological theories of motivation and development (examples of the evolution can be found in Biber, 1967b, 1977b; Biber & Franklin, 1967; Biber, Shapiro, & Wickens, 1977; Shapiro & Biber, 1972; Shapiro & Weber, 1981). Those involved in the process recognized that finding congruence among educational assumptions and psychological theories required choices, and this realization reinforced their historical concern with clearly explicating and elevating their educational values as educational guides (for example, Biber, 1977b; Biber & Franklin, 1967; Franklin & Biber, 1977; Shapiro & Biber, 1972).

In contrast to the Montessori method, belief in the interplay between theory and practice as an ongoing interaction has sustained the fluidity of the Developmental-Interaction approach. This characteristic is reinforced further by the way in which the Developmental-Interaction approach has been formalized—it is the conceptual framework, rather than practices, that is prescribed.

♂ ESSENTIAL TENETS

The Developmental-Interaction approach has been informed by three main sources: (a) the dynamic psychology of Sigmund Freud and his followers, including Anna Freud, Erik Erikson, Heinz Hartmann, and Harry Stack Sullivan, especially as their ideas relate to the understanding of motivation and autonomous ego processes; (b) gestalt and developmental psychologists concerned with cognitive development, especially Max Wertheimer, Kurt Lewin, Heinz Werner, and Jean Piaget; and (c) educational theorists and practitioners who either have been influenced by these psychologists or developed their own approach, specifically

John Dewey, Harriet Johnson, Susan Issacs, Lucy Sprague Mitchell, and Caroline Pratt (Shapiro & Biber, 1972; Shapiro & Mitchell, 1992).

Internal consistency among these theories comes from the fact that both psychodynamic processes and developmental theory rely on stage theories of development that conceptualize development in terms of qualitative shifts in modes of experiencing and reacting, that occur in an invariant sequence, the earlier being necessary precursors for the later (Biber, 1977b; Shapiro & Biber, 1972). Stage theory provides a framework for understanding and interpreting children's changing behaviors, rather than a literal informant of what children can be expected to do—or should be expected to know—at various points in their development.

Additional coherence is established by linking the values implicit within chosen theories with those explicitly promoted by the Developmental-Interaction approach. "A common purview of optimal human functioning establishes kinship between the educational practices and the psychological theories" (Biber, 1977b, p. 426). Thus, it is recognized that theories of development are not value free.

Presentation of the specifics of the Developmental-Interaction approach follows an outline used by Biber (1977b): value priorities, developmental-educational goals, teaching strategies, and organization. The essentials of this approach already have been described. It is a child-centered, experience-based, process-oriented early childhood program focused on promoting every aspect of a child's development in the direction of optimal human functioning.

It is still a program organized for children from the early preschool years through the elementary grades. So much of the work published about the Developmental-Interaction approach particularizes principles relative to the preschool years because that is the level at which its proponents have experienced the most pressure to explain and defend their approach. The essential elements of the approach, however, are not age specific. Finally, it still is an approach to early childhood education that believes advancing a child's total psychological functioning—social and emotional, as well as intellectual—should define schools' overarching aims and functions.

What is different about the Developmental-Interaction approach from what already has been presented about the Bank Street approach is the expanded breadth, depth, and detail that have been created by embedding and substantiating long-term practices and understandings within a comprehensive theoretical framework. A comprehensive, articulated formulation of the Developmental-Interaction approach now exists that can be provided as a framework and psychological rationale for influencing others' practices.

This formulation represents an important, historical shift in focus. At its beginning, ongoing practice and ongoing research informed each other. Then, gradually, practice was related to theory. With the advent of the Developmental-Interaction approach, theory now informs practice.

Given the character of the Developmental-Interaction approach, specifics are distilled conceptual principles/guidelines for informing teacher practice and decision making, not particulars of implementation. As noted by Evans (1975), these guidelines are a "set of profound, variously abstruse principles" (p. 73). Because

Biber attempted to rationalize every program element and elucidate the multiple interconnections among them, program descriptions often require attentive reading—and rereading. It is impossible for summaries, including the one that follows, not to oversimplify the approach's detailed operational statements. Most frustrating is the extent to which overviews dilute the complex psychological conceptualization of the educational process. The frequent use of quotes is an attempt, in part, to convey the intricacies of the approach's psychological rationalizations.

Value Priorities

According to Biber (1981, 1984), the values of the Developmental-Interaction approach have remained constant throughout the curriculum's evolution. The stated values are those humanistic views of optimal human functioning "generally acceptable across the broad sweep of Western culture" (Shapiro & Biber, 1972, p. 61) and are linked with John Dewey's philosophy of democratic living. These values are grounded in the progressive ideals of individuality and social potential. Educationally, this dual focus generates a continuing search for the kinds of educational experiences that will promote optimal development of individuality and ongoing exploration for the "images of society" that should inform the classroom's social dynamics (Biber, 1981, p. 11). Biber (1981) also stated that "[i]n the broadest sense, the basic value system is an amalgam of ideas about social change, process of maturing, and selection of preferred learning-teaching strategies" (p. 11), thus highlighting that every aspect of the Developmental-Interaction approach is related to its expressed values.

Educational Goals: A Vehicle for Promoting Developmental Processes

The program's psychological rationale, which provides the underpinnings for practice, is drawn from psychodynamic and cognitive-developmental theory. Even though the Developmental-Interaction approach does not believe that psychological theories, in and of themselves, can specify what the immediate or ultimate purposes of education shall be, it does view them as important screening devices when organizing curriculum and making decisions about content and choice of methods and strategies. Six theoretical formulations, reflecting overarching beliefs about the developmental process (see Figure 3-1), provide "the channels through which to navigate toward selected educational goals" (Biber, 1977b, p. 428).

These six formulations, in turn, are reduced to four primary psychological constructs that determine the program's developmental-educational goals and teaching strategies: competence, individuality, socialization, and integration. It is assumed that growth in each of these four areas proceeds developmentally and will be actualized differently by children in different stages of their development.

Therefore, the educational emphasis of the Developmental-Interaction approach is the child's developmental progress (as informed, and particularized, by various stage theories) toward increased competence, individuality, socialization, and integration. Growth occurs by supporting the developmental processes

Figure 3-1 **Six Essential Theoretical Formulations**

1. The autonomous ego processes of the growing organism synchronize with increasingly strong motivation to engage actively with the environment, to make direct impact upon it and to fulfill curiosity about it.
2. The course of development, characterized by qualitative changes or shifts in the individual's means of organizing experience and coping with the environment, may be viewed overall in terms of increasing differentiation and hierarchic integration. This general line of development can be discerned within different stages and with regard to the pattern of growth in various spheres (for example, motor activity, emotional development, perceptual-cognitive functioning).
3. Progress from earlier to later levels of functioning in any domain (emotional, intellectual, or social) is characterized by moments of equilibrium in which the individual's schemata are adequate for the task at hand, and by moments of instability in which currently operative structures are breaking down but new ones are not sufficiently developed to take over completely.
4. An individual does not operate at a "fixed" developmental level, but manifests in his behavior a range of genetically different operations. Earlier or more "primitive" modes of organization are not eradicated, but become integrated into the more advanced modes of organization.
5. The self is both image and instrument. It emerges as the result of a maturing process in which differentiation of objects and other people becomes progressively more refined and self-knowledge is built up from repeated awareness and assessment of the powers of the self in the course of mastering the environment. The shape and quality of the self reflect the images of important people in the growing child's life.
6. Growth and maturing involve conflict. The inner life of the growing child is a play of forces between urgent drives and impulses, contradictory impulses within the self and demanding reality outside the self. The resolution of these conflicts bears the imprint of the quality of interaction with the salient life figures and the demands of the culture.

These statements are quoted from Biber, B. (1977b). A developmental-interactional approach: Bank Street College of Education. In M. C. Day & R. K. Parker (Eds.), *The preschool in action: Exploring early childhood programs* (2nd. ed., pp. 426–28. Boston: Allyn & Bacon. They can also be found in Biber, B., & Franklin, M. B. (1967). The relevance of developmental and psychodynamic concepts to the education of the preschool child. *Journal of the American Academy of Child Psychiatry.* 6 (1–4), 5–24.

underlying these four constructs. This emphasis is in intentional contrast with discrete, concrete behavioral achievements sequenced toward a specified accomplishment.

The teacher, consequently, is primed to be sensitive to children's individual behaviors in terms of their underlying developmental processes. It is the development of these underlying processes, rather than specific behaviors, that is the focus of the teacher's educational efforts.

Educational goals (see Figure 3-2), therefore, do not define behavioral end points. Instead, they are informants for supporting, stimulating, and guiding developmental processes that can help actualize each child's optimal functioning. Given the complementary concern for social potential, these goals also help establish priorities for the social organization of the classroom.

Figure 3-2   **Developmental-Educational Goals**

1. To serve the child's need to make an impact on the environment through direct physical contact and maneuver
2. To promote the potential for ordering experience through cognitive strategies
3. To advance the child's functioning knowledge of his environment
4. To support the play mode of incorporating experience
5. To help the child internalize impulse control
6. To meet the child's need to cope with conflicts intrinsic to this stage of development
7. To facilitate the development of an image of self as a unique and competent person
8. To help the child establish mutually supporting patterns of interaction

These developmental educational goals are excerpted from Biber, B. (1977b). A developmental-interaction approach: Bank Street college of Education. In M. C. Day & R. K. Parker (Eds.), *The pre-school in action: Exploring early childhood programs* (2nd ed., pp. 435–445). Boston: Allyn & Bacon.

The emphasis on underlying developmental processes means that the approach's educational aims are extended developmentally. As a result, program effectiveness cannot be validly assessed in terms of short-term objectives. This factor contributed to the defensiveness of proponents of the developmental-interaction viewpoint because their approach was placed at a distinct disadvantage when competitive evaluations of curriculum models focused on short-term gains in cognitive functioning. (This is discussed further in Chapter 6.)

Competence. The primary learning associated with this developmental construct involves bringing a child's individual potential to its highest possible realization—becoming competent in body and mind. Functionally, this includes concern for how the child uses her knowledge and skills in negotiating the environment and in interactions with others.

Individuality. The enhancement of individuality focuses on promoting the child's sense of self as unique—"a distinct, thinking, feeling being capable of emotional investment, with a sense of worth based on knowledge and feelings of his own competence as much as on reflections of himself in people around him" (Biber, 1977b, p. 430). High priority is placed on autonomous functioning, which in this instance (in contrast to Montessori's conceptualization of autonomy [see Chapter 2] and Kamii and DeVries's [see Chapter 5]) refers to the ability to make choices, develop preferences, take initiative, risk failure, set an independent course for problem solving, and accept help without sacrificing independence.

Socialization. This developmental process, when framed in terms of an educational goal, involves helping children learn control over their impulses in order to participate in classroom life, adapt their behavior to a rational system of controls and sanctions, and become self-regulating. This goal also addresses relationships with others.

Integration. The goal of integration is concerned with helping children merge disparate experiences, both personal and impersonal—"to integrate thought and feeling, thought and action, the subjective and the objective, self-feeling and empathy with others, original and conventional forms of communication, spontaneous and ritualized forms of response" (Shapiro & Biber, 1972, p. 62). When teachers respond to children with this goal in mind, they help children see connections among their various reactions to an incident, to appreciate a situation more completely. Functionally, this means teachers avoid strategies that fragment learning. The process of integration is seen as especially critical to creativity and maximum engagement in learning (Biber, 1977b; Shapiro & Biber, 1972).

Teaching Strategies

Teaching strategies are intermediaries between the developmental principles and developmental-educational goals and the specific content and organization experienced by children. Teaching strategies have been carefully deliberated based on the assumption that chosen strategies influence the selection of program content and learning experiences, an insight later confirmed by research (See chapter 6).

Teaching strategies are informed by three components: the teacher–child relationship, curriculum content and instructional principles, and motivation (Biber, 1977b). These three components are the same elements emphasized by Shapiro and Biber in their elucidation of the term *interaction*. These programmatic components are seen as essential to achieving developmental-educational goals because they describe characteristics of the learning environment that either facilitate or impede a child's actualization of his potential. The Developmental-Interaction approach, however, does not limit its focus to learning within the classroom. It also extends children's learning opportunities into the community (i.e., field trips) and actively seeks continuity between home and school environments.

Teacher–Child Relationship. The primary task of the teacher in the teacher–child relationship is to establish a mutually trusting relationship. A trusting relationship is foundational because it enables the teacher to become effective as a mediator of children's learning experiences, provides a reflective surface for the child's developing self-concept, ensures the child's identification with the teacher (which is prerequisite to a child taking as his own the learning goals that the teacher holds for him), and serves as a model for human interchange.

The nature of the teacher–child relationship, therefore, is a defining, interactional element of this approach. The teacher is given theoretical and actual responsibility for structuring and nurturing this relationship. She is designated as the respondent and activator; the child's active influence on the teacher, other children, and the learning environment is mentioned less frequently.

To establish and sustain a trusting relationship, teachers are expected to be able to:

- listen in order to understand a child's underlying thinking when immature verbal discourse may deflect it;
- help formulate and channel children's semiformed intent into a realizable activity;

- establish herself as a resource for meeting problems of confusion, fear, loss of direction, anger, or loneliness;
- understand behavior in the context of the characteristics of the stage of development; and
- establish a personalized, differentiated relationship with each child (Biber, 1977b, p. 431; these descriptors were chosen from a listing of 19 expectations).

Curriculum content and instructional principles refer to the program of activities and the nature of the learning experience. Biber (1977b) provided a list of 18 statements to describe instructional principles for preschool children. These principles are meant to inform the knowledge and skills children should be expected to master at this stage of development, the role of the child in the mastery process, and the most effective organization of learning experiences. Examples of these principles include:

- intellectual mastery is conceived in terms of the organization of knowledge and an active stance toward learning;
- children's varied ongoing experience in the classroom is the primary material for advancing the functional use of language and the thinking processes;
- curriculum content reflects two dominant themes: the "how" processes of making, doing, and fixing; and the questions of origin—where things come from, where they end, what it is to be born, and what it is to die;
- optimal learning is active learning in which the child is given the role of questioning, probing, exploring, and planning;
- the curriculum is organized flexibly so as to provide many opportunities for children to make choices, select from alternatives, and determine their own course within an established program;
- the teacher uses every appropriate opportunity to encourage differentiated observation and comparison, the search for causes and origins, and the organization of experience in terms of continuity and transformation;
- ideally, thinking becomes part of continuous experiencing, in the same stream with doing, feeling, and imagining. (p. 432)

> The teaching role envisioned here . . . requires the capacity to empathize with the mental processes of young children, to deal without anxiety with the ambiguity necessarily associated with exploration-search patterns rather than right-wrong paradigms, to deal with variations not only in rate of mastery but in cognitive style, and thus to carry a multiple series of evaluative criteria by which to judge when learning is being productive for different children. (Biber, 1967b, p. 120)

In Bank Street's recent dissemination effort, the role of social studies is emphasized as the core of the integrated curriculum for children 4 through 8 years old (see Mitchell & David, 1992). Social studies has long provided a vehicle for integrating themes of concern and subject matter knowledge (Cuffaro, 1977; Gilkeson et al., 1981).

Gilkeson et al., (1981), for example, describe a primary grade project where students explored Weeksville, a community of former slaves located where the school in question now stands. Children dug up artifacts, read historical records, and recreated the clothing, tools, and activities of Weeksville, acquiring a "host of skills" (p. 258) throughout the project's completion. At the primary level, academic skills are interconnected and integrated throughout children's learning activities.

It is noteworthy, within this context, that despite continuous reference to John Dewey's influence, the Developmental-Interaction approach does not incorporate his strong concern for teachers' knowledge of subject matter. Consistent with its psychological emphasis on developmental processes, interest in intellectual development focuses on processes such as reasoning and problem solving; but little attention is given to what children should think about beyond what they are immediately experiencing and/or are interested in knowing—even in the most recent curriculum guide (Mitchell & David, 1992). The issue of subject matter knowledge rarely is addressed.

Yet, as Dewey (1938) has pointed out, the critical question for progressive education is "What is the place and meaning of subject-matter and of organization *within* experience?" (p. 20). The Developmental-Interaction approach does not address this question. Extensive expectations for teachers relative to their psychological knowledge of the child are not joined by similar expectations for a thorough familiarity with organized knowledge as represented in the disciplines. This tilt toward the child, and away from Dewey's dual and integrated thrust, is consistent with the direction taken by many educators during the progressive education era (Cremin, 1961/1964).

It logically follows, given its process orientation and concern with integrated developmental processes, that advocates of the Developmental-Interaction approach oppose programs in which stimulation of cognitive development is disassociated from meaningful experience and occurs apart from consideration of other interacting developmental processes (Biber, 1981, 1984). Yet behavioral curriculum models with a focus on discrete intellectual and academic tasks dominated the compensatory education movement, and thus were an irritant to advocates of the Developmental-Interaction approach (see Chapter 4). Objection to over reliance on direct instruction was of long standing. As a teaching strategy, direct instruction is consistent with conventional public school practice which contributors to the Developmental-Interaction approach have consistently criticized.

Finally, *motivation* as a program factor refers to what constitutes positive motivation within this approach. It is framed by six statements that emphasize children's intrinsic drive toward competence, the satisfaction of meaningful learning, and the linkage between motivational concepts and the child's development as an autonomous individual (Biber, 1977b, p. 433).

Organization

One of the challenges to discussing the Developmental-Interaction approach stems from the fact that, for so many early childhood educators, characteristics of this approach have become mainstream practice. Because they are so pervasive in present practice, it is difficult to ferret out the approach's distinguishing characteristics.

Depiction of classroom organization and materials is an especially good example of this predicament. The classroom organization developed by Bank Street's founders and integral to the Developmental-Interaction approach has become standard description in undergraduate, early childhood textbooks.

Organizational characteristics represent a critical component of the learning environment and are necessary for fulfilling program goals. The classroom arrangement should allow children to speak and move about freely, work individually and in groups, choose activities, and access a variety of materials. In a typical preschool classroom, there are clearly marked areas for painting, water play, block building, dramatic play, and looking at books. Table groupings serve as places for snacks, art-related activities, table games, and lunch. The organization of primary classrooms is based on similar tenets, though, obviously, available materials would reflect the interests of older children as well as teacher concerns with basic skills (Gilkeson et al., 1981).

Criteria for material selection are derived from the developmental-educational goals and teaching strategies. In general, priority is given to open-ended materials, such as blocks, paints, sand, clay, wood, planks, climbing equipment, animal and people figures, dress-up clothes, and housekeeping setup, that offer multiple and varied opportunities for child-initiated exploration, experimentation, and representation. More structured materials, such as pegs, form boards, and puzzles, are provided to strengthen perceptual discrimination and manipulative problem solving. For primary children, written materials, such as books, catalogs, and magazines, and math and science equipment, such as kits, scales, thermometers, attribute blocks, geoboards, and Cuisenaire rods, plus games become the classroom staples.

Mass-produced and home-made materials are arranged functionally on open shelves where children can have easy access, and are labeled with pictures, symbols, or written labels, depending on what children can understand. Children are given responsibility for properly using materials and returning them to their appropriate location. Finally, for preschoolers, activities are scheduled in a regular sequence so children know what to expect and can develop a sense of temporal order.

All of these organizational aspects are also intended as statements about how the room is to be used and the way in which the teacher expects children to be engaged in learning. The classroom is planned not only in terms of practical needs but also in terms of the teaching value (Biber, 1977b; Gilkeson et al., 1981).

Teachers plan activities to achieve predetermined learning goals for individual children and the children as a group. Most especially, teachers will be careful observers of children and their activities and will be responsive to the learning possibilities embedded within children's ongoing experiences with classroom materials, with each other, and in interaction with her. Ultimately, therefore, it is the teacher who operationalizes Bank Street's carefully integrated conceptual framework, who sensitively responds to children's underlying motivations, recognizes the sources of confusion, seizes opportunities for new insights, and optimizes moment-by-moment interactions. "The teacher is the most important figure in the developmental-interaction approach because it is she who creates the climate in the classroom, the physical and psychological learning environment of the young child's life in the school" (Shapiro & Biber, 1972, p. 68).

Appreciating the complexity of the Developmental-Interaction approach for beginning teachers, attempts have been made to simplify the approach. A single volume published by Bank Street provides a framework for choosing activities (Mitchell & David, 1992). A more ambitious series of guides, videos, and manuals for supervisors and trainers for infant-toddler, preschool, and primary practitioners have been published by Teaching Strategies, Inc. (see, for example, Dodge, 1992, 1993).

◈ FROM REFLECTIVE PRACTICE TO THEORY INTO PRACTICE

The Developmental-Interaction approach is the most comprehensive enduring approach to early childhood curriculum because of its encompassing concern with social-emotional and intellectual development. It also is among the most flexible because, as an approach *to* rather than a model *for* early education, it chose to develop principles to inform practitioners' daily decision making rather than provide them specifics of practice.

Yet, even so, evolving to the form and status of a formalized approach has significantly, even if subtly, transformed its historical approach to early childhood education. Biber (1988) herself unwittingly identified the most significant "aftereffect" of formalizing an approach to early childhood education, of exchanging evolving, dynamic, individualistic practice for practice prescribed within a formal theoretical framework.

In a paper addressing the challenges of professionalism in early childhood education, Biber (1988) identified the integration of theory and practice as the paramount difficulty. Notably, before placing this challenge at the feet of teachers, she reminisced about the contributions of Lucy Mitchell and Harriet Johnson as pioneers of a new form of education for young children. And then she lamented, "Theory and practice were woven together. Today, theory and practice are separate provinces; seldom does the same individual operate in both. Often they don't even talk to each other. New lines of connection and communication must be built from both domains" (p. 37).

Formalizing an approach to curriculum, in effect, creating a curriculum model, regardless of how flexible and dynamic, promotes this detachment of theory from practice, of teaching from research and theorizing, and teachers from researchers and theoreticians. It undermines relationships between teachers and theoreticians/researchers as equal partners and co-informants, which *had* characterized the Bank Street approach. It promotes a relationship of dependency, where practice becomes dependent on research and theory "to tell it what to do"; and it encourages teachers to become recipients of others' knowledge and know-how, rather than co-creators.

Biber and her colleagues seemed to be unaware of these repercussions, however. Their critical sensitivities were directed more toward the theoretical impact of having formalized their conceptual framework. They questioned, for example, "To what extent does adherence to a given psychological theory as the basis of an educational design restrict the comprehensiveness of the program—the extent to which it provides for the multiple aspects of learning, ego development, and socialization?" (Franklin & Biber, 1977, p. 25). Biber also (1984) asked, "Is it spurious or at least premature to posit a body of theory or theories sufficiently comprehensive to be the foundation for the multitudinous aspects of an educational design?" (p. 303).

Those espousing the Developmental-Interaction approach recognized, as well, that how one arrives at the formation of a value system is problematic (Biber, 1981), and they pondered the lack of articulation between individual variation and developmental theory. They questioned whether developmental theories direct attention toward characterizing behavior in terms of what it has not yet become, and whether developmental stage theories divert attention from the uniqueness of the individual (Shapiro & Wallace, 1981).

Yet, there was no apparent awareness of a movement, in which they unintentionally participated, that has shifted the balance between theory and practice. Biber (1984, 1988) urged theorists to interact with teachers as a source for greater understanding of how individual children, from year to year, function within the educational sequence, and she has argued, "Theory should not be insulated from application, nor should practice be allowed to escape responsibility for articulating theoretical foundations since cross-fertilization is essential to sound progress in both spheres" (Biber, 1984, p. 304). But despite these expressions of concern for collaboration between theory and practice, subtle shifts in Biber's analyses of the Developmental-Interaction approach indicate a different kind of relationship.

When Biber (1977b) wrote about the decision in 1959 to critically examine the rationale for their practices, she said,

> Knowledge of the growing field of child development and psychology of learning had indeed influenced these assumptions (about learning), but they had been primarily derived from the direct experience of observing and teaching children in school. . . . To what extent would formulations and viewpoints in the field of psychology, arrived at independently of the field of education, corroborate these assumptions and thus provide a firmer theoretical base for the practices? (p. 425)

In contrast, when justifying the change in name to Developmental-Interaction approach more than a decade later, Biber (1977b) argued it was time to be known by their essential *theoretical* characteristics.

And, when writing retrospectively about the era of the seventies, there no longer is any mention of corroborating the relationship between theory and practice:

> By the seventies, our thinking was directed toward clarifying the developmental-interaction point of view: the implications for education of perceiving identifiable successive patterns of growth as a function of chronological age, of placing emphasis on the child's interaction with the social and physical environment within the context of preferred values, and, finally, of recognizing the interaction between cognitive and affective spheres of experience. (Biber, 1984, p. 310)

Lucy Mitchell's contention that Bank Street's teacher education program would not perpetuate any particular "school of thought" (as cited in Antler, 1982, p. 583) now seems debatable.

Since its formalization as an approach to early childhood education, the Developmental-Interaction approach no longer is infused with the conjectural, experimental practice that characterized it during the era of progressive education. Its rationalization now relies mostly on the thoughtful deliberations of theorists such as Biber, rather than the reflective practices and ideas of practitioners. Although Biber's writings relied on the pioneer insights of practitioners such as Harriet Johnson, Lucy Mitchell, and Susan Issacs, their contemporary counterparts are conspicuously absent. Similar to other curriculum models developed during the 1960s, the notion of experimental practice became associated with how to implement a preconceived conceptual framework.

One only need read *I Learn from Children* by Caroline Pratt (1948/1990) to appreciate the energy, commitment, and intellectual vitality that came from practitioners and researchers mutually creating and recreating the meaning and purpose of an educational setting. Even though the Developmental-Interaction approach has maintained an experimental quality to daily practice and avoided mechanizing the acts of teaching, by shifting its attention away from practice, and toward theory as a primary stimulus for decision making, the teacher's role has shifted from that of creator to implementer—even though as noted throughout the chapter, the complexity of implementation is daunting and therefore problematic to a field in need of "qualified" practitioners.

The existence of a formalized conceptual framework, by definition, constrains the possibilities considered and subtly redirects teacher thinking and behavior from contemplating how to maximize individual and group potential to how best to implement a chosen approach. Silin (1986), in his review of Biber's book *Early Education and Psychological Development*, speaks to this particular point:

> One would wish [that Biber's] command of the psychological literature and her openness in assimilating new research findings were matched by an equal willingness to deal with developments in sociological and political theory. Biber would never limit her psychological insights to the work of one person, yet this is exactly what she does in the realm of sociopolitical analysis by relying so completely on John Dewey. The developmental-interaction approach claims to be a comprehensive one, yet its knowledge base is confined to developmental psychology; its politics to the liberal, democratic view of a large faction within the progressive movement; and its social vision to the description of individual personality traits deemed desirable for an ill-defined world of the future. (p. 615)

In response to this and other challenges to developmental theory as a determinant of educational practice (see Chapter 7), proponents of the Developmental-Interaction approach have begun exploring "new pathways for revitalizing the approach" (Nager & Shapiro, 2000, p. 33).

There is no way of knowing if the Bank Street perspective would have been formalized as the Developmental-Interaction approach if the external pressures that were present during the 1960s had not existed: concern with the nation's capacity to respond to international competition, discouragement with the educational status quo, and an incredible demand for early childhood programs coexisting with the early childhood profession's insufficient capacity to respond. Nor is there any way to forecast what might have happened to an appreciation of, and concern for, the "whole child" if Biber and others had stayed outside the fray.

The pressures faced by the Bank Street approach during the 1960s are not unlike the ones the field of early care and education continues to confront. These shared historical factors make the experience of the Developmental-Interaction approach especially informative to current deliberations concerned with how to ensure increasing numbers of children consistently high quality early childhood care and education in ways that also elevate the professional knowledge and expertise of those who provide it.

☞ FOR FURTHER READING

Biber, B. (1984). *Early education and psychological development.* New Haven, CT; Yale University Press.

> In this book, Biber presents many of her original writings, extending from 1939 until 1977, and then reassesses her thinking, sometimes validating it anew, at other times extending it to reflect her current interests or thinking. As such, it is a comprehensive theoretical and personal review of Biber's thinking over 5 decades.

Biber, B. (1977a). Cognition in early childhood education: A historical perspective. In B. Spodek & H. Walberg (Eds.), *Early childhood education: Issues and insights* (pp. 41–64). Berkeley, CA: McCutchan.

> Because changing perspectives on cognition are so integral to the history of the Developmental-Interaction approach, we found this historical review by Biber to be especially informative.

Biber, B. (1977b). A developmental-interaction approach: Bank Street College of Education. In M. C. Day & R. K. Parker (Eds.), *The preschool in action: Exploring early childhood programs* (2nd ed. pp. 421–460). Boston: Allyn & Bacon.

> Although focused on its preschool program, this chapter presents a detailed discussion of the Developmental-Interaction approach that, more than other descriptions, reveals the intricacy of the approach and its psychodynamic underpinnings.

Greenberg, P. (1987). Lucy Sprague Mitchell: A major missing link between early childhood education in the 1980s and Progressive Education in the 1890s-1930s. *Young Children, 42,* 70–84.

> Greenberg uses her review of Antler's (1987) biography of Lucy Sprague Mitchell not only to describe Mitchell's contributions to the early childhood profession but also to provide a historical review of early childhood education prior to the 1960s. Greenberg presents a passionate review of early childhood education's U.S. history from the 1930s to the 1960s.

Chapter Four

The Direct Instruction Model

It seems to me somewhat misleading to go on treating the traditional approach as one among a host of alternative approaches to teaching young children. It is better seen, not as a distinctive approach to teaching, but as a system of custodial child care that may incorporate to a greater or lesser extent various educational components similar to those found in instructional programs for young children, but that is primarily distinguished by its minimization of teaching. The true issue between the traditional approach and the various instructional approaches in not how young children should be taught but whether.

Carl Bereiter, "An Academic Program for Disadvantaged Children: Conclusions from Evaluation Studies," 1972

In the beginning, there was the response. And the behaviorist looked at the response and saw that it was good. At least it was real, and the behaviorist was weary of creativity. There had passed considerably more than six days, during which numerous psychologists had invented even more numerous souls, minds, instincts, feelings, drives and mediating mechanisms, all to explain the response. But the behaviorist who had started with the response because it was clearly there, began to explain the response with what was also clearly there, which was the external environment. And indeed, the response proved responsive to the external environment, indicating that the word was good, too. Therefore, another word was made to name those parts of the clearly there external environment to which the response was responsive; and the new word was called stimulus. And together the two words were functional, and begat many new words, such that the land was filled with them.

Donald M. Baer, "In the Beginning, There Was the Response," 1975

The Bereiter-Engelmann preschool curriculum, which was the forerunner to the Direct Instruction model, was one of the first curricula expressly developed as a preschool model after the advent of Head Start. As the tone of the first introductory quote suggests, the Bereiter-Engelmann preschool served as a critical, and often belittling, protagonist to early childhood programs with a "traditional" focus. Hence, examination of the Bereiter-Engelmann preschool continues the drama that unfolded when academically oriented models challenged early childhood programs that advanced intellectual development as an untutored process.

As detailed in Chapter 3, the Developmental-Interaction approach was placed in a defensive posture almost from the onset of the curriculum model era. In this chapter, an "assailant's" viewpoint is presented. In the process, the competitive climate created by the curriculum model era and its search for the most effective early childhood programs becomes more visible.

97

The experiences of the behaviorally grounded Bereiter-Engelmann and Direct Instruction models during this era are almost the complete reversal of those encountered by advocates of the Developmental-Interaction approach. Proponents of the Developmental-Interaction approach were placed on the defensive because of the contrast between their holistic, child-centered viewpoint and that of more cognitively oriented programs. In contrast, the Bereiter-Engelmann and Direct Instruction models were catapulted to center stage by the alignment of their curricular premises with educational norms and societal expectations.

This alignment sustained the prominence of their and other academically oriented models despite shifts occurring in behavioral theory toward more cognitively oriented interpretations of learning (Case & Bereiter, 1984; White, 1970; Wittrock & Lumsdaine, 1977) and in spite of impassioned challenges by members of the early childhood profession. As expressed by one detractor, the Bereiter-Engelmann model created

> . . . an environment in which work and play are polar opposites, in which the pleasurable interpersonal affective factors in learning are avoided while material (cookies) rewards are permitted. It is, in short, an atmosphere of puritanical zeal in which difficult tasks are dutifully pursued, while delight in an original expression, deviation, personal view or recounting are devil's pleasure. (Moskovitz, 1968, p. 27)

The Direct Instruction model built on the approach developed by Bereiter and Engelmann. Developed as a part of Project Follow Through, the Direct Instruction model, which targets kindergarten through third grade, has endured as an active curriculum model (see, for example, Carnine, Grossen, & Silbert, 1995). Even though only the Direct Instruction model remains a viable curriculum model, both models serve as the focus of this chapter for two reasons. First, and most obvious, as a precursor to the Direct Instruction model, knowing the Bereiter-Engelmann model helps our understanding of its successor. Second, as a leading advocate for intense and direct academic instruction as the most appropriate curriculum for disadvantaged preschoolers, review of the Bereiter-Engelmann model provides a graphic example of the opposing perspectives that came to inhabit early childhood education during this era.

In contrast to the Montessori method and the Developmental-Interaction approach, the Bereiter-Engelmann model, and then the Direct Instruction model, grew out of and were nurtured by the particular tenor of the 1960s. As a result, examination of these two models provides a chance to consider the influences that shaped model development during this time. Finally, as a new, and radical,[1] addition to curriculum possibilities in preschool and kindergarten education, these two models furnish an opportunity to examine the impact wrought by the onset of curriculum models.

The degree of support for an approach that "shocked early childhood education establishmentarians" (Evans, 1975, p. 141) was apparently unanticipated. According to Biber's (1984) reflection, "We thought we were the wave of the future.

---

[1]Heretical might be a better word choice!

We could not have imagined the important place that behavior modification as applied to preschool education would attain in the 1960s and thereafter as part of government planning in particular and in academic circles in general" (p. 25). Appreciating the history and impact of these two curriculum models requires understanding how this level of support came to be.

The Bereiter-Engelmann and Direct Instruction models, in conjunction with other academically oriented models spawned during this period, brought the tensions between developmental and academic orientations, heretofore deliberated in elementary education, into the arena of kindergarten and preschool education. In the arena of early education, however, with its established child-centered focus, the tensions quickly escalated into warfare.

The downward movement of this debate from elementary to preschool, in turn, further exacerbated the prevailing distinction between the (child) care and education of young children. The advent of Head Start not only affirmed the educational purpose of nursery schools, it spurred acceptance of nursery education as the start of children's schooling, regardless of socioeconomic background. No longer was the argument about the educational nature of nursery programs but rather how their educational purpose was best achieved and whether educational purpose differed for children of different socioeconomic status (see, for example, Elkind, 1970; Sigel, 1991).

Kindergartens were undergoing a matching evolution for similar reasons (Weber, 1969). As a result, the historically separate pathways of nursery and kindergarten education began to merge in their opposition to academic curricula for young children. (Chapter 1 details the beginning of this history.) Child care, however, continued to carry the burden of its history and its negative character as a substitute for mothering; its custodial focus remained intact and outside the purview of educational institutions. By the end of the zenith of the curriculum model era in the early 1970s, the educational purposes of preschool and kindergarten education often were juxtaposed against the custodial function of "day care."

Debate regarding how educational purpose was best achieved in early childhood programs was operationalized in the diversity of curriculum models that emerged during the 1960s. Until the mid-1960s, *systematic* variety in early childhood curricula for nursery schools and kindergarten programs had been minimal. Programmatic differences reflected differences among sponsoring agencies rather than conscious decisions to vary curriculum in terms of specified learning goals and objectives (Spodek, 1973; White & Buka, 1987).

Propelled by the search for effective educational interventions for disadvantaged preschoolers and the infusion of federal dollars into their research and development, the curriculum model approach to early childhood education flourished during the 1960s and early 1970s. The 1967 initiation of Project Follow Through and its method of planned variation among curriculum models systematized the effort, intensified the competitive overtones of the search for the best model, and framed the question of which curriculum was best as a problem to be resolved by science.

The idea of curriculum models, consequently, emanated from outside the field of early childhood education. Both in concept and in practice, they were imposed on the field. Examination of the Bereiter-Engelmann and Direct Instruction models uncovers how the advent of curriculum models in early childhood education provoked not only the creation of diverse curriculum possibilities but also initiated curricular repercussions that still reverberate.

℘ THE PSYCHOLOGICAL FRAMEWORK FOR DIRECT INSTRUCTION

The Tenets of Behaviorism

The Bereiter-Engelmann and Direct Instruction models are based on learning principles derived from behavioral psychology. Derived from the stimulus–response psychology of Edward Thorndike and John Watson, who usually is credited as the father of behaviorism, behavioral psychology substituted observable stimuli and responses for mentalistic ideas and images.

In contrast to the other curriculum models under discussion, the Bereiter-Engelmann (B-E) and Direct Instruction (DI) models are not built from a theory of child development. Behavioral changes and individual differences are explained in terms of learning, not development. As defined by Hilgard and Bower (1975), learning "refers to the change in a subject's behavior to a given situation brought about by repeated experiences in that situation, provided that the behavior change can not be explained on the basis of native response tendencies, maturation, or temporary states of the individual (e.g., fatigue, drugs, etc.)" (p. 17). Learning is understood as the result of an external event. Consistent with its dismissal of mentalistic ideas and images, behavioral psychology viewed the child as a recipient of, rather than participant in, learning.

According to White (1970), learning theories can be characterized by five statements:

1. The environment is characterized in terms of stimuli.
2. Behavior is characterized in terms of responses.
3. Stimuli called reinforcers, when applied contingently and immediately following a response, increase or decrease the response in measurable ways.
4. Learning can be understood in terms of the associations among stimuli, responses, and reinforcers.
5. Unless there is evidence to the contrary, all behavior is learned, manipulable by the environment, extinguishable, and trainable, (pp. 665–666)

The B-E and DI models are based on the application of these behavioral principles and laws of learning to instruction. Movement from learning in theory to prescribing learning in practice means that the structure of the subject matter content being taught also has to be considered (Case & Bereiter, 1984; Hilgard & Bower, 1975). Siegfried Engelmann, who helped design both curriculum models, is credited with employing learning principles and programming strategies to construct the programmed lessons in reading, arithmetic, and language (Becker, Engelmann, Carnine, & Rhine, 1981; Bereiter, 1968).

The efforts of Bereiter and Engelmann and their colleagues are part of what is variously labeled theories of instruction, instructional psychology, instructional design (Case & Bereiter, 1984; Glaser, 1990; Hilgard & Bower, 1975; Wittrock & Lumsdaine, 1977), and, more recently, educational learning theory (Bereiter, 1990). According to Case and Bereiter (1984), a behaviorist technology of instruction emerged primarily as a result of B. F. Skinner's work in conceptualizing the notion of shaping or successive approximations. Whereas the principle of reinforcement deals with strengthening behaviors that already are part of an individual's repertoire, the shaping process conceptualizes a means for modifying existing behavior by reinforcing behavioral variations that are in the direction of a desired behavior. With this behavioral principle, it became possible to promote new (versus merely reinforce existing) behaviors.

Individuals involved with this field of study are predominately educational and behavioral psychologists, rather than developmental psychologists. In an examination of the relationship between the learning theory tradition and child psychology, White (1970) pointed out that no learning theory has been constructed from studies of children or been specifically directed toward them.

Consequently, many of the educational psychologists developing early childhood curriculum models had limited knowledge of, or experience with, early childhood education. Nor, given their underlying assumptions about learning and their disinterest in the construct of development, was such knowledge or experience needed. Based on the assumption that all behavior is learned and subject to predictable laws of learning, the architects of the B-E and DI models created an instructional environment to teach young children directly and systematically the prerequisite skills in reading, arithmetic, and language that were believed necessary to secure their future academic achievement.

The early childhood community, however, was aghast. Based on her observation of the B-E classroom, Weber (1970) wrote:

> As a total learning theory, operant conditioning, dependent as it is upon the key words "operants" and "reinforcement" can be accepted only by those who are willing to view the learner as passive and non-purposive and who tolerate the assumption of determinism. . . . This mechanical approach leaves no place for feelings, sensitivities, creativity, or a sense of autonomy in learning.[2] (p. 27)

Bereiter countered in terms consistent with behaviorists' fundamentally different approach to children and the purposes of education:

> On the contrary, we cared about the children, and we considered their emotional future as carefully as we considered their academic future. Concern for the children's

---

[2]Although Weber's comment was directed toward the Bereiter-Engelmann preschool, it should be noted that Bereiter and Engelmann did not view their program as based on operant conditioning. According to Bereiter (1986), their model "was not a Skinnerian behavioral management program. It was . . . a rationalist program of concept teaching not even remotely Skinnerian in theory" (p. 290). This distinction was explained further in the earlier discussion about theories of instruction. For examples of curriculum models based on operant conditioning, the reader is referred to Bushell (1973, 1982) and Ramp and Rhine (1981).

emotional stability was the justification for such careful programming of skills—to make learning a less frustrating experience. (Anderson & Bereiter, 1972, p. 341)

Finally, the B-E and DI models were informed by the thinking prevalent during the 1960s regarding the learning needs of young children from economically disadvantaged home environments. In particular, their decisions regarding program content and instructional design were heavily influenced by their acceptance and interpretation of the notion of cultural deprivation.

The notion of cultural deprivation was constructed in the mid-1960s in an attempt to understand why children from low-income families, in contrast to their middle-class counterparts, were unsuccessful learners in public schools. The widely accepted interpretation was that children from low-income families were deprived of adequate learning experiences, especially in language development. Their "culture" deprived them of the adult–child interactions and stimulating experiences common for their middle-class peers, and thus they arrived at school intellectually unprepared to learn.

This interpretation was a prevalent explanation for the different performance levels of children from low-income and middle-class families. Variation among curriculum models resided not in their acceptance of the concept but in their programmatic responses to this presumed deficiency. The Developmental-Interaction approach, for example, assumed the same underlying developmental processes needed nurturing and support regardless of a child's socioeconomic status (Biber, 1967a, 1984). Architects of the B-E and DI models developed a program based on the premise that preschoolers and kindergartners from low-income backgrounds enter school with fewer skills and concepts than their advantaged peers. From their way of thinking, delaying academic instruction because children are not "ready" only serves to widen the gap. Given their adherence to behavioral theory, it was logical that they would advocate minimizing the gap in achievement through direct means.

Understanding the disparity between these two views is relevant because it clarifies their differing approaches. In addition, although the concept of cultural deprivation has been discarded, debates regarding the most appropriate curriculum for young children identified as at risk still revolve around similar questions: Do all children thrive with similar learning experiences, or do the "needs" of children from low-income families necessitate an academic curriculum?

The following two quotes, the first by Biber and the second by Bereiter and Engelmann, effectively contrast the difference in approach. According to Biber (1967a):

> What the child misses . . . is not only a model of spoken language but, much more fundamentally, a lack of rich, meaningful communication beyond just the necessities of practical living. These lacks are deterrents for language use, indeed. Eventually, they become deterrents for learning to read. But, more than that, more deeply, they are deterrents for being able to learn in general because it is through the active relationship with people, it is through being known and felt and understood as a person, that the child's basic curiosity and interest in the world begins to flower and develop. (p. 112)

In contrast, Bereiter and Engelmann (1966b), who identified the B-E model as a remedial course for preschoolers deficient in language and verbal reasoning, asserted:

> From the beginning there is a lag in learning that must be overcome if disadvantaged children are to emerge from school with the same skills and knowledge as more privileged children. If the lag is to be made up during the school years, then schools for disadvantaged children have to provide higher quality and faster-paced education than that provided for advantaged children. Another possible solution is to provide this kind of education before the school years—the motivating idea for preschool education for disadvantaged children. (p. 6)

Thus, Bereiter and Engelmann's academic curriculum model was based on the belief that the critical issue confronting disadvantaged children was their learning deficit, which increased in magnitude as children from low-income families progressed through grade school (this was known as the cumulative deficit). The most effective way to remedy this deficit, according to proponents of the B-E and DI models, was by directly and systematically teaching the skills children needed in order to succeed in school (Bereiter & Engelmann, 1966b; Carnine, Carnine, Karp, & Weisberg, 1988; Gersten, Darch, & Gleason, 1988; Gersten & George, 1990).

Thirty-four years later, it is difficult to read *Teaching the Disadvantaged Preschooler* wherein Bereiter and Engelmann provide a detailed rationale for, and explanation of, the B-E curriculum model. Their 1966 interpretation of cultural deficit, in light of our changed understandings about cultural diversity in 2000, is unnerving. According to their interpretation, cultural deprivation and language deprivation were synonymous. As explained by Horowitz and Paden (1973):

> [Bereiter and Engelmann] worked from a deficit model which could almost be described as a dismissal model. In the area of language, for instance, they sometimes have appeared to assume that for all practical purposes the "disadvantaged" child has no language, that he cannot think, and that he has nothing to think about. . . . They argue that whatever his language, it is insufficient for functional operation in the middle-class, mostly white culture where the child must ultimately operate. (pp. 374–375)

At this point, it is important to note that even though the Direct Instruction model built on the Bereiter-Engelmann model, it did not speak to the issue of "cultural deprivation." Instead, it justified the effectiveness of its direct instruction and "catch-up" approach by arguing that low-income, at-risk students should be prepared "to enter first grade with a similar knowledge base in reading, mathematics, and language concepts as children not at risk" (Gersten et al., 1988, p. 228).

Science, Method, and a Science of Education

Science and Method. With its emphasis on observable behaviors and environmental manipulation, the history and practice of behavioral psychology is closely aligned with experimental methodology (Hilgard & Bower, 1975; White, 1970). Experimental methodology attempts to impose environmental control over the experimental situation and to manipulate clearly defined variables in search of quantifiable cause and effect relationships. The theoretical relationships between behavioral psychology and experimental methodology assumed practical and political significance for the B-E and DI models when policy makers decided to determine program effectiveness by assessing children's learning in terms of standardized test scores, an assessment tool particularly well matched to the learning objectives and teaching style of these two models.

First funded as part of Project Follow Through (and then Head Start Planned Variation), the systematic evaluation of curriculum models was instituted to determine the most effective curriculum for equalizing the academic success of children from low- and middle-income families. Curriculum models were regarded as whole units. The curriculum model was the environmental manipulation, in effect the "treatment," which was evaluated in terms of its educational impact. Program evaluation results were to provide an objective, scientifically derived answer to the policy question regarding how most effectively to improve the school success of children from low-income families. Given the theoretical consistency between behavioral psychology and experimental methodology, the B-E and DI models had a competitive edge in comparative evaluations, which reaped political advantage for their models of early education.

Experimental methodology is considered the hallmark of objective, scientific research and the most valued source of confirmation for specified practice and policy. This belief gave the empirically validated practices of the Bereiter-Engelmann and Direct Instruction models an added aura of validity. Later, it augmented their boasts of programmatic superiority, assertions that were (and are) based on the superior standardized test scores and academic performances of children attending their programs (see, for example, Becker et al., 1981; Carnine et al., 1988; Gersten et al., 1988).

Method and Science of Education. A basic premise of the B-E and DI models, both of which rely on direct instruction, is that the *how* of teaching is as important as the *what* (Becker et al., 1981; Bereiter & Engelmann, 1966a, 1966b). Bereiter and Engelmann felt most early childhood programs were focused on the issue of program content to the exclusion of teaching method. They contended that failure to develop "more effective teaching methods is perhaps to fail completely in equalizing the educational attainment of children from different cultural backgrounds" (Bereiter & Engelmann, 1966a, p. 55).

In the B-E and DI models, the *how* of teaching and *what* is taught are intimately correlated. In reference to the Bereiter-Engelmann model, Bereiter (1972) contended that no other preschool intervention program presented instructional goals in such a clear-cut fashion or had procedures so exclusively devoted to achieving those goals in the most efficient manner. "I would assert that the program is . . . at bottom distinguished entirely by the degree to which content and method are combined into a fully engineered instructional program" (Bereiter, 1972, p. 5).

Reliance on direct instruction to teach carefully structured academic content is consistent with behavioral psychology's emphasis on observable behaviors, systematic manipulation of environmental input, and attention to quantifiable outcomes.

The program architects believed that "children can be taught competencies more rapidly if teachers are provided with well-planned educational procedures, including pretested curriculum materials" (Becker et al., 1981, p. 96).

The reliance on direct instruction and focus on academic content affronted early educators who trusted and valued children's interests as sources of curriculum content. This discrepancy indicated more than a difference in style and beliefs about the nature of children and their learning. It revealed as well a fundamental difference in educational purpose.

Whereas advocates of the Montessori method and the Developmental-Interaction approach saw their efforts as part of a larger reform of public education, the B-E and DI models did not challenge existing public school objectives and practices. "Certainly, the emphasis was not on changing the society and schools to fit the disadvantaged but on changing the disadvantaged to fit the school" (Anderson & Bereiter, 1972, p. 339).

Designers of the B-E and DI models did aim their efforts at improving schooling, however. But rather than wanting to restructure public schooling, their interest was in making public school curricula more effective and efficient. They were especially critical of the basal series used to teach language skills, reading, and arithmetic. They consistently attacked the limitations of basal readers and highlighted the organizational and structural advances found in their programmed lessons. Their goal was to improve on the status quo by providing increased consistency and efficiency in procuring greater academic achievement for all children.[3]

This goal, and the method chosen to achieve it, provides the connection that links experimental methodology to a science of education. A science of education strives to systematically apply the findings from science to the problems of education and thereby improve education's predictability, efficiency, and effectiveness.

Psychology's vision of a science of education can be traced to Thorndike's work in the 20th century (Cremin, 1961/1964). The vision was shared and reinforced by early 20th-century curriculum theorists. These curriculum theorists, categorized as social efficiency educators by Kliebard (1986), were inspired by the power of experimental methodology and the possibility of using it to devise curricula that efficiently prepared individuals for their future roles as adults.

Emerging at the same time as the United States' rapid growth as an urban and industrial nation, social efficiency educators strived for efficiency, social utility, and

---

[3]Although Bereiter (1986) credited *Teaching the Disadvantaged Child*, published in 1966, with being the first explicit formulation of direct instruction, direct instruction has by no means been limited to these two curriculum models. It was a central component of the teacher effectiveness movement (see, for example, Brophy, 1979) and popularized by educators such as Madeline Hunter (1976, 1977, 1979). DI proponents like to point out that direct instruction received official support from the U.S. Department of Education in the 1986 publication *What Works*. Theories of instruction, however, have been shifting from their reliance on behaviorism to include cognitive theory. To the extent that these theories now contemplate learning in less mechanistic ways, their interpretation of its applicability seems less mechanistic as well. For discussion of some of these changes, see Iran-Nejad, McKeachie, and Berliner (1990b).

scientific management (Kliebard, 1986).[4] Amazing correspondence exists between the axioms of social efficiency educators and those of Bereiter[5] and Engelmann and their associates.[6] As architects of the B-E and DI models, they approached the ideals of efficiency, social utility, and scientific management by focusing on clearly stated academic objectives and standardizing teaching strategies and curriculum.

ᘒ TEACHING DISADVANTAGED CHILDREN IN THE PRESCHOOL: THE BEREITER-ENGELMANN MODEL

The Bereiter-Engelmann preschool was established by Carl Bereiter and Siegfried Engelmann at the University of Illinois at Urbana-Champaign in the mid-1960s. A 2-hour-per-day program, it was designed to provide intensive direct instruction in reading, arithmetic, and language to disadvantaged children, 4 to 6 years of age (Bereiter & Engelmann, 1966b).

According to Anderson and Bereiter (1972), the decision to develop their model for preschoolers was a strategic one. They anticipated that the preschool would be more amenable to change because it had fewer educational commitments, fewer explicit goals, fewer ties to the educational establishment, and fewer years of existence (a rationale also articulated by Weikart; see Chapter 5). The age of the children also was considered a plus because they were willing learners, "more teachable," and not yet tainted by the arbitrary nature of the school system. Finally, Bereiter and Engelmann felt they would be more likely to find cooperative adults who wanted to help children. "And, if changes seemed impossible within the schools themselves, then early education was the *only* place to prepare children for what they had in store" (Anderson & Bereiter, 1972, p. 340).

The choice of an academic program that taught skills in language, reading, and arithmetic was based on their belief that disadvantaged children needed these skills to succeed in public school. These three subjects were taught as separate classes, each with its own teacher. Children circulated in groups of five from class to class, each session lasting 20 minutes. Singing was the only other major educational activity. Teachers sung specially written songs to give children further practice in skills being taught in the classes. During the remaining hour of the day, the

---

[4]It is generally agreed that the curricular views associated with social efficiency educators dominate public schooling.

[5]Carl Bereiter's views about learning and instructional design have evolved since 1966. In a 1990 article, for example, he wrote

. . . the distinctive requirement of an educational learning theory [would seem to be] to explicate the students' role as intelligent agents in the learning process, to take account of the variety of resources that may come into use in achieving difficult learning objectives, and to embed explanations of particular learning processes within larger descriptions of the cognitive structures by which people adapt to various contexts so that they can achieve personal goals within them. (Bereiter, 1990, p. 619)

[6]Interested readers should read Chapter 4 of Kliebard's (1986) text.

whole class participated in "minor activities," including snack time and a semi-structured activity.

Curriculum. Two different strategies were used to determine curriculum content (Bereiter, 1970). First, Bereiter and Engelmann looked at what children were expected to know when they encountered first-grade curriculum materials. Second, they worked backward from the content of the Stanford-Binet intelligence test to define a "universe of conceptual content" (p. 205). From these exercises, they determined that the conceptual content of their program should include concepts of color, size, shape, location, number, order, class, action, use, material, and part–whole relations as applied to concrete objects and events.

The B-E model identified 15 goals (Bereiter & Engelmann, 1966b). The first 9 goals pertained to words and constructions that occur in ordinary speech, such as "ability to use both affirmative and *not* statements in reply to the question, 'What is this?'" and "ability to use the following prepositions correctly in statements describing arrangements of objects: on, in, under, over, between." Objectives 10 to 15 addressed numerical and reading skills, including "ability to count objects correctly up to ten" and "ability to recognize and name the vowels and at least 15 consonants." These goals, in turn, were carefully analyzed to determine the prerequisite learning for their achievement.

Teaching Methods. According to Bereiter and Engelmann (1966a), their instructional method had five distinguishing characteristics:

1. It was fast paced. During a 20 minute period, five or more different kinds of tasks would be presented and as many as 500 responses might be required of each child.
2. Task irrelevant behavior was minimal. The efforts of both the teacher and the children were task-oriented. Spontaneous exchanges were intentionally minimized by the teacher.
3. There was a strong emphasis on verbal responses. Children often produced them in unison so that each child's total output could be maximized.
4. The curriculum was comprised of carefully planned, small-step instructional units and continuous feedback. Although the teacher discouraged "irrelevant exchanges," she was to be sensitive to possible difficulties, quickly correct mistakes, and anticipate and avert misunderstandings.
5. The curriculum placed heavy work demands on children. Children were required to pay attention and work hard and were rewarded for thinking (pp. 55–56).

Instruction was carried out "in a business-like, task-oriented manner" (Bereiter & Engelmann, 1966b, p. 59). The pace and intensity of the academic instruction led to charges that the program was unhealthy for young children. Bereiter and others associated with the B-E and DI models persistently reiterated, however, that children experienced no negative emotional side effects from learning academic subjects in demanding and rigorous ways (Bereiter & Engelmann, 1966a, 1966b; Carnine et al., 1988; Gersten & George, 1990).

Despite reassurances, concerns regarding the effects of academic environments in preschool and kindergarten persisted (see, for example, Gallagher & Sigel, 1987; Rescorla, Hyson, & Hirsh-Pasek, l991b). Although the debate has generalized to declarations about the advantages and disadvantages of developmental and academic curricula, and more recently to comparisons between developmentally appropriate and inappropriate curricula (see, for example, Burts, Hart, Charlesworth, & Kirk, 1990; DeVries et al., 1991; Schweinhart, Weikart, & Larner, 1986), the opposing claims have remained relatively unchanged.

The language program was based on five basic teaching "moves" (the term "moves" is Bereiter's; see Figure 4.1). These moves are less teaching strategies than articulation of various sentence structures that, once mastered, were presumed to enable different levels of reasoning and thinking. These structures progressed from basic statements of object identity to if–then statements and finally language for deductive reasoning.

An underlying assumption was that language structured thought; children could not think logically unless they had the language with which to reason. The B-E language curriculum directly taught disadvantaged children the sentence structures deemed necessary to support their ability to think logically.

Language concepts were grouped together based on the rules governing their manipulation rather than on thematic associations such as the zoo (Bereiter, 1968). The objective was not for children to learn content, but for them to learn conceptual

Figure 4.1   **Basic Teaching Moves Organized by Task Difficulty**

1. Verbatim repetition:
   Teacher: This block is red. Say it. . . .
   Children: This block is red.
2. Yes-no questions:
   Teacher: Is this block red?
   Children: No, this block is not red.
3. Location tasks:
   Teacher: Show me a block that is red.
   Children: This block is red.
4. Statement production:
   Teacher: Tell me about this piece of chalk.
   Children: This piece of chalk is red.
   Teacher: Tell me about what this piece of chalk is not.
   Children: *(ad lib)* This piece of chalk is not green . . . not blue, and so on.
5. Deduction problems
   Teacher: (with piece of chalk hidden in hand) This piece of chalk is not red. Do you
        know what color it is?
   Children: No. Maybe it is blue . . . maybe it is yellow. . . .

Taken from Bereiter, C. (1968). A nonpsychological approach to early compensatory education. In M. Deutsch, I. Katz, & A. R. Jensen (Eds.), *Social class, race, and psychological development* (p. 342). New York: Holt, Rinehart & Winston. Copyright © 1968 by Holt, Rinehart & Winston, Inc. Reprinted by permission.

strategies for organizing content information. Consequently, conceptual strategies were selected based on their capacity to be applied to more than one content area. By the program's end, the majority of time was spent on deduction problems, although at each new step in the program, teachers and children went through all of the moves, even if in condensed form.

Instruction in reading and arithmetic was similar in conception to the language program. They were highly verbal, with emphasis on learning generalizable rules through the repetitive and patterned practice of tasks that embodied the rule. (This is called learning rules by analogy.) The essential arithmetic principle to be learned from the example presented in Figure 4.1 is that saying that something is *not* a member of one set is equivalent to saying that it *is* the member of another set. And because learning rules by analogy requires children to figure things out, designers of the B-E model disavowed the criticism that children's academic achievement was the result of rote memory.[7]

Bereiter (1970) credited his efforts, along with others in the compensatory education movement, with formulating a common content for preschool intervention programs and initiating consensus regarding instructional goals. He characterized preexisting early childhood programs as sharing a common set of activities, but lacking in a shared set of learning expectations:

> Their commonality resides not in what they are trying to get children to learn but rather in a set of activities, such as free play, certain games, story reading, painting, housekeeping and dress-up, field trips, etc., that constitute the traditional school fare.
>
> When Project Head Start began, this fund of common activities was about all there was to draw upon in forming a compensatory educational program for young children. Since then, in an effort to put wheels under one or another view of the cognitive needs of disadvantaged children, educators have begun to introduce new elements into the preschool curriculum that were not merely considered to be good things for children to do but that were intended to produce particular effects. Now, regardless of what long-range effects one wishes to produce, it is necessary to have children doing something in the short run that entails learning.[8] (pp. 204–205)

Teacher Characteristics. The B-E model designated three teachers for every 15 children. Teachers taught particular subjects, not groups of children. Their ability as managers was of paramount importance. "In a preschool that is concerned

---

[7]As part of its evolution toward the Direct Instruction model, the original B-E curriculum model was replaced with DISTAR (the instructional programs in reading, arithmetic, and language), which was written by Engelmann and others (and is described as part of the DI model), the Conceptual Skills Program written by Bereiter and other associates, and the Open Court Kindergarten Program written by Bereiter and Hughes—all of which, according to Bereiter (1972), differ from each other and the program set forth in *Teaching Disadvantaged Children in the Preschool.*

[8] In explaining why academically trained psychologists might have missed the important emphasis given to thinking in traditional preschools, Biber (1977a) suggested that "They may not have recognized attention to cognitive processes when these did not appear as specifically structured lessons but were, instead, interwoven with the total experiential scheme of learning" (p. 49).

with enabling every child to extract the maximum amount of learning from every minute of the school day, efficient and intelligent management becomes of the utmost importance" (Bereiter & Engelmann, 1966b, p. 66).

Teachers also had to master the teaching strategies associated with the model. The teacher acted as a clinician; her responses were always to be premeditated and purposeful. They also were scripted.

> Slight variations can make the difference between successful learning and discouraging confusion. This is not to say that there is only one way to present a concept, any more than there is only one way to perform a surgical operation. But it takes a very sophisticated practitioner to know which variations are optional and which are dangerous. (Bereiter & Engelmann, 1966b, p. 104)

Consequently, teachers were encouraged to study the chapters depicting teaching methods and to use them as they "would a detailed cookbook, recognizing that it is possible to be a very good cook without being an expert in the science of cookery, but that when one is not a thorough master of the science of cookery, it is necessary to stay close to the recipes if one is to avoid failures" (Bereiter & Engelmann, 1966b, p. 104).

Bereiter and Engelmann identified elementary school teachers as preferable teacher candidates because they "more or less" spoke the language of the intensive preschool. They found elementary teachers more inclined toward direct instruction, to work toward specific learning goals, and to maintain discipline. They discouraged hiring nursery school teachers because they "must usually unlearn a great deal before they can become effective. . . . Their conception of child development and the emergence of skills is usually diametrically opposed to the viewpoint on which the intensive preschool rests" (Bereiter & Engelmann, 1966b, p. 69).

✐ THE DIRECT INSTRUCTION MODEL

It is unclear when the Direct Instruction model received its current name, but it appears to have been in place by 1981. Wesley Becker, who strengthened several behavioral components of the program, joined Engelmann in 1967, following Bereiter's departure earlier that same year. The model then became known as the Engelmann-Becker model. In a 1980 discussion of Follow Through models, it was identified as the Engelmann-Becker Direct Instruction model, and in a 1981 publication, the designers labeled it the Direct Instruction model. The model and its staff left the University of Illinois at Urbana-Champaign and moved to the University of Oregon in 1970.

The DI model is designed for children in kindergarten through third grade. Because research findings indicate the model achieves greater success when children begin the program as kindergartners, the designers stress the importance of children beginning the program before first grade (Gersten, et al., 1988).

The designers suggest that the kindergarten year is so important because it provides a gradual, but systematic transition between a child-centered, "accepting" preschool and the structured environment of most first grades (Carnine et al., 1988; Gersten et al., 1988). The DI kindergarten year builds, step-by-step, the skills and knowledge necessary for student success in first grade. Proponents argue that program evaluations document that even extremely disadvantaged 5-year-olds can be taught to read in kindergarten, without negative side effects (Carnine et al., 1988; Gersten et al., 1988). Advocacy for academic kindergartens and direct instruction for students from low-income families (Carnine et al,. 1988; Carnine, Grossen, & Silbert, 1995; Gersten, 1991; Gersten et al., 1988; Gersten & George, 1990) continues the model's historic role as protagonist to traditionally oriented early childhood programs.

The model's short-term goal is to help students achieve grade-level performance on major school achievement tests by the end of third grade. The long-term goal is to teach basic academic skills to low-income students "that will equip them to compete with their more advantaged peers for higher education and the opportunities available in our society" (Becker et al., 1981, p. 109).

Usually 3 hours of a 5-hour day are devoted to teaching academic skills, with the remaining 2 hours designated for other activities. Although the program's primary focus is on children's academic achievement, the designers express an interest in promoting children's affective and social development and suggest students receive "instruction in these areas" in ways appropriate to local circumstances (Becker et al., 1981).

Advocates contend (with accompanying evaluation data) that their instructional methods engender positive self-esteem. Their explanation is that as children become more academically competent, they feel better about themselves and others respond to them more positively. "From this perspective, a positive self-concept occurs as a by-product of good teaching" (Becker et al., 1981, p. 109).

The Direct Instruction model[9] is built on two premises: (a) that the rate and quality of children's learning in the classroom is a function of environmental events and (b) that educators can increase the amount of children's learning in the classroom by carefully engineering the details of students' interactions with that environment. "When these details are chosen and sequenced according to a rational plan, efforts to improve the rate at which children learn are likely to be successful" (Becker et al., 1981, p. 98).

Program Content

Instructional programs in reading, arithmetic, and language are the core of the model and are published under the trade name DISTAR. Each instructional program contains objectives for three curriculum levels, creating a total of nine programs. These nine programs, in turn, contain programmed lessons derived from

---

[9]Becker et al. (1981) provide a complete description of the Direct Instruction model, including detailed analysis of its program design and curriculum content. Their chapter served as a primary informant for this review of the model's program and design.

learning principles and programming strategies that were field tested to ensure empirical validity.

Teachers focus first on decoding skills and then on comprehension in DISTAR Reading I and II. In Reading III, students learn to read to obtain and use new information. In DISTAR Arithmetic I, students learn basic addition and subtraction operations and their related story-problem forms. In DISTAR Arithmetic II, they are introduced to multiplication and fractions along with further instruction in addition, subtraction, and various measurement concepts. Then in Arithmetic III, students receive instruction in algebra, factoring, and division, as well as continued practice in addition, subtraction, multiplication, and division.

Finally, the first two language programs teach object names, classes, and properties and relational terms. Children learn to make complete sentences and describe their world. Language comprehension and language production are stressed. Students learn to ask questions to obtain information and are taught logical processes, including causality, deductions, opposites, and multiple attributes. The third language program expands students' logical use of language and basic grammatical rules. There also are activities designed to improve writing and spelling skills.

During each group session, teachers present six or seven brief 3-minute teaching sequences. These lessons include frequent teacher–student verbal interaction through games and races. Students actively participate in lessons; engagement rates might be as high as "ten responses per minute, with 80 to 90 percent of the responses being correct" (Carnine et al., 1988, p. 75).

In addition, students spend 30 minutes a day in academically related independent activities. Supplementary gamelike activities provide additional practice and mastery of key concepts (Gersten et al., 1988).

Decisions regarding which concepts to include were heavily weighted in terms of a skill's generalizability and its success quotient. According to Gersten et al. (1988), a central image that guided the conceptualization of the DI model was of students learning new concepts and skills in such a way that they "experienced unremitting success" (p. 229).

Programmatic Design

Three primary sources informed the construction of the DI model: (a) empirical behavior theory, (b) logical analysis of the use of classroom resources, and (c) logical analysis of concepts and tasks (Becker et al., 1981).

Empirical Behavior Theory. Behavioral principles that informed the model are reinforcement, conditioned responses, stimulus control, prompting, shaping, punishment, extinction, and fading. (Each of these learning principles refers to strategies that increase or decrease the presence of desired behaviors.) These learning principles were used in the construction of the DISTAR instructional programs and in developing teaching procedures for eliciting and maintaining students' attention, securing their responses, and dispensing reinforcers. These behavioral principles also guided procedures for regulating the verbal behavior of teachers and students, monitoring students' academic progress, and using praise and other reinforcers to encourage students' acquisition of desirable behaviors.

Logical Analysis of the Use of Classroom Resources. In response to limited resources, the DI architects used logical analyses to determine potential benefits and costs of alternative uses of classroom resources. Their analysis informed decisions regarding the choice of small-group rather than individualized instruction; use of parents as paraprofessionals rather than employment of additional teachers; prioritizing academic instruction over play, art, music, and similar activities; and the use of scripted lessons versus teachers' selection of their own instructions.

Logical Analysis of Concepts and Tasks. According to Becker et al. (1981), identifying the structural relationships among concepts and tasks is a prerequisite for designing efficient educational programs. For example, the concepts hot–cold and wet–dry are sets of polar concepts that share a common characteristic; they are two-member groups. If this structural relationship is understood, then you know that if something does not have one characteristic, it must have the other. Becker et al. (1981) also identified hierarchical structures that illustrate the characteristics shared among concepts; for example, collies are dogs; dogs are mammals; mammals are animals; and animals are living things. Conceptual and task complexity was analyzed so that teaching could progress from simple to more difficult learning.

The findings from these analyses were used to design the DISTAR instructional programs. Objectives were characterized as sets of related problems that children could solve by using a common strategy; concepts were identified that could be taught as general cases. Program designers used this information to create systematic lessons in reading, language, and arithmetic. The information also was used to devise strategies for teaching basic concepts, teaching systematically related concepts, teaching rules, and teaching cognitive operations, which, in the DISTAR program, represent four different classes of tasks. Mastery of these lessons, it was assumed, would result in students learning skills and concepts that could be generalized and transferred to new learning situations.

Finally, as students progress through kindergarten and the primary grades, teaching and task requirements shift in terms of six criteria (Becker et al., 1981). At first glance, these six teaching criteria might seem commonplace; yet they specify the application of learning principles. Their systematized and systematic application distinguishes them from conventional classroom practices.

1. *From overt to covert problem solving.* When teachers use an overt problem-solving strategy, they make every step in the strategy explicit. Eventually, via the application of appropriate learning principles, the problem-solving process becomes covert until only the response is overt. Covertization provides an essential link between the work that students perform under close supervision and their eventual independent effort.

2. *From simplified contexts to complex contexts.* When teachers introduce a discrimination in simplified contexts, they emphasize the relevant features of the task. In more complex contexts, students are expected to apply their knowledge in settings characterized by a wide range of irrelevant detail.

3. *From providing prompts to removing those prompts.* Early in instruction, a teacher may use modified examples or special wording to focus the learner's attention on relevant features. Later, these prompts are removed.

4. *From massed practice to distributed practice.* Massed practice is designed to bring about mastery and occurs when new skills are being learned; distributed practice (in other words, less frequent practice) aids retention of what already has been learned.

5. *From immediate feedback to delayed feedback.* As learners become more capable, teachers reduce the amount of feedback they provide.

6. *From an emphasis on the teacher's role as a source of information to an emphasis on the learner's role as a source of information.* As learners increase their repertoire of skills, teachers decrease their role as providers of information and become more of a guide to assist students in using information previously acquired. The learner must decide how to apply previously learned skills and information in a variety of problem-solving situations (p. 102).

Teaching Methods

Each DISTAR instructional program includes scripts indicating exactly what the teacher should say and do during classroom instruction. The scripts provide teachers with directions, sequences of examples, and sequences of subskills and wording that have been tested for effectiveness. Scripted presentations reduce the time required for supervising and training teachers. A supervisor need only pinpoint a teacher's deficiency and provide appropriate remedies.

Proponents discourage deviation from the script because it has been found that teachers lose their effectiveness when they attempt to individualize instruction for individual students (Gersten, Carnine, Zoref, & Cronin, 1986). Individualization occurs in terms of a student's entry level, motivating procedures, techniques for making corrections, and the number of practice trials to mastery. In one case study, Gersten et al. (1986) found that although kindergarten teachers initially resisted changing their teaching style because they thought the model too academic, they changed their minds once they saw the program's effects.

Small-group instruction is considered a central feature of the model. A class usually is divided into four groups of four to seven individuals, and students rotate through subject areas and seatwork. Small-group instruction lasts about 30 minutes in each subject area at levels I and II. At level III, each 15 minutes of instruction is followed by 30 minutes of self-directed practice in workbooks.

Top ability groups are expected to complete 1.5 lessons per day and the lowest ability groups 0.7 lesson per day. Teachers systematically use positive consequences such as behavior-specific praise and point systems to strengthen students' motivations for learning.

Finally, parents are expected to work with their children at home using home practice books to reinforce skills students have recently mastered.

☞ THE NEXT ITERATION: THE SUCCESS FOR ALL MODEL

Continuing efforts to meet the needs of children identified as being academically at risk have sustained interest in curriculum models providing direct instruction. One of the most popular is Success for All, a schoolwide program originally designed in 1987 for the Baltimore City Public Schools by Robert Slavin and Nancy Madden of Johns Hopkins University. In 1999, 150 schools used Engelmann's Direct Instruction program, kindergarten through sixth grade (American Institutes for Research, 1999). Success for All is used in more than 1,130 schools in 44 states (American Institutes for Research, 1999), and is funded primarily with Title I dollars (federal funds targeted to increasing school achievement of students from low-income families).

Success for All is representative of newer models by going beyond curriculum reform to address schoolwide reform needs. Intent on increasing the academic achievement of children from low-income families, many recent reform efforts take a more comprehensive approach, attempting to influence what happens in classrooms by also restructuring the organization and management of the entire school. Success for All emphasizes this distinction in its materials. Schools that adopt the Success for All model are required to make changes in instruction, curriculum, and support services available to students and families, including specially trained tutors and family support staff to serve all children, prekindergarten through sixth grade. Reflecting growing belief in literacy as the cornerstone for school achievement, Success for All places primary emphasis on the "prevention of reading failure" (Slavin, Madden, Dolan, & Wasik, 1996, p. 224).

The Success for All model includes a half-day prekindergarten and full-day kindergarten. In contrast to the Direct Instruction model, the curriculum is "thematically based" and its goals, which are more inclusive, focus on developing oral language, literacy listening skills, numeracy, creative expression, and positive self-esteem (Slavin et al., 1996).

Teachers are provided with thematic units. Each unit includes:

- an introduction describing the "learning essentials" of the unit;
- a letter to families describing the unit;
- a dictionary of terms associated with each unit;
- "learning lessons" for each theme;
- literacy activities, including a structured "story telling and retelling" (STaR) exercise;
- activities for phonemic awareness, writing, learning centers, math, science/social studies, music/creative activities, movement/circle game, home learning;
- a unit assessment.

Teachers are not expected to complete each activity in the unit. Instead, teacher select specific learning essentials and activities that correspond to the needs developmental levels of the children. Thematic units for prekindergarter kindergarten include Special Me and My Five Senses, Community Helpers, Plants in Our Lives, Space, Multicultural, Famous Black Americans, Dinosaurs, Recycling, Transportation, and Tools and Machines (Slavin et al., 1996, p. 98–99).

Teacher-directed instruction is most focused during StaR. Teachers use a set of procedures and materials in a whole-class format. Sessions are designed for teachers to devote 5 minutes to introducing the story, including its setting, theme, vocabulary, and questions that ask children to guess what the story might be about. The next part of STaR is a 20-minute "interactive storyreading" in which the teacher reads the story, following the story kit's suggestion to interrupt her reading with frequent requests for children to summarize, predict, and recall story events. Finally, teachers are instructed to provide 10 minutes for "story structure review," in which the teacher asks children to recall the title, names, and descriptions of the main characters, and significant story events. Follow-up StaR guide sheets provide ideas for dramatization. Children later are assigned to teacher assistants who use questions provided with each StaR exercise to prompt individual children to "retell" the story.

The Peabody Language Development Kit is used daily to provide "lessons on such concepts as shapes, colors, classification, neighborhoods, foods and clothing, and such language concepts as over/under and before/after" (Slavin et al., 1996, p. 104).

Program designers describe the curriculum as a "balance between child-initiated and teacher-directed instruction" (Slavin et al., 1996, p. 98). However, the carefully scripted guidelines for learning center activities suggest limited opportunity for child-initiated activities as they generally are understood in the field of early childhood care and education. The program designers note:

> Center time is not considered "free-play." Instead, center time is carefully planned to support the specific concepts that relate to the theme. For example, if the class is working on the Community Helpers unit, an art center activity presented in the unit suggests that the children make a fire fighter ladder. Such concepts as counting the number of rungs on the ladder, spacing the rungs of the ladder, and comparing and contrasting are highlighted when doing this activity. Teachers are instructed to incorporate higher-order concepts into the center activities and guide children to think about the many concepts that can be learned from the tasks as they circulate from center to center (Slavin et al., 1996, p. 104).

While Success for All provides a highly structured curriculum, the model represents a significant shift from early intervention strategies developed in the 1960s. Whereas the Bereiter-Engelmann and Direct Instruction models relied on classroom instruction as a means of preparing preschool children for school, Success for All reflects the current focus on comprehensive intervention strategies. (See Chapter 6 for more detail.) Success for All schools must agree to restructure their staffing, grouping of children, instructional strategies, and home/school relationships, including:

- grouping students across age and grade for reading instruction;
- providing one-on-one reading tutors (teachers or paraprofessionals);

- restricting use of special education and grade retention;
- relying on cooperative learning (small-group activities designed to maximize the ability for students to learn from and with one another) as a central teaching strategy;
- providing formal assessment of student progress at least every 8 weeks;
- creating family support teams (teams typically include the principal or assistant principal, the Success for All facilitator, and others including social workers, counselors, attendance monitors, teachers, and volunteers) that encourage parent support and involvement, and address problems at home that affect a student's ability to learn (for example, by providing referrals to social services); and
- providing a local full-time program facilitator and staff support team to assist the school and teachers in implementing the model (American Institutes for Research, 1999).

Responding to increasing pressures at the federal and state levels for replicable, research-based models, Success for All has become a prominent model in the schoolwide reform movement. Longitudinal studies in 23 schools suggest that the greatest positive effects are for children most at risk, including language-minority students (Fashola & Slavin, 1998).

๙ EXPLAINING THE UNANTICIPATED SUCCESS OF ACADEMICALLY ORIENTED CURRICULA

The rapid rise of Success for All is reminiscent of the unanticipated success of the Bereiter-Engelmann and Direct Instruction models. To understand the rapid acceptance of the B-E and DI models as a valid approach to early childhood education and the rising popularity of highly structured, academically oriented programs such as Success for All, it is necessary to reinsert the Bereiter-Engelmann and Direct Instruction models into the sociopolitical context that birthed them so successfully during the 1960s. An appreciation of this context helps explain the staying power of direct instruction models.

The discussion of the B-E and DI models that follows focuses on their position as powerful representatives of, and advocates for, academic early childhood programs—rather than as discrete models. This discussion discloses some of the ways in which the introduction of curriculum models in the mid-1960s influenced the evolution of early childhood education.

The Timing Was Right

Prior to the onset of Head Start and other preschool intervention programs, most preschool and kindergarten programs were child centered and nonacademic. Although considerable activity in the learning theory tradition had been occurring in psychology, it had had little if any impact on child development theory/child psychology (White, 1970).

Preschool programs, as exemplified by the Developmental-Interaction approach, were heavily influenced by psychodynamic theory and focused on nurturing children's development. Kindergartens, after an early alliance with Thorndike's behavioral theory and habit-training (Bloch, 1987; Weber, 1969), became almost totally maturational in approach, using the then-new normative data about child growth being generated by university-based child study centers. This normative data, according to Weber (1969), was used "to define those conditions that would foster growth organismically—including physical, intellectual, social, and emotional development. These were developmental needs formulated by adults who then used them to formulate a program" (p. 184).

Before the onset of curriculum models, the programmatic emphasis in preschool and kindergarten education, even with their differences, was on assuring the appropriate environmental conditions, deduced from child development theory, for nurturing each child's potential. Thus, when the B-E model burst onto the early childhood scene, it represented an approach to early education that was diametrically opposed to the status quo. The question is, why, under these circumstances, did it not only survive, but also succeed in changing the landscape of early childhood education?

The answer seems to lie in the timely convergence of at least six factors that emerged almost simultaneously from psychology, education, and societal dissatisfaction:

1. challenges to the notion of fixed intelligence;
2. "discovery" of widespread poverty in the United States;
3. the 1957 Russian launching of *Sputnik,* which punctured America's pride;
4. escalation of interest in cognitive development nurtured by the rediscovery of Piaget's theory of cognitive development; Piaget's theory, in turn, was positively reassessed, in part, because of society's concern with reestablishing its competitive intellectual edge;
5. dissatisfaction with the educational status quo; and
6. the additional potency of applied learning theory following B. F. Skinner's "discovery" of operant conditioning.

These factors, for the most part, also helped launch Head Start in 1965. The nation's search for a solution to poverty, in conjunction with optimism that modifying the experiences of young children could change the trajectory of their development and academic achievement at a time when the U.S. public was embarrassed by the apparent inferiority of their educational system, converged in enthusiastic public support for compensatory education. (Chapter 1 discusses these changes in more detail.)

It would be easy to argue that the focus on academically oriented programs resulted from the fact that once the purpose of Head Start was narrowed to school readiness, program designers, such as those who developed the B-E and DI models, thought it logical to accomplish this purpose by focusing on the academic skills needed by disadvantaged children. This explanation, however, *only* achieves its explanatory value when understood in terms of the forces that made this approach to compensatory education appear more valid than others. In fact, adoption of a behaviorally defined academic approach to early education rested on three supports: (a) reestablishment of academic learning as the mission of schooling, (b) behaviorism's focus on changing behavior through modifying the environment, and (c) the alignment between these two factors and school practices.

A Justification for Academic Early Childhood Programs

The U.S. public was in the mood for effective academic solutions. "While American schoolchildren were learning how to get along with their peers or how to bake a cherry pie . . . Soviet children were being steeped in the hard sciences and mathematics needed to win the technological race that had become the center piece of the Cold War" (Kliebard, 1986, p. 265). The "scientific" language of behaviorism fit right in with the U.S. search for technological superiority, and programmed learning made sense as the most effective means for alleviating the consequences of disadvantaged environments.

In addition, according to Egan (1988), behaviorism's discussions of process and product and teaching as a technological enterprise are analogous to the notion of assembly lines, thus aligning it in powerful ways with some of the most deeply held beliefs in the United States about progress and how to achieve it efficiently— at least as defined in the mid-1960s and early 1970s.

Now, link this information with the underlying assumption of the first early intervention programs—that providing disadvantaged children with a changed environment would alter the course of their future academic development. Behaviorism was founded on exactly the same premise—that the determining factor in changing behavior resided not within the individual, but in the environment. Traditional early childhood programs, in contrast, placed their faith in defining "those conditions that would foster growth organismically" (Weber, 1969, p. 184). When the political and educational search for environments that would stimulate intellectual development erupted, psychologists with a behavioral focus were positioned to respond.[10]

The final and critical element in understanding the unanticipated success of behaviorally derived academic programs was their alignment with the practice of most public schools. Unlike the Developmental-Interaction approach, or the Piagetian-based models to be discussed in Chapter 5, the B-E and DI models created a

---

[10]White (1970) chronicles a similar development in child psychology. He explains learning theory's lack of impact on child psychology until the mid-1950s by the fact that a genetic point of view dominated child psychology:

Watson's behaviorism, and the subsequent elaboration of learning theories, did not have a significant influence on child psychology in the early decades of this century because child psychologists had a rival theoretical scheme, more or less implicit and unrehearsed, in the genetic-rationalist tradition. (p. 665)

first-time, close alliance between the curricula of early childhood programs and that of the public schools. Even the Montessori method, which shares B-E's and DI's academic focus, structures its program very differently from conventional classrooms.

The relationship between early childhood and public school curricula is an important consideration because a major purpose of Head Start and Follow Through had been to improve public schooling (Hodges et al., 1980; Maccoby & Zellner, 1970; White & Buka, 1987). In contrast to early childhood curriculum models that proposed alternative views on curriculum and the purposes of education, the B-E and DI models sought to help schools do a more efficient job of teaching basic academic skills. The improvements sought for the primary grades by the B-E and DI models and similar academically oriented curricula were theoretically and practically consistent with existing school practice, and certainly less threatening to the status quo.

A Changing Relationship Between Early Childhood and Elementary Education

Since the onset of preschool early intervention programs, a critical transformation in the relationship between preschool and kindergarten education and the primary grades has materialized. Cognizance of this transformation seems critical for understanding the success of academic curriculum models. Simultaneously, it reveals reverberations from the curriculum model era on the subsequent progression of early childhood education.

This transformation emerged from the reality that, despite programs and rhetoric to the contrary, most preschool intervention programs have focused on enhancing the ability of children from low-income families to succeed at the next level of the educational system. In actuality, if not in theory, a majority of preschool intervention programs has understood their purpose in terms of school readiness rather than child development.

It was not the persuasiveness of progressive early educators and their arguments regarding nursery education as a lever for promoting educational change that convinced the public about the importance of early education. Rather, it was dismissal of the notion of fixed intelligence, designation of the preschool years as the most susceptible to redirection, and a societal reason for using this knowledge that propelled public acceptance of early education as a counteragent to children's disadvantaged circumstances.

At the same time, public appreciation for the benefits of nursery education extended to children from middle-income families. And, once nursery education was reconfigured as "pre-school" and recognized as an "educational" program, it became subjected to the same struggles as other parts of the educational system regarding curriculum priorities.

This deduction is supported by the work of Kliebard (1986), who argued that four competing interest groups (humanists, social efficiency proponents, developmentalists, and social meliorists) have struggled for control of the American public school curriculum since the 1890s. In the case of early childhood education, however, the appearance of various educational factions vying for control over the curriculum did not emerge at the onset of the 20th century. Instead, the struggle was introduced and systematized through the medium of curriculum models.[11]

The advent of curriculum models, of course, cannot be credited as the sole cause of this transformation. But both as a participant in, and an artifact of, this transformative process, the emergence of curriculum models has affected early childhood education in at least two significant ways. First, the development and evaluation of curriculum models furthered the notion of a science of education within early childhood education. Second, competition among curriculum models thrust early childhood education into the struggle for control of the U.S. curriculum that Kliebard (1986) described.

In the specialized realm of early childhood education, this struggle has pitted developmentalists against those who Kliebard labeled social efficiency educators. The fact that early childhood education's participation in this decades-long struggle did not occur until recently, rather than during the early 1900s when the developmental faction first emerged, highlights the catalytic value provided by the onset of preschool intervention programs and the systematic variation of curricula. At the time that the four factions identified by Kliebard were emerging, kindergartens were dismantling their connection with Froebel, and progressive and laboratory-based nursery schools were emerging. The interest group labeled developmentalist was shaping, almost single-handedly, the notion of early childhood education (see Bloch, 1987, 1991; Weber, 1969).

Nursery schools were almost totally separate from public schools in the early and mid-1900s (though exceptions linked to targeted public policies, such as Depression-era preschools, existed; see, for example, Beatty, 1995; Michel, 1999). Public school kindergartens, which were limited in number, developed a curriculum derived primarily from maturational theory. Until recently, in the minds of most educators, elementary school began with first grade. Discussions about preschool and kindergarten curriculum usually were separate from those about primary schools and, as a result, were unaffected by the struggle Kliebard described.

After the launching of Project Head Start and similar preschool intervention programs, this relationship changed. Preschool education was gradually reconceptualized as an appropriate beginning for primary schooling (especially for children from low-income families). This reconceptualization has enabled public school programs for 3- and 4-year-olds to proliferate. The changed relationship between preschool and elementary education illuminates why interest in prekindergarten programs and

---

[11]In an attempt to understand the challenges confronting kindergartens in the 1980s, Walsh (1987) used a similar line of reasoning to conclude that kindergartens have become assimilated into the elementary school and entangled in the ongoing struggle over which position shall have control over the curriculum. His title question of "Why here? Why now?" is misleading, though. According to the reasoning just presented, this conflict was instigated 25 years earlier when the purpose of nursery schools was reinterpreted as preschool education.

curriculum models now comes from state policy makers—where education policy is made—and from public schools (Goffin, in press; Powell, 1987a).

Developmentally Appropriate Practice: Reclaiming Traditional Early Childhood Education

Early childhood education's entry into the struggle over the structure and content of school curriculum has sustained the conflict between proponents of developmental and academic curricula (and opens early childhood education to criticism from curriculum theorists; see Chapter 7). Early childhood educators and developmental psychologists still frame the debate in child development terms (e.g., Charlesworth, 1998; Elkind, 1986; Rescorla, Hyson, & Hirsh-Pasek, 1991a; Sigel, 1991), and social efficiency educators remain focused on issues related to academic outcomes (e.g., Carnine et al., 1988; Carnine et al., 1995; Gersten et al., 1988; Gersten & George, 1990; Slavin et al., 1996).

Reflecting their perspective, early childhood educators reframed the controversy between academic and developmental programs as a battle between developmentally appropriate and developmentally inappropriate curricula. The change in terminology reflected more than a particular ideological stance, however. It pointed to a critical alteration in the way the issues came to be debated.

In the decade between the mid-1980s and the mid-1990s, early childhood advocates for a developmental curriculum moved from a defensive to an offensive position. With what some may consider sweet irony, programs characterized by what currently is labeled developmentally appropriate practice began to place academically oriented (i.e., developmentally inappropriate) programs on the defensive. As a result, proponents of the Direct Instruction model contended that there need not be a dichotomy between programs that address academic skills and those that address socialization. They argued that kindergarten programs for economically disadvantaged children should include effective academic instruction and child development experiences (Carnine, et al., 1988; Gersten et al., 1988; Gersten & George, 1990; Slavin et al., 1996). Of interest to this discussion are the changing circumstances that supported this reversal of positions.

Few would disagree that the most successful challenge to the validity of academic early childhood programs was the 1986 position statement of the National Association for the Education of Young Children (NAEYC) entitled "Developmentally Appropriate Practice in Early Childhood Programs" (DAP; Bredekamp, 1987; the document was expanded in 1987 to address children from birth to age 8, and revised in 1997 [Bredekamp & Copple, 1997]). According to Bredekamp (1991), escalation of public school programs for 4-year-olds provided a major impetus for the document's development. In response to membership request, and in hopes of influencing public school prekindergarten and kindergarten programs, the NAEYC Governing Board appointed a Commission on Appropriate Education for 4- and 5-year-olds.

Bredekamp's overview of events takes on a deeper hue when considered in light of the unanticipated success of academically oriented preschools and kindergartens and the increasing number of children in these programs. By the mid-1980s when NAEYC first articulated the concept of DAP, 90% of 5-year-olds were attending kindergartens, which, by then, were almost universally offered by public schools (Spodek, 1986). Consistent with the trend begun in the mid-1960s, when only half as many children attended kindergarten, kindergartens had become increasingly academic (e.g., Egertson, 1987; Graue, 1993), and there was every indication the same trend would characterize the development of the new prekindergartens.

Early childhood educators, consequently, did not want only to exert influence on public school prekindergarten and kindergarten programs. They also wanted to stay the tide of academic curricula. The DAP position statement, therefore, reflected more than just an attempt to influence public school decision making. It also represented an attempt by the early childhood profession to reassert—and reinsert—its developmental tradition into the public school curriculum.

Bredekamp (1991), who edited the NAEYC position statements, acknowledged the document's political motivation. She also affirmed that "[i]t is reasonably safe to say that the developmentalist perspective of the document reflects the consensus position of the early childhood profession" (p. 202).

Explaining the Unanticipated Success of Developmentally Appropriate Practice

NAEYC's stated purpose for developing DAP has been advanced beyond expectations. The DAP position statement has been enormously effective both internally and externally. Internally, the concept of DAP has helped to unify early childhood education's various strands (nursery education, child care, Head Start, kindergartens, and prekindergarten programs; Kagan, 1989). This unanticipated outcome can be attributed to the galvanizing effect of the profession's attempt to reclaim its heritage.

Externally, the concept became familiar rhetoric in reports commissioned by businesses seeking high-quality early childhood programs to help ensure the competence of their future labor force (e.g., Committee for Economic Development, 1991) and by educational associations committed to educational reform (e.g., National Association of Elementary School Principals, 1990; National Association of State Boards of Education, 1988, 1991). Acceptance by these groups enabled the concept of DAP to influence the curriculum of primary grades. Even proponents of the Direct Instruction model reframed their presentation. They, too, spoke to developmentally appropriate practice and used its terminology, even though, programmatically, the model remained unchanged. As expressed by Gersten et al., (1988), "Teaching reading in a developmentally appropriate fashion to [low-income] students is a challenge—but it can lead to enduring benefits to the students involved" (p. 238).

The degree and extent of current support for a developmental orientation to early childhood education is in sharp contrast to the reception given to proponents of the Developmental-Interaction approach in the mid-1960s. How did this come to be? What changed to make the public and other educators more receptive to an approach they had summarily dismissed for the preceding two decades? And does this change mean that the dream of progressive early educators to reform schooling "from below" (i.e., via nursery and kindergarten education) may at last be coming to fruition?

A critical turning point in the complexion of the competition between developmental and academic approaches to early education appears to have been the 1984 publication by David Weikart and his associates describing the lasting effects of the developmentally oriented High/Scope Curriculum (see Chapter 5). Prior to High/Scope's publication, the Consortium for Longitudinal Studies (1979) released its study on the long-lasting impact of early intervention programs. The findings of this influential study (discussed in greater detail in Chapter 6), which demonstrated that children who participated in early childhood interventions were less likely to be retained in grade or placed in special education programs and were more likely to graduate from high school, renewed public confidence in the value of preschool intervention programs, irrespective of the curriculum model.

The findings regarding the long-term impact of the High/Scope Curriculum not only reinforced the consortium's optimistic conclusions, they also linked the outcomes to a particular curriculum model. High/Scope's results credited its curriculum model with improving children's cognitive performance during early childhood; improving scholastic placement and achievement during the school years; decreasing delinquency, crime, use of welfare assistance, and incidence of teenage pregnancy; and increasing high school graduation rates, frequency of enrollment in postsecondary education programs, and employment (Berrueta-Clement et al., 1984). Enthusiasm for these findings was augmented by an economic evaluation of the data in terms of costs and benefits, which enabled educators and policy makers to contemplate the value of preschool education in economic terms. (This receives further discussion in Chapter 6.)

The well-publicized findings provided developmentally oriented early childhood programs what years of heated debate had not—scientific validity. By verifying the benefits of a developmentally oriented early childhood program in terms of measurable outcomes through scientific research, and hailing the outcomes in terms of their cost effectiveness for society, Weikart and his associates succeeded in aligning a developmental approach with society's technological norms. This strategy, which has been amazingly successful with policy makers and public school decision makers, set the stage for NAEYC's unveiling of its 1986 position statement on developmentally appropriate practice.

In 1986, High/Scope researchers published results of yet another longitudinal study that compared outcomes for children who had participated in preschool intervention programs between 1967 and 1970 using the High/Scope Curriculum, a traditional curriculum, and direct instruction (Schweinhart et al., 1986). Based on participants' self-reports at age 15, Schweinhart and colleagues concluded that children participating in the Direct Instruction model were more likely to engage in delinquent acts than children participating in the other two curriculum models. Although the study's methodology has been questioned (e.g. Bereiter, 1986; Engelmann, 1999; Gersten, 1986; Powell, 1987a), the possibility that direct instruction models might have harmful effects was influential in promoting the concept of developmentally appropriate practice.

With the passage of time, however, advocacy on behalf of developmentally appropriate practice less frequently is couched in terms of achieving holistic educational goals. Rather, traditional early childhood practices now tend to be promoted in terms of their ability to achieve school readiness, secure conventional educational objectives cost effectively, and meet societal needs without harmful side effects. Curriculum possibilities for young children have been narrowed to achieve more conventional educational outcomes.

Thus, in response to the earlier question as to whether the dream of progressive early educators to reform public schooling "from below" is at last coming to fruition, the answer seems to be "yes" . . . but "no." The movement toward developmental early childhood programs for children prekindergarten through third grade continues to gain momentum. Yet advocates for programs described as developmental are more likely to tout children's intellectual (albeit not academic) and social-emotional development rather than their overall psychological adjustment, are less likely to position their struggle as part of a larger educational effort, and are unlikely to propose revolutionary changes in the goals of education.[12] These latter aspirations, unfortunately, are more difficult to support with scientific justifications and in terms of social efficiency.

⌁ FOR FURTHER READING

Becker, W. C., Engelmann, S., Carnine, D. W., & Rhine, W. R. (1981). Direct instruction model. In W. R. Rhine (Ed.), *Making schools more effective: New directions from Follow Through* (pp. 95–154). New York: Academic Press.

> This chapter is a comprehensive and detailed description of the Direct Instruction model written by its designers.

Gersten, R., Darch, C., & Gleason, M. (1988). Effectiveness of a direct instruction academic kindergarten for children from low-income families. *The Elementary School Journal, 89,* 227–240.

> This description and defense of the Direct Instruction model provides not only a succinct summary of the program but also one "enlightened" by the rhetoric of developmentally appropriate practice.

Kliebard, H. M. (1986). *The struggle for the American curriculum, 1893–1958.* New York: Routledge.

> This book chronicles the struggle among four interest groups to achieve control over the public school curriculum. This is a fascinating text, not only because of its thesis, but also because the information is presented through the lens of a curriculum theorist.

---

[12]These last three outcomes are taken from Zigler's (1984a) summary of Barbara Biber's contributions to early education.

Chapter Five

Two Models Derived from Piagetian Theory

So what do we do with stages? What is there beyond the rhetoric of generalities and vague long-term goals? . . . What teachers need are not descriptions of stages on Genevan tasks, but descriptions of developmental stages (or levels) in classroom activities—that is, in activities justifiable on the basis of cognitive-developmental theory and research.

Rheta DeVries, *Developmental Stages in Piagetian Theory and Educational Practice*, 1984

Evidence of the cost-effectiveness of . . . high quality preschool programs has enabled them to become part of the social "safety net." So, the Perry Preschool Project began as a "suspect" innovation, then became one of a multitude in a surge of public support for such efforts, and has played a major role in legitimating preschool education through the research evidence of its cost-effective nature as a social investment.

David Weikart, in Preface to *Changed Lives: The Effects of the Perry Preschool Program on Youths Through Age 19*, 1984

This chapter is unique because it explores two early childhood curriculum models—the Kamii-DeVries approach and the High/Scope Curriculum—both of which rely on the theory of Jean Piaget. As a result, this chapter highlights how different interpretations of the same theoretical framework can generate distinctive approaches to early education.[1] The program designers also continue to modify their thinking, thereby presenting examples of evolving curriculum models.

Examination of the Kamii-DeVries approach and the High/Scope Curriculum helps illustrate the challenge of deriving definitive educational implications from developmental theory. Although these two models—and their three program architects—rely on the same theory to rationalize their practices, they appeal to different aspects and interpretations of the theory to do so.

---

[1]Numerous approaches to early childhood education have been derived from Piagetian theory. Lavatelli's (1970) approach used many of Piaget's experiments as a means for advancing children's cognitive development. Less literal applications include the approach of Forman and his colleagues (1977, 1980) and Copple, Sigel, and Saunders (1979). The High/Scope and Kamii-DeVries approach were selected for review because they are better known, more systematized, and included in numerous comparative program evaluations.

The extent of the two models' reliance on Piaget's theory also differs. Whereas the Kamii-DeVries approach is almost totally reliant on Piaget's theory, the High/Scope Curriculum incorporates the ideas of non-Piagetians as well. As expressed by Weikart in his introduction to the model's first rendition, "While there is a growing congregation of 'high church' Piagetians in preschool education, I would classify this curriculum as the product of 'store front' Piagetian theory utilization" (Weikart, Rogers, Adcock, & McClelland, 1971, p. ix). In contrast, Kamii and DeVries have prided themselves on achieving a coherent, internally consistent curriculum.

These particular two models also present contrasting rationales for creating curriculum models. As the introductory quotes intimate, the Kamii-DeVries approach and High/Scope Curriculum emphasize different programmatic concerns.

The High/Scope Curriculum, through the efforts of the High/Scope Educational Research Foundation, has generated sustained interest in curriculum models as a vehicle for disseminating a "proven" curriculum that will pay back society for its investment in early childhood education. As one of the first experimental early childhood programs initiated in the early 1960s (before the advent of Head Start), advocates of the High/Scope Curriculum have effectively promoted the results of longitudinal studies describing the positive long-term effects of the curriculum on program graduates. (See Chapter 6 for reviews of these studies.) The effectiveness of the High/Scope Foundation's advocacy on behalf of early childhood education has demonstrated policy makers' responsiveness to educational programs that can be empirically and economically justified.

Most of the extensive writings by designers and advocates of the High/Scope Curriculum argue the importance of early childhood education as part of society's resolution of its many ills, and the unique efficacy of the High/Scope Curriculum in this regard (see, for example, Berrueta-Clement et al., 1984; Epstein et al., 1996; Schweinhart & Weikart, 1998; Weikart & Schweinhart, 1993). In contrast, Kamii and DeVries rarely address early childhood education as a public policy issue. The bulk of their writings, both individually and collaboratively, mine the educational implications of Piaget's theory, justify the superiority of his theory as a framework for early education, and refine the explication of their approach.

Kamii and DeVries confidently express not only the superiority of Piaget's ideas as a theoretical framework for early education, but also contend that their approach represents the most faithful implementation of Piaget's ideas (DeVries, 1993; DeVries & Kohlberg, 1987; Kamii, 1998; Kamii & DeVries, 1978/1993). Thus, the soundness of their approach to early education is highly dependent on the validity of Piaget's theory as an explanation for human development in general, and cognitive development in particular. (Critique of Piaget's theory can be found in Karmiloff-Smith, 1992; for critiques accompanied by implications for education, see Gardner, 1991, 1999; Inagaki, 1992; Lubeck, 1996; Silin, 1995).

The writings of Kamii (1981a, 1981b, 1985, 1994, 1998, 2000) and DeVries (1984, 1993, 1997; DeVries & Kohlberg, 1987) advocate not so much the importance of early childhood education, but the possibility of a scientifically informed approach to early education, thus continuing the search initiated during the 1960s with the advent of Project Follow Through. DeVries's efforts, in particular, have continued the lengthy effort to develop a science of educational practice and to rationalize, conceptually and empirically, the superiority of a Piagetian approach such as hers to early education (DeVries, 1991, 1997; DeVries & Goncu, 1987; DeVries & Kohlberg, 1987; DeVries et al., 1991). As a result, DeVries's ongoing work is less about promoting a particular curriculum model than about her continuing desire to explore the educational implications of Piaget's theory of cognitive and moral development during early childhood and beyond.

These two curriculum models, therefore, were designed with different purposes. Although Weikart and Kamii and DeVries each selected Piagetian theory as a basis for their decision making, they did so with different intentions and for different reasons.

Weikart based his curriculum on Piaget's theory of cognitive development because his theory provided a coherent, cognitively oriented framework for a curriculum designed to ameliorate the scholastic difficulties of disadvantaged youth. The Kamii-DeVries approach relied on Piaget's theory because its coherent explanation of cognitive development provided a framework for a scientifically valid approach to early education. As a logical outcome of these choices, Weikart and Kamii and DeVries use curriculum models to achieve different outcomes.

The High/Scope Curriculum has provided the High/Scope Educational Research Foundation a vehicle for widely disseminating its curriculum and for expanding accessibility to a "proven" early childhood program that promises to improve children's life chances. For DeVries, the structure of a curriculum model provided a vehicle for designing a theoretically coherent, empirically validated approach to early education—a framework for creating, at long last, "a science of educational practice" (DeVries, 1991, p. 547).

Uniquely, these two approaches to early childhood education are still evolving. Their architects continue to develop and refine their curricula. The work of Weikart, in particular, reveals contemporary thinking regarding curriculum model development and issues of implementation. Due to this fact, this chapter does not benefit from the historical commentary that has been available for the other four curriculum models.

☞ EARLY HISTORY: APPLYING PIAGETIAN THEORY TO EARLY CHILDHOOD EDUCATION

David Weikart and Constance Kamii became involved with early childhood education during their tenure with the Ypsilanti, Michigan, public schools in the early 1960s. One of the impressive facts about the High/Scope and Kamii-DeVries approaches is the sustained length of time their architects have been committed to curriculum development.

Prior to their entry into early childhood education, David Weikart was a school psychologist and Constance Kamii a diagnostician and adolescent counselor. The Perry Preschool Project was initiated in the Ypsilanti Public Schools in fall 1962 as part of a long-term effort to improve the scholastic performance of Ypsilanti's disadvantaged youth. Frustrated by the lack of alternatives within the existing school system, Weikart decided to explore the potential of preschool intervention for 3- and 4-year-olds. Weikart became the Perry Preschool Project director and Kamii served as a research associate.

The curriculum developed for the Perry Preschool Project evolved over 10 years. The first significant revision occurred during spring 1964 when the Perry Preschool Project staff rejected the instructional emphasis on visual-motor skills, number concepts, and language enrichment activities and focused their attention on the developmental theory of Jean Piaget (Hohmann, Banet, & Weikart, 1979; Weikart et al., 1971). In the foreword to their 1979 curriculum description, the program architects noted:

> It is difficult . . . to imagine the dearth of information about preschool curriculum that the Perry Preschool faced. In 1960, when the first planning for the project began, there were few guidelines on how to operate a nursery school . . . . Published discussions of curriculum that the staff turned up stressed group dynamics and physical, social and emotional development, but programs specifically aimed at school success and/or cognitive development were not accessible to us if they were in fact available. (Hohmann et al., 1979, pp. xii–xiii)

Shortly thereafter, Kamii was awarded a postdoctoral fellowship, and from 1966 to 1967, she studied at the University of Geneva under Jean Piaget and his colleagues. In 1967, she became curriculum director in the Ypsilanti public schools for a separate early childhood program, the Ypsilanti Early Education Program, and began directing the development of another preschool curriculum based on Piaget's theory. Kamii focused her effort on articulating a framework for preschool curriculum based on Piaget's theory.

For both Weikart and Kamii, Piaget's theory of cognitive development offered a structured, theoretical framework for developing a cognitively oriented curriculum. Their separate intentions, however, were already evident. Weikart chose Piaget's theory as a basis for curriculum because, after a frustrating search for a useful conceptual framework, Piaget's theory addressed the issues of cognitive development he and his staff were confronting (Hohmann et al., 1979). Weikart's efforts were focused on developing a preschool curriculum to alleviate the academic disadvantages experienced by Ypsilanti's children. Piaget's theory provided a needed, cognitive conceptual framework: "Piaget offered a conceptual structure around which a preschool curriculum model could be built, an explicit rationale for preschool activities" (Weikart & Schweinhart, 1987, p. 255).

Kamii, unlike Weikart, was interested primarily in probing the educational implications of Piaget's theory for preschool education. As her understanding and interpretation of Piagetian theory evolved, she became increasingly dissatisfied with her early efforts. Ultimately Kamii cited her early thinking and writings as an example of how one should *not* interpret Piaget for education (see, for example, Kamii, 1971, 1972; Kamii & Radin, 1967, 1970; Sonquist & Kamii, 1967).

As a result of her continuing study, and in contrast to the curricular emphasis of the High/Scope model at that time, Kamii shifted her focus away from Piaget's stages of cognitive development and behaviors characteristic of thinking at various stages. She focused instead on the constructive processes that advanced cognitive development and logical reasoning. Kamii's efforts accelerated when she began her collaboration with Rheta DeVries at the University of Illinois–Chicago campus in 1970. (DeVries also studied at the University of Geneva under Piaget and his colleagues.)

Prior to pursuing the outcomes of Weikart's and Kamii's divergent routes, a brief analysis of why, in the 1960s, Piaget's theory of cognitive development generated such excitement in the educational community deserves explanation. Recall from the discussion in Chapter 3 of the Developmental-Interaction approach, for example, that Lucy Sprague Mitchell and her progressive colleagues had read Piaget in the 1930s and been unimpressed. Barbara Biber and her Bank Street affiliates read Piaget again in the 1960s, and although they thought his ideas useful and incorporated them into their conceptualization of the Developmental-Interaction approach, they argued that his ideas were insufficient as the basis for an entire curriculum. What, then, about Piaget's theory in the 1960s so galvanized psychologists such as Weikart, Kamii, and DeVries (and so many others)?

The Piagetian Mystique

The phrase *Piagetian mystique* is borrowed from Evans (1975), who credited most of the attention to children's cognitive development in the 1960s and 1970s to Piaget's ideas. Weber (1984) attributed the long delay in recognizing Piaget's ideas to three factors, two of which are primarily methodological. Weber explained the delay of interest in Piaget's ideas first in terms of the discrepancy between his clinical research method and the scientific, statistical treatment of findings prevalent in the United States. The second methodological factor was Piaget's persistent blending of empirical description with theoretical speculation; this lack of empirical clarity apparently rankled psychologists seeking to build a science of human behavior. It was reversal of the third factor, however, that set the stage for Piaget's educational impact.

Prior to the 1960s, as already has been stated many times, interest in intellectual development was limited because it was presumed to be predetermined and fixed by heredity. Reassessment of this long-held judgment shifted psychologists' focus from the contribution of biology to the contribution of environment to intellectual development. And, as we already know, this reassessment, aligned with society's increasing concern with alleviating poverty, led to a federal focus on early childhood education as a mechanism for promoting school success and social equality. In the 1960s, therefore, Piaget's theory of cognitive development, with its emphasis on intellectual growth as the result of interactions between a child and her environment, found a socially and politically responsive milieu.

This responsiveness was nurtured further by an emerging educational interest in intellectual functioning and public expectation that the public school system should promote intellectual prowess, especially in mathematics and the sciences. It may be remembered from discussion in previous chapters that public school education during the 1940s and 1950s focused on students' life adjustment. This focus had led to curricula based on children's perceived psychosocial needs. During the 1950s, educational criticism focused once again on making training of the intellect the central function of schools (Kliebard, 1986).

This change in direction became firmly secured when, on October 5, 1957, *Sputnik* was launched by the former Soviet Union. As described by Kliebard (1986):

> Within a matter of days, American mass media had settled on a reason for the Soviet technological success. Just as Prussian schools were widely believed to be the basis for the victory of the Prussians over the Austrians in the Battle of Konigratz in 1866, so, implausibly, did the Soviet technological feat become a victory of the Soviet educational system over the American. Quickly, life adjustment education was seen as the prime example of America's "soft" education in contrast to the rigorous Soviet system. While American schoolchildren were learning how to get along with their peers or how to bake a cherry pie, so the explanation went, Soviet children were being steeped in the hard sciences and mathematics needed to win the technological race that had become the centerpiece of the Cold War. (pp. 264–265)

Thus by the mid-1960s Piagetian theory found a receptive psychological, social, and political climate in the United States. It was not only that Piaget's theory focused on cognitive development at a time when the nation was interested in intellectual development or that his theory saw cognitive development as the result of children's active interaction with stimulating environments. Interest in his theoretical ideas also was ensured by the fact that his theory specifically conceptualized the development of logical reasoning.

Piaget's theory focuses on the logical operations considered the underpinnings of mathematics and science. Student mastery of these disciplines was going to ensure the United States' technological superiority over its competitors, and victory in the Cold War competition between the then-Soviet Union and the United States.

Murray (1979) concluded that these converging factors made adoption of Piagetian theory virtually inevitable. "Given that the content of Piaget's theory and research was largely children's reasoning in mathematics, science, and logic, and the lack of similar content anywhere else in psychology, it was all but inevitable that Piaget would dominate these curricular reforms" (p. 34).

These factors, though, speak primarily to Piaget's acceptance by the general education community. Murray also noted that Piaget's claim that intellectual development progressed in terms of a hierarchically organized sequence rooted in sensorimotor activity ensured, as well, the interest of early childhood educators. In contrast to the mechanistic and instructional emphasis of behavioral theory, Piaget's theory offered early childhood educators a framework for incorporating cognitive development into early childhood education that was compatible with their existing notions of teaching and learning as interactive and developmental.

✑ THE KAMII-DEVRIES APPROACH

The Kamii-DeVries approach (a) was built on Piaget's distinction among different types of knowledge; (b) incorporated educational implications of Piaget's distinction between heteronomous and autonomous moral reasoning (these terms are defined below); and (c) provided a constructivist perspective on traditional school objectives in number and arithmetic, and reading and writing. The first two components are unique to their approach and are the basis for two program components: physical-knowledge activities and group games. Kamii and DeVries contended that Piaget's work had educational implications for children's moral, social, affective, *and* cognitive development.

The Kamii-DeVries approach was developed primarily for preschool, although Kamii's and DeVries's work in sociomoral development, number and arithmetic, and reading and writing has been extended into the primary grades (see, for example, DeVries & Zan, 1994, 1995; Ferreiro & Teberosky, 1979/1982; Kamii, 1985, 1994, 2000; Kamii & Joseph, 1989).

Although Kamii (currently at the University of Alabama at Birmingham) initiated the first curricular components for what became known as the Kamii-DeVries approach, DeVries (at the University of Houston for 12 years, and currently at the University of Northern Iowa) framed their collaborative work as a specific approach to early childhood education. DeVries's formal designation of her collaborative work with Kamii as a specific approach to early education became popularized in 1987 with the publication of *Programs of Early Education: The Constructivist View*. In this text, DeVries reasserted the importance of Piaget's stage theory and incorporated Kohlberg's stages of moral development and Selman's stages of interpersonal understanding into the Kamii-DeVries approach (DeVries, 1984, 1992; DeVries & Kohlberg, 1987). These changes reflected a third alteration to the Kamii-DeVries approach—from Kamii's original focus on Piagetian stages, to Kamii and DeVries's shared emphasis on constructivism, to DeVries's reinsertion of Piaget's stages (structuralism) as an important curricular element.

Until the mid-1980s, Kamii and DeVries had minimized the educational relevance of advancement to the next stage of cognitive development. They argued that Piaget's stages held little usefulness for teachers in terms of helping them know what to do in their classrooms (DeVries, 1978; Kamii & DeVries, 1977, 1978/1993). Then in the late 1980s, DeVries aligned with her former colleague Lawrence Kohlberg and championed a carefully delineated definition of development. DeVries's endorsement of development as the aim of education refers to children's progression through universal stages of intellectual and moral development consistent with Piaget's stages of operational reasoning (DeVries, 1992, 1997; DeVries & Kohlberg, 1987). DeVries and Kohlberg (1987) contended that "development as the aim of education is the most legitimate because it avoids the pitfall of value relativity" (p. xii–xiii).

When advancement toward the next developmental stage was reincorporated into the approach as programmatically relevant, it became possible to articulate and scientifically validate desired developmental outcomes, as well as preferable practices for their achievement. Previously, developmental outcomes had been defined in terms of global characteristics: "We advocate development as our educational objective because it is the only way by which individuals can become intelligent, autonomous, mentally healthy, and moral. . . . Curriculum objectives, therefore, can only be stated in general terms" (Kamii & DeVries, 1977, pp. 392–393).

Reinserting Piaget's structuralism into curriculum development was necessary, DeVries (1984; DeVries & Kohlberg, 1987) explained, in order to tighten interpretation surrounding such general terms. Their original educational goals, which had relied on Piaget's constructivism, had become disassociated from his theory (1984; DeVries & Kohlberg, 1987). "The generality of constructivist objectives has led to a lack of consensus about the practical definition of constructive activity" (DeVries & Kohlberg, 1987, p. 48).

Omitting the theory's structural component, DeVries argued, made it possible to justify a variety of loosely connected generalities, such as "hands-on-learning," "learning by doing," or "play." Although generally accurate, these generalities lacked guidelines for discriminating the relative value of specific activities and ways of teaching (DeVries, 1984).

By reinserting the theory's structural component (stages of cognitive development) into the approach, DeVries felt that she rectified this concern. Piaget's stages provided tangible boundaries within which curriculum possibilities could be justified in terms of their likelihood for promoting cognitive and moral development. Simultaneously, stages provided a clear frame of reference for assessing children's progress (see, for example, DeVries, 1992; DeVries & Fernie, 1990; DeVries et al., 1991). DeVries's reemphasis on the educational significance of Piaget's stages of cognitive development provided the framework needed for a defined approach to curriculum development.

In 1977, Kamii and DeVries asserted, "We do not aim to move children to the stage of concrete operations" (p. 390). At that point in its evolution, the Kamii-DeVries approach emphasized the educational significance of Piaget's notion of constructivism and offered general proposals for improving early childhood curriculum (e.g., Kamii, 1982; Kamii & DeVries, 1977, 1978/1993, 1980). Later DeVries claimed that "[t]o deny the aim of concrete operations [is] to rob the rationale of what is uniquely Piagetian" (DeVries, 1984, p. 86). With the reinsertion of Piaget's structuralism, the Kamii-DeVries approach became a framework for early education that was linked to measurable outcomes (e.g., DeVries, 1992; DeVries & Kohlberg, 1987).

These revisions placed DeVries's thinking at odds with that of Kamii, who continued to emphasize constructivism as the primary educational implication of Piaget's work and autonomy as the indisputable educational goal derived from his theory (Kamii, 1984, 1985, 1992). According to DeVries and Kohlberg (1987), although Kamii's goal of autonomy has been a distinguishing characteristic among constructivist programs, "it introduces the difficulty of understanding differences in objectives at less rarified levels of concern" (p. 58) and is too open to multiple interpretations. DeVries and Kohlberg (1987) argued that the goal of autonomy was susceptible to the danger of becoming a vague generality that can be linked with a variety of theoretical possibilities. In their view, "reduction of aims to autonomy is too one-sided, omitting what the notion of structural stages contributes to educational planning" (p. 58).

These alterations to the Kamii-DeVries approach had practical as well as conceptual consequences. No longer was the continuing development of the Kamii-DeVries approach a collaboration between its two namesakes, a fact easily overlooked on reading the program name. This state of affairs added to our challenge of presenting a complex approach to early childhood education. Sometimes the collective pronoun *they* is accurate when discussing program specifics. But often it is misleading because the statement is not representative of the shared views of Kamii and DeVries, or, because in some circumstances, the "they" refers to the thinking of DeVries and Kohlberg. At other times DeVries's thinking has evolved independently or with new collaborators. This challenge has been complicated still further by the fact that Kohlberg, who became DeVries's collaborator in the 1980s (and whom she credits for the shift in her thinking [DeVries, 1984]), died in 1987 just before the publication of their seminal description of the Kamii-DeVries approach.

At this writing, DeVries's interests have evolved still further. She no longer organizes her work within the context of the Kamii-DeVries approach. Consistent with her exploration of the educational implications of Piaget's theory—versus development of a formalized curriculum model—she now uses the broader term "constructivist education" when referring to her work.

Yet it was DeVries who anointed the Kamii-DeVries approach and continues to serve as its primary advocate. The description that follows relies heavily on her presentation of the approach, especially as articulated in *Programs of Early Education: The Constructivist View* (later retitled *Constructivist Education: Overview and Comparison with Other Programs*). This text incorporates the thinking DeVries developed with Kamii. It also indicates the ways in which their previous work has been altered to reflect DeVries's evolving thinking, especially relative to Piaget's stage theory, development as the aim of education, sociomoral development, and educational assessment.

Because DeVries advanced the most developed version of the Kamii-DeVries approach, she should be credited with the rationale and justifications that follow, even though her thinking clearly builds on her earlier collaboration with Kamii. Their coauthored works (Kamii & DeVries, 1976, 1977, 1978/1993, 1980) form the core of the Kamii-DeVries preschool curriculum. The Kamii-DeVries approach was derived from deep and extensive study of Piaget's theory; an overview of their approach, therefore, must presume readers have knowledge of his complex ideas.

Deriving Educational Implications from Piaget's Theory of Cognitive Development

The first revisions to the Kamii-DeVries approach relied both on Piaget's psychological theory of cognitive development and on his epistemological[2] framework. The approach was framed as a cognitive-developmental *and* constructivist approach

---

[2]Epistemology is concerned with assumptions about the nature of knowledge and how it is acquired.

to early education. DeVries explained her reliance on Piaget's ideas as being based on her belief that his work represented the most advanced theory of mental development (DeVries & Kohlberg, 1987). Drawing from Piaget's theory of cognitive development as well as his epistemological framework resulted in a two-pronged focus: Piaget's structural stages and the concept of constructivism.

Piaget's Structural Stages. The focus on structural stages emerged from Piaget's theory of cognitive development. Piaget's clinical study of children led him to conclude that intellectual development progressed through four qualitatively different stages from birth through adolescence: (a) sensorimotor, (b) preoperational, (c) concrete operational, and (d) formal operational.[3]

Children during the preschool years are characterized by preoperational thinking. Their thinking is different from that of older children and adults not only because they usually know less but also because they differently interpret and make sense of what they know. Piaget's stage theory shaped his description of the form, content, and sequence of intellectual development/logical reasoning. In turn, this knowledge provided an important underpinning for the educational practices proposed by the Kamii-DeVries approach. Teachers embrace children's preoperational thinking; they plan for it and use it to conceptualize their teaching (DeVries & Kohlberg, 1987).

Following Piaget, DeVries emphasizes development as being composed of invariant, sequential, and hierarchical stages in mental evolution. As a result of these characteristics, Kohlberg (1984) categorized Piaget's stage theory as an example of a "hard" stage model. And, constructivist education, according to DeVries and Kohlberg (1987), should aim at hard structural development.

These stages are presented as universal and structurally whole. Cultural factors may speed up or slow down development, but the sequence remains unchanged. A given stage represents an underlying thought-organization that a child applies to all her experiences, regardless of the experiences that have informed her development. Culture and the specifics of one's experiences are not considered significant as explanations of individual development.

DeVries contends that cognitive organization is present in every area of the child's development "where a self thinks about the physical and social world and its own relation to that world" (DeVries & Kohlberg, 1987, p. xii). Kamii and De-Vries (DeVries & Kohlberg, 1987; Kamii, 1975) viewed cognitive development as explaining and integrating all aspects of development—sociomoral and personality, as well as cognitive development. This conclusion, which permeates Kamii's and DeVries's collaborative writings, extended the original parameters of their approach beyond cognitive development to include concern for the whole child.

---

[3]Actually, Piaget designated three stages of cognitive development: sensorimotor, concrete operational, and formal operations. The concrete operational stage, in turn, is composed of two subperiods: preoperational and concrete operational. More often, though, the subperiods are ignored, and Piaget's theory is described as having four stages.

Kamii's and DeVries's interest in the "whole child" included children's interests, sociability, character, and general self-esteem. It was based on an appreciation that children's active involvement with their environment, which is viewed as an essential ingredient for cognitive and sociomoral development, depends on social-emotional well-being.

For example, the Kamii-DeVries approach encourages cooperative relationships among children and between children and teachers. The value of cooperative activities rests not so much with interest in creating harmonious, mutually beneficial social relationships or in enhancing children's social skills, but with the fact that the social context offers possibilities for children to become aware of differences in perspective (which is essential to cognitive and sociomoral development). And to the extent that children continue a particular social interaction, cooperative activities provide a special motivation to coordinate (create relationships among) these differences. The interactions promoted by cooperative activities, in turn, facilitate children's cognitive structures of reasoning. Thus, Kamii and DeVries explained their interest in personality and affective development in terms of its supportive role to cognitive and sociomoral development versus its legitimacy as an equal and uniquely contributing partner in the multifaceted development of children.

Piaget's contention that an individual's thinking becomes more adequate with each stage of cognitive development provided the underpinning for DeVries's conclusion that development, defined in terms of Piaget's stages of cognitive development, should be the aim of education.[4] DeVries acknowledged, however, what has been labeled the psychologist's fallacy.

The psychologist's fallacy is the conviction that educational aims can be derived directly from descriptions of optimum psychological development. The psychologist's fallacy represents an important issue because it questions the nature of the relationship between developmental theory and educational practice—whether developmental theory is more appropriately an informant to, or determinant of, educational goals. (See Chapter 7 for further discussion of this issue.)

DeVries contended that developmental theory, specifically Piaget's theory of cognitive development, can and should determine the identification of educational outcomes. Following Kohlberg's (1981; Kohlberg & Mayer, 1972) classic argument, DeVries tried to avert the psychologist's fallacy and defended Piaget's developmental outcomes as educational goals by aligning developmental end points (e.g., logical reasoning) with philosophical arguments:

> Cognitive-developmental psychological theory postulates that movement through a sequential progression represents movement from a less adequate to a more adequate psychological state. This formal standard is not itself ultimate, but must be elaborated as a set of ethical principles and justified in philosophical and ethical terms. (DeVries & Kohlberg, 1987, p. 9)

---

[4]This conclusion was actually formulated earlier by Kohlberg and Mayer (1972) and defended by Kohlberg (1981) in a later publication.

The progression of this defense is important to note. DeVries contended that philosophical principles regarding valued behaviors can be stated as educational aims only when they can be expressed psychologically and assessed empirically.

> This means translating [philosophical values] into statements about a more adequate stage of development. Otherwise the rationally accepted principles of the philosopher will only be arbitrary concepts and doctrines for the child. Accordingly, to make a genuine statement of an educational end, the educational philosopher must coordinate notions of principles with understanding of the facts of development. (DeVries & Kohlberg, 1987, p. 10)

To do otherwise, according to DeVries, was to fall prey to arbitrary, often contradictory, objectives that are subject to multiple interpretations.

DeVries justified transposing the cognitive-developmental outcomes outlined by Piaget into the educational aims of the Kamii-DeVries approach because they represented the "natural" outcomes of cognitive development. In contrast, general societal values are considered arbitrary.

Kohlberg and Mayer (1972) coined the phrase "bag of virtues" to categorize what they called value-relative objectives. They contrasted these objectives with developmental progressions that they viewed as natural laws of mental development validated by scientific research. DeVries argued that the educational values of the Kamii-DeVries approach were more valid than others because they are not arbitrarily drawn from a bag of virtues (DeVries & Kohlberg, 1987).

A summary of DeVries's analysis of the Developmental Interaction approach clarifies her point of view. Recall that adherents of the Developmental-Interaction approach identified educational goals in terms of preferred values and relied on the integration of complementary theories to inform their educational actualization. They argued that this approach to curriculum development enabled them to holistically address the whole child. In contrast, DeVries contended that this approach to selecting goals and theories is arbitrary and fragmented (DeVries & Kohlberg, 1987). Given her belief in the dominant position of cognitive organization in child development, DeVries argued that the Developmental-Interaction approach lacked a coherent conceptual framework because it draws on multiple theories of emotional and cognitive development. Finally, the contention that educational aims, rather than psychological theory, provided unification to curriculum decisions caused DeVries to categorize the Developmental-Interaction approach as eclectic (DeVries & Kohlberg, 1987).

In resurrecting Piaget's structuralism as significant for educational practice, DeVries realized that she had to avoid the mistakes of early education programs that had attempted to directly promote the operational characteristics associated with Piagetian stages. Rather than examining Piaget's stages for their educational implications (DeVries, 1978; DeVries & Kohlberg, 1987), early programs had literally translated Piaget's stage descriptions into educational practice, especially as represented by the experimental tasks Piaget used to identify a child's stage of cognitive reasoning. In these programs, practice with specific Piagetian tasks, such as experiments with conservation of liquid and solids and classification of objects with varying number of attributes, often supplied curricular content (see, for example, Lavatelli, 1970). Programs that organized their curriculum around Piagetian tasks assumed that teaching preschool children how to master these cognitive tasks would accelerate their development beyond preoperational thought into the next stage of operational thinking.

According to DeVries (1978, 1984; DeVries & Kohlberg, 1987), literal translation of Piaget's work into educational practice has three limitations. First, it confuses children's sequential progress on individual Piagetian tasks with the sequence of general cognitive development. This reduced the theory to the development of scientific knowledge and isolated operations (the term *operations* refers to the mental "devices" individuals use to make sense of their physical and social environments). Although Piaget's stages describe children's thinking at various stages of cognitive development, they do not explain how a child moves from one stage to the next. The *how* of development, according to DeVries, is derived from Piaget's epistemology, in particular, the concept of constructivism.

Second, progress from one stage to the next occurs over time, and practice with Piagetian tasks does not offer pedagogical insights that teachers can use to support children's progress. Third, although Piagetian tasks are useful in demonstrating stages of thought, they do not meet the criteria of good educational activities from a constructivist perspective. Specific Piagetian tasks are unrelated to children's interests, and the next stages of reasoning are not achieved through direct instruction. Children advance toward more operational reasoning by being given opportunities to interact directly with objects and people. (The discussion following on constructivism addresses this more fully.)

To overcome the limitations of literal translations of Piaget's stages, as well as the weaknesses associated with focusing on Piaget's notion of constructivism to the exclusion of the theory's structural features, DeVries (1984, 1992; DeVries & Kohlberg, 1987) concluded that it was necessary to identify stages or levels of cognitive development *within daily classroom activities.* This focus, according to DeVries, retained the clear and necessary connection with Piaget's structural stages but did so in a way that is meaningful to teachers and their everyday experiences with children.

> The aim is a redefinition of structural stages or levels in terms of signs that are visible to the teacher observing the constructive process as it occurs in classroom activities. . . . The educational integration of structuralism and constructivism requires understanding the structural history and future of a child's present structures as these are observable in the active constructive context. That is, the kind of research with classroom activities and content that Piaget did with his tasks and the broad domains of knowledge needs to be done. . . . This kind of research also may be a vehicle through which the development of the educational translation can progress to more coherence and consensus. . . . *Constructivist education must demonstrate that it facilitates structural progress,* and stages in activities may provide a good focus for both formative and summative evaluation. (DeVries, 1984, p. 87, emphasis in original)

DeVries worked as a consultant to Missouri's Project Construct to develop such an assessment technique (see, for example, DeVries, 1992, 1993). By assessing structural progress in terms of children's daily activities, the pedagogic meaningfulness of Piaget's theory was retained. "We are looking for indicators observable in classroom activities that not only give the teacher information on the stages of development but also provide a basis for planning further intervention" (DeVries, 1992, p. 19).

Furthermore, evaluation of children's structural progress, according to DeVries (1984, 1992, 1993; DeVries & Kohlberg, 1987), validated constructivist education. The increased specificity of practice engendered by delineating, through research, the progressive development of logical and moral reasoning in everyday classroom activities supports the development of a behavioral science of education (DeVries, 1984). This possibility is part of DeVries's, as well as Kamii's, long-held belief that early childhood teaching needs a more scientific basis for educational practice. Kamii (1981b) has cogently expressed their viewpoint:

> Education has developed over the centuries by personal opinions called philosophies, and by trial and error, and by tradition, to meet certain practical needs. To educate the young generation of their society, teachers have used their best common sense. But a profession cannot develop on the basis of common sense alone. . . . Just as agriculture and medicine advanced with scientific research and theory, education can go forward only by raising fundamental questions once again and getting scientific answers to these questions. (pp. 7–8)

By identifying stages of cognitive development within typical classroom activities, DeVries hoped that teachers would have clear developmental targets to inform their teaching decisions, guide and justify their selection of specific activities, and evaluate individual children's developmental progress. Classroom activities, according to DeVries (1984, 1992, 1993; DeVries & Kohlberg, 1987), need to be justifiable in terms of developmental theory and research, and indicators used to assess children's development should be justifiable "in terms of how they fit into a sequential developmental progression" (DeVries, 1992, p. 19).

DeVries and Kohlberg (1987) suggested that assessing children's developmental understanding of diverse disciplines also provided a strategy for sequencing the teaching of subject matter. To inform this line of reasoning, DeVries relied on her research of children's progressive strategies in playing Tic-Tac-Toe (DeVries & Fernie 1990) and the game Guess Which Hand the Penny Is In (DeVries, 1970), her investigation of children's understanding of shadows (DeVries, 1992; DeVries & Kohlberg, 1987), and Selman's (1980) extensive chronicling of children's growth in interpersonal understanding (DeVries, 1992; DeVries & Kohlberg, 1987; DeVries et al., 1991). Activity-specific developmental knowledge, according to DeVries (1984), permitted a specificity in practice that was lacking because of overreliance on the constructivist implications of Piaget's theory.

Constructivism. The concept of constructivism is the second linchpin in the Kamii-DeVries approach. DeVries explains constructivism as the functional aspect of Piaget's theory; it is the process by which cognitive and sociomoral development are facilitated. Stages are the by-products of the constructive process; they are the *results* of development. In turn, children's development of increasingly adequate cognitive structures (i.e., later stages of cognitive development) is the means by which they become more intelligent (DeVries & Kohlberg, 1987).

For this reason, according to DeVries and Kohlberg (1987), constructivism is the heart of Piaget's theory. The curriculum of the Kamii-DeVries approach revolves around creating individual and group activities that mentally engage children in ways that provoke constructivist activity that will facilitate cognitive and sociomoral development.

Kamii and DeVries were both creative and inventive in analyzing the extent to which individual activities can motivate constructivist activity (see, for example, Kamii & DeVries, 1978/1993, 1980). Their writings provide not only a clear articulation of their rationale, but also practical principles relevant for teaching and a wide range of activities appropriate for classroom implementation. Depending on the type of knowledge involved (see following) and its associated content, these suggestions range from broad generalities to specific recommendations for sequencing content-specific knowledge.

The constructive process is characterized by two features: (a) children's interaction with their physical and social environments and (b) the internal, mental interaction between children's current way of understanding an event or phenomena and input from a new experience. These interactive processes are formally known as *assimilation* and *accommodation.* Through these dual interactions, children progressively reorganize their understandings of the physical and social world. In other words, children actively create their knowledge of the world, and children's cognitive/structural development results from their first-hand interactions with the environment. Neither direct biological maturation nor direct instruction[5] explain development.

Although the specifics of a child's interactions with the environment are unique to the child and her interests, the cognitive developmental outcomes of these interactions are not. This assumption provides the conceptual and programmatic linkage between constructivism and stage theory.

Constructivism undergirds Kamii's and DeVries's emphasis on children's active participation in learning. Constructive activity, especially during the preschool years, is prompted best by children's spontaneous interactions with their physical and social environments. Cognitive structures develop in the course of children's thinking about their physical actions on objects and interactions with people.

The Kamii-DeVries approach relied heavily, and uniquely, on Piaget's distinction between two types of action that arise from two different types of psychological experience: physical experiences and logico-mathematical experience (DeVries & Kohlberg, 1987; Kamii & DeVries, 1976, 1978/1993, 1980). Physical experience consists of individual actions on objects and leads to knowledge of the objects themselves. For example, when a child drops an object, such as a ball or a piece of

---

[5]General disregard for direct instruction explains their denunciation of didactic approaches such as Direct Instruction.

glass, a child can observe the object's reaction to being dropped. This type of action is called *simple* or *empirical abstraction.*

In contrast, logico-mathematical experience provokes children to mentally create relationships between and among objects that do not exist directly in the object. For example, number does not exist in an object; it is not a physical property of objects. Children have to mentally put objects into a relationship with each other in order to conclude that, for instance, there are three objects. This mental action, which also is required for spatial and temporal reasoning, is called *reflective abstraction.*

These two action types result in two different types of knowledge: physical knowledge and logico-mathematical knowledge. Physical knowledge results from individual action, whereas logico-mathematical knowledge results from an individual mentally coordinating two or more actions and reactions. Logico-mathematical knowledge emerges from the knower's mental coordination of information; as a result, it cannot be taught directly.

Children's level of logico-mathematical knowledge is essentially synonymous with their level of cognitive development. According to Piagetian theory, logico-mathematical knowledge defines an individual's way of knowing. During early childhood, however, children's ways of knowing still are dependent on direct versus mental action on their environment. Physical experience, therefore, is crucial to preschoolers' cognitive development. "At least for babies and young children, there can be no logico-mathematical experience without objects to put into relationship with one another" (DeVries & Kohlberg, 1987, p. 21).

From an adult's point of view, the relationships construed by children may appear in error, but within a Piagetian framework, such errors are anticipated and appreciated as signs of children's progressive development. Children's early stages of intellectual development are characterized by particular kinds of errors; these errors are developmental and reflect children's increasingly sophisticated attempts to make sense of their experiences.

Piaget also discussed a third type of knowledge—social-arbitrary knowledge. This type of knowledge has people, rather than physical or mental action, as its source. Social-arbitrary knowledge refers to those facts and conventions that have been socially accepted, such as the names of objects or the ways in which particular holidays are celebrated.

In actuality, these three types of knowledge are interdependent. All content, whether social-arbitrary or physical-knowledge, must be structured within some logico-mathematical framework. A child's logico-mathematical framework, in turn, is formed from the mental coordination of understandings derived from physical and social-arbitrary knowledge. Kamii and DeVries used these theoretical distinctions to create their curricular approach.

Curriculum and Activities

Kamii and DeVries built on the child development approach as represented by the Developmental-Interaction approach and the classic nursery school text written by Katherine Read (DeVries & Kohlberg, 1987; Kamii, 1981a; Kamii & DeVries,

1977; Read, 1966). Kamii and DeVries valued the child development approach's respect for children's pursuits and its insights into children's intrinsic interests, such as block building, painting, play, and table games.

They considered the child development tradition weakened, however, by its dependence on teachers as knowledge transmitters, its largely intuitive methods, and an insufficient appreciation for the nature of preoperational intelligence. They believed that their approach improved on the child development tradition by providing a scientific framework that could contribute greater precision to teacher behaviors. In addition, they believed that Piaget's theory provides teachers a theoretical rationale and more powerful justification for decisions (DeVries & Kohlberg, 1987; Kamii, 1981a; Kamii & DeVries, 1977). The Kamii-DeVries approach, therefore, incorporated the child-centered, child-development approach, much of its daily routine, and a majority of its developmentally oriented activities (see Chapter 3), but redirected these elements toward an emphasis on children's moral and intellectual activity.

Specifically, children's activity is nurtured and augmented in ways that promote their creation of new intellectual relationships. Meaningful constructivist activities provoke purposeful experimentation. To the extent that children are mentally engaged in an activity, either singly or with others, they are thinking and creating new intellectual relationships that will advance their operational thinking.

Kamii and DeVries used the distinctions among physical, logical-mathematical, and social-arbitrary knowledge as a basis for selecting among activities traditionally associated with nursery education, analyzing their cognitive possibilities, creating meaningful adaptations, and generating new possibilities. So, for example, opportunities for experimentation, especially as incorporated into physical-knowledge activities, are a prominent curriculum component. Group games, based on Piaget's investigation of games with rules and description of moral development, have been given an expanded role. And, what is popularly known as sociodramatic play is retitled symbolic play and encouraged because of its contributions to children's ability to represent their thinking symbolically.

Creating a learning environment that meaningfully and mentally engages children requires that teachers create possibilities of interest to young children. Piaget designated interest as the "fuel" of the constructive process (DeVries, 1993, 1997; DeVries & Kohlberg, 1987). Kamii and DeVries incorporated the child development approach into their own because it successfully identified activities of natural interest to preschoolers. In the absence of interest, children do not extend the effort needed to make sense out of experiences (i.e., attempt to assimilate the experience to existing structures) or modify their current way of knowing (i.e., accommodate existing cognitive structures).

Facilitating Moral Reasoning. The value system of Piaget's cognitive-developmental viewpoint focuses not only on cognitive universals, but also ethical universals. Ethical universals are defined in terms of Kohlberg's stages of moral justice, which were derived from Piaget's early work on moral development. Within this frame of reference, moral development proceeds parallel to cognitive development. Increasing adequacy in logical reasoning is necessary, though not sufficient, for attainment of the parallel stage of moral development[6] (DeVries, 1997; DeVries & Kohlberg, 1987).

Piaget distinguished between heteronomy and autonomy. Individuals who are heteronomous rely on the thinking of others in their decision making, rather than their own. But, if not restricted by adults' overuse of their authority, children naturally evolve toward autonomous thinking and action. In contrast to those who argue that children learn to behave morally through direct instruction, the Kamii-DeVries approach contends that moral development is the result of active mental construction.

As a result, the Kamii-DeVries approach addresses what DeVries (1992, 1997; DeVries et al., 1991; DeVries & Kohlberg, 1987; DeVries & Zan, 1994, 1995) calls the sociomoral atmosphere of the classroom. The term *sociomoral atmosphere* refers to the entire network of interpersonal relations that comprise a child's experiences in school, including children's interactions with their teachers. It includes both social perspective taking and moral judgment (DeVries, 1997; DeVries & Zan, 1994, 1995; Kohlberg & Lickona, 1987). Teachers' respect for children's thinking, reduction of adult authority, alleviation of arbitrary rules, and opportunities for cooperative interactions necessitating coordination of diverse perspectives are each valued for their contributions to children's moral development. So are opportunities for children to create classroom rules and negotiate conflicts with peers and teachers, both of which are seen as characteristic of a democratically run classroom. In each of these instances, the classroom's social life is explicitly appropriated as curriculum.

The Kamii-DeVries approach also gives a significant position to group games, which are described shortly. Mention of group games is pertinent at this point in the discussion, however, because Piaget stressed that games, such as Marbles, have a rules component and thus involve attitudes of respect for rules and authority.

At one point the moral discussion and group decision methods of Selman and Kohlberg (1972a, 1972b; Selman, Kohlberg, & Byrne, 1974a, 1974b) were incorporated into the Kamii-DeVries approach. Classroom time was set aside to view filmstrips presenting hypothetical dilemmas, followed by teacher-facilitated discussion. The presumption was that social and moral reasoning was advanced by providing children opportunities to apply their reasoning to real-life situations (Kohlberg & Lickona, 1987).

Recently, DeVries (DeVries & Zan 1994, 1995) dismissed the use of hypothetical situations and replaced them with ideas for promoting children's sociomoral reasoning during daily routines and events found in preschool and primary classrooms. For example, clean-up time is viewed as an occasion for children to "think about the care of their class environment in terms of consideration and fairness toward everyone in the class community" (DeVries & Zan, 1994, p. 218).

---

[6]Kohlberg's theory of moral development has been extensively critiqued; for examples of this criticism, the reader is referred to Flanagan (1993) and Gilligan (1977, 1988).

Physical-Knowledge Activities. Physical-knowledge activities originated from Kamii's and DeVries's use of Piaget's distinction between simple and reflective abstraction and the two types of knowledges—physical and logico-mathematical—with which they are linked (DeVries & Kohlberg, 1987; Kamii & DeVries, 1978/1993). Intelligence, as conceptualized by Piaget, is fostered by action, both physical and mental. Because the preoperational thought of preschool children is closely linked to physical action, activities to promote the development of thought must be tied to children's interests in figuring out how to do things—in effect, physical-knowledge activities. In turn, the thinking instigated by physical-knowledge activities provokes reflective abstraction. Coordinating new and existing understandings induces children to mentally reorganize what they know.

Physical-knowledge activities involve children's actions on objects and their observations of the reactions. Children initiate these actions because they want to see what will happen, want to verify an anticipation of what will happen if they act on an object in a particular way, or desire to experiment in a way that involves some combination of these two reasons (DeVries & Kohlberg, 1987; Kamii & DeVries, 1978/1993). While acting on objects during physical-knowledge activities, children have the possibility of constructing correspondence between actions and reactions, and these gradually evolve into causal explanations. DeVries (1992; DeVries & Kohlberg, 1987) has also presented physical-knowledge activities as an example of how Piaget's structural and constructivist components can be integrated through assessment of children's cognitive progress with physical-knowledge activities.

Examples of physical-knowledge activities include activities with rollers, inclines, pendulums, and water play. *Physical Knowledge in Preschool Education: Implications of Piaget's Theory* (Kamii & DeVries, 1978/1993) provides detailed discussion of physical-knowledge activities, guidelines for their creation, and teaching principles. There is an obvious correlation between physical-knowledge activities and science education, but Kamii and DeVries (1978/1993; DeVries & Kohlberg, 1987) emphasized that the objective of physical-knowledge activities is not to teach scientific concepts, principles, or explanations, but rather to build the foundation for physics and chemistry.

Kamii and DeVries (1978/1993) identified three types of physical-knowledge activities:

- activities that involve the movement of objects, for example, children's actions on objects to make them move by pulling, pushing, kicking, swinging, and so forth;
- activities that entail changes in objects, including cooking and mixing paints; and
- activities, such as sinking and floating objects or shadow play, that share elements of the first two activity types but cannot be neatly categorized.

Good physical-knowledge activities, regardless of which type, are characterized by four criteria that enhance the possibility that children will be able to construct relationships between their actions and an object's reactions: (a) Children must be able to produce phenomena by their own actions, (b) children must be able to vary their actions, (c) reactions of objects must be observable, and (d) the reaction of the object must be immediate (DeVries & Kohlberg, 1987; Kamii & De-Vries, 1978/1993).

Group Games. Whereas physical-knowledge activities promote children's construction of knowledge about the physical world, Kamii and DeVries (1980) conceived group games to promote children's adaptation (in the Piagetian sense) to the social world. Group games are geared particularly toward development of the twin objectives of autonomy and cooperation. In conjunction with her revised thinking, DeVries later elaborated their rationale and objectives and described stages in children's way of playing games (DeVries, 1992; DeVries & Kohlberg, 1987).

The sociomoral objective of the Kamii-DeVries approach is long-term progress in the structure or stage of moral reasoning. The stages outline the developmental construction of inner moral convictions about what is good and necessary in one's relationships with others. Generally,

> . . . the sociomoral goal is for children to develop autonomous feelings of obligation (or moral necessity) about relations with others that are not just dictates accepted from adults. Rather, a feeling of moral necessity reflects an internal system of personal convictions. Such a personal system is autonomous in so far as it leads to beliefs and behavior that are self-regulated rather than other-regulated. It is co-operative insofar as it reflects a view of the self as part of a system of reciprocal social relations. (DeVries & Kohlberg, 1987, p. 121)

Group games foster interactions based on conventional rules that specify how players relate to each other and the preestablished climax that is to be achieved. The relations between players should be interdependent, opposed, and collaborative (DeVries & Kohlberg, 1987; Kamii & DeVries, 1980). Using their example of the game of Hide and Seek, the roles of "hider" and "seeker" are interdependent; neither can exist without the other. The roles are opposed because the intentions of the hider and seeker are to prevent what the other is attempting to do. Finally, the roles are collaborative because the game depends on the players mutually agreeing on the rules and abiding by them.

Group games promote autonomy by providing a context in which children can voluntarily accept and submit themselves to rules. Importantly, however, these rules are self-imposed by the players rather than dictated by adults (at least as implemented in the Kamii-DeVries approach). Development toward autonomy, and away from heteronomy, is prompted by children's freedom to choose to follow or not follow rules, reflect on the consequences, and eventually to understand that the reasons for rules are rooted in maintaining desired relations with others. Group games are particularly facilitative in this regard because the egalitarian relationships among peers remove the force of coercion, permitting autonomous co-operation to emerge and develop, fueled by interest in playing with others.

The Kamii-DeVries approach identifies eight types of group games, which are detailed in *Group Games in Early Education; Implications of Piaget's Theory* (Kamii & DeVries, 1980):

- aiming games,
- races,

- chasing games,
- hiding games,
- guessing games,
- games involving verbal commands,
- card games, and
- board games.

Educationally worthwhile games provide something interesting and challenging for children to figure out how to do, allow children to judge their own success, and permit children to participate actively throughout the game. Their value is achieved when teachers reduce their use of authority, encourage children to regulate the game, and modify games as needed in terms of how children think so there will be something they want to try and figure out. In addition to their contributions to sociomoral development, each type of group game promotes cognitive development in distinctive ways.

Traditional School Curricula. Finally, the Kamii-DeVries approach offers a constructivist perspective on traditional objectives in arithmetic and reading and writing. Piaget and his colleagues amassed extensive research and theory on children's construction of number. As a result, this aspect of the Kamii-DeVries approach drew from a deep knowledge base and presumed a great deal of theoretical understanding. According to DeVries (DeVries & Kohlberg, 1987), Piaget's work suggests that knowledge of number involves a single system of logical classes and relations that includes conservation of number, class inclusion, and seriation; specific numbers can be understood fully only as a part of this system.

The child's construction of number and the development of logic progress in a coordinated fashion; hence, their development is interdependent. The cognitive structures available during concrete operations enable children to understand many specific number and spatial concepts. From an educational standpoint, this implies that by promoting children's cognitive structures, teachers simultaneously are advancing children's construction of number and spatial concepts.

All of these aspects of number, however, are logico-mathematical in nature. Thus, numerical reasoning cannot be achieved through direct instruction nor can it be learned from action on objects. Children's understandings of number result from a gradual organization of relations that is the result of their mental construction. Based on these understandings, math education should focus on the development of children's general logical ability and cognitive structures before attempting to introduce numerical questions and formal symbolism. In addition, children need opportunities to invent mathematical relations, a possibility that is enhanced within a classroom where the teacher is knowledgeable about the developmental nature of children's mistakes and cultivates an atmosphere conducive to thinking (DeVries & Kohlberg, 1987).

Kamii and DeVries first outlined their approach to the teaching of number in *Piaget, Children, and Number* (Kamii & DeVries, 1976). This work was revised by Kamii in 1982 and then the approach was extended into first grade (Kamii & De-Clark, 1985). Kamii has since continued her research into the second and third grades (Kamii, 1994, 2000; Kamii & Joseph, 1989). Because construction of number cannot be taught directly or through physical-knowledge activities, the Kamii-DeVries approach promotes young children's construction of number through classroom activities of daily living and through group games.[7]

Teachers are encouraged to take advantage of routine situations in which number is a natural issue and to create situations in which children need to think about number in order to accomplish something they want. Examples include the distribution of materials, the division of objects, the collection of things, keeping records, clean-up, and opportunities for voting. In each of these instances, teachers avoid providing needed answers (for example, by asking how many napkins are needed so every child at snack has one or how to divide a deck of cards so all the players have an equal number) so children can be confronted with the opportunity to figure out the relationships involved. Similarly, in group games that involve number, such as board games with dice and spinners or aiming games that involve score keeping, children are given the opportunity to devise and negotiate their own system with peers.

DeVries and Kohlberg (1987) relied on the work by Ferreiro and Teberosky (1979/1982 especially) for their presentation of a constructivist perspective on reading and writing. Ferreiro was a student of Jean Piaget and Hermaine Sinclair at the University of Geneva. Based on their clinical study of children learning to read and write, Ferreiro and Teberosky conceptualized how children continually construct and refine their understandings about print and identified some of their constructive errors.

Ferreiro and Teberosky's work suggested that learning to read and write involves an active process of constructing and testing hypotheses about print. From this body of knowledge, DeVries and Kohlberg (1987) identified a list of 14 pedagogical principles, such as,

- begin with what a child knows,
- respect children's constructive errors and encourage their predictions and self-corrections,
- support children during times of conceptual conflict,
- expose children to written language in all its variety,
- foster social interaction about how to read and write,
- allow sufficient time for the constructive process, and
- encourage children to write in terms of their understandings.

For the most part, subject matter knowledge in the Kamii-DeVries approach is located in the content of constructivist activities. Reading, for example, is embedded in group games, cooking, and symbolic play. Science is represented in physical-knowledge activities; and elementary arithmetic is developed in group games and daily living activities. As already noted, DeVries and Kohlberg (1987) believed

---

[7]Kamii's work with children's construction of number, as noted previously, extends into the primary grades, but it is not part of the Kamii-DeVries approach, which is a preschool–kindergarten model. DeVries and Kohlberg (1987) acknowledged that Kamii's work substantially extends their own.

that teaching subject matter needed to begin with understanding how children think about subject matter, rather than with subject matter analysis. "Teaching informed by Piaget's theory must be based on knowledge of mental development within a subject-matter domain" (DeVries & Kohlberg, 1987, p. 381).

Expectations for Teachers

Kamii and DeVries presume that teachers are child centered, relate well to children, and understand how to manage a classroom and provide traditional nursery school activities. To successfully implement the Kamii-DeVries approach, teachers must also be able to execute a number of additional roles. Specifically, DeVries and Kohlberg (1987) identified four teacher functions: evaluator, organizer, collaborator, and stimulator.

As an evaluator, teachers are expected to have extensive knowledge of children and a thorough understanding of mental development in order to assess children's spontaneous activity, to appraise how a child is thinking about or understanding a particular interaction. And, in order to promote a child's intellectual reasoning, teachers need to be able to coordinate this knowledge with the provision of appropriate learning activities (organizer role) and questions that extend children's ideas and stimulate their reasoning in ways consistent with the type of knowledge involved (collaborator and stimulator roles). For example, if an interaction involved social-arbitrary knowledge, the teacher probably would respond with the correct answer, but if the interaction targeted physical knowledge, the teacher would encourage children to find the answer directly from an object's reaction to a physical action. If logical-mathematical knowledge was central, then the teacher would avoid providing any response and, instead, encourage mental reflection.

> Our view is that when children reason preoperationally, they are usually unable at that moment to correct themselves or to understand correction by others. . . . [O]perational thought evolves out of preoperational thought as the child becomes more and more conscious of new aspects to think about in situations in which interests motivate thinking. (DeVries & Kohlberg, 1987, p. 85)

Thus, teachers' decision-making skills are consequential. Actions based on their decisions serve as catalysts for children's development toward progressively higher levels of reasoning. Teachers need, therefore to be very knowledgeable about Piaget's theory, especially children's preoperational ways of interpreting experiences, and be able to convert their theoretical understandings into practical knowledge of individual children.

The Kamii-DeVries approach also argues the importance of creating egalitarian relationships with children. Not that teachers never exert their authority, especially when children's safety is in question. But children's active, mental construction of knowledge, as opposed to their passive acceptance of adults' conclusions, necessitates that teachers minimize their authority and respect children's ways of knowing.

Children are encouraged to take intellectual risks and develop their intellectual and moral autonomy—in effect, to construct personal rules of behavior for self-governance. Hence, children's interpretations of the moment are accepted and respected. Kamii and DeVries expressed concern that when adults impose their answers, children learn to distrust their ability to make sense of their own experiences (DeVries, 1997; DeVries & Kohlberg, 1987; DeVries & Zan, 1994, 1995; Kamii & DeVries, 1978/1993).

Without this supportive context, according to Kamii and DeVries, children learn to behave in ways that unthinkingly accept and conform to adult expectations. Piaget identified this type of social reasoning as heteronomous (DeVries & Kohlberg, 1987; Kamii & DeVries, 1978/1993, 1980). Children (and adults) with heteronomous attitudes tend to rely on others to inform their thinking and decision making. In Piaget's view, according to DeVries (1997), a life dominated by "the rules of others through a morality of obedience will never lead to the kind of reflection necessary for commitment to a set of internal or autonomous principles of moral judgement" (p. 5).

As noted earlier, neither Kamii nor DeVries reference their current work as the "Kamii-DeVries approach." Their approach no longer formally functions as a self-contained framework. They instead have aligned their independent investigations with the growing interest in "constructivist education" in early childhood, primary, secondary, and postsecondary classrooms.

As a result of their new alliance with constructivist education—versus the Kamii-DeVries approach—their investigations inform an emerging psychological tradition rather than define a program's scope of work. Kamii continues to investigate and refine the implications of Piaget's constructivism for understanding children's mathematical thinking (Kamii, 1994, 2000). DeVries has turned her attention to developing the ideas, set forth in collaboration with Lawrence Kohlberg (DeVries & Kohlberg, 1987), on the sociomoral climate of constructivist classrooms (DeVries, 1997; DeVries & Zan, 1994, 1995). Her current writing addresses the explicit role of teachers in fostering "cooperation among children by promoting their construction of emotional balance [for example, withholding judgment and seeking to understand the intentions of others] and coping abilities, interpersonal understanding, and moral values" (DeVries & Zan, 1994, p. 78). Development as the aim of education continues, however, to be a centerpiece of DeVries's thinking.

✂ THE HIGH/SCOPE CURRICULUM

Overview of the High/Scope Curriculum

The Preschool Curriculum. The first version of the High/Scope[8] Curriculum for preschool and K–3 emerged in 1962 and 1978, respectively. In 1964, when the Ypsilanti Perry Preschool Project came under the influence of Piagetian theory, its curriculum was named the Cognitively Oriented Curriculum. *The Cognitively Ori-*

---

[8]An interesting aside: the High/Scope name was invented by David Weikart and colleagues to connote "high" aspirations and a broad "scope" of interests. It was first used in conjunction with a summer camp for teens in the early 1960s (Weikart, 1990).

ented Curriculum: A Framework for Preschool Teachers by Weikart, Rogers, Adcock, and McClelland (1971) describes the resultant curriculum. At this point in its evolution, the curriculum gained its developmental focus. Teachers still were didactic in their interactions with children. Only now, instead of focusing on specific motor and perceptual skills, teachers taught specific Piagetian experimental tasks in hopes of accelerating children's progress to the next stage of cognitive development (Hohmann et al., 1979).

The third revision to the curriculum was presented in *Young Children in Action: A Manual for Preschool Educators* by Hohmann, Banet, and Weikart (1979). This version replaced the curriculum presented earlier in *The Cognitively Oriented Curriculum.* In this third phase, the notion of children as active learners and constructors of knowledge became central. This shift emerged, according to Hohmann et al. (1979), with the organization of the program around a set of "key experiences." This new organization freed teachers from their instructional focus and permitted them to share the process of developing learning experiences with children.

Higher level reasoning in domains of interest to Piaget remained the model's educational target, but now its advancement was fostered through active learning rather than direct instruction. In their description of the model's evolution, program designers noted, "in adopting the term 'key experiences,' High/Scope staff placed the emphasis on children's thinking abilities in varied contexts with new materials and challenging situations rather than on precisely timed interventions aimed at moving children from one level of development to the next" (Hohmann & Weikart, 1995, p. 300).

In 1995, the High/Scope Curriculum underwent a fourth revision resulting in *Educating Young Children: Active Learning Practices for Preschool and Child Care Programs* (Hohmann & Weikart, 1995). *Educating Young Children* is a manual for those wishing to implement the High/Scope Curriculum with preschool-aged children. Topics include room arrangement, materials, daily routine, staffing needs, and activities and teaching strategies associated with each of 10 key experience categories. The importance of working with families also is emphasized. Considerable detail will be provided about the differences between the latest two versions of the model in order to document the model's evolution.

In the fourth version, active learning has been elevated from its designation as a key experience, to become the centerpiece of the curriculum. Active learning is valued not only for stimulating the child's construction of knowledge, but for promoting dispositions associated with the child's role as an active learner. In the process, the High/Scope Curriculum has added operating principles similar to those found in the Kamii-DeVries approach.

Active learning is defined "as learning in which the child, by acting on objects and interacting with people, ideas, and events, constructs new understanding" (Hohmann & Weikart, 1995, p. 17). Active learning is characterized by four elements that describe the nature of the child's involvement with the learning experience:

1. *The child's direct actions on objects.* The physical activity of acting upon objects provides the child with something "real" to think about and discuss with others.

2. *The child's reflection on the outcomes of her actions.* Action alone is not sufficient for learning to occur. Active learning must involve the child's mental activity of interpreting outcomes and fitting interpretations into a more complete understanding of her immediate world.

3. *The child's interests as the source of learning.* The child's personal interests, questions, and intentions serve as the catalyst for exploration, invention, and construction of new knowledge.

4. *The child's discovery of compelling problems.* Real-life problems encountered by actions on objects and interactions with people, and the arising need to reconcile new experiences with what the child knows of her world, stimulates learning and development (Hohmann & Weikart, 1995, pp. 17–18).

Hohmann & Weikart (1995) summarize these four elements as (a) direct action on objects; (b) reflections on action; (c) intrinsic motivation, invention, and generativity; and (d) problem solving (p. 17).

Initially, the High/Scope Curriculum primarily addressed issues of cognitive development (Hohmann et al., 1979). Social and emotional development were nurtured only indirectly. The reasoning had been that "it's easier and more productive to focus directly on, say, children's planning than on group dynamics, on classifying objects and events than on interpreting fantasies—the one is concrete and intelligible, the other abstract and esoteric" (Hohmann et al., 1979, p. 1). Social and emotional development were indirectly addressed through open acceptance of children and their parents and through the curriculum's structure. Positive social and emotional development were appreciated as positive by-products of the model's cognitive orientation. Children's sense of personal responsibility, self-worth, and independence, for example, was nurtured via children's direct involvement in planning and assessing their activities and teachers' concerns with engaging children in meaningful learning opportunities. Now, however, in response to their own research highlighting the significance of positive social and emotional development to later personal and academic success (see Schweinhart & Weikart, 1993, 1997a, 1997b; Schweinhart et al., 1986), the "by-products" of learning have become the critical outcomes to be fostered through the active learning process:

> The High/Scope Curriculum works because it empowers children to follow through on their interests purposefully and creatively. In the process, children develop initiative, interest, curiosity, resourcefulness, independence, and responsibility—habits of mind that will serve them well throughout their lives. (Hohmann & Weikart, 1995, p. 10)

Program designers attribute their new emphasis on active learning to their research comparing the long-term effects of the High/Scope Curriculum with other curriculum models (discussed in greater detail in this chapter and in Chapter 6). As a result of the changes, movement from preoperational to concrete operations no longer is viewed as the curriculum's primary outcome for children. Instead, the dispositions associated with active learning—initiative, reflection on actions, intrinsic motivation, and problem solving—are now valued as the significant child outcomes of the High/Scope Curriculum.

The most recent version of the High/Scope Curriculum assimilates the major content of its predecessor. But what differs—and thus what is spotlighted—is the greater importance accorded the dispositions associated with active learning as the critical component of school readiness. This emphasis further distances the High/Scope Curriculum from academically directed programs such as the Direct Instruction model and Success for All. As a result of their longitudinal studies, High/Scope's program designers have concluded that the most important purpose of their curriculum is to set the stage for the child's successful "life pattern" as a self-supporting and law-abiding citizen through promoting the child's sense of personal and social responsibility, independence, and goal-oriented approach to life (Weikart, 1995, p. 299).

The K–3 Curriculum. The decision to extend the curriculum into the primary grades in 1978 came about because of an invitation from the U.S. Office of Education to participate in Project Follow Through and the urging to do so from several public school districts. Weikart and his associates initially were hesitant to become involved with Project Follow Through because they questioned public schools' willingness to change their ways of educating children. Now High/Scope credits its involvement with Project Follow Through as instrumental to the development and expansion of the K–3 curriculum (Wallgren, 1990; Weikart, 1990; Weikart, Hohmann, & Rhine, 1981).

High/Scope's curriculum developers initially focused on revising their preschool program to suit the needs of K–3 children and teachers in public school settings. They quickly confronted the challenge of effecting individual and systemic change. When funding for Project Follow Through declined, so did High/Scope's involvement with K–3 curriculum development. Their learnings from this experience, though, were carefully considered when interest in developmentally appropriate curricula for kindergarten and primary grades reemerged in the mid-1980s.

Interest in resurrecting and revising their K–3 curriculum came from two sources: (a) agencies implementing the High/Scope preschool curriculum that were interested in extending the curriculum upward and (b) the push toward making developmentally appropriate curriculum available to all children in early childhood programs, not just those living in poverty.

High/Scope staff knew, though, from their experiences with the K–3 curriculum in Project Follow Through that their existing program needed refinement and expansion. The decision not to simply rewrite *Young Children in Action* (the version of the curriculum at that time) using public school vernacular was a strategic one. High/Scope staff consciously chose to extend and reorganize the K–3 curriculum in a way that would be appealing to, and implementable in, public schools. This decision was made in order to increase the possibility of developmentally appropriate practices in school settings (Wallgren, 1990; this is further discussed shortly). As of 1998, the High/Scope staff provides "full-service to 27 schools and partial services for more than 500 schools. In addition, several thousand schools use High/Scope materials" (American Institutes for Research, 1999).

Materials for the updated K–3 curriculum, which were pilot-tested in High/Scope's ongoing Follow Through programs, began to appear in 1990 and were completed in 1995. There now are six K–3 curriculum guides in the High/Scope K–3 Curriculum Series:

- *Foundations in Elementary Education: Movement* (Weikart & Carlton, 1995)
- *Foundations in Elementary Education: Music* (Carlton & Weikart, 1994)
- *Language and Literacy* (Maehr, 1991)
- *Mathematics* (Hohmann, 1991)
- *Science* (Blackwell & Hohmann, 1991)
- *Learning Environment* (Hohmann & Buckleitner, 1992a)

These six curriculum guides describe the physical setting, daily schedule, and teacher–child strategies. Four of the guides are accompanied by a video that demonstrates the curriculum in action in primary classrooms, presents the theoretical premises of the High/Scope approach, details the supportive research, and describes specific aspects of the curriculum's implementation. Also included are extensive lists of suggested activities. The curriculum's stated thrust is intellectual maturation and conceptual understanding (Wallgren, 1990).

High/Scope's preschool curriculum is probably best known, but both the preschool and primary curricula have been replicated nationally since 1968. The preschool curriculum has been implemented in rural, urban, and suburban settings and has been used with mildly handicapped, economically disadvantaged, and bilingual children, as well as typically developing middle-class preschoolers and primary grade children. The preschool curriculum now is being used internationally, as well. Because of their interest in, and commitment to, dissemination, High/Scope Curriculum developers have been particularly sensitive to the necessity of describing their program in terms that are clear to practitioners (Hohmann et al., 1979; Hohmann & Weikart, 1995).

Organization of the Curriculum. Both levels of the curriculum are organized around small-group, teacher-initiated interactions, and child-initiated activities. The content of these activities and interactions is informed by a set of "key experiences" derived primarily from Piaget's description of cognitive development. Teachers, often in teams of two, use the list of key experiences to help ensure that they recognize and plan for interactions and activities that advance children's cognitive development. The curriculum, however, is not a package with sets of consumable workbooks or prescribed activities—a disclaimer the program architects frequently emphasize (Epstein et al., 1996; Hohmann et al., 1979; Hohmann & Buckleitner, 1992b; Hohmann & Weikart, 1995; Weikart & Schweinhart, 1987, 1993). Rather, the curriculum is a set of recommended activities framed by a daily routine, learning experiences linked to Piaget's theory and description of cognitive development, and a programmatic emphasis on child initiative, problem solving, and representation.

The High/Scope Curriculum draws from Piaget's theory of cognitive development and researchers working within a Piagetian framework, plus the instructional techniques of Sara Smilansky (1968), an Israeli psychologist. Smilansky helped the High/Scope staff integrate some of the traditions of early childhood curriculum, especially sociodramatic play, that were being ignored during the 1960s because they did not directly address children's cognitive development (Hohmann et al., 1979). She also supplied the three-part sequence of children's planning, working, and self-evaluation that became the organizing principle for the daily routine. The program designers' years of practical experience also are credited as a critical contributor to the model's development.

Weikart and his associates selected Piaget's theory as a framework because, at the time, it seemed to be the most complete and coherent theory available for addressing cognitive development and ensured them of creating a developmentally valid curriculum (Hohmann et al., 1979; Weikart & Schweinhart, 1987). They developed curriculum strategies and goals based on what they saw as Piaget's most salient principles, "rather than on the esoteric, controversial fine-points" (Hohmann et al., 1979, p. 2). Piaget's theory of cognitive development is used by the High/Scope Curriculum as an overarching conceptual framework for selecting learning experiences that will enhance children's cognitive development. In contrast to the Kamii-DeVries approach, Weikart and his associates have not extensively and intimately studied Piagetian theory for its educational implications. In fact, they caution just the opposite. "We urge that (our curriculum) not be viewed as a narrowly Piagetian curriculum but rather as a general framework for an approach to education that stresses problem-solving and decision-making by both child and adult" (Hohmann et al., 1979, p. vi).

In particular, the High/Scope Curriculum extracted two basic principles from Piagetian theory (Hohmann et al., 1979; Hohmann & Weikart, 1995; Weikart & Schweinhart, 1987). These two basic principles define the process and content components of the High/Scope Curriculum:

1. Human beings develop their intellectual capacities in predictable sequences. The High/Scope Curriculum is organized around the notion that learning progresses in terms of stages identified by Piaget's theory of cognitive development and description of the preoperational and concrete operational child (approximately 3–8 years and 8–12 years of age). Piaget's description of age-related cognitive changes helps set programmatic limits on the range of tasks children are expected to master at any given age level, and
2. Changes in logical reasoning occur as a result of changes in a child's underlying thought structures. These changes are not directly teachable; they are the result of children's active construction of new understandings. Weikart and his associates concluded that changes in these underlying thought structures represented the preparation children required for effective school learning (Weikart et al., 1981).

The High/Scope Curriculum conceptualizes the teacher's responsibility as supporting children's development. This is accomplished by promoting children's active learning. Children's active learning is so important because it is the catalyst for cognitive restructuring and hence for development. For similar reasons, the High/Scope Curriculum stresses the importance of children's initiative and the shared responsibilities of children and teachers in defining classroom learning experiences. Curriculum developers contend that the curriculum is neither laissez-faire nor directive:

> The supportive climate advocated by High/Scope prevails in an early childhood setting where adults and children share control over the teaching and learning process. In this climate, adults provide an effective balance between the freedom children must have to explore as active learners and the limits needed to permit them to feel secure in the classroom or center. . . . Adults make their presence known by joining children as *partners* who are genuinely interested in and committed to watching, listening to, conversing with, and working with children. (Hohmann & Weikart, 1995, p. 49, emphasis in original)

The High/Scope Curriculum provides a framework for adults so they can support children's development through active learning (Hohmann & Weikart, 1995). It is presumed that facilitating preschool children's natural development will prepare them scholastically for kindergarten and first grade, especially if economically disadvantaged (Hohmann et al., 1979; Schweinhart & Weikart, 1997a, 1997b; Weikart, 1988; Weikart & Schweinhart, 1987). The K–3 curriculum promotes children's academic growth through developmentally appropriate learning experiences that develop problem-solving and verbal and written communication skills.

The important cognitive changes that occur during the preoperational and concrete operational stages of development provide the basis for the curriculum's content. The preoperational child is described as being able to mentally represent her actions and experiences, communicate verbally with others, reflect on her own actions, recall past events, predict consequences in familiar cause-and-effect sequences, mentally resolve simple, everyday problems, and distinguish symbols or representations from the things for which they stand. These mental processes still are intuitive, however, and have not yet been organized into the integrated systems characteristic of the next stage of cognitive development.

The mental operations preoperational children needed to advance to the next stage were a primary focus of the 1979 High/Scope Curriculum. The 1995 revision, however, places less emphasis on the child's advancement toward the Piagetian stage of concrete operations (which is described under the heading "The Preschool Curriculum Framework"), and instead speaks more broadly of "developmental change" (Hohmann & Weikart, 1995).

Finally, in addition to active learning as an important learning mechanism, the High/Scope Curriculum recognizes social and communication skills as strategies that facilitate development of logical reasoning. It also emphasizes the important role of *representation*. Weikart attributes the importance of representation to Piaget's statement that children acquire knowledge through a representational process and to the work of others that link children's representation of ideas and objects with their cognitive development[9] (Weikart et al., 1981).

---

[9]The stress on representation has been criticized by DeVries as a misinterpretation of Piaget's thinking by confusing representational acts with a network of coordinated mental actions underlying specific knowledge and reasoning, in effect confusing representation with mental operations (DeVries & Kohlberg, 1987, pp. 54–55).

Because of its perceived importance, representation is integrated into the model's daily routine, known as "plan-do-review" (which is described under the heading of "Daily Routine"). The High/Scope Curriculum emphasizes the representational process as a powerful mechanism for helping children conceptualize and consolidate their understandings across activities and subject matter domains. In addition, representation provides the model an important linkage to traditional academic exercises in reading and mathematics (Hohmann et al., 1979; Hohmann & Weikart, 1995; Weikart et al., 1981).

From these and other characteristics of preoperational and concrete operational thinking, in conjunction with the beliefs that active learning, social and communication skills, and representation promote development, the designers identified "key experiences." Key experiences serve as guideposts for teacher planning and for evaluating the preschool curriculum. Key experiences for the K–3 curriculum also include the developmental sequence of subject matter. Fundamental skills and concepts in the subject areas are articulated as emerging capacities; these, in turn, provide the sequence of key experiences in each curriculum area (Hohmann & Buckleitner, 1992a, 1992b; Hohmann & Weikart, 1995).

In the most recent revision (Hohmann & Weikart, 1995), the key experiences were expanded and revised. They were expanded to include key experiences on social and moral development, derived from the work of developmental psychologists Lawrence Kohlberg, Erik Erikson, Howard Gardner, Sara Smilansky, and Stanley Greenspan (Hohmann & Weikart, 1995). They were revised so children's social and emotional development could assume a more central position in the model.

The Preschool Curriculum Framework

Key Experiences. Key experiences were designed to provide teachers a way to think about the curriculum and free them from the use of workbooks and scope and sequence charts. They permitted interactions with children to be more individually responsive (Weikart & Schweinhart, 1987). "The key experiences should each appear many times—they are not goals to 'attain' and check off but are more like vitamins and other nutrients: their repeated presence in many different forms is important for good 'intellectual nutrition'" (Hohmann et al., 1979, p. 60).

Key experiences for the preschool curriculum initially were organized under the headings of active learning, language, experiencing and representing, classification, seriation, number spatial relations, and time. To reflect the model's new emphasis on social learning and recent interest in literacy development, key experiences have been reorganized into 10 categories: creative representation, language and literacy, initiative and social relations, movement, music, classification, seriation, number, space, and time (Hohmann & Weikart, 1995). These categories are further divided into types of learning experiences that promote cognitive growth within a particular domain. For example, key experiences in classification include:

• exploring and describing similarities, differences, and the attributes of things;
• distinguishing and describing shapes;

- sorting and matching;
- using and describing something in several ways;
- holding more than one attribute in mind at a time;
- distinguishing between "some" and "all"; and
- describing characteristics something does not possess or the class it does not belong to (Hohmann & Weikart, 1995, p. 449)

Teachers originally were encouraged to sequence classroom activities around a key experience so activities moved from concrete to abstract, from simple to complex, and from the "here and now" to more distant events (Hohmann et al., 1979). Teachers continue to be reminded of the general sequence of development, but they no longer are urged to use these experiences to help children acquire more advanced mental operations. Key experiences now serve to

> . . . broaden adults' understanding of what children do, think about, and enjoy. This appreciation of the complexity of children's pursuits enables adults to support children's emerging capabilities with appropriate materials and interactions rather than to focus on children's mistakes and deficits (Hohmann & Weikart, 1995, p. 304)

Activities and interactions involving key experiences are not mutually exclusive; any single activity might incorporate several key experiences. Key experiences are not intended as concepts for direct instruction or individual focus. They are designed as reminders to teachers of the content knowledge and intellectual processes inherent in children's activity and accessible to their facilitation. They can be realized through an infinite number of activities across a range of developmental levels and can be initiated either by children or adults.

In addition to providing structure to the curriculum, key experiences provide a mechanism for maintaining the model's openness to new possibilities. As new curriculum is added in areas such as computers or music and movement, High/Scope staff have a mechanism for outlining additional experiences (Hohmann & Weikart, 1995; Weikart & Schweinhart, 1987, 1993). Further, key experiences provide a framework for practitioners in the 19 countries where High/Scope now has training projects (Epstein et al., 1996), demonstrating that "child development occurs in similar progressions in all cultures and geographic locations" (Hohmann & Weikart, 1995, p. 302)

The key experiences also are linked to child and program assessment. They provide the framework adults use to observe each child (Hohmann & Weikart, 1995; Weikart & Schweinhart, 1993). The High/Scope Child Observation Record (COR) takes each of the key experience areas and divides them into developmental steps; these are formatted as a checklist that the teacher completes on each child once or twice a year, thereby providing a developmental record of each child's progress.

The COR was revised in 1992. Now for children ages 2.5 to 6 years, it includes six developmental domains: initiative, social relations, creative representation, music and movement, language and literacy, and logic and mathematics. These domains, in turn, are organized into five assessment levels, sequenced from low to high (Schweinhart & McNair, 1991; Weikart & Schweinhart, 1993). According to Schweinhart and McNair (1991):

> Good measures of child development provide parents and the taxpaying public with information on whether their investment in early childhood programs is paying off. In addition, by mapping out the various dimensions of child development for everyone concerned, good measures present an operational definition of goals for the care and education of young children. (p. 5)

Hence, key experiences were designed as an organizational tool for teacher planning as well as program accountability. They provide teachers a framework for planning educational experiences, extending children's involvement with activities, and assessing children's developmental progress, which, in turn, provides an accountability measure of program success (Hohmann & Weikart, 1995; Weikart & Schweinhart, 1987).

Daily Routine. Whereas key experiences are a central feature of the curriculum for teachers, the "plan-do-review" sequence is the "centerpiece of the High/Scope active learning approach" for children (Hohmann & Weikart, 1995, p. 167). As stressed by program designers, "We cannot emphasize enough the importance we place on the plan-do-review process in assuring successful implementation of the High/Scope active learning approach" (Hohmann & Weikart, 1995, p. 167).

The plan-do-review sequence, in conjunction with small-group time, large-group time, and outdoor play, make up the daily routine. The plan-do-review cycle is the curriculum device that permits children to exercise their individual choices about activities without excluding the teacher from the learning process. The plan-do-review cycle also is the primary means through which representation is integrated into the curriculum. Regardless of when other parts of the daily routine are implemented, the planning time, work time (including clean-up), and recall follow each other in sequence.

Although planning time, work time, and recall are distinct segments of the daily routine, they also occur throughout children's work time. Depending on her interest, a child might plan, do, and recall several activities with a teacher during a single work time.

During planning time, children tell the teacher of their choice activity and what they intend to do. In the previous version of the High/Scope Curriculum (Hohmann et al., 1979), program designers contended that this process helped children form mental images of their ideas and develop a plan of action. As Weikart and Schweinhart noted in 1993, "Children make choices and decisions all the time, but most programs seldom have them think about these decisions in a systematic way or help them realize the possibilities and consequences of their choices" (p. 198). At the same time, planning time provides teachers an opportunity to gauge and extend children's thinking.

The current version identifies the planning process less in terms of cognitive outcomes and more in terms of its contributions to children's sense of "initiative and enterprise" (Hohmann & Weikart, 1995, p. 168), including their opportunities to

- establish a problem or goal,
- imagine and anticipate actions,
- express personal intentions and interests,
- shape intentions into purposes,
- deliberate, and
- make ongoing modifications (pp. 168–170).

This shift in emphasis responds to findings from High/Scope's longitudinal research showing the importance of these behaviors to children's future productivity as adults.

Teachers are encouraged to support the child's planning process by asking careful questions of the child about "what" the plan entails and "how" it will be carried out. Teachers are urged to use a form of conversational "turn-taking," always being attentive to following the child's idea. A sound understanding of the key experiences helps teachers appreciate the child's plan in relation to the abilities being promoted by the High/Scope Curriculum.

The "do" part of the cycle is work time. High/Scope classrooms are arranged with learning centers or work areas. The four basic work areas in the earlier version were a house area, block area, art area, and quiet area. In the current revision (Hohmann & Weikart, 1995), work areas have been expanded to include a sand and water area, block area, house area, art area, toy area, book and writing area, woodworking area, music and movement area, and computer area. During work time, which is supposed to be the longest single time period of the day, children are involved in implementing their plans in various areas (for example, following through with a plan in the block area, engaged in the house area, or reading a book in the quiet area). During this time, teachers are coached to "ask questions sparingly" (p. 216). Through the use of carefully selected questions, a child can "consolidate what he knows and recognize how he knows it" (p. 217).

Clean-up time, which immediately follows work time, is considered an integral part of work time. Formerly, clean-up time was viewed as another opportunity for children to engage in classification and sorting activities. Children, for example, returned materials to their proper place, often by superimposing an object over a matching visual image, such as laying a spatula on top of a corresponding paper cut-out. Clean-up time now is viewed as an opportunity for teachers to encourage problem solving (for example, how to save a block construction for later work) or initiate "put-away" games that involve other children in a cooperative effort (for example, "setting up a 'fire-brigade' line in which items are passed from child to child until they reach their shelf or container" (Hohmann & Weikart, 1995, p. 223).

Recall time occurs with the teacher and a small group of children. During this time, children represent their experiences for their teacher and peers using a variety of techniques, for example, verbalizing, drawing, or pantomiming what occurred during their work time. Teachers can choose to focus children's recall on different aspects of their experience, such as recounting the names of other children involved in their plans, sharing any problems they encountered, or providing an overview of their activities.

Recall is intended to bring closure to children's planning and work, create relationships in children's minds between plans and actions, and provide opportunities for children to represent their thinking (Hohmann et al., 1979; Hohmann & Weikart, 1995). It also is recognized as an occasion for children to make public their accomplishments.

In an interesting shift from an early emphasis on the ways children are different from adults, Weikart and his associates now link recall time to the practices of adults, and to the long-term benefits of certain skills and "habits of mind":

> Remembering and reflecting on their [children's] original intentions, associating plans with actions and the outcomes of these actions, and talking with others about meaningful experiences are important to the intellectual and social-emotional life of all of us, not just children. These mental and social processes allow us to search through the past for clues to the present and future. Recalling events and experiences is a skill that will benefit children throughout their lives. (Hohmann & Weikart, 1995, p. 228)

During small-group time, teachers present an activity in which all the children participate. Usually, at least two small-group times are occurring simultaneously. Because of the small group size, children can actively participate in the activity, and teachers have a focused time during which they can observe children's capabilities and developmental progress (Hohmann et al., 1979). Small-group time is also now valued for bringing children together for social experiences. Working with the same materials, children are encouraged to share ideas and to help and learn from one another (Hohmann & Weikart, 1995).

Large-group time (referred to as "circle time" in the 1979 version) is a time when all the children and adults gather for shared activity. Circle time originally was defined as a brief time for teachers to provide "key experiences in a social setting," including finger plays, brief games, and movement exercises (Hohmann et al., 1979, p. 96). However, large-group time now is envisioned as a time to promote children's social and emotional development by creating

- a repertoire of common experiences,
- a sense of community,
- group membership and leadership, and
- group problem-solving experiences (Hohmann & Weikart, 1995, p. 268).

Outside time provides an opportunity for children to engage in energetic play, and explore the natural world and the neighborhood (Hohmann & Weikart, 1995). Teachers are encouraged to appreciate the benefits of outdoor exercise to children's health and well-being, as well as notice further opportunities for children to have key experiences.

Throughout the daily routine, teachers are observers, assessors, and guides. In the 1979 version of the model, teacher questioning was viewed as a primary way to extend children's logical thinking (Hohmann et al., 1979). To do this effectively, teachers needed to recognize the key experiences embedded in children's activity, be knowledgeable about a child's current developmental status, and pose open-ended questions to encourage problem solving and independent thinking. Proponents of the High/Scope Curriculum argued that these interactions distinguished a cognitive-developmental approach from conventional early childhood programs. Even though children's activities and their organization are derived from a traditional child development approach (similar to the Kamii–DeVries approach), teachers were encouraged to direct children's active learning through questions rather than waiting for it to emerge spontaneously (Hohmann et al., 1979; Hohmann & Weikart, 1995; Weikart & Schweinhart, 1987, 1993).

Reflecting new appreciation for children's initiative, teachers now are cautioned to ask questions sparingly (Hohmann & Weikart, 1995). Teachers are given a broader range of strategies for listening, observing, and reflecting on a child's actions and representations. These additional strategies are designed to promote the teacher's appreciation and understanding of the developmental benefits of active learning when it is child initiated. Prior emphasis on the teacher's role in using questions to promote cognitive development has been diminished. Guided by the framework of key experiences within the various categories, teachers are instead encouraged to support children's dispositions toward initiative, responsibility, independence, curiosity, friendliness, and cooperation (Weikart, 1995). These traits now are viewed as the direct outcomes of a well-designed and implemented curriculum.

Finally, the 1995 revision of the High/Scope Curriculum includes a significant shift in thinking about teacher/family relationships (Hohmann & Weikart, 1995). In the earlier version of the model, the primary responsibility of teachers was to establish positive relationships with parents, and provide information about child development and the classroom curriculum (Hohmann et al., 1979). In the revised curriculum, teachers are discouraged from assuming a deficit approach to families and children, and encouraged, instead, to be self-reflective about their own beliefs and values about child rearing, and to create a climate of family support that is respectful of diversity.

The K–3 Curriculum Framework

The K–3 curriculum is an upward extension of the preschool curriculum. The guiding principles from Piaget's theory remain intact, and the preschool daily routine (plan-do-review and small- and large-group times), classroom design, and manipulative materials are extended into the primary grades. The K–3 curriculum presumes a standard public school class size of 25 children with one teacher. Active learning and child-initiated and individualized learning still are emphasized.

Work areas and key experiences are keyed to the subject matter areas of math, language and literacy, and science and reflect the grade level structure of public schools. In the area of mathematics, for example, almost 100 developmentally sequenced key experiences are identified. Suggested work areas in first grade include a reading/writing area, math area, computer area, art area, and construction area; or work areas might be organized around a theme, such as book making. Small-group instruction during small-group workshops (the term used for small-group time)—versus teaching to the whole class—and cooperative projects are encouraged. During small-group workshops, teachers plan activities to present new skills and concepts and introduce projects and problem situations. There may be two or more workshop periods during a day. In addition to mathematics, language and literacy, and science, three additional subject areas—movement, music, and computers—are incorporated into the curriculum (Hohmann & Buckleitner, 1992b; Wallgren, 1990).

Key experiences in the K–3 curriculum are structured as detailed sequences of developmental milestones. Similar to key experiences in the preschool curriculum, they are not intended as content for direct instruction. Rather, they are introduced to teachers as experiences children should encounter repeatedly in interactions with materials, teachers, and other children (Hohmann, 1991).

The level of detail found in the key experiences permits them to serve as a teacher's guide for planning appropriate activities and assessing children's developmental progress. The carefully sequenced detail is seen as especially important for K–3 teachers used to relying on workbooks and instructional guides.

Based on High/Scope's experiences with Project Follow Through and the prevalent criticism that developmental programs lack focus, the key experiences are accompanied by specific activity ideas, teaching suggestions, and instructional strategies. High/Scope staff hopes thereby to demonstrate to schools that developmentally sequenced, age-appropriate education can be systematic (Hohmann & Buckleitner, 1992b; Wallgren, 1990).

Serving as Change Agents Through Program Dissemination

In his remarks celebrating High/Scope's 20th anniversary, Weikart (1990) asserted, "We're trying to put in place nationwide a high-quality program that has been validated by 30 years of research. We know the program works; we know we can change children's lives for the better; we *have* to deliver" (p. 14, emphasis in original). The High/Scope Educational Research Foundation is Weikart's vehicle for fulfilling this aspiration.

Weikart launched the foundation in 1970 as the complexities of his project work, and its potential national and international scope, became evident (Weikart et al., 1981). The foundation is a center for research, curriculum development, professional training, and public advocacy. Its programs focus on children from infancy through adolescence. In addition to its work with the High/Scope preschool and K–3 curriculum, it sponsors, among other things, an adolescent summer camp and the Ypsilanti-Carnegie Infant Education Project.

Through its years of developing the High/Scope Curriculum, researching its effectiveness, and implementing it in classrooms, the foundation has acquired extensive knowledge regarding program development and implementation. They have been especially sensitive to the value of clearly framing their curriculum's benefits to education and public policy makers. Their presentations on the economic benefits of well-developed early childhood programs, especially their own model, has capitalized on society's implicit view of early childhood education as an instrument of social reform and has shaped public interpretation of early childhood education as a cost-effective social investment.

Yet, they also know the frustration of trying to effect and sustain change. "A common problem in education," according to Weikart (1990), "is that after a few years, the quality of any program installed diminishes" (p. 14). As a result, finding ways to maintain high-quality early childhood programs has become a central thrust for the foundation.

The foundation offers extensive professional training opportunities around its preschool and K–3 curriculum. Professional supports include

- one- and two-day workshops, week-long institutes, and multiple-week programs either at High/Scope Foundation headquarters in Ypsilanti, Michigan, or on-site;
- in-service training;
- consultation and planning;
- a training of trainers program;
- an annual High/Scope Registry Conference that serves as a network and support system for High/Scope teachers, trainers, and administrators; and
- extensive publications and videos published by the High/Scope Press, which was established in 1978. The High/Scope Press also publishes a magazine entitled *High/Scope ReSource* and *Extensions,* a subscription newsletter for practitioners (High/Scope Educational Research, 1999).

Although the High/Scope training and materials have played an important role in informing teachers and administrators about the High/Scope Curriculum and in supporting their efforts, it is High/Scope's research accomplishments (which are discussed in more depth in Chapter 6) that have helped propel early childhood education, in general, and the High/Scope Curriculum, in particular, into the national limelight and onto the agenda of public policy makers and school district administrators. Clearly, the turning point in their dissemination efforts was the 1984 publication of findings regarding the long-term effectiveness of the Perry Preschool Project. (Weikart, 1990, called it a dream come true.)

The study of the Perry Preschool Project, which lasted from 1962 until 1965, was designed as a classic scientific experiment. It had both a control and experimental group to which children were randomly assigned, and it was longitudinal in design. As a result, its positive finding of the effectiveness of preschool education (versus no preschool) can be stated clearly and assertively. The results of their study through age 19, reported in *Changed Lives,* documented that high-quality preschool education can have lasting effects in improving scholastic achievement during the school years; in decreasing delinquency and crime, the use of welfare assistance, and the incidence of teenage pregnancy; and in increasing high school graduation rates and the frequency of enrollment in postsecondary programs and employment (Berrueta-Clement et al., 1984). Cost–benefit analysis of these findings highlighted the economic benefits derived from investing in preschool education (Berrueta-Clement et al., 1984). A follow-up study by Schweinhart, Barnes, and Weikart, released in 1993, provided continuing data that the positive effects of preschool endured through age 27.

Two years after the publication of the landmark study, *Changed Lives* (Berrueta-Clement et al., 1984), another study was released with the findings from High/Scope's age 15 follow-up of children in the Ypsilanti Preschool Curriculum Demonstration Project. Initiated in 1968, this study compared three different preschool curriculum models—a direct instruction curriculum, the High/Scope Curriculum, and a traditional nursery school curriculum—in terms of gains in children's school performance. Although no differences among curriculum approaches had been found initially, High/Scope researchers concluded that, at age 15, children who participated in a direct instruction curriculum were more prone to delinquent behaviors than participants in the other two curriculum models (Schweinhart et al., 1986). In 1997, analysis of new data extended program effects through age 23 (Schweinhart & Weikart, 1997a, 1997b). Due to these findings, High/Scope's focus on child-initiated learning has become even more pronounced and their focus on the social consequences of early education more prominent.

Following publication of these results, Weikart and his associates became increasingly vocal about their beliefs regarding the content of early childhood programs—in particular, that they involve child-initiated learning—and the need for more consistent program quality (Schweinhart & Weikart, 1998; Weikart, 1987, 1992; Weikart & Schweinhart, 1993). This concern has led Weikart (1992, 1995) to propose a solution to the problem of program quality in early childhood education. A 1992 quote by Weikart says it most directly:

> There is a strategy that, if fully implemented, may deliver high-quality programs more consistently than current strategies do. Why not commit the field to the finest preservice training it is possible to afford and then have programs operate according to the standards of a model curriculum program? *It was a model curriculum program, after all, that produced the permanent effects on children, families, and the community documented in the High/Scope Perry Preschool Project.* (Weikart, 1992, p. 11, emphasis in original)

Weikart (1995) states that the High/Scope curriculum is uniquely prepared to meet this challenge because it is:

- based on a coherent theoretical base,
- validated by research,
- capable of implementation on a wide scale,
- clearly articulated and easily understood by practitioners in a variety of different programmatic settings,
- supported by an effective staff training system, and
- defined by an assessment system of broadly defined child outcomes.

The characteristics outlined above by Weikart as uniquely preparing the High/Scope Curriculum to promote uniform program quality and improved child outcomes have been honed over a period of 38 years, expressed through four different iterations of their curriculum manual, and supported by the High/Scope Educational Foundation's ever-expanding organizational capacity. Each curriculum iteration has been informed by findings from their research, and from reports provided by program training staff as they assist practitioners in the model's implementation across the nation and internationally.

In this regard the High/Scope Curriculum represents an early childhood curriculum model that continues to evolve (albeit within its Piagetian framework). Through the structure of key experiences, the High/Scope Curriculum has created a mechanism for its ongoing evolution. This aspect of the curriculum deflects complaints regarding the static nature of curriculum models, such as those expressed in regards to the Montessori method (see Chapter 2). Noteworthy, however, is the question of who is privileged to inform the model's evolution.

In response to concern that the broad use of curriculum models may contain teacher practice and restrict intellectual engagement with the dynamic and uncertain terrain of teaching and learning (Goffin, 1993), High/Scope program designers countered:

> We believe that teachers should have the same balance of autonomy and responsibility as scientists and artists. In all three cases, the practitioner intelligently interprets principles to develop raw materials into refined product. The teacher intelligently interprets principles of learning and child development to contribute to children's learning and development. Such interpretation of principles is what treatment replication is all about and thus is what permits program providers to generalize findings from a study like the High/Scope Perry Preschool study and apply them to their own programs. (Epstein et al., 1996, p. xii)

In the next three chapters, issues such as these that swirl around the use of early childhood curriculum models— regardless of the model in question—are explored. These chapters provide information that needs to be considered before responding to Weikart's proposal to rely on "proven" curriculum models to increase community access to high quality early childhood programs.

☞ FOR FURTHER READING

DeVries, R., with Kohlberg, L. (1990). *Constructivist education: Overview and comparison with other programs.* Washington, DC: National Association for the Education of Young Children. (Originally published as *Programs of early education: The constructivist view* by Longman in 1987)

> This is DeVries's seminal work on the Kamii-DeVries approach. In addition to describing in detail her own approach to early education, she carefully compares it to other curriculum models, including High/Scope, Montessori, and Bank Street. Her lucid writing style makes even difficult Piagetian concepts understandable. Readers interested in pursuing constructivist activities

will also want to read Kamii and DeVries's books on physical knowledge activities (1978/1993), group games (1980), and number concepts (1976).

Hohmann, M., & Weikart, D. P. (1995). *Educating young children: Active learning practices for preschool and child care programs.* Ypsilanti, MI: High/Scope Press.

This is the most recent definitive text on the High/Scope Curriculum. It includes many brief introductory sections that summarize the changes in the High/Scope model from its inception to its most current form.

Part III

An Examination of the Underpinnings of Curriculum Models in Early Childhood Education

*T*his final section moves beyond examination of individual curriculum models to investigate curriculum models from the perspectives of program evaluation and curriculum development. Chapter 6 reviews findings from comparative evaluations of early childhood curriculum models and assesses their impact on public policies related to early childhood education and on the continuing popularity of curriculum models. Chapter 7 reviews significant shifts that have occurred within child development research and theory since the mid-1960s. Research on, and deliberations about, teacher effects are similarly examined. New understandings about child development, reassessment of the relationship between child development knowledge and early childhood curriculum, and research on teacher effects are considered in terms of the challenges they elicit for early childhood curriculum models as tools of education. Chapter 8 returns to the book's overarching question: "What is the purpose, function, and the impact of curriculum models in early childhood education?" Chapter 9 examines the work of teachers in Reggio Emilia, Italy, and implications for the early care and education field. Curriculum models are being used to address an array of social, educational, and professional challenges. The Reggio Emilia approach poses new questions, as well as directing attention to "old" questions in new ways.

Chapter Six

In Pursuit of Answers
Comparative Evaluations of Early Childhood Curriculum Models

*T*his chapter reviews research regarding the relative effectiveness of early childhood curriculum models. It returns our investigation of curriculum models in early childhood education to their original purpose: identification of the most effective curricula for children from low-income families. Given the focus in the United States on results and faith in scientific outcomes, findings from these program evaluations have been particularly influential with policy and other decision makers.

A chronicle of the search for the most effective curricula[1] reveals more than an answer to the central, competitive question of effectiveness. It also exposes the simplicity of evaluators' initial thinking about children, educational programming, and the nature of change. As these assumptions have become explicit, they have been reassessed. These assumptions, though, have provided the basis for policy support of early childhood curriculum models. Consequently, challenges to the validity and reliability of program evaluations pose comparable challenges to the purpose and function of curriculum models in early childhood education.

Our review of evaluation findings is organized historically, first in terms of studies investigating the short-term impact of early childhood curricula, followed by more recent findings regarding their long-term effectiveness. This historical organization parallels the history of early childhood curriculum models presented in Chapter 1.

Because the histories of early intervention programs and curriculum models are so intertwined, discussion of the former's effectiveness is necessarily included. The meaning and conceptualization of early intervention programs has expanded since their onset in the mid-1960s, however. This reality complicates usage of the term "early intervention" when discussing research of more recent vintage; hence we use the term "preschool intervention programs" to distinguish these programs from those more inclusive and comprehensive in their focus.

---

[1]Frede (1995) called these evaluations a "theory-driven 'horse race' to determine if a curriculum derived from Theory A is more effective than curricula derived from Theories B and C by comparing model programs in which each curriculum is implemented as completely as possible" (p. 117).

Review of curriculum model effects occurs alongside discussion of issues associated with interpreting program evaluation results. This is done to highlight the restraint needed when interpreting these results. Such caution is necessitated, in part, because of a tendency to overgeneralize these findings when deliberating federal and state policies regarding early childhood intervention.

Consideration also is given to the extent early childhood curriculum models have accomplished their intended goal: preparing economically disadvantaged preschoolers to enter kindergarten on an equal footing with their middle-class peers. Early childhood curriculum models have competed not only in terms of their relative effectiveness, but also on their conceptualizations of the best way to educate children from low-income families. As a result of evaluation findings, deliberations regarding the best way to assist children have expanded beyond curriculum reform (via curriculum models) to classifying the essential characteristics of effective early intervention programs.

✐ EMPIRICAL EVALUATIONS OF EARLY CHILDHOOD CURRICULUM MODELS

> The variety among early childhood curricula today enriches the early childhood field. But within this variety lies disputes about educational practice that ought to be resolved. We trust that researchers will continue to seek such resolutions by conducting the necessary curriculum evaluations and fine-tuned research. (Schweinhart, 1987, p. 10)

Curriculum models, by definition, present ideal representations of education programs. Program implementation converts an abstract program ideal into a practical reality. This reality, in turn, becomes the substance assessed by program evaluation.

One of the major challenges confronting program evaluations is the extent to which a program-in-action accurately reflects its conceptual representation. Failure to accurately implement a curriculum model obscures differences among program types and makes it difficult to assess the extent to which models differ in their effects (Barnett, Frede, Mobasher, & Mohr, 1987; Frede, 1995; Frede & Barnett, 1992; Lawton & Fowell, 1989; Rivlin & Timpane, 1975; Travers & Light, 1982).

The findings from a study by Barnett and colleagues (1987) highlight the significance of "accurate" implementation. In assessing the impact through third grade of a new public school preschool program for at-risk 4-year-olds in South Carolina, Barnett and his associates found that preschool programs using the High/Scope Curriculum increased children's school readiness *only* when the quality of program implementation also was assessed. They concluded that if their study had proceeded without measuring accuracy of implementation, it might have been assumed that the preschool program was ineffective.

Accurate implementation has been a consistent source of frustration in large-scale, multisite comparative studies of curriculum models (House & Hutchins, 1979; Rivlin & Timpane, 1975; Travers & Light, 1982). It also has been a source of enlightenment. Variations in implementation of the same curriculum model have helped direct attention to the effects exerted by different settings (Rivlin & Timpane, 1975; Travers & Light, 1982).

The term *evaluation* is defined as determining the worth or value of something according to criteria that are clearly explained and justified (House, 1990). Evaluation involves systematic inquiry into the operations of a program, including the services delivered, characteristics of those served, the process by which services are delivered, and the program outcomes (Travers & Light, 1982). With respect to early childhood curriculum models, program evaluations have attempted to determine the worth or value of early childhood models in relation to particular outcomes. In practical terms, evaluations have functioned to justify the existence or expansion of programs, improve program functioning, and demonstrate the program's impact on participants (Hauser-Cram, 1990).

Program evaluations can provide information about the effectiveness of different curriculum models relative to specified outcomes. This information can then be used for program comparisons. Policy makers have found this information particularly useful. Because of their focus on program outcomes, global program evaluations are less informative for advising practice or for generating understanding of children's lived experience in a particular program. However, evaluations of overall program effectiveness enable us to compare measured effects of curriculum models with their theorized impact and in relation to other models.

Empirical comparisons of early childhood curriculum models have been dominated by two questions:

1. Are the programs experienced by children really different from each other?
2. Are some programs better than others in producing desired outcomes?

Early answers to these two questions primarily came from two sources: experimental preschool programs initiated during the 1950s and early 1960s, and evaluations of early childhood programs that were part of Head Start and Follow Through Planned Variation. The majority of these studies involved experimental preschool programs serving African American children from low-income families, with the intention of helping these children begin their formal school careers on an equal footing with their more advantaged peers (Barnett, 1995; Powell, 1987a; Schweinhart & Weikart, 1985). More recent early intervention programs extend beyond experimental preschool programs to include preventive health, parent education, and family support components.

Initial Findings: Short-Term Effects

The most consistent finding from evaluations of preschool intervention programs has been an immediate increase in IQ scores of program children, as compared to program controls (children who did not attend a preschool program prior to first grade). These increases almost always fade by third grade, however (Entwisle, 1995; Karnes, Shwedel, & Williams, 1983; Miller & Bizzell, 1983b; Powell, 1987a; Schweinhart & Weikart, 1985; Stallings & Stipek, 1986; Weikart, 1981). Immediate gains in IQ scores have been especially pronounced for children in programs with highly structured curricula and a strong academic focus. But the loss of superiority over children without preschool experience has affected all program participants, regardless of the curriculum they experienced.

Recall that Project Follow Through began in 1967 as a comprehensive education program for economically disadvantaged children in kindergarten through third grade. Its purpose was to fortify short-term outcomes achieved by Project Head Start, in order to offset children's declining IQ scores following school entry. Budget problems, however, reduced the project to a small program, and its goals changed accordingly. Follow Through became known for its planned variation of educational approaches. The hope was that study of these variations would increase understanding of program effects (Hodges & Sheehan, 1978; Kennedy, 1978). Head Start Planned Variation was initiated 1 year later. According to Bissell (1973), Planned Variation—meaning variation among curriculum models—was designed to explore five issues:

1. the processes involved with implementing preschool intervention programs;
2. the nature of experiences provided by different preschool intervention programs;
3. the effects of different programs on Head Start children and their families;
4. the contributions of intervention programs during preschool versus the primary grades; and
5. the benefits of continuous, sequenced intervention when the same educational strategies were used over several years.

Head Start Planned Variation incorporated 12 curriculum models, 11 of which were also represented in Project Follow Through (see Figure 1.2). This made it possible to compare not only a variety of curricula at the Head Start level, but also to follow children interacting with the same curriculum through the early grades.

Children who participated in Head Start Planned Variation classrooms had substantially higher test scores than would be expected of children who did not attend a Head Start program, but they did not perform significantly better than the children with whom they were compared who had attended regular Head Start classes (Rivlin & Timpane, 1975). In addition, no single Head Start Planned Variation curriculum model emerged as significantly better than another (Rivlin & Timpane, 1975).

The cross-model evaluation of Follow Through compared 13 early childhood curriculum models implemented at 80 sites throughout the United States (Follow Through curriculum models are listed in Figure 1.1). Curriculum models were organized into categories based on their programmatic emphasis: basic skills, cognitive capabilities, and affective development. Even though the most academically structured curriculum models produced the greatest academic gain for participating children, this gain was not consistently found at each of the program sites (House & Hutchins, 1979; Kennedy, 1978; Rivlin & Timpane, 1975). In fact, the lack of consistency among program sites for the *same* curriculum models (i.e., within model variation) was the only consistent finding (House & Hutchins, 1979; Kennedy, 1978; Rivlin & Timpane, 1975).

No consistent pattern of differential effectiveness emerged among curriculum models in comparison to other models or control groups. Based on their reanalysis of the Follow Through evaluation data, correcting for what they saw as statistical flaws in the original statistical analysis, House and Hutchins (1979) concluded that local conditions, parents, teachers, peers, and the home and school environments had more impact on program outcomes than program type. Note, however, that even though Head Start and Follow Through provided comprehensive services, these Planned Variation studies focused only on the educational component and did not assess the effects of the companion health, nutrition, and psychological and social services (Bissell, 1973).

As these and other findings accumulated, they were accompanied by the conclusion that no significant differences existed among early childhood curricula in terms of measured child outcomes (Karnes et al., 1983; Miller & Dyer, 1975; Ramey et al., 1985; Weikart, 1981, 1983). Given less attention at this time were findings that program outcomes usually were consistent with program goals and content (Bissell, 1973; Miller, 1979) or that a relationship existed between curricular approach and ease of implementation. It is noteworthy, for example, that teachers rated highest in terms of program implementation taught in academically oriented programs (Bissell, 1973).

Despite the absence of strong support for any one curriculum model, highly structured, academic preschool and primary programs consistently were more successful in initially increasing children's IQ scores and promoting academic success in the primary grades. Attention to these findings, of course, was consistent with the high priority accorded academic development. Not surprisingly, these findings intensified the debate between those who asserted the priority of social-emotional and general intellectual development and those who advocated academic training during early childhood.

Program developers whose models emphasized a developmental focus argued that the measures used to assess program success—IQ scores and gains on academic achievement tests—did not measure their programs' intentions. Proponents of curriculum models, such as the Developmental-Interaction approach (see Chapter 3), that were less structured and emphasized the importance of social-emotional development and child-initiated activity, argued that their program goals were not fairly or adequately assessed (Cohen, 1975; Hodges & Sheehan, 1978; Takanishi, 1979; Zimiles, 1977). Less personally involved researchers also have pointed out that because program evaluations relied on standardized tests, curriculum models emphasizing the academic skills found on such tests should have been expected to score higher (House & Hutchins, 1979; Stallings & Stipek, 1986).

This problem, to some extent, was inherent to the questions program evaluations were attempting to answer. Early studies of curriculum models were primarily interested in discovering which model was best for advancing the school success of economically disadvantaged children. To conduct a comparison among curriculum models, global measures were needed, measures that could assess program effects on similar outcomes (Clarke-Stewart & Fein, 1983; Peters, 1977; Powell, 1987a). But as lamented by Rivlin and Timpane (1975), because standardized tests are explicitly designed to give comparable measures of children's academic performance, regardless of curriculum, they are "singularly ill-suited for use as discriminators among curricula" (p. 14).

A second, critical aspect of the problem was availability of valid and reliable measures of program impact. In measurement terms, validity concerns the extent to which a particular test or other means of assessment accurately measures the behaviors being assessed. Reliability refers to whether or not, on repeated testing, the same outcomes are being measured.

Debate on the validity of cognitive abilities as a program outcome was hindered by existing capabilities in the field of measurement. Available measures of children's affective, motivational, and social competence were not sufficiently reliable and valid (Clarke-Stewart & Fein, 1983; Condry, 1983; Gray et al., 1982; White & Buka, 1987). Cognitive measures were. According to White and Buka (1987), "Since the initiation of the earliest of the modern wave of experimental programs, evaluation efforts have been tethered to the current state of the art of objective measurement of children" (p. 69).

By the mid-1970s, lackluster findings regarding the impact of Head Start programs and curriculum models began to have their effect on policy makers and others. The once exuberant enthusiasm for the possibilities of environmental intervention began to dissipate.

Follow-Up Findings: Long-Term Impact

Knowledge about the long-term effectiveness of preschool intervention programs, in general, and curriculum models, in particular, has been heavily informed by the findings from The Consortium for Longitudinal Studies. The Consortium for Longitudinal Studies was formed in 1975 to ascertain whether early education programs had long-term effects on the school performance of children from low-income families (Condry, 1983). It was formed in response to the threatened demise of Head Start in the mid-1970s (Condry, 1983; Lazar, 1980).

The threat materialized, in part, from the disappointing, well-publicized findings of the Westinghouse-Ohio study[2] (Condry, 1983; Lazar, 1980). Given hindsight, this threat to survival could have been anticipated. Theories and programs of early intervention had been overstated and distorted. As a result of these exaggerations, both politicians and the press assumed that Head Start would eradicate poverty and ignorance (Zigler & Anderson, 1979).

The Westinghouse-Ohio study (Cicirelli, 1969) evaluated the effectiveness of the first 3 years of Head Start (including the period when it was a summer-only program). Compared with children who had not attended Head Start, the study found few advantages for Head Start participants on standardized tests 1, 2, and 3 years into their public school experience. These findings spurred initiation of Project Follow Through. They also provided a rationale for the Nixon White House to develop a 3-year phase-out plan for Head Start (Zigler, 1984b).

To try to frame a well-informed counterargument to this threat, 11 investigators, who had implemented experimental early intervention programs during the late 1950s and early 1960s, agreed to collaborate in assessing the long-term effectiveness of preschool intervention across program types. As members of The Consor-

---

[2]The Westinghouse study is frequently targeted for Head Start's loss of public favor at this time. Cicirelli (1984) argued, however, that the study was maligned.

tium for Longitudinal Studies (CLS), participants agreed to send their original raw data, plus new data collected from their original subjects, to a group at Cornell University who had no connection with any of the original studies. The group at Cornell merged the data and provided independent analysis (Condry, 1983; Lazar, 1980).

The immediate policy need for information regarding the long-term impact of early childhood intervention programs informed the decision to use experimental programs launched during the early 1960s versus initiating a new longitudinal study of Head Start (Condry, 1983; The CLS, 1979; Lazar, 1980). The possibility of evaluating existing Head Start programs was discarded because the critical elements needed for an experimental research design were missing—such as controls (children who are just like those attending Head Start except for the fact that they are not in the program), baseline measures (knowledge about the children prior to their program experience), and random assignment (children who are arbitrarily assigned to a group that will either become participants or controls) (Condry, 1983; Lazar, 1980).

Without these elements, the outcomes of program evaluation cannot be attributed to children's program participation; factors not controlled by the study design remain as possible explanations. The use of random assignment is especially critical to being able to conclude that a specific program is directly responsible for changes in participating children (Clarke-Stewart & Fein, 1983; Ramey et al., 1985). Yet random assignment was becoming a source of tension because of the ethical dilemma of withholding services from eligible participants (the control group) and arbitrarily assigning subjects to control and experimental groups without regard to need (Campbell, 1987; Cohen, 1975; Hauser-Cram, 1990; Seitz, 1987).

The experimental programs that contributed data to the CLS primarily served children who were eligible for federal assistance, and they contained many of the elements critical to an experimental research design. They thus provided reassurance that the findings might serve as a basis for federal policy (Lazar, 1980).

The CLS began collecting follow-up data in 1976–1977. Each participating program collected parent and youth interview data (children who had participated in the early childhood programs were now between 9 and 19 years of age), school records and achievement test results, and Wechsler Intelligence Test data (The CLS, 1979). The study included all major preschool curricula and delivery systems (home-based, center-based, and combination programs). Programs involved children of various ages, lasted over various periods of time, differed in intensity, and used staff with varying levels of previous training. This diversity suggested that the CLS's findings could be broadly generalized (Lazar, 1983).

The CLS found that, on average:

1. Preschool programs increased individual scores on standard intelligence tests. These increases remained statistically significant for three to four years after the preschool experience.
2. During most of the elementary school years, arithmetic and reading achievement scores of program graduates were higher than those of controls.

3. Preschool graduates had higher self-esteem, valued achievement, and had higher occupational aspirations than the controls. The parents of preschool graduates also had higher occupational aspirations.

4. Preschool graduates were less likely to be placed in special education or remedial classes than their control counterparts. They were more likely to meet standard school requirements and to graduate from high school. (Lazar, 1983, p. 461)

The consistency of these findings across curricula led the CLS to conclude that the search for a "perfect" curriculum was futile. What mattered as far as the outcomes they measured was implementation of a well-designed, professionally supervised curriculum, with specific goals (Lazar, 1983). David Weikart (1981, 1983), who developed the High/Scope Curriculum, concluded that the basic issue for successful early childhood programs was quality of program implementation rather than a curriculum model's particular philosophy. His frequently cited conclusion was based on the lack of differential effectiveness among curriculum models in promoting sustained increases in children's IQ scores.

The CLS findings, particularly those regarding decreased grade retention, special education placement, and increased high school graduation rates, succeeded in having a significant impact on federal and state policies. They helped to generate widespread support for preschool intervention programs. In addition, the use of functional outcome measures, which assessed the effectiveness of preschool intervention programs based on criteria of successful school performance, undermined reliance on IQ scores and achievement measures as sole indicators of program effectiveness (Condry, 1983). However, given the small differences found among curriculum models on assessed outcomes, the results did little to boost their popularity.

The findings of the CLS were fortified by the independent findings of Weikart and his associates, published in 1984, on the long-term effectiveness of the Perry Preschool Project, which used the High/Scope Curriculum (Berrueta-Clement et al., 1984). A consortium participant, Weikart had already begun to assess the long-term impact of the Perry Preschool Project when the CLS was conceived. His findings extended those of the CLS by addressing not only functional measures of school success, such as special education placement and high school graduation, but also program effects on children's success as members of their communities, including labor force participation, crime and delinquency, and arrest rates.

Evaluations of the Perry Preschool Project, which began when program children were 3 and 4 years old, have assessed children annually from ages 3 to 11, and again at ages 14, 15, 19, and 27 (compared with controls who had no preschool experience).[3] Assessment of the results through age 27 credit children's preschool education with:

- improving cognitive performance during early childhood;
- improving scholastic placement and achievement during the school years;

---

[3] The effects of the Perry Preschool Project through age 27 were released in 1993. Findings at age 27 for program participants, as compared with the no-program group, found that program participants had higher monthly earnings, higher percentages of home ownership and second-car ownership, higher levels of schooling, fewer arrests, and lower usage of social services during the preceding 10 years (Schweinhart & Weikart, 1993).

- decreasing delinquency, crime, use of welfare assistance, and teenage pregnancy; and
- increasing high school graduation rates, frequency of enrollment in postsecondary programs, and employment (Berrueta-Clement et al., 1984; Schweinhart & Weikart, 1993).

The dramatic findings from the 1984 study focused attention on the High/Scope Curriculum and redirected attention to the question of relative effectiveness of different curriculum models.

Using Findings from Program Evaluations

The CLS's decision to investigate the long-term effectiveness of early childhood programs based on especially well-planned and implemented experimental programs made the findings and their policy implications vulnerable to challenges regarding their generalizability to local, nonexperimental programs, which traditionally are supported by federal funding (Evans, 1985; Haskins, 1989; Hebbeler, 1985). The most frequent warning associated with reports of these studies, therefore, is caution in generalizing their conclusions to other than very high quality, preschool intervention programs for African American children from urban, low-income families (Barnett, 1986; Evans, 1985; Haskins, 1989; Powell, 1987a).

The experimental programs evaluated by the CLS were implemented under unique conditions. They were well designed, implemented by skilled practitioners, and evaluated by knowledgeable researchers. As Grubb (1987) observed, the frequent citations of the Perry Preschool Project fail to note that it consistently emerges as the program with the highest ratios, highest salaries, and highest costs, "an extraordinarily expensive program by any standard" (p. 42). These concerns have persisted and led to questions of whether the effects of exemplary programs can be produced by typical programs (Barnett, 1986; Clarke-Stewart & Fein, 1983; Evans, 1985; Frede, 1995; Haskins, 1989).

Evaluations of more "ordinary" preschool intervention programs have, in fact, found less dramatic outcomes. Evans (1985), in an assessment of urban high school minority students, found no differences between students who had attended preschool and those who had not. A critical review of preschool intervention programs by Haskins (1989) concluded that, although there is strong support for the immediate impact of typical Head Start programs on children's intellectual performance, there is "virtually no evidence" (p. 278) of long-term impact on specific measures of life success such as those found for participants in the Perry Preschool Project. This discrepancy has led to calls for further investigation of "ordinary" early childhood programs (Evans, 1985; Haskins, 1989; Jacobs, 1988; Reynolds, 1997; Weiss, 1988; Zigler & Styfco, 1994).

Explaining Program Effects

A consistent lament of researchers involved in evaluating curriculum models has been the inability to determine which program elements are connected with which program outcomes (Barnett et al., 1987; Clarke-Stewart & Fein, 1983; Karnes et al.,

1983; Miller & Bizzell, 1983b; Miller et al., 1985; Powell, 1987a; Ramey et al., 1985; Travers & Light, 1982). It is difficult to disentangle the effects of content, activities, and materials from teaching techniques (Miller et al., 1985). Interpretation of program effects has consistently been thwarted by an inability to link program dimensions, such as type of teacher–child interaction, with program outcomes.

Researchers trying to resolve this issue attempted to vary teaching techniques while holding program content constant (Powell, 1987a). The research of Miller et al. (1985), in particular, illustrated the complexity of relationships among curriculum, instruction, and program outcomes.

Their research tried to disentangle these three elements. They found that program content varied with technique, and that some teaching techniques were used only with certain tasks (Miller et al., 1985). What one teaches, in other words, varies with how one teaches, and how one teaches varies with what is being taught. Similar findings regarding the confounding influence of content and technique have been described by those involved in research on teacher effects (e.g., Shulman, 1987).

Another difficulty has been identifying a "teaching unit" for purposes of evaluation. Miller et al. (1985) suggested that some teaching strategies may be comprised of several components and that some teaching elements may only be important in combination with others or be influential only at certain levels of intensity. Uncertainty regarding what comprises a teaching segment makes it difficult to determine what teaching strategies are responsible for which outcomes.

Finally, determination of which program elements are associated with which program outcomes is confounded by the relationship between the goals of a curriculum and its content and teaching techniques. Program philosophy modified teachers' implementation of similar teaching techniques (Miller et al., 1985). In combination, these findings suggested that understanding the effects of early childhood programs requires conceptualizing early education as something more than a mixture of discrete activities and interactions.

✑ A CHANGING PICTURE: AN EMERGENT PATTERN OF DIFFERENTIAL IMPACT

Into the early 1980s, it was generally accepted that differences among curriculum models were negligible. In comparison to the absence of significant, differential effects on cognitive growth, findings from Head Start and Follow Through Planned Variation indicating that curriculum models produced outcomes consistent with program goals received limited attention.

Two experimental programs that were part of The Consortium for Longitudinal Studies research, however, included comparisons of curriculum models within a single study (Karnes et al., 1983; Miller & Bizzell, 1983a, 1983b). This time the finding of consistency between program emphasis and program outcome drew more notice.

A study by Karnes et al. (1983) examined the extent to which five different preschool programs for low-income children prepared them for public school. It also attempted to determine if any one of these five approaches would be more successful in accomplishing this outcome.

The five programs consisted of two highly structured, didactic programs; two traditional nursery programs that focused on social, emotional, physical, and general language development; and a Montessori program. The impact of the five programs immediately following children's participation and up through third grade was, on the whole, consistent with those discussed earlier, with two exceptions.

First, children who participated in the Montessori program showed continued gains in intellectual functioning through first and second grade. Second, children who participated in one of the highly structured programs *and* received a second year of intensive training showed an increase in IQ scores. Karnes et al. (1983) interpreted these findings as evidence of the benefits of sustained, intensive intervention, a hypothesis reinforced by the findings from long-term follow-up of students who participated in Direct Instruction Follow Through (Stallings & Stipek, 1986).

Although students' achievement in the elementary grades is attributed to continued program contact (Stallings & Stipek, 1986), Miller (1979) pointed out that Karnes and her colleagues' (1983) findings do not necessarily indicate which programs produced better cognitive results. The study's results might, instead, indicate the effect of a sustained academic focus. In addition, in both the Karnes and Louisville studies (see later discussion), the most detrimental effects on achievement test scores were obtained when children experienced a pre-academic preschool and then attended a program that was either less academic or nonacademic (Miller, 1979).

By the time students who participated in the Karnes et al. (1983) study graduated from high school, there no longer were significant differences among the groups in terms of school performance. Follow-up data collected after high school graduation showed considerable variability, however. Although there were no statistically significant differences among the five groups, the Montessori and traditional nursery school programs contained the largest number of high school graduates. The Montessori group also had the fewest number of retained students.

The success of children who participated in the Montessori program led Karnes et al. (1983) to conclude that task persistence and the ability to work independently, both important elements of the Montessori method, might be important for long-term school success. Unfortunately, their research could not distinguish which elements of the preschool programs were critical for long-term school success.

The Louisville experiment, a stronger study methodologically, attempted to address the question of differential program effectiveness by comparing the effects and characteristics of four different preschool programs: Montessori, a traditional preschool, Bereiter-Engelmann's direct instruction model, and DARCEE, another highly structured, academically oriented program (Miller & Bizzell, 1983b; Miller & Dyer, 1975). Only the traditional preschool program focused on children's emotional needs, and all but the Montessori program stressed language development (Miller & Dyer, 1975).

The Louisville experiment was designed to (a) assess behaviors that were consistent with program goals, (b) determine if programs so different in goals and philosophies really differed in terms of teacher behaviors and children's experiences, and (c) distinguish which program aspects were crucial to program differences and differential effects (Miller & Bizzell, 1983b).

The researchers were able to answer only their first two questions. They later conducted another study (Miller et al., 1985, discussed previously) to determine which program dimensions contributed to which outcomes.

Their classroom observations revealed that the four programs clearly differed from each other in terms of both teacher and child behaviors. Depending on the program in which they were placed, children's experiences varied. In addition, both the immediate and long-term effects of the four programs differed, and the differences tended to be in line with the program's goals. Miller and Bizzell presented evidence that there might be one curriculum model that was "better" than another in terms of producing academic benefits, that a determination of which was better might vary according to whether a child was male or female, and that the effects of a preschool program may not be revealed until later in a child's schooling (Miller & Bizzell, 1983a, 1983b).

Although immediate program effects on IQ were greater for the didactic programs, they also faded more quickly, especially for children who attended the Bereiter-Engelmann program, a finding that was accentuated for females. Miller and Dyer (1975) concluded that raising IQ might not be a particularly desirable goal for prekindergarten children and that prekindergarten achievement, versus IQ, was a better predictor of first-grade success. Miller and Dyer also found a delayed, positive effect for males who participated in the Montessori program, a finding that did not emerge until second grade.

The same children were compared on IQ and school achievement when they were in the sixth, seventh, and eight grades (Miller & Bizzell, 1983a). This follow-up study found that IQs did not differ significantly among the four program groups. In reading and math achievement, however, there were differential effects in all three grades that related both to the type of preschool program the children experienced and a child's gender.

Males in the two nondidactic programs performed significantly better in reading and math achievement than males who participated in the two didactic programs. Females who participated in didactic early childhood programs achieved slightly better than girls who attended nondidactic programs, but only in reading. However, IQ scores of females showed the greatest decline, especially if they attended the didactic Bereiter-Engelmann program. The middle school males who attended the Montessori program were consistently in the highest group on school performance. (Other studies investigating the impact of early childhood experiences also have found program effectiveness to be tied to gender [Evans, 1985; Gray et al., 1982; Jordan, Grallo, Deutsch, & Deutsch, 1985; Lally et al., 1988; Larsen & Robinson, 1989; Marcon, 1999; Schweinhart & Weikart, 1993].)

Miller and Bizzell (1983a) concluded that early childhood programs emphasizing academic skills might require continued intervention in order to achieve maximum impact. Reynolds (1994, 1997) recently reached a similar conclusion regarding the importance of extended support. His evaluation of the effects of preschool on 1,106 African American children participating in a large federally funded early intervention program in Chicago found greater school success for children whose preschool intervention was extended through grade 3.

Miller and Bizzell (1983a) also suggested, as did Karnes et al. (1983), that successful school performance might be better achieved by helping children learn strategies that can be generalized to later school experiences, a conclusion, with slight modifications, also advanced by Gray et al. (1982) and more recently by Weikart (1995).

In attempting to explain the enhanced effectiveness of the Montessori program for males, Miller and Bizzell (1983a) hypothesized that males, perhaps because of their relative immaturity in comparison to girls, responded better to individualized attention within a structured program format, which is characteristic of Montessori programs. Their findings led them to challenge the appropriateness of drill and didactic instruction in prekindergarten programs. They hypothesized that children's first school experiences may set different learning paths in motion, depending on what type of program is first encountered (Miller & Bizzell, 1983a, 1983b).

Concern regarding the potential negative impact of highly structured academic preschool programs has been reinforced by comparative findings reported by Schweinhart and colleagues (1986; Schweinhart & Weikart, 1997a; 1997b). Their follow-up study compared outcomes among three curriculum models that served children 3 and 4 years old between 1967 and 1970: the High/Scope Curriculum, a direct instruction curriculum based on the Bereiter-Engelmann model, and a traditional nursery school program.

Schweinhart et al. (1986) found little difference at age 15 in intellectual and scholastic performance among participants in the three program groups. However, based on participants' self-reports, the researchers found that students who attended the direct instruction program as preschoolers reportedly engaged in twice as many delinquent acts as did participants in the other two curriculum groups. Adolescents from the direct instruction group also reported relatively poor relations with their families, less participation in sports and school job appointments, lower expectations for educational attainment, and less willingness to seek help from others for personal problems.

High/Scope's second follow-up study of participants at age 23 indicated that the pattern of differences between students who had experienced the direct instruction and High/Scope models became more prominent. Students in the direct instruction program had three times as many felony arrests, and 47% higher rates of emotional disturbance during schooling than students who had participated in High/Scope or a traditional nursery school program (Schweinhart & Weikart, 1997a, 1997b). High/Scope participants also were more likely than participants in the direct instruction group to remain married to their spouses, and participate in community activities such as voting and volunteer work.

Designers of the didactic approach have challenged the validity of High/Scope's findings because of methodological limitations, including small sample size, lack of comparability among students in the three groups, and evaluation and interpretation by a potentially self-interested researcher (Bereiter, 1986; Engelmann, 1999; Gersten, 1986). These concerns have caused the findings to be cautiously received by others (e.g., Karweit, 1988; Powell, 1987a; Sigel, 1990).

Controversy therefore surrounds the Schweinhart et al. (1986; Schweinhart & Weikart, 1997a, 1997b) findings. The first study, in particular, renewed the long-standing debate between academic and developmental approaches to early childhood education. The findings helped to reformulate the academic versus child development debate of the 1960s as one between direct instruction versus child-initiated learning. Their conclusions intensified competition among models by framing the findings as the long-awaited answer to the question regarding differential effectiveness of early childhood curriculum models. Referring to Weikart's (1981) earlier judgment that limited differences existed among curriculum models of high quality, Schweinhart et al. (1986) reignited the debate by concluding:

> For some years, we interpreted the early findings of the High/Scope Preschool Curriculum study to imply that high-quality early childhood education could be built upon *any theoretically* coherent model. The Curriculum Study, with its age 15 data, no longer permits that conclusion. The latest interpretation from the study, tenuous though the data are, now must be that a high-quality preschool curriculum is based on *child-initiated learning* activities. (p. 43, emphasis in original)

Earlier evidence of the potential negative effects of intense didactic programs came from a study by Stallings (1975), as well as the studies previously reviewed by Karnes et al. (1983) and Miller & Bizzell (1983a). Stallings found that third-grade students attending a Direct Instruction Follow Through Program were more likely to attribute their classroom achievement to their teachers rather than to themselves. She also found that these same children scored lower on a test of nonverbal problem solving abilities. In an assessment of this study as part of a review of research on early childhood programs, Stallings and Stipek (1986) suggested that children's highly structured relationships with teachers and learning materials provided students with little opportunity to experience taking things apart, putting them back together, and seeing how things fit together. They suggested that this lack of experience with concrete materials might have contributed to children's poor performance in nonverbal problem solving.

Stallings and Stipek's (1986) conclusions have been augmented by DeVries's investigations comparing the level of interpersonal understanding exhibited by children attending constructivist, didactic, and eclectic (i.e., traditional preschool) kindergartens (DeVries, Haney, & Zan, 1991; DeVries, Reese-Learned, & Morgan, 1991). Children attending a constructivist kindergarten, which stressed problem solving and autonomy, were consistently found to be more advanced in their level of interpersonal understanding with peers and more skillful in their social interactions compared to children attending the eclectic and didactic kindergartens. These findings, though, need to be considered in light of the fact that DeVries, who was the lead researcher for both of these studies, is also a primary architect of the constructivist Kamii-DeVries approach.

A more recent comparative study of preschool programs supplements these findings. Developed in response to persistent questions about the impact of variations across early childhood programs, Marcon (1992, 1999) examined the differential effects of three curriculum approaches in public school prekindergarten and

Head Start classrooms in the District of Columbia. Based on teachers' espoused beliefs about teaching and learning, 65 early childhood classrooms were organized into three clusters: child-initiated, academically directed, and middle-of-the-road. Randomly selected 4-year-olds from these classrooms were followed and tested 1 year later. The study found differential effects of the three approaches. Children whose teachers held beliefs that corresponded to a single, coherent theory did better than children whose teachers attempted to blend instructional approaches. Child effects coincided with the philosophy and approach of the program. Further, children in the child development-oriented programs mastered more basic skills than the children in the academically directed approach. According to Marcon (1999), this finding was especially notable in the performance of African American children.

The conclusions from DeVries's multiple studies (DeVries, Haney, & Zan, 1991; DeVries, Reese-Learned, & Morgan 1991), Marcon's research (1992, 1999), and the High/Scope Preschool Curriculum study (Schweinhart et al., 1986; Schweinhart & Weikart, 1997a, 1997b), in conjunction with the rejoiners to their conclusions (Bereiter, 1986; Engelmann, 1999; Gersten, 1986, 1991), sustain the debate between academically focused and child-oriented approaches. They also spotlight the shift away from a solitary focus on IQ and academic gains to one that includes social-emotional factors as critical contributors to children's school readiness.

Explaining How Early Childhood Programs Effect Change

As evaluation results have accumulated, researchers have attempted to explain the process by which preschool intervention programs effect change. In light of the "fade-out" of IQ gains by third grade, other, often indirect, explanations for long-term effects are being expressed. In attempting to explain why program type, level of teacher preparation, and intensity of program participation seemed irrelevant, Lazar (1983, 1988), who supervised and directed The Consortium for Longitudinal Studies, speculated that what these programs affected were parents' expectations and the extent to which they valued educational achievement. The important role of parent involvement in the effectiveness of preschool intervention programs was also stressed in an oft-cited report by Bronfenbrenner (1974).

A more recent explanation by Weikart (1995) attributes the long-term effects of the High/Scope Curriculum to children's opportunities to develop the social values of personal and social responsibility, independence, and a goal-oriented approach to life—dispositions that contribute to successful life patterns. Internalization of these dispositions, according to Weikart, enables children to assume more responsibility for their lives and engenders different relationships with significant adults.

In contrast to Weikart's programmatic and child-focused explanation, Reynolds (1992, 1994, 1997) attempts to explain the mediating factors through which preschool intervention exerts its effect on school success. He has tried to understand how positive outcomes from participation in preschool intervention programs later emerge as higher academic achievement, reduced grade retention, and other outcomes now commonly associated with effective preschool intervention programs.

Following their participation in a Chicago-based government-funded preschool program, Reynolds followed 266 low-income, mostly African American preschool children and 125 comparison group children from kindergarten through third grade (1986–1989). As a result of his findings, Reynolds concluded that the influence of preschool intervention on later outcomes is largely indirect and is mediated by intervening factors such as cognitive readiness, teacher ratings of social-emotional maturity, parent involvement, and school stability. According to Reynolds, in the absence of support from these intervening factors, the positive outcomes obtained from preschool intervention programs are less likely to have long-term effects. Reynolds's findings reinforce the importance of sustained support for young children identified as at risk and challenge those who argue that 1 or 2 years of preschool are sufficient to ensure lasting effects for children.

Missing Pieces of the Puzzle. Missing from these evaluations is consideration of children's influences on program outcomes. Program evaluations that ignore child input assume that children passively receive a program's "treatment." Program effects are investigated as if they equally affect participating children, regardless of individual differences, and fail to examine how children experience the program (Clarke-Stewart & Fein, 1983; Powell, 1987a; Takanishi, 1979).

Do individual children respond differently to different types of learning environments? Some empirical basis for insight into this question is provided by the Miller et al. (1985) study. They noted that most comparisons of program approaches had used classrooms as the unit of analysis. Consequently, little information existed on how individual children functioned in different classrooms.

Their research attempted to investigate the effects of specific teaching techniques and individual child behaviors on child outcomes. They found that children's behaviors in response to the demands of the educational situation were the most significant predictor of what children learned.

Teacher behaviors appeared to be important in terms of how they structured children's responses. But children's responses to learning experiences, versus the teaching technique per se, were a more significant predictor of child outcomes. Consequently, Miller et al. (1985) concluded that similar methods could not be expected to have the same effects for all children, a conclusion reinforced by Ramey and Ramey (1998) in their review of what is known about effective early intervention programs.

Also absent from consideration is assessment of the tensions between the intentions of program designers and of teachers who implement curriculum models. A case study of public school prekindergarten programs in Virginia, for example, investigated teachers' responses to required use of the High/Scope Curriculum (Walsh, Smith, Alexander, & Ellwein, 1993). Researchers found teachers frustrated by a curriculum that appeared to dictate how they were to interact with children. As a result, teacher response to the model ranged from confusion about "what they were allowed to do and when they were allowed to do it" (p. 324) to teachers creating their own curriculum "under the guise of the imposed one" (p. 328).

Traditional approaches to program evaluation also have omitted examination of tensions between the content and teaching practices promoted by a particular curriculum model, and family, community, and administrative expectations and values. For example, in a case study of teachers implementing the High/Scope Curriculum in a Head Start program serving Southeast Asian families, Inoway-Ronnie (1998) recorded families' disappointment with the absence of direct instruction in letters, colors, and numbers; the informality of teacher–child relationships; and the value placed on individualism, initiative, and autonomy. Inoway-Ronnie reported that teachers cared both about the learning promoted by the High/Scope Curriculum and the concerns families expressed. But in deciding how to navigate the dissonance between program and family priorities, they concluded that if they did not follow the High/Scope Curriculum they would be "written up by their program managers and might face discipline and possibly the loss of their jobs" (p. 192).

Revised Interpretations of Program Effectiveness. These studies provide mounting evidence that challenge earlier conclusions that no differences exist among curriculum models and their effects. Newer findings imply that, even on global outcomes such as IQ or school achievement, curriculum models may produce different effects. These findings bolster the relevance of an educationally significant consideration: learning environments created by different curricula affect program outcomes. Findings that program outcomes tend to be consistent with a program's expressed intent directs attention to the importance of program goals and content.

These findings also supply empirical support for the theoretical contention that particular environmental conditions foster different developmental consequences, depending on the personal characteristics of the individuals living in that environment. They substantiate pleas for research to consider both the learner *and* the learning context (Bronfenbrenner, 1989; Clarke-Stewart & Fein, 1983; Horowitz & O'Brien, 1989; Kessen, 1983; Ramey & Ramey, 1998; Takanishi, 1979; White & Buka, 1987). Finally, these findings hint at program differences subjectively experienced by children.

These conclusions dispute the long-standing premise that early childhood curriculum can be effective independent of child, teacher, or context. This "new" conclusion is reminiscent of Franklin and Biber's (1977) ardent contention that different approaches "involve children in qualitatively different encounters with people, problems, and ideas in the school setting" (p. 3). Suransky's (1982) and Polakow's (1993) vivid portrayal of children's lived experiences in diverse early childhood programs underscores the pertinence of this conclusion.

Returning to a Habitual Question: How Is Program Effectiveness to Be Defined?

By the early 1980s, in a throwback to criticisms of the first wave of research on curriculum effects, a reconceptualization of program outcomes was repeatedly recommended (Clarke-Stewart & Fein, 1983; Hauser-Cram, 1990; Hauser-Cram & Shonkoff, 1988; Takanishi, 1979; Travers & Light, 1982). "Past approaches to assessing program impacts on children focused on attributing importance to what was measurable. Future effort must be directed more toward measuring what is important" (Hauser-Cram & Shonkoff, 1988, p. 90).

Demand for change in the conduct of program evaluations on preschool intervention programs appears to be in response to at least four related factors. These four factors span interest in the content of programs to concerns with the purpose of early childhood interventions. All four factors move beyond an interest in comparative evaluations of curriculum models to a broader investigation of early intervention and determinants of effectiveness.

Acknowledging Program Complexity. There is mounting recognition of the complexity and dynamic character of early childhood programs and program participants. Findings such as those discussed previously have provoked program evaluators to move beyond conceptualization of early childhood programs as single, static treatments (Clarke-Stewart & Fein, 1983; Hauser-Cram 1990; Huston, McLoyd, & Garcia Coll, 1994; Jacobs, 1988; Ramey & Ramey, 1998; Reynolds, Mann, Miedel, & Smokowski, 1997; Schorr, 1997; Travers & Light, 1982; Weiss, 1988; Zimiles, 1986). "Treatment," according to Clarke-Stewart and Fein (1983), "involves a configuration of factors on multiple dimensions, including personal qualities of the educator, content of the curriculum, its theoretical underpinnings, instructional methods, location, and intensity" (p. 935). These calls challenge researchers to evaluate children and families in ways more responsive to their individuality and diversity and to the complexity of change.

Understanding What Works and Why. Interest is growing to determine not only the effects of early childhood programs but also to understand how these effects occur. Joined with recognition of program complexity is interest in discerning how a program affects a child's development, how this effect occurs, and under what conditions (Clarke-Stewart & Fein, 1983; Horowitz & O'Brien, 1989; Huston et al., 1994; Jacobs, 1988; Karoly et al., 1998; Powell, 1987b;). This issue is of particular importance to policy makers. Based on a comprehensive review of a broad range of early intervention programs for young children (in other words, not just preschool early intervention programs), Karoly et al. (1998) concluded that "one of the big unknowns is why successful programs work—and others don't" (p. xx). They go on to argue that "These unknowns will have to be resolved if wise decisions are to be made among early intervention alternatives and if the programs chosen are to be designed to fully realize their potential for promoting child development—and saving money. Otherwise inferences cannot be drawn about new program designs, and every such design would be unproven until tested and evaluated" (p. xxi). Finally, some program evaluators suggest a retreat from hunting "causes" of program effects to seeking "contributions" (Clarke-Stewart & Fein, 1983; Jacobs, 1988; Phillips, 1987). "The task for evaluation thus becomes one of determining which aspects of a program are valuable, for whom, and in which way" (Hauser-Cram, 1990, p. 589).

Outlining a Theory of Change. By the late 1980s, Powell's (1987a) conclusion reflected the viewpoint of many (Clarke-Stewart & Fein, 1983; Horowitz & Paden, 1973; Miller, 1979; Miller et al., 1985): the "bottom line of research on preschool practices . . . is finding an effective match between curriculum and child characteristics" (Powell, 1987a, p. 208). By the end of the 1990s, many were placing less emphasis on curriculum reform as a change strategy and more on the theory of change, the means by which services and supports hypothesize to change participants (Ramey & Ramey, 1998; St. Pierre & Layzer, 1998). In light of what now is known about the complexities of poverty and individual change, arguments have resurfaced to bring a broader, ecological approach to program design and evaluation (Huston et al., 1994; Schorr, 1997).

Identifying Essential Program Characteristics. It is widely recognized that high-quality, intensive center-based early childhood programs can make an important difference in children's lives (Barnett, 1995; Karoly et al., 1998; Ramey & Ramey, 1998; St. Pierre & Layzer, 1998). Studies that inform this conclusion attend less to the specific curriculum model being implemented than to the presence of a well-organized curriculum accompanied by additional program characteristics. Ramey and Ramey (1998), in their review of the early intervention literature, identify as critical program characteristics the onset and duration of the intervention program, its intensity (in terms of variables such as number of home visits per week, number of hours per day), comprehensiveness of services, and the availability of environmental supports after the child's participation concludes—in addition to curriculum design. These program characteristics exceed what most people associate with high-quality early childhood programs and argue for higher levels of program and financial support.

Beyond Definitions of Program Effectiveness

That an ideal early childhood program can be objectively constructed is another assumption under assault. (Some would even suggest that the notion of objectivity has been invalidated; see, for example, Barone, 1992; Eisner, 1992.) Evaluations, by definition, determine the worth or value of something according to predetermined criteria (House, 1990, 1993). Yet, the value component inherent to evaluations only recently has been confronted.

Initially, evaluators of early childhood curriculum models were assigned the task of discovering which educational programs worked best (Cohen, 1975; House, 1990; House & Hutchins, 1979; Rivlin & Timpane, 1975; Travers & Light, 1982) "as a strategy to find grand solutions to social problems" (House, 1990, p. 27). It was assumed, that as representatives of an impartial science, researchers could identify causes of social problems and objectively construct and assess best solutions to their amelioration. The definition of "best" and the process of evaluation were presumed to be objective and value free. The realization surfaced only recently that the question was actually "best for whom and for what purpose."

Evaluators now acknowledge that every aspect of the evaluation process, from the formulation of initial questions to the development of conclusions, requires choices that are resolved, even if at an unconscious level, by applying value judgments (House, 1990, 1993; Weiss, 1983). The fact that program evaluations are judged against some criterion of success (expected program outcomes, another program, or the absence of a program) negates the possibility of program findings being fully neutral and objective (Apple & Beyer, 1983; House, 1990, 1993; Royce, Murray, Lazar, & Darlington, 1982; Waters, 1998; Weiss, 1983).

Advocates' efforts to link evaluation findings to policy decisions underscore the extent to which the meaning of "best" is connected to preferred outcomes—both educational and political (Barnett, 1986, 1995; Haskins, 1989; Royce et al., 1982; Takanishi, 1979; Waters, 1998; Weiss, 1983; Woodhead, 1988; Zimiles, 1986). In reference to the preschool intervention programs initiated during the 1960s, Horowitz and Paden (1973) acknowledged, "Despite the scientific admonition against 'belief' and for 'objectivity,' there [was] much faith that environmental interventions [could] have effects upon developmental outcomes" (p. 391). To the extent that the values of program evaluators can inadvertently drive program design (analogous to the way that the availability of cognitive measures drove program outcomes during the 1960s and 1970s), awareness of this factor lessens the likelihood that designers of early childhood programs or their evaluators will sidestep the question of program values.

The Policy Connection

The majority of evidence for early childhood program effectiveness comes from evaluations of sophisticated curriculum models developed for African American children from low-income families who were identified as being at risk for school failure. As a result, arguments in support of preschool education tend to be linked with policy discussions concerned with moderating the ill effects of poverty. Policy makers ask if early childhood programs prevent social problems, including school failure, delinquency, antisocial behavior, teen pregnancy, and dependency on public welfare programs (Barnett, 1995; Clarke & Campbell, 1998; Yoshikawa, 1995).

High-quality early childhood programs make a difference; of concern is the tendency to overgeneralize the findings from available research (Barnett, 1995; Clarke-Stewart & Fein, 1983; Haskins, 1989; Karoly et al., 1998). No evidence exists, for example, that the benefits of preschool intervention programs also accrue for children from middle-class families (Grubb, 1987; Zigler, 1987).[4] Nor is there

---

[4]Small-scale research by Larsen and Robinson (1989) found evidence of higher second- and third-grade achievement scores for middle-class males who attended a preschool program compared with males who had not. A second study associated with the same longitudinal project concluded that the positive impact could be attributed to the preschool program itself versus the mandatory parent education component (Harris & Larsen, 1989). This particular finding contrasts with the importance attributed to parent participation in programs that target children from low-income families.

convincing evidence that the effects of high-quality early intervention programs will materialize for minorities other than African Americans (Barnett, 1995; Laosa, 1982; Lee, Brooks-Gunn, & Schnur, 1988; Ramey, Bryant, & Suarez, 1985). Finally, the extent to which program results for vulnerable children can be attributed to the curriculum rather than to additional program supports also is being questioned (Haskins, 1989; Ripple et al., 1999; Stallings & Stipek, 1986; Zigler, 1987).

Additionally, questions are being raised about transferring expectations from an experimental program to its large-scale implementation. For example, the 45 children participating in the Perry Preschool Project entered the program at age 3 and attended for 2 years; center-based classes were accompanied by weekly 90-minute teacher home visits; child–teacher ratios were 6:1; and teachers were highly qualified and trained. Is it possible to anticipate similar child outcomes from a program that does not provide the same conditions, which often is the case when experimental programs "go to scale" (Karoly et al., 1998)?

Another concern is the extent to which program achievements match the intentions originally associated with curriculum models: to assist economically disadvantaged preschoolers enter the public school system on an equal footing with their more advantaged peers. Several researchers suggested that this question had not been adequately addressed and investigated how well Head Start graduates performed in school. Hebbeler (1985) and Lee et al. (1988) found that even though participation in Head Start provided advantages, especially in comparison to disadvantaged children without preschool experience, it did not substantially reduce the educational discrepancy between advantaged and disadvantaged children. After describing her findings, Hebbeler (1985), a school district employee, protested that if "a program has been advertised as capable of eliminating the 'gap' between two groups, citing positive findings which show only improved performance does not prove the program has lived up to its advertising" (p. 214).

The desire for federal support and funding often drives programs to provide evidence of effectiveness that will please policy makers (Jacobs, 1988; Takanishi, 1979; Weiss, 1988; Zervigon-Hakes, 1995; Zigler & Freedman, 1987). The policy impact of the Perry Preschool Project findings was considerably enhanced by an economic evaluation of the data in terms of cost–benefits because this analysis enabled policy makers to contemplate the worth of early childhood programs in economic terms.

Economic evaluation is an assessment of the costs and outcomes of a program for society as a whole, in order to determine a program's desirability relative to other alternatives (Barnett, 1986; Karoly et al., 1998). Cost–benefit analysis, in particular, attempts to estimate the monetary value of the resources consumed by a particular program. The monetary value of the program's outcomes (such as the monetary worth of avoiding the stigma of being placed in special education) also is assessed, in order to determine the worth of the outcomes relative to the costs of achieving them. This relationship is represented in a cost–benefit ratio. Cost–benefit analysis asks, in economic terms, whether the results of a program are worth more than what it costs to achieve them (Barnett, 1986; Karoly et al., 1998; Levin, 1988; White, 1988).

Cost–benefit analysis of the Perry Preschool Project, based on program impact through age 27, concluded that for every dollar spent for children in 1 year of preschool, there was a savings of $7.16 to society by reducing costs for special education, additional years of schooling, welfare support, and the criminal justice system (Schweinhart & Weikart, 1993). Benefits also included contributions of future productivity as a consequence of employment. These cost–benefit findings have been persuasive with policy makers. They have built policy support at both the federal and state levels for preschool intervention programs, in general, and the High/Scope Curriculum, in particular.

However, several researchers investigating the long-term effectiveness of preschool education have noted that subjects continue to live in conditions of poverty and to attend inadequate public schools (Jordan et al., 1985; Lally et al., 1988; Lee, Brooks-Gunn, Schnur, & Liaw, 1990). St. Pierre & Layzer (1998) concluded that despite the positive effects of early childhood programs, there is no evidence that an early childhood program, by itself, can move children out of poverty.

Others emphasize the contradiction of promoting the benefits of high-quality preschool education in the absence of commitment to fully funding program costs (Grubb, 1987; Powell, 1987b; Ramey & Ramey, in press). "It makes no sense to cite evidence about the educational benefits of exemplary, high-quality programs and then to enact programs with low expenditures, low ratios, low salaries, and inadequate teacher preparation" (Grubb, 1987, p. 42). Still others question the point of trying to improve the life chances of children during preschool if public school practices that contribute to academic failure are not also addressed (Ellsworth & Ames, 1998; Entwistle, 1995; Horowitz & Paden, 1973; Jordan et al., 1985; Lee et al., 1990; Woodhead, 1988)—issues of increasing relevance given the rapid expansion of state-funded prekindergarten programs for children from low-income families. Horowitz and Paden (1973) and Vinovskis (1993) even questioned whether changing practices in public school classrooms might, in and of themselves, produce desired effects in academic achievement among poor and minority children, thus removing the need for preschool intervention programs as deterrents for public school failure.

Woodhead (1988) has asserted that isolated focus on the positive effects of preschool intervention programs places unrealistic emphasis on the early years as a period for effecting permanent individual change, distracting attention from community and school processes that help determine a child's future success, a concern repeatedly expressed by Lazerson during the height of early intervention activity (1970; 1972). Gray, Ramsey, and Klaus (1982), in assessing the impact of their preschool intervention program on the lives of participants over a 16-year period, also argued the complexity of human experience. They felt the findings of their study could only be understood in terms of "exchanges among changing people with other changing people and institutions during changing times" (p. 267). Woodhead argued that a narrow focus on preschool education reinforced political preference for simple strategies and inexpensive educational solutions to complex social and economic problems.

Recent findings regarding children's early neurological development has heightened persistent belief in the critical importance of the early childhood years.

A stimulating environment during the first 3 years is being stressed as critical for ensuring the intellectual and social-emotional development of individual children, and therefore, the future well-being of society (see Chapter 7).

Melton (1987) and Polakow (1986, 1993) shift the focus and argue that emphasis on the long-term consequences of early childhood deprivation devalues the well-being of children in the present. When problems of childhood are evaluated and promoted as serious only in terms of their long-term consequences, it implies that help can be forthcoming only when the effects are expressed in terms of adult nonproductivity and social pathology. The critical political question, according to House (1990), is: "Whose interests does the evaluation serve?" And, it might be added, "Whose social values?"

This expansive list of issues and concerns reinforces the complexity involved and highlights the challenges that remain in creating positive developmental contexts for children from low-income families. It also spotlights differences among change agents regarding appropriate targets for public policy. Current measures of long-term effectiveness focus on indicators of change that are making meaningful differences in children's lives and society's well-being. Yet Clarke-Stewart and Fein (1983) concluded that "[p]ositive findings may reassure policy makers that the investment in early childhood programs is cost-effective, but they are unlikely to reassure those concerned with broader social values" (p. 941).

✐ FOR FURTHER READING

Barnett, W. S., & Escobar, C. M. (1987). The economics of early educational intervention. *Review of Educational Research, 57,* 387–414.

> This article explains economic analysis with particular reference to preschool intervention programs.

The Consortium for Longitudinal Studies. (1983). *As the twig is bent . . . The lasting effects of preschool programs.* Hillsdale, NJ: Lawrence Erlbaum.

> This book describes the history of individual preschool intervention programs and The Consortium for Longitudinal Studies (CLS). Chapters written by program developers describe their studies and program effects. Two chapters describe the study conducted by the CSL and its findings. This book provides a comprehensive overview of the CSL and the programs that informed its results.

The Future of Children, 5. (1995). Long-term outcomes of early childhood programs [Special issue] [Online]. Available: http://www.futureofchildren.org.

> This issue of the journal reviews research on early childhood programs and examines implications for public policy. Of particular note are Barnett's review of 36 studies of model demonstration projects and large-scale public programs for children from low-income families; Frede's analysis of common elements linked to long-term effectiveness in preschool programs; and Zervigon-Hakes's discussion of the relationship of research to public policy.

Chapter Seven

Identifying the Source of Early Childhood Curriculum

Noting that this was the sixth edition devoted to early childhood education, Kagan (1991) identified four recurring themes in her preface to the ninetieth Yearbook of the Society for the Study of Education: (a) discerning the relationship between child development theory and educational practice, (b) confirming the appropriate content and method of teacher preparation, (c) defining early childhood education comprehensively and holistically, and (d) using research to inform pedagogy. "These fundamental issues," according to Kagan, "transcend time and place, bespeaking a generational continuity of enduring challenges that confront the field" (p. ix). Though accurately reflecting the scarcity of debate, the issue of curriculum is notably absent from Kagan's list.

Developed in part for the purpose of comparing different curriculum approaches to early childhood education, curriculum models provide structures for shaping, containing, and transporting early childhood curriculum. In the process, deliberations regarding what knowledge is of most worth (a critical curriculum question; Schubert, 1986)—and why—have been sidestepped.

Until recently, the field of curriculum focused primarily on the development and management of curriculum. It is only within the last 30 years—basically the life span of systematic dissemination and implementation of early childhood curriculum models—that curriculum studies have moved beyond developing and managing curriculum to investigating educational experience in terms of its political, cultural, gender, and historical dimensions (Pinar, 1988, 1999). Pinar has labeled this 30-year time period one of *curricular reconceptualization.* Within the last decade, this reconceptualization began to influence discussions of early childhood curriculum.

As academic content continues its encroachment into early childhood programs, its legitimacy as a primary source of early childhood curriculum continues to be debated. The clash between advocates of a developmental approach versus school content is not new, of course, but its prominence has escalated alongside the increasing number of early childhood programs in public schools (see, for example, Bredekamp, 1991; Elkind, 1986, 1989; Goffin, Stegelin, & Walsh, 1992; Hiebert, 1988; Warger, 1988).

Recently a third stakeholder entered the fray: early childhood curriculum theorists. Early childhood curriculum theorists transferred the premises of curricular reconceptualization to discussions of early childhood curriculum (see, for example,

Cannella, 1997; Kessler, 1991a; Kessler & Swadener, 1992; Lubeck, 1994, 1996, 1998; Swadener & Kessler, 1991b). They have challenged the appropriateness of *both* developmental theory and academic content as informants for early childhood curriculum, arguing that both limit consideration of the historical, political, and sociological dimensions of what children should learn. Early childhood curriculum theorists such as Swadener and Kessler (1991a) argue that early childhood curriculum should be analyzed in terms of whose interests are being served, and marginalized, by curricular decisions. For example, Delpit's (1988, 1995) concern that developmentally oriented curricula fail to meet the school readiness needs of poor minority children frequently is cited to support the argument that curriculum choices cannot be isolated from a community and its concerns.

As a result of these exchanges, curriculum issues are becoming part of the dialogue in early childhood education. As part of this curriculum debate, the soundness of creating and replicating preconceptualized curricula is being questioned on different terms.

Weikart and Schweinhart (1993; see also Weikart, 1995) asserted that "[d]elivery of high-quality programs is the most important task the early childhood field faces, as programs move from laboratory and demonstration schools into large-scale service to children and their families" (p. 195). Weikart and Schweinhart's assertion reminds us that the architects of curriculum models presume that curricula can be preconceptualized, transported to diverse locations, and uniformly implemented by teachers.

Recent theorizing, however, describes curriculum as knowledge-in-the-making, which differs from the idea of transporting preconceptualized programs. And, increasingly, teachers are being described as creators and interpreters of curricula, not just as its implementers. Arguments in support of the emergent character of curriculum and dynamic quality of teaching question curricula developed in laboratories and demonstration schools rather than in the daily interactions among children and teachers. These arguments also question the extent to which curriculum models, which were designed to increase uniformity, can be responsive to children, particular environments, and dilemmas resistive to standardization.

The reconceptualization of curriculum and reassessment of teaching are examples of shifts in thinking that have occurred since the era of curriculum models. These and other shifts are the focus of this chapter. When considered as part of an examination of curriculum models, these shifts in thinking uncover models' structural characteristics and offer insight into their educational purpose and function. Concurrently, concern for the low academic achievement of poor and minority children, alongside increased demand for public accountability, has elevated school and policy interest in research-based, transportable instructional programs.

∽ DEVELOPMENTAL THEORY AND EARLY CHILDHOOD CURRICULUM

Theories of child development have provided the basis for curriculum development in early childhood education since the late 1800s. The relationship between developmental theory and early childhood curriculum was reinforced during the 1960s when developmental psychologists assumed leadership positions in developing experimental early childhood programs. The relationship was confirmed when NAEYC approved its far-reaching position statement: Developmentally Appropriate Practice in Early Childhood Programs Serving Children Birth Through Age 8 (Bredekamp, 1987).

During the last 15 years, the relationship between developmental theory and early childhood curriculum has been strongly challenged (Kessler, 1990, 1991a; Lubeck, 1996, 1998; New, 1994a; Silin, 1985, 1987, 1988, 1995; Spodek, 1988), leading to a revised version of NAEYC's position statement on developmentally appropriate pratice (Bredekamp & Copple, 1997). Questions regarding developmental theory as a primary source for curriculum development challenge its appropriateness as a teacher guide for promoting child growth (Greene, 1989; Haberman, 1988; Polakow, 1989, 1993; Suransky, 1982; Sutton-Smith, 1989), its role in determining practice (Egan, 1983; Fein & Schwartz, 1982), and the extent to which it responds to the multiple purposes of early education and values of participating families (Delpit, 1988, 1995; Lubeck, 1996, 1998; Silin, 1995; Stott & Bowman, 1996).

Child development knowledge as *an* informant to practice is *not* the issue being deliberated. Rather, critics are questioning the overly dependent relationship between developmental theory and early childhood curriculum. These challenges come from the disciplines of philosophy, anthropology, linguistics, and curriculum studies, as well as early childhood education.

Further, developmental theory is informed by an ever-expanding knowledge base about child development. Another aspect of this discussion, therefore, concerns the extent to which the assumptions and research that provided the foundation for developmental theory and early childhood curriculum models during the 1960s and early 1970s remain valid.

Review of the developmental premises that undergird initial construction of curriculum models discloses that the developmental knowledge base has been altered in significant ways. Because, by definition, curriculum models have established parameters, the progressive nature of knowledge is problematic for them. In addition, changing understandings about child development from ongoing research and thought are not easily incorporated into early childhood curriculum models "in the field." Consequently, programs implementing specific models often inadvertently continue to promote practices based on dated understandings (Moore, 1983; Stott & Bowman, 1996). This discrepancy provided the basis for Simons and Simon's (1986) conclusion, for example, that "Montessori education, as practiced today, is misguided in its attempt to keep alive a system of education that may have been effective and appropriate in the past, but which, being fossilized, is inappropriate for the children of today" (p. 218). The unavoidable divergence between newly created knowledge and a model's particular frame of reference highlights a tension inherent to reliance on others' research and theory as templates for practice.

Questioning Old Assumptions and Making New Ones: Changing Understandings About Child Development

Faith in the positive, developmental effect of early childhood programs has largely reflected optimism regarding the impact of children's early experiences on their future success with society's educational and economic systems. Kagan (1983, 1998) attributed this linkage to the presumption of connectivity, an assumption that children's earlier experiences are causally related to their later experiences, and to our commitment to the idea of the early years as a determinant of future development. Embedded within this assumption are presumed answers to two questions that have existed throughout the history of developmental psychology (Cole & Cole, 1996): (a) Is development explained primarily by heredity or environment? and (b) Is the process of development continuous or discontinuous?

During the 1960s and early 1970s, bolstered by the conclusions of psychologists such as Hunt (1961) and Bloom (1964) regarding children's intellectual development, environmental influences, in general, and early experiences, in particular, were elevated over heredity as a primary explanation for developmental outcomes and individual differences. Further, these outcomes were believed to be the result of a continuous process of growth. Later developmental outcomes were assumed to be predicated on earlier ones; human development was characterized as a cumulative process.

Under the influence of Freudian psychology and the prevailing assumption that children's intellectual abilities were fixed by heredity, early childhood programs in the 1940s and 1950s focused on nurturing children's social-emotional development and providing supportive environments for their evolving capabilities. With the emphasis on cognitive development during the 1960s, the focus changed from nurturing children's social-emotional development to stimulating their cognitive abilities. Educationally, this shift was reflected in the then-new programmatic emphasis on providing young children from economically disadvantaged circumstances a "head start" on school success.

According to Bronfenbrenner (1974), interest in early stimulation originated from theory emerging in the early 1950s that pointed to the beneficial effects of early stimulation on animal and human development. The changed attitude toward cognitive development also is attributed to the discovery of Jean Piaget's work on cognitive development (in part due to English translations of his writings). His work was repeatedly cited to emphasize the importance of early, stimulating experiences in the growth of children's mental abilities (White & Buka, 1987).

The assumption of developmental continuity was integral to discussions about the detrimental impact of accumulated negative experiences. Called the cumulative deficit hypothesis, this assumption provided a psychological rationale for preschool intervention programs (Evans, 1975), which, in turn, spawned the development of curriculum models.

Since the height of curriculum model development, there is

- renewed interest in the interplay of heredity and environment in child development,
- differentiated understanding of the environment's contributions to child development,
- recognition of development's social nature and children's contributions to the process,

- appreciation for the role of adults in children's development and learning,
- renewed interest in social competence and emotional development, and
- reassessment of developmental psychology as an objective science.

These shifts reflect changing assumptions and understandings about child development. Because early childhood education and its curriculum models have been so reliant on developmental theory for curriculum design, knowledge of these shifts provides a basis for assessing the theoretical currency of enduring early childhood curriculum models.

New Understandings About the Interplay of Heredity and Environment.

When enthusiasm for preschool intervention programs first emerged, it was fueled by the then-new belief that children's intelligence was malleable. Especially for young children living in poverty, there was an expectation that their intelligence could be modified by providing enriching experiences. This view credited the environment, rather than heredity, with determining cognitive development.

Recent research on heredity's contributions to individual development, however, has redirected the pendulum's swing regarding the relative roles of heredity and environment (Cole & Cole, 1996; Horowitz & O'Brien, 1989; Kagan, 1983, 1998; Plomin, 1989, 1997; Rutter & Rutter, 1993). Findings from behavioral genetic research document that genetic influence on individual, developmental differences is significant and substantial (Plomin, 1989, 1997). Individual malleability, consequently, now is understood in a more restricted way.

Recognition of the contribution of genetic factors to development does not mean that the importance of environmental contributions is being dismissed. Rather, respect has grown for the complex interplay between environmental and genetic variables:

> With respect to the major determinants of behavioral development, a consensus is beginning to emerge. This consensus involves the notion that the general outlines of behavioral development have strong biological bases and will develop in most normal environments. But the specific behaviors that must be acquired are very much influenced by the availability of opportunities for learning in the child's environment. (Horowitz & O'Brien, 1989, p. 441)

Associated with the concept of plasticity, or malleability, of intellectual development has been the issue of timing, of when best to intervene to compensate for a poor environment. The concept of *critical period* contends that unique times exist in a child's growth during which specific environmental or biological events must occur for development to proceed normally. The work of psychologists, such as Bloom (1964), reinforced the idea of a child's first 5 years as critical to, and predictive of, later intellectual development

Preschool intervention programs were designed to intervene in the lives of disadvantaged children to modify the course of their early development. The field of compensatory education, as a result, contains numerous experimental studies relevant to the modifiability of intellectual ability.

Twenty years after the onset of compensatory education, Clarke (1984) concluded that exposure to a good early childhood program might temporarily alleviate some of the difficulties experienced by disadvantaged children, but it could not be expected to provide an effective, long-term barrier to ongoing environmental risks. The recent research of Ramey and Ramey (1998) and Reynolds (1994, 1997) supports this conclusion. Their research has found that continued environmental support is essential to sustaining the positive impact of preschool intervention programs. In their analysis of the issue over a decade ago, Horowitz and O'Brien (1989) argued:

> Development is not a disease to be treated. It is a process that needs constant nurturance. There is no reason to expect that an intensive program of early stimulation is an inoculation against all further developmental problems. No one would predict that a child given an adequate amount of vitamin C at 2 years of age will have no vitamin deficiency at 10 years of age. Currently, according to the most viable model of development that applies to both at-risk and normal children, developmentally functional stimulation is desirable at every period of development and not only in the early years. (p. 444)

Although research supports the concept of "the earlier the better" (St. Pierre & Layzer, 1998), findings that an adverse early environment can be mitigated by later, supportive experiences have challenged interpretations of the early years as a sole predictor of later ability (Bruer, 1999b; Clarke & Clarke, 1976; Kagan, 1984, 1998; Rutter & Rutter, 1993). In 1983, Kessen predicted, "The commitment to the special, even unique importance of the child's encounters during the infantile years—a commitment old and almost universal—is under such serious attack these days, we can wonder if it will survive the decade" (p. 31).

Research on Early Brain Development.

Research on Early Brain Development. Kessen's prediction never materialized. Recent advances in neuroscience and cognitive science have provoked dramatic new interest by policy makers to the first 3 years of childhood, provided new evidence that the environment plays an important role in early brain development, and bolstered advocacy on behalf of programmatic interventions during early childhood. Emphasis on the first years of life has directed attention away from the preschool years, however, and underscored anew the question of timing in early intervention programs. This new research dismantles once and for all polarization of heredity's and the environment's contributions to child development as an either–or question. The implications of this research for policy and practice, however, are hotly debated.

According to Bruer's (1999b) review of research, three major strands of investigation on brain development have fueled this revival. The first strand is evidence that the brain's structure and complexity continue to develop during the first decade of childhood, rather than being genetically determined and complete at birth, as previously understood. Current research defines two periods in early brain development: the growth of the structure or architecture of the brain, and the creation of neural connections or synapses. Brain structure begins developing before birth, and although genes play an important role, environmental factors such as health and nutrition of the mother exert significant influence on the brain's development.

Neural connections emerge before birth in the form of spontaneous brain activity, but during the first 3 years of a child's life the building of synapses occurs in a "biological exuberance" of activity (Bruer, 1999b, p. 11). Although significant neurological development occurs before a child is born, neuroscientists speculate that important developmental work remains in order for infants to "fine-tune" neural mechanisms to specifics of their environments. The process of fine-tuning involves both production and pruning of neural connections.

The second strand identified by Bruer (1999b) to emerge from neuroscience is return of the idea of critical periods. As the brain's structure and neural connections develop, there are periods when activity appears to intensify in different parts of the brain. For example, in human infants, synaptic formation in the auditory cortex reaches peak levels about 3 months, and in the frontal cortex, at 2.5 to 3 years. Implications have been drawn from this research to suggest that there are "prime times" for development (Shore, 1997, p. 38), and that an absence of appropriate stimulation disrupts development for the brain area under construction at that time. The Committee on Developments in the Science of Learning commissioned by the National Research Council has concluded that further research is needed on "which things are tied to critical periods . . . and for which things is the time of exposure less critical" (Bransford, Brown, & Cocking, 1999, p. 115).

Finally, a third strand of research conducted on rats indicates that greater synapse formation occurs in certain portions of the brain for animals raised in complex, stimulating environments than for those animals raised in less elaborate settings. Implications drawn from this line of study suggest that the early years offer a unique timeframe during which to enrich children's environments with language, songs, and music; provide opportunities for exploration and play; and establish warm, caring relationships with responsive adults.

Bolstered by scientific evidence for long-held beliefs, early childhood advocates have used this research to reignite discussion about programs for young children and their families (see, for example Carnegie Corporation of New York, 1994, 1996; Karoly et al., 1998; Schorr, 1997). These efforts have resulted in a broadened group of stakeholders becoming interested in early childhood issues, development of new programs, the addition of new resources, and numerous new public policy initiatives, especially in states and communities.

The success of early childhood advocates in publicizing their perspective on the implications of neuroscience research has fostered expressions of concern about linkages between science and public policy. Some advocates for early intervention are claiming irreversible effects on children's developing brains if they do not receive experiences critical to healthy development. Such bold statements, however, have led to counterarguments (see, for example, Bruer, 1999a, 1999b; Kagan, 1998; Nelson & Bloom, 1997):

> It may be useful to question the simplistic view that the brain becomes unbendable and increasingly difficult to modify beyond the first few years of life. Although clearly much of brain development occurs late in gestation through the first years of postnatal life, the brain is far from set in its trajectory, even at the completion of adolescence. (Nelson & Bloom, 1997, p. 983)

Of concern is that popular interpretations of the research on early brain development may resurrect the discarded notion from the mid-1960s of the cumulative deficit hypothesis. Kagan (1998) cautions that as concern grows for children from low-income families, the idea of critical periods in its current guise may be "more political than scientific" (p. 89). Reminiscent of Ramey et al.'s (1985) assessment of policy makers' embrace of the early experience paradigm during the 1960s and 1970s (see Chapter 1), Kagan concludes, "It is considerably more expensive to improve the quality of housing, education, and health of . . . children living in poverty today than to urge their mothers to kiss, talk to, and play with them more consistently" (1998, p. 91).

Further Contributions of the Environment to Child Development. When curriculum models were systematically initiated during the late 1960s, psychologists and educators focused primarily on constructing environments that would stimulate children's cognitive development. The nature and intensity of the stimulation varied by curriculum model, but, in general, "the environment" was a global, undifferentiated concept. Few questioned that the home environment of poor children, in comparison to their middle-class peers, was inferior in terms of stimulating cognitive development. This assumption, of course, provided justification for early intervention (Clarke-Stewart & Fein, 1983; Evans, 1975; Ramey et al., 1985; Ramey & Suarez, 1984).

The meaning of the term *environment* now has been more deeply analyzed, however. Initial findings from comparative evaluations of curriculum models, which explained program variance by site variations rather than by differences among specific models, contributed to this reassessment. Findings challenged the belief that children's learning environments and developmental trajectories could be homogenized if they experienced the same curriculum model.

Attention then was directed to studying the uniqueness of various environments in which learning and development occurred and how, in turn, learning and development are influenced by their particular context (Bronfenbrenner, 1989; Bruner & Haste, 1987; Cole, 1998; Horowitz & O'Brien, 1989; Rogoff, 1990). Contextual influences now include factors such as neighborhoods, living arrangements, poverty, and the influence of racism (Chase-Lansdale & Gordon, 1996; Garcia Coll et al., 1996).

In addition, researchers point to the "funds of knowledge" overlooked when development is viewed only through the lens of white, middle-class child-rearing practices (Moll, Amanti, Neff, & Gonzalez, 1992, p. 132). Ethnographic studies indicate that opportunities exist for developing culturally valued skills and knowledge in many different types of environments (see, for example, Delgado-Gaitan, 1994; Goncu, 1999; Moll et al., 1992).

Thus diverse environments are now studied in terms of how they provide for and promote different kinds of learning opportunities. This apparently benign statement derives its controversy from the fact that it challenges the universality of development—an assumption inherent to most theories of child development

(Gardner, 1999; Lubeck, 1985). Relative to our examination of curriculum models, this reassessment parallels conclusions from program evaluations (see Chapter 6). Curriculum models are more than simply different approaches to early education; they are sources for creating significantly different learning environments and child outcomes.

Bronfenbrenner (1986) suggested that individuals live simultaneously in multiple environments. He described these multiple environments as a series of embedded, concentric circles, starting with the closest environment, home and neighborhood, and extending to encompass societal norms, policies, and cultural expectations. This ecological framework identifies various circles of influence and proposes that their interactions with each other become the environmental in which we live.

Understanding the complexity of environmental influences challenges simplistic faith in the ability of early childhood experiences, organized as early childhood programs, to totally and easily transform children's lives. This understanding helps explain interest in expanding preschool intervention programs to include health services, and parent education and support.

Cole (1998) extends Bronfenbrenner's description of embedded environments by placing these environments within a cultural context. Whereas other theoretical frameworks study development in terms of the interaction of heredity and environment, the cultural context perspective incorporates culture as a third contributor to the developmental process. Bruner (1990, 1996) would argue that human development can *only* be understood in light of one's cultural context, a factor almost totally neglected in discussions of curriculum models.

Culture is based on the accumulated knowledge of a people and is reflected in their language, beliefs, values, and customs (Cole, 1998). It is "a way of life shared by members of a population. It is the socio-cultural adaptation or design for living that people have worked out in the course of their history" (Ogbu, 1987, p. 156).

Those who advocate the significance of culture contend that biological and environmental factors have different consequences for development depending on the specific cultural context in which they are embedded. These differences in turn have implications for planning early childhood learning environments (Bowman & Stott, 1994; Ogbu, 1987, 1994; Phillips, 1994; Tharp, 1989; Tobin, Wu, & Davidson, 1989).

Lubeck's (1985) and O'Brien's (1993) ethnographic studies of preschool programs affirm this conclusion in terms of the learning environments provided by teachers from different cultural groups. O'Brien's findings are particularly noteworthy because she studied Head Start teachers who were implementing the High/Scope Curriculum in a rural, impoverished community. Despite the use of a highly developed and carefully articulated curriculum model, "[t]he varying social milieus of the teachers seem to have been important to their conceptions of the skills, knowledge, and values they believed ought to be transmitted to the children in their charge" (O'Brien, 1993, p. 15). As a result, children's learning environments varied with the cultural priorities of their teachers.

Current sensitivity to cultural differences contrasts with interpretations that dominated psychological thinking during the 1960s and early 1970s. At that time, home environments that differed from those of white middle-class families were seen as inferior learning environments for young children. The terms *culturally deprived* or *culturally disadvantaged* were frequently applied, and clearly implied the superiority of the majority culture. Some preschool intervention programs were designed to provide disadvantaged children with experiences to make up for their presumed deficiencies. The Bereiter-Engelmann model, it will be recalled, was an especially strong example of this viewpoint.

In contrast, culturally sensitive approaches attempt to avoid devaluation of cultural differences and to understand variation from the perspective of a cultural group (see, for example, Garcia Coll et al., 1996; Greenfield & Cocking, 1994; Ogbu, 1994). Studies of differences in cultural values reveal distinctive familial and community strategies for socializing young children (Goncu, 1999; Greenfield & Cocking, 1994).

Further, increased appreciation exists for the role of "cultural frames of reference" or "cultural identity" in development, as critical frameworks for how children and families perceive themselves in relation to the dominant social group (Ogbu, 1994; Ogbu & Simons, 1998). Garcia Coll et al. (1996) describe, for example, the complexities encountered by minority families in raising children to function within two systems of cultural values and beliefs, particularly when the home culture is subject to discrimination and racism.

In terms of cultural impact on early childhood education, Edwards and Gandini (1989) studied teacher expectations for the timing of developmental skills in Italian and American early childhood programs. Their cross-cultural study found that the two cultures had different expectations regarding the ages at which children should master various developmental tasks. Differences in cultural expectations also extend to the function of preschools, as Tobin et al. (1989) vividly portrayed in their comparison of preschools in three cultures.

Labov's (1969) classic study of differences in how African American children used language in formal (such as the classroom) and informal settings highlighted the misconceptions that insensitivity to cultural differences can generate. In informal settings with an interviewer from the same ethnic group, African American children were found to have highly complex and differentiated language skills. By studying young African American children's language skills in a setting more familiar to them, Labov's study punctured the perception that African American youth were racially deficient in their language and reasoning abilities.

Early childhood curricula, however, have been based primarily on white, middle-class perspectives of society and families (Bloch, 1991; Bowman & Stott, 1994; Henry, 1996, Lubeck, 1994, 1998; Williams, 1994). So, for example, in studies of Head Start and public prekindergarten programs, efforts to socialize children from culturally different experiences to the norms and practices of public schools have revealed differences in expectations that can heighten tensions for children, teachers, and families (see, for example, Inoway-Ronnie, 1998; Polakow, 1993; Quintero, 1999; Wilson, 1999).

Appreciation of culture as a third, and significant, contributor to development argues for a reexamination of reliance on white, middle-class norms. This recommendation is bolstered by the increasing cultural diversity of children in the United States who participate in early childhood programs, expanding understanding of cultural differences, and increasing appreciation for the fact that different cultural settings provide different (versus deficient) backdrops and opportunities for learning.

The Social Nature of Development. Bruner and Haste (1987) contended that

> [a] quiet revolution has taken place in developmental psychology in the last decade. It is not only that we have begun to think again of the child as a *social being*—one who plays and talks with others, learns through interactions with parents and teachers—but because we have come more to appreciate that through social life, the child acquires a framework for interpreting experiences, and learns how to negotiate the meaning in a manner congruent with the requirements of the culture. (p. 1, emphasis in original)

Primarily because of the influence of Jean Piaget's theory of cognitive development, children's developing understandings about the world often are described in terms of their independently constructed interpretations of experience. Critics have argued that this description presumes that children construct their views of the world in isolation of their social and cultural context, in effect that context does not significantly inform how one's world can be interpreted (Bruner, 1990, 1996; Bruner & Haste, 1987; Goncu, 1999; Rogoff, 1990).

As highlighted in the previous section, newer interpretations of child development and learning attend to the impact of the social and cultural contexts in which children participate (Cole, 1998; Garcia Coll et al., 1996; Greenfield & Cocking, 1994). Publication of Vygotsky's (1978) writings in the United States helped prompt interest in the role of adults in guiding children's participation in culturally valued activities. Vygotsky theorized human development as having two dimensions: a biological and a cultural. The cultural dimension of development emerges as children participate in activities and learn to use the tools valued by their culture.

Children learn to function as members of their communities by participating within their *zone of proximal development*—a dynamic range of performance defined as the distance between a child's abilities when working alone and what she can accomplish with the assistance of a more accomplished member of the culture. Adults who provide experience for a child within her range of ability assist the child in moving along the developmental pathway valued by her community. Thus, from a Vygotskian perspective, learning leads development. Appreciating adults' contributions to children's learning by supporting and extending children's performance beyond that which they can accomplish independently has challenged the view of the child constructing meaning independently of culture. It also challenges the Piagetian view that development precedes learning.

Interest in Vygotsky flourished in the 1990s, stimulating developmental psychologists to explore the sociocultural context of development and provoking educators to examine the implications of this view of development and learning for their teaching practice. These questions contributed to reexamination of the first version of the position statement of the National Association for the Education of Young Children on developmentally appropriate practice (Bredekamp, 1987; see Chapter 4). The revision incorporates a new awareness of the social context of children's development, including a more intricate role for teachers in interactions with children, and a more complex understanding of families as contexts for children's learning and development (Bredekamp & Copple, 1997).[1]

Current interpretations of child development also incorporate the child as a contributor to his or her own development (Bronfenbrenner 1989; Iran-Nejad et al., 1990b; Lerner, 1987; Matusov, 1998). By influencing how others respond to them and thus changing the context that, in turn, influences their own behavior, children are now credited as "*co*-producers" of their own development (James, Jenks, & Prout, 1998; Lerner, 1987; Matusov, 1998).

Emphasis on the social, versus self-sufficient, nature of children's learning and development directs attention to the significance of social relationships in all areas of a child's growth: moral (Gilligan, 1988), interactions with adults and peers (Bukowski, Newcomb, & Hartup, 1998; Corsaro, 1988, 1997; Greenfield & Cocking, 1994; Hartup, 1984, 1989), and intellectual (Bruner, 1996; Bruner & Haste, 1987; Rogoff, 1990; Rutter, 1985; Vygotsky, 1978). Appreciation for the social nature of child development highlights the importance of contemplating early childhood curriculum models in terms of the relationships they foster among and between children and teachers.

Revisions to conceptualizations of "intelligence" have further enlarged interest beyond cognitive development to include an appreciation of "interpersonal" (Gardner, 1983) or "emotional" intelligence (Goleman, 1995). According to Elias (1997) in a publication targeted to public school administrators, persistent concern with student alienation, disaffection with school, and diminishing willingness to participate in the roles of citizenship and family life have led to reconsideration of the importance of social and emotional learning in public schools.

The abilities to cooperate with others, solve problems, and set personal goals are becoming valued as skills and dispositions necessary for academic success, as well as essential life skills—a conclusion, it will be recalled, that led Weikart and his colleagues to revise the High/Scope Curriculum to give more emphasis to fostering similar dispositions (see Chapter 5).

Developmental Psychology as Objective Science: A Reassessment.

As a science, developmental psychology has attempted to describe general laws of behavior that are applicable regardless of circumstances. As developmentalists became aware of the ways in which individual behavior is socially and culturally organized, they lessened their search for laws of development that apply across circumstances.

This is because such laws can be derived only from study of those things that are culturally and environmentally indifferent (Kessen, 1983; White, 1983b). If different settings can facilitate a variety of developmental outcomes, then developmental laws or principles must be related to the setting(s) in which behavior is occurring.

---

[1]Berk and Winsler (1995) and Bodrova and Leong (1996) provide useful discussions of the implications of Vygotsky's theory for early childhood practitioners.

Relative to curriculum models, this is a challenging position for program architects who must assume that child development principles can be decontextualized and applied across settings with similar results.

Similarly, insights regarding the significance of cultural circumstances have changed our understanding of childhood. The idea of childhood as a separate developmental period has existed as a concept for more than 100 years (Postman, 1982/1994). Since then, society, with the help of psychology, has invented different kinds of children. The idea that our notions of childhood are culturally constructed, rather than the natural result of a predetermined developmental process, is now a recurring theme (Cahan, Mechling, Sutton-Smith, & White, 1993; James et al., 1998; Kagan, 1983; Kessel & Siegel, 1983).

For example, according to Elkind (1987), during the 19th century, the dominance of religious thinking helped create the image of the "sinful" child. In the early 20th century, which was dominated by Freudian psychology, the concept of the sinful child gradually was replaced by the "sensual" child. Contemporary emphasis on the intellectual ability of children, accompanied by research findings detailing the abilities of infants, gradually has replaced the concept of the sensual child with that of the "competent" child. (For in-depth descriptions of changing social conceptions of children and childhood, see also Cosaro, 1997; Elder, Modell, & Parke, 1993; Liljestrom, 1983; and Zelizer, 1985.) Major theorists in developmental psychology, consequently, have "gathered an assembly of vastly different children" (White, 1983b, p. 28).

Psychology's attempts to describe these "different" children have been informed by Darwin's theory of evolution (Bronfenbrenner, Kessel, Kessen, & White, 1986; Weber, 1984; White, 1983a), which proposed that development of the species resulted from improvements in its adaptability. As a consequence of this thinking, developmental psychology came to assume that the process of development followed a natural order that resulted in a known end point, a goal toward which development was progressing (Brofenbrenner et al., 1986; White, 1983a, 1983b).

Some developmentalists, however, challenge whether the process of development can, in fact, be objectively described as traveling toward a known end point. Perhaps, some are suggesting, no single, clear end point or standard of development exists toward which all individuals evolve (Bronfenbrenner et al., 1986; Burman, 1994; Greene, 1989; Haberman, 1988; Morss, 1996; Suransky, 1982; Vandenberg, 1993).

White (1983b) argued that "all technical problems that command our interest and our concern and our enthusiasm and our passion have buried within them questions of value" (p. 15). Even descriptions of the developmental process are statements of value. Silin (1995), for example, noted that Piaget's theory and its concern for the development of rational thought arose "in a culture obsessed with technological accomplishments and scientific approaches to the management of human problems. What Piaget's theory excludes from consideration are nonrational, but not necessarily irrational, modes of thought: intuitive, mythical, religious, aesthetic, imaginative" (p. 90). Silin goes on to argue that these omissions are not neutral; they reflect a value system consistent with a highly rationalized, scientifically oriented culture. This value system is present not only in Piaget's focus on the development of rational thought but also in his description of the process of adaptation by which rational thought develops. "The implication is that education, in promoting intelligent behavior, promotes adaptation to the environment. In the end, every psychology is embedded in a politics as well as a world view, and the politics of adaptation is certainly not the politics of resistance or revolution" (p. 91).

These insights are of particular importance to early childhood education. Many early childhood educators unknowingly promote values implicit in developmental theories as if they were objectively determined end points for development. For example, Lubeck (1996) notes that Piaget's developmental studies reflect a child who is "Western, White, and middle class; indeed, a child similar to his own" (p. 155). When Piaget's theoretical framework became a "universal norm" of development, "differences in non-Western children and children of color within Western nations were interpreted as indications of 'developmental lag'" (p. 154).

The research of Durkin (1987) and Silin (1987, 1988, 1995) demonstrates how early childhood education's dependence on developmental theory has fostered the belief that teachers should use child development knowledge to facilitate children's developmental progression in ways consistent with a particular developmental theory. As summarized by White (1983a):

> If the summum honum of child development is formal operations (the final stage of Piaget's theory of cognitive development), then it is good to do anything that helps bring about formal operations. . . . If it is decentration—or active play, or taking the role of the other, or metacognitive activities—that drives a child toward formal operations, then we know what is good for educators to do with children. (p. 74)

The High/Scope Curriculum (mostly in its earlier versions and less so in its most recent iteration) and Kamii-DeVries approach provide examples of how theories of development have been used to construct educational environments designed to promote children's growth along a prescribed developmental trajectory.

But, increasingly, the question is being asked: "Should child development theory serve as the source of educational values for early childhood education" (Greene, 1988; Kessler, 1990, 1991b; Lubeck, 1996, 1998; Silin, 1995; Spodek, 1988; Swadener & Kessler, 1991a)? Uncertainty regarding the appropriate relationship between developmental theory and early childhood curriculum is deepened by disputes over the objectivity of developmental theories and their individualist perspectives on learning and development.

Child Development Theories and Early Childhood Curriculum: Challenges to the Status Quo

Developmental Theory as the Source of Education Objectives.

In advocating the pivotal position of developmental theory relative to early childhood education, Sigel (1972) contended that

> [d]evelopmental theory ideally describes patterns of growth in cognitive, social, perceptual, and affect areas. Armed with this knowledge, program builders can proceed to construct programs that follow the course of growth. . . . The rationale for advocating "the match" is that such a match is essential if we are to create curricula that are relevant and appropriate for maximizing the development of young children. (p. 13)

One of the best known arguments for constructing early childhood programs that pursue the course of development was advanced by Kohlberg and Mayer (1972). Their argument made "explicit how a cognitive-developmental psychological theory can be translated into a rational and viable progressive educational ideology, i.e., a set of concepts defining desirable aims, content and methods of education" (p. 450).

When Kohlberg and Mayer wrote "Development as the Aim of Education" in 1972, there were, as reflected in the diversity of curriculum models, multiple educational programs and methodologies emphasizing different educational outcomes. The challenge then, as now, was how to choose among these outcomes. Their classic paper supplied a justification for why development, as detailed in Piaget's theory of cognitive development, provided the appropriate aim for education.

Kohlberg and Mayer (1972) identified three prevalent educational streams of thought informing the selection of educational outcomes: romanticism, cultural transmission, and progressivism. According to Kohlberg and Mayer, the romantic view, associated with maturational theory, promoted nurturing the innate, predetermined capacities of children. They criticized this perspective because it lacked a clear theoretical rationale for pursuing particular educational outcomes.

The cultural transmission view is associated with behavioral theory that explains growth primarily in terms of environmental inputs. Children, for the most part, were construed as relatively passive recipients of environmental stimuli.[2] Because the source of behavioral change is external to the individual, educational objectives aligned with this approach emanate from social consensus, rather than fulfillment of one's innate capacities. Kohlberg and Mayer (1972) censured this view for its failure to recognize ultimate standards of worth in learning and development.

In contrast, according to Kohlberg and Mayer (1972), Piaget's cognitive developmental theory provided a clear theoretical rationale for moving from "is" to "ought" that could withstand the logical and philosophical criticisms that undermined the other two perspectives (also see Kohlberg, 1981). Cognitive developmental theory, according to Kohlberg and Mayer, avoided the cultural relativity associated with the romantic and cultural transmission streams of educational thought. This same reasoning, it will be recalled, undergirded the latest iteration of the Kamii-DeVries approach.

Kohlberg and Mayer's (1972) rationale assumed a predetermined direction and outcome for human development that, in light of its universality, was objective and independent of context:

> Searching for the "objective" in human experience, the progressive seeks universal qualitative states or sequences in development. Movement from one stage to the next is significant because it is a sequence in the individual's own development, not just a population average or norm. At the same time, insofar as the sequence is a universally observed development, it is not unique to the individual in question. (p. 463)

---

[2]As noted in Chapter 6, behavioral theory has undergone considerable revision since the 1960s. Thus, Kohlberg & Mayer's description of behavioral theory should be considered in light of the authors' arguments regarding educational aims, but not as a current description of behavioral theory.

This line of reasoning, however, contradicts contemporary thinking regarding the significance of environmental and cultural circumstances. It advances development as context free and developmental theory as a valid source for educational goals, as long as implicit values are articulated and supported by a complementary philosophical framework (also see Weber, 1984). By relying on this line of reasoning, desired educational outcomes are detached from deliberations regarding preferred, and often conflicting, values.

Challenges to Developmental Theory as the Source of Educational Outcomes. Challenges to development as the aim of education stem, in part, from developmental theory's fall from the pedestal of scientific objectivity; this "fall" derails the possibility of rationalizing the notion of "is" to "ought."

Challengers further argue that emphasis on development as an educational outcome directs attention to what children can do, rather than what they should be doing. Yet, the argument goes, it is the question "What should children be doing?" that is educationally significant, and further, this is a question that should be addressed philosophically and ethically, rather than in terms of developmental theory. Critics contend that overreliance on developmental theory has prompted early childhood educators to sidestep the issue of societal values and to ignore discussion—and responsibility—regarding what outcomes are most educationally worthwhile for young children (Kessler, 1991a; Silin, 1995; Spodek, 1988).

The search for universal behaviors in the developing child has resulted in a framework of developmental "needs" that guides to adult decision making. Reliance on developmental theory to determine educational outcomes obscures the political dimensions of what is taught by implying that curriculum choices can be determined by developmental appropriateness, rather than political and moral priorities (Kessler, 1991a; Lubeck, 1998; Silin, 1995). As expressed by Martin Woodhead (1997),

> . . . if needs can be identified with children's nature, with universal qualities of their biological and psychological make-up, then the evidence of scientific enquiry can provide the basis of social and educational policy and practice. But, if, on the other hand, needs have to be seen as cultural construction, superimposed on children "in their best interests" as future adult members of society, personal values and cultural ideologies have a much bigger part to play and the politician's or practitioner's authority is substantially diminished. To put it bluntly, the one appears mainly a matter of establishing "the facts," the other appears as also a matter for personal choice and political discussion. (p. 68)

Moreover, according to Bloch (1991), focusing on individual development places responsibility for change with the individual and "serves (whether intentional or not) to distract attention from structural analyses of the problems that help to maintain oppression and inequities in achievement" (p. 105). Using this reasoning, it is possible, for example, to construe school readiness as an issue of individual, rather than institutional, responsibility.

Others express concern regarding the ways theories of development limit early education's promotion of children's individuality and self-creation by restraining perceptions of the learner (Burman, 1994; Greene, 1988, 1989; Haberman, 1988; Suransky, 1982; Sutton-Smith, 1989; Zimiles, 1986). Polakow (1989) argued that discussions of child development remake children into objects "conditioned, driven, modeled, matured, or staged" (p. 78).

According to Haberman (1988), any theory of child development makes two implicit assumptions: (a) What can be explained and predicted about child development and behavior by using a theoretical explanation exceeds that portion of growth and behavior that is unpredictable and (b) regardless of the specific theory, there is an acceptance of regularity of behavior undergirded by a systematic set of explanations. Consequently,

> [t]eachers committed to a theory of development will hold expectations of what is normal and typical which they will inevitably transform into what is desirable. They will then develop and hold expectations for preferred behavior which supports their particular theory and makes them insensitive to other explanations and understandings. (p. 37)

Such restraints, according to Polakow, deprive children "of their own history-making power, their ability to act upon the world in significant and meaningful ways" (p. 8).

In light of our investigation, these provocative concerns are of more than passing interest. They are troublesome critiques for curriculum models because models depend on a consistent model of the child in order to ease dissemination and replication.

Educational dependence on developmental theory affects teachers as well. For one, when children become objects of study, adults are placed in the role of developers; and adults, according to Suransky (1982), have become developers of an increasingly rational, controllable, and predictable image of the child. Second, they diminish the opportunity for substantive (and often more contentious) conversations about educational values. Third, by creating the notion that all that needs to be known about children exists in an outside body of knowledge, teachers become defined as consumers of knowledge rather than its creators (Lubeck, 1996, 1998; Silin, 1987, 1995; Zimiles, 1986). As a result, Zimiles (1986) pointed out, teachers tend to be deflected from doing their own thinking. However, as we learned from examining the history of the Developmental-Interaction approach (see Chapter 3), this dependent, consumer-oriented relationship between practitioner and theory is a relatively new phenomenon:

> Whereas in the past, there was a partnership between early education and developmental psychology in the quest for understanding the young child, the vast expansion and differentiation of developmental psychology have assigned dominance to research and left early education in the role of consumer. Yet the level of analysis of most research and its quest for certainty and substantiation rather than theoretical elucidation and elaboration is more browbeating than useful to the educational practitioner. After intimidating and silencing the educator of young children by their masses of data and pose of authoritative mastery, psychologists rush in to fill the vacuum created by their dominance. This sometimes leads to the development of teacher-proof methods that further diminish the level of initiative and resourcefulness to be expected from teachers. (Zimiles, 1986, p. 201)

Relation Between Theory and Practice. Sigel (1972) described the relationship between developmental theory and early childhood programming as a necessary match between theory and practice. His focus on practice as a mirror of theory assumed a dependent relationship that, as we have now seen, has been challenged empirically, philosophically, and practically. In part, continued acceptance of this relationship derives from the failure to distinguish between the functions of psychology and education.

Generally, psychology's purpose is to describe behavior as it is, not in terms of what it ought to be (Egan, 1983; Fein & Schwartz, 1982; Katz, 1991; Silin, 1988, 1995; Spodek, 1988). In contrast, a theory of education, in addition to addressing individual growth, confronts questions of what kind of person society hopes will result from the educational process. As a result, the function of education is to try and shape the forces that produce desired educational outcomes (Egan, 1983; Fein & Schwartz, 1982; Pinar, 1999; Silin, 1995; Spodek, 1988).

Whereas psychological theories strive to be descriptive and as value free as possible, educational theories are intentionally prescriptive and value laden:

> Educators are not trying to describe a process of development in a value-free way; they are trying to prescribe the best way of actualizing a range of preferred potentials. The value-laden nature of the end does not present a problem for educators; it is a part of the job in hand to deal constantly and explicitly with value matters. (Egan, 1983, p. 8)

Egan (1983) concluded that by failing to recognize this distinction, we confuse psychological with educational development. It is perhaps easier, now, to recognize that Kohlberg and Mayer (1972) were trying to construct a bridge between psychological and educational development. They were uncomfortable, however, with the "subjectively" chosen values associated with the romantic and cultural transmission viewpoints. So, they attempted to demonstrate the "natural" superiority of educational objectives associated with Piaget's cognitive-developmental theory.

But the contention that developmental theory depicts "natural" end points of growth—and hence a justifiable source of educational objectives—has been severely challenged by revelations of developmental psychology's subjectivity. Skrtic (1991) argued that we are moving away from belief in the objectivism of science and mechanical change toward a more subjective interpretation of knowledge. He suggested that this shifting acceptance of subjectivity is part of a larger paradigm shift being experienced by Western civilization.

A shift away from the "objectivity" of science, though, surfaces the dreaded specter of relativism (Bruner, 1996). Bruner (1996), however, is quick to argue that the complex diversity of value commitments inherent to any culture does not equate with "free-for-all relativism" (p. 61), as Kohlberg and Mayer apparently feared. The prevalence of multiple choices need not imply that each is of equal merit nor eliminate requirements for their justification (Bruner, 1996; Buchmann, 1984, 1990).

This perspective concurs with the recommendations of a growing number of early childhood educators and theorists, especially early childhood curriculum theorists: determination of educationally worthwhile experiences should be derived from discussions of our commitments, including community and societal values, and issues of equity and justice (Egan, 1983; Kessler, 1991a; Lubeck, 1996,

1998; New, 1997; Silin, 1987, 1988, 1995; Spodek, 1988; Swadener & Kessler, 1991a). These issues, however, rarely have been raised as an explicit part of discussions on early childhood curriculum models.

As we will discover in Chapter 9, as a result of encounters with educators in Reggio Emilia, Italy, these issues are being exposed to a broader group of early educators. Their broad consideration will confront the field with arguments for different purposes for providing early childhood education (Goffin, in press).

To avoid misinterpretation of this discussion, it is important to repeat a caution provided earlier. These concerns should not be construed as suggesting that developmental theory is educationally irrelevant. The issue under deliberation is not the educational relevance of child development research or developmental theory; nor is the issue the developmental nature of education.[3] It is the legitimacy of developmental theory as the primary *determinant* of early childhood curriculum that has been identified as problematic. Expressions of concern regarding the limitations associated with developmental theory, therefore, frequently are accompanied by recommendations that early childhood education broaden its perspective to incorporate other disciplines, including sociology, philosophy, anthropology, linguistics, and curriculum studies, as additional informants to goal setting, decision making, and practice (Almy, 1988; Greene, 1988; Kessler, 1991a; Lubeck, 1996; Silin 1987, 1995; Swadener & Kessler, 1991a; Takanishi, 1981).

Research on Teacher Effects

One of the challenges to the practical conceptualization of early childhood education as birth to age 8 years is the fact that early childhood and elementary education have evolved from different institutional histories. Bloch (1991, 1992) suggested that the histories of early childhood's and elementary education's different institutional affiliations explain early childhood education's greater reliance on developmental theory in comparison to elementary education's dependence on efforts aimed at social efficiency.

Perhaps elementary education's historical roots explain its interest in research on teacher behaviors that increase student achievement, a search primarily directed toward improving teacher practice. Opportunities to apply the findings to educational decision making—with hopes of increasing student achievement and teacher accountability—fueled interest in this research (Zumwalt, 1989) and were based on faith in the power of scientific knowledge to resolve societal problems. Under the rubric of teacher effectiveness research (which was especially prominent from the 1960s through the early 1980s), researchers sought to explain relationships between classroom processes (usually teacher behaviors) and educational outcomes. Limited attention was directed to the curriculum or subject matter being taught (Zumwalt, 1989).

---

[3]For an interesting discussion of education *as* development, see Blenkin and Kelly (1987).

Teacher effectiveness research assumed effectiveness could be achieved by teacher application of those strategies and methods the research identified as increasing student achievement. Researchers assumed that teaching consisted of tactics "made rigorous by the application of scientific theory and technique" (Schon, 1983, p. 21; see also Doll, 1988).

Despite intense interest in teacher effectiveness research, Goffin's (1989) search for a similar body of knowledge specific to early childhood education found it to be virtually nonexistent. What *was* occurring in early childhood education during this time were program evaluations of early childhood curriculum models. And similar to the research on teacher effectiveness, these evaluation studies hoped to identify the best means for promoting student achievement. Whereas educational researchers probed for the most effective teacher behaviors, evaluators of early childhood curriculum models sought confirmation regarding the most effective early childhood curriculum—which, of course, directs teacher behavior. So when the complexities of classroom life confounded the identification of effective curriculum models, evaluators searched for the best match between curriculum and child by attempting to tease apart the effects of specific teacher behaviors (see Chapter 6).

Thus, although these two research agendas were differently designed, they sought similar outcomes. This correspondence makes assessment of the teacher effectiveness research pertinent to our own inquiry. The findings weaken expectations that teaching—or the anticipated by-product, educational achievement — can be improved by structuring education as a technical enterprise, whether pursued via research on teacher effectiveness or evaluations of the differential effects of early childhood curriculum models.

Based on the premise that research findings regarding the effectiveness of elementary teachers could be translated into effective teaching behaviors, research on teacher effectiveness became the content for teacher education and staff development programs. Zumwalt (1982) and Darling-Hammond (1985) called this linear process of reinterpreting research results into teacher practices a technological orientation. This technological orientation was criticized for assuming that knowledge about effective teaching can be transformed into production rules for making teachers more effective. Similar to program evaluators' failure to consider children's influence on their own development, educational researchers have been criticized for neglecting to consider the extent to which teacher effects are mediated by teacher knowledge, purposes, and values (Buchmann, 1984; Fenstermacher, 1979; Kerr, 1981; Macmillan & Garrison, 1984; Shulman, 1987; Stodolsky, 1984; Zumwalt, 1982, 1986). (Recall that this issue recently has been identified as affecting implementation of early childhood curriculum models as well. See Chapter 6.)

Critics of teacher effectiveness research claim that teachers do not become more effective merely by acting differently toward students; if this were so, teaching would be simply a technical vocation (Darling-Hammond, 1999) and learning a passive act. As discussed previously, the notion of children's passivity in their own learning and development has been severely criticized. So has the notion that teachers are passive in learning how to teach and technical in implementing what they know. To the contrary, it now is argued that teachers become more effective by thinking about and reflecting on what makes the activity of teaching worthwhile (see, for example, Irwin-DeVitis & DeVitis, 1998; Zeichner & Liston, 1996). Embedded within these arguments is a shift in thinking about the teacher's role that is supported by contemporary interpretations regarding the nature of teaching.

New Judgments About the Nature of Teaching

New conceptualizations of teachers and teaching are distancing themselves from the technical images portrayed by the teacher effectiveness literature and school-wide reform efforts that rely on scripted instruction. Revisions are informed by what is touted as a central characteristic of teaching: the need to act in an uncertain world (Berlak & Berlak, 1981; Buchmann, 1984, 1990; Cuban, 1992; Lampert, 1985, 1999; McDonald, 1992).

> When the template of technical rationality is laid over a messy social or educational problem, it seldom fits. The entangled issues and their ambiguity spill over. There are no procedures to follow, no scientific rules for making decisions. Worse yet, the template hides value conflicts. These so-called "problems" are complex, untidy, and insoluble. They . . . are dilemmas. (Cuban, 1992, p. 6)

As currently described, the choices that teachers confront are rarely made among clear-cut alternatives. This is the characteristic that defines them as dilemmas. It is not feasible, for example, to choose *either* to build curriculum around children's interests *or* around subject matter, or to choose between meeting the needs of the group *or* the needs of individual children (Berlak & Berlak, 1981; Cuban, 1992; Elliott, 1989; Lampert, 1985, 1999). Many of the dilemmas teachers confront are unsolvable. Thus teaching requires coping with equally weighted alternatives, or sometimes contradictions, and attempting to do so in ways that reflect one's educational values (Buchmann, 1984; Lampert, 1985, 1999; Smylie, Bay, & Tozer, 1999; Welker, 1991). From this perspective, teaching rarely entails making purely rational choices and applying technical solutions.

In her conceptual investigation of the use of research knowledge in teacher education and teaching, Buchmann (1984) extended this notion by distinguishing between the functions of research and teaching. Reminiscent of the distinction between developmental theory and educational practice, Buchmann claims that problems in practice are not the result of deficiencies in knowledge. She argued:

> Good practice, not truth, is the goal of action, and knowledge utilization and wise action are not the same. . . . . [P]roblems in the practicing professions do not primarily derive from deficiencies in knowledge. They arise instead because of tensions or deficiencies in the moral framework in which professional practice is embedded. (pp. 421–422)

Although these conclusions have not been articulated specifically for early childhood education, the dilemma has been recognized. Many analysts of curriculum models have noted that child development theories are not geared to the world of practice. Child development theories provide little guidance for how a program is to be implemented with differing populations on a day-by-day basis (Day, 1977; Fein & Schwartz, 1982; Peters, Neisworth, & Yawkey, 1985; Spodek, 1973). In addition, given the incompleteness of child development theories, Day (1977) pointed out that it is impossible to prescribe an entire curriculum without extensive inferences. Consequently, in reality, most curriculum models eschew precise implementation and are bound by the inferences program designers bring to bear.

Fein and Schwartz (1982) specifically contrasted theories of development with practice. They labeled theories of child development as passivist in orientation with the objective of describing how certain behaviors develop as a result of specified encounters with the environment. In contrast, theories of practice are activist in orientation. Theories of practice assume that certain behaviors or types of knowledge are more desirable than others and describe for the practitioner how to cultivate desired behaviors. Theories of practice are expected to formulate strategies for constructing environments that ensure the greatest beneficial impact within the practitioner's particular environment.

As a result of these distinctions, both in and out of early childhood education, there is growing recognition that advancing teaching involves acknowledging its distinctive context and focusing on the generation of what Elliott (1989) and Buchmann (1984) have independently labeled practical wisdom (see also Clandinin & Connelly, 1995; Schon, 1983, 1987). "Wisdom can be defined as a holistic appreciation of a complex practical activity which enables a person to understand or articulate the problems (s)he confronts in realizing the aims or values of the activity and to propose appropriate solutions" (Elliott, 1989, pp. 83–84).

Teaching also is increasingly appreciated as an interplay among personal, practical, and political knowledge, shaped by different and changing contexts of teaching. For example, in studies by Deborah Ceglowski (1998) of teachers in a rural, Midwestern Head Start program, and by Catherine Wilson (1999) of teachers in an urban Head Start classroom, the multiple ways teachers negotiated the "official curriculum" in a manner more congruent with their beliefs and values were documented. These two studies dismantle views of teachers as neutral figures, implementing a prescribed model with predetermined educational goals.

Whether intended or not, curriculum models steer teacher attention away from these complexities of teaching. By presenting teachers with a predetermined curricular framework (regardless of how flexible), curriculum models direct teacher energy toward issues of implementation and away from the complexities of schooling and classroom life. A study by Walsh et al. (1993) supports this conclusion. Their case study examined teacher efforts to implement the High/Scope Curriculum during the first year of a statewide pilot prekindergarten program. Walsh et al. found that teachers never felt secure regarding what they were supposed to be doing and constantly sought practical information regarding how to implement the model. One teacher even asked whether it was okay to use scissors!

Guided by newer interpretations of teaching, an alternative definition of "effective" teachers has emerged. Within this framework teachers less frequently are described as those who apply the knowledge of others. The critical shift in thinking about teaching is that expertise develops *in* practice (Buchmann, 1984; Clandinin & Connelly, 1995; Schon, 1983, 1987), not from repeated practice of predetermined teaching strategies.

Reflecting on one's practice to discover better approaches to teaching's complex practical problems is essential to this view of teaching. This element is necessitated because from this perspective no definitive solutions exist for the practical problems of teaching (Buchmann, 1984, 1990; Cuban, 1992; Lampert, 1985, 1999). This conceptualization of teaching explicitly challenges technological interpretations of teacher effectiveness.

Simultaneously, this conceptualization seeks to elevate appreciation for teachers' contributions to educational deliberations. Problems in practice have been expanded beyond those of a technical or "practical" nature. Teachers are being viewed as intellectuals who can generate knowledge and wrestle with the questions of what kind of people and what kind of society will result from their teaching (see, for example, Cochran-Smith, 1991; Greene, 1978; Noddings, 1992, 1999). In this framework, various specialized disciplines, such as psychology, philosophy, sociology, linguistics, and so forth, become intellectual resources that enable teachers to become better at dealing with the complexities associated with achieving educational goals (Scheffler, 1991); becoming agents of change in educational reform (Smylie et al., 1999); and transforming the relationship between theory and practice (Clandinin & Connelly, 1995; Cochran-Smith & Lytle, 1993).

This complex and dynamic portrait of practice competes with the coexisting view of teaching as a technical activity with a primary focus on academic achievement. A view of teaching as a technical activity is especially to be found in research-based reform models presently being implemented as strategies for raising the academic performance of students in high-poverty schools. Prompted by federal legislation providing funds for schoolwide reforms, models that provide clearly defined instructional components, such as Success for All (Slavin et al., 1996; see Chapter 4), are promoted as more effective than those with a less specific set of guiding principles.

Their program designers argue that schools need not "reinvent the wheel" (Fashola & Slavin, 1998, p. 371; also Pogrow, 1996). Effective schoolwide models are touted as those with materials and services that provide explicit, replicable directions for teachers. Expecting teachers to develop their own curriculum and pedagogy is viewed as unrealistic and as an unwanted burden (Fashola & Slavin, 1998; Pogrow, 1996). As argued by Pogrow (1996), "While there are many talented teachers who can come up with highly innovative techniques, it's too demanding and too hit-or-miss a process, especially for major changes. Most practitioners (or academicians) do not have the skill or time to develop new processes" (p. 40).

Further, since reform is based on efforts to change past teaching practices, Stringfield, a researcher associated with Success for All, argues:

> You basically have to replace what's going on and make it more difficult for teachers to go back to what they were doing before. . . . There has to be a specificity about what the teacher does on Tuesday morning, if you want to change what happens on Tuesday morning. (quoted in Olson, 1998, p. 18)

Consistent with the belief found in each of the enduring curriculum models, interactions between teachers and students are viewed as the most important for creating change in student outcomes. In this instance, this belief underscores the critical importance of structuring the nature of these interactions. Further, "teacher-proof" models are seen as a necessary response to the urgent pressures being placed on schools to improve academic outcomes (Fashola & Slavin, 1998; Olson, 1998).

✑ BEYOND A SEARCH FOR EFFICACY

Changing views about the nature of teaching and classroom life challenge original expectations that comparisons among curriculum models can produce an answer regarding the most effective way to educate young children. Even if one model were found to be statistically more effective on any given measure, the important influence of context and values—whether in one's choice of models or one's daily practice—stimulates questions about issues other than relative effectiveness.

Thus, the distinction between educational means and ends has been clarified. Conceptualization of teaching as limited to technical activity has been questioned. And acknowledgment of the value decisions implicit in all of our choices makes attempts to neutralize or "objectify" curriculum options inappropriate. Clearly, our continued inquiry needs to set a different course.

Of course, early childhood curriculum models have always been characterized by differences in their learning contexts and the values they promote as most worthwhile. But the implications of these differences have received limited attention or analysis. Curriculum models emerged and flourished during a period when science was considered an objective and authoritative means for discriminating among educational alternatives. It was assumed that effective models for early education could be identified through research and evaluation and then uniformly implemented.

But what happens when the outcomes of science no longer are recognized as the sole, authoritative basis on which to decide how best to educate children? Skrtic (1991) contended that the social sciences no longer provide criteria for judging one knowledge claim as superior to another. He suggested that the process of science has become a subjective activity that produces "possible knowledges" (p. 19) that are predicated on a particular frame of reference. Framing an investigation of early childhood curriculum models from this perspective establishes a different landscape for contemplating the multiple curriculum models that co-inhabit early childhood education. It becomes necessary to assess them in terms of the learning contexts they create and the values they foster—for both children and teachers.

Bruner (1990) addressed the loss of science as a definitive authority (not to be confused with science as a method of inquiry) by pointing to the importance of open-mindedness (also Buchmann, 1990):

> I take open-mindedness to be a willingness to construe knowledge and values from multiple perspectives without loss of commitment to one's own values. . . . It demands that we be conscious of how we come to our knowledge and as conscious as we can be about the values that lead us to our perspectives. It asks that we be accountable for how and what we know. But it does not insist there is only one way of constructing meaning, or one right way. (p. 30)

⌗ FOR FURTHER READING

Goncu, A. (Ed.). (1999). *Children's engagement in the world: Sociocultural perspectives.* London: Cambridge University Press.

> For readers interested in studies derived from Vygotstky's sociocultural perspective of development, the contributors to this collection explore children in various cultures at play, work, school, and home, with particular interest in examining the economic, social, and physical conditions that influence how children participate in different activities.

Kohlberg, L., & Mayer, R. (1972). Development as the aim of education. *Harvard Educational Review, 42,* 449–496.

> In this classic and frequently cited article, Kohlberg and Mayer compare various approaches to understanding child development and defend their conclusion that Piagetian cognitive-developmental theory provides a logical and defensible framework for promoting development as the aim of education.

Mallory, B. L., & New, R. S. (Eds.). (1994). *Diversity and developmentally appropriate practices: Challenges for early childhood education.* New York: Teachers College Press.

> Contributors to this volume challenged the theoretical framework and implications for practice of the National Association for Early Childhood Education's position statement on developmentally appropriate practice, and played an important role in shaping the issues for the 1997 revision. The collection provides readers with a sense of the continuing tensions as the early care and education field grapples with the need to inform the public of young children's developmental characteristics, while, at the same time, reexamines the relationship of child development knowledge to teaching practice.

Silin, J. G. (1987). The early childhood educator's knowledge base: A reconsideration. In L. G. Katz & K. Steiner (Eds.), *Current topics in early childhood education* (Vol. 7, pp. 17–31). Norwood, NJ: Ablex.

> Silin challenges early childhood education's reliance on developmental theory as the source for curriculum decisions. He argues that recognition of early childhood education as a profession demands that early childhood educators create their own distinctive knowledge base.

Zelizer, V. A. (1985). *Pricing the priceless child: The changing social value of children.* New York: Basic Books.

> In a fascinating analysis, Zelizer chronicles how economic and social events in the United States have directly influenced the cultural meaning of childhood. Special emphasis is given to analyzing the ways in which children's changing "worth" has been framed by social and economic occurrences and in illustrating the social impact of economic events.

Curriculum Models and Early Childhood Education

A Quandary

Almost 40 years have passed since curriculum models were a focal point in early childhood education. Following a period of declining interest during the late 1970s and early 1980s, interest in their use reemerged during the late 1980s (see Chapter 1). In response to renewed interest, an updated review of five enduring early childhood curriculum models has been provided.

The central question posed by the book's first edition was whether early childhood curriculum models should be returned to the prominent position they held during the 1960s. Changing social and economic circumstances, including dramatic expansion of early childhood programs since this question first was posed, required that the question be updated. Since their zenith in the mid-1960s, curriculum models have become woven into the fabric of early childhood education. Though not at their former position of prominence, use of curriculum models is sustained by at least four factors:

1. the galvanizing power of Goals 2000 and its first education goal that all children will enter school ready to learn;
2. heightened concern with the low academic achievement of children from low-income families;
3. the response of state policy makers to findings from neuroscience on early brain development; and
4. empirical evidence documenting the overall low quality of center-based and family child care.

These four factors not only have sustained interest in early childhood curriculum models, they have modified the conversation about their use. The conversation now is less about *which* curriculum to use in educating young children, as first suggested by Powell (1987a), than it is about whether "proven" curriculum models should serve as vehicles for improving the consistency and quality of early childhood education. Driven by public demands for program results and child outcomes (see, for example, Kagan & Cohen, 1997; Kagan et al., 1997), the sense of urgency surrounding school reform, and the prevalence of poor-quality child care, curriculum models are being advanced as the solution to ensuring that public dollars are wisely spent and that children enter school ready to learn (see, for example, Weikart, 1992, 1995).

In pursuit of further understanding, the notion of curriculum models and the origin and evolution of individual models were considered in the context of both historical and contemporary issues and concerns. In the process, the purpose and function of curriculum models began to emerge. Chapter by chapter, it became increasingly apparent that curriculum models, by intent, are designed to bring uniformity to early childhood programs. Seven years after publication of the first edition, this insight perhaps seems obvious. But at the time, curriculum models still were being used primarily as a vehicle for finding the most effective early childhood education program for economically disadvantaged preschoolers. The quest still focused on finding which curriculum to use in educating young children. Although now it seems obvious that once "an ideal" curriculum was found, the next step would be its broad dissemination, the challenges associated with identifying the "ideal" curriculum deflected attention away from this issue.

The idea of curriculum models is derived from an industrial notion of standardization that assumes "one size can fit all"—a notion now under attack not only within education but also within the private and public sectors (see, for example, Osborne & Gaebler, 1993; Schorr, 1997; Senge, 1990). To achieve standardization, curriculum models—regardless of their internal flexibility—operate by using predictable representations of teaching and learning, relying on fixed interpretations of the nature of children and teachers, and minimizing variation across sites. Curriculum models value uniformity over diversity; they assess results in terms of predetermined outcomes rather than unanticipated examples of enhanced overall competence. And they direct their attention to teachers as the instrument through which uniform results are achieved. This view of curriculum models has been clearly revealed by our investigation. But, as the early history of the Developmental-Interaction approach (see Chapter 3) and the story of the Reggio Emilia approach (see Chapter 9) portray, other options can exist.

Yet as revealed throughout these pages, the general idea of curriculum models and the individual histories of enduring models have been shaped profoundly by social and historical circumstances. The question as to whether curriculum model use should be encouraged is similarly bounded. Contemporary characteristics of the early childhood field and their intersection with current societal needs and expectations create a particular frame of reference for considering the value and contribution of curriculum models.

Within this context, curriculum models offer positive and negative educational possibilities. Consequently, their broad use raises complicated questions for the early childhood field. When these questions are deliberated collectively, it is clear that the field has a dilemma. The intent of this chapter is to pose this dilemma for public debate and to highlight the circumstances that have generated the context for its creation.

✢ AN EXPANDED AGENDA FOR EARLY CHILDHOOD EDUCATION

Current interest in curriculum models as a systematic approach to early childhood education, similar to interest during the 1960s, is linked with concerns for the education of young children from economically disadvantaged circumstances. Current interest, however, has been narrowed from the broad reform framework that launched the "Great Society" and used early childhood education as a means to alleviate poverty and promote social equality. As linkages between early childhood education and the public schools have deepened (see Chapter 4; Goffin, in press), early childhood education increasingly is being incorporated as a component of comprehensive school reform efforts.

In addition, present interest in early childhood curriculum models reflects a desire to improve the quality of child care for the growing number of children who participate in it daily. Heightened by a public policy shift that requires low-income parents to work and be independent of cash assistance, the continued influx of women into the labor force, and dramatically low unemployment rates, demand for child care has soared. Financial resources to support the provision of quality child care, however, have not. In addition, rarely are child care issues considered in the context of school reform, thereby perpetuating the image of child care as custodial and continuing a two-tiered system response by policy makers.

In the 1960s, public and professional interest in early childhood education converged around concern for the economically disadvantaged and was embedded in the civil rights movement. Now, almost 40 years later, early childhood care and education and its curriculum models are tied to a changed policy context, pushed to be responsive to the nation's robust economy, and conjoined with concerns for improving the academic achievement produced by the nation's public schools.

Changes since the mid-1960s have not been restricted to changing economic and societal circumstances, however. The field of early childhood care and education and its knowledge base also has evolved. As a result, during the 1990s, early childhood curriculum models were implemented in a different societal, as well as professional, context. Their future use no doubt will be accompanied by continuing change.

These differences in context are not new to this discussion; they first were introduced in Chapter 1. As part of the book's introduction to curriculum models, descriptions of contemporary interest in early childhood programs and the changing configuration of early childhood care and education provided an up-to-date backdrop for the subsequent examination of individual curriculum models. When reconsidered in light of what has been learned about curriculum models, this contextual information discloses the circumstances that create tension among what we now know to be the purpose and function of curriculum models, intensified expectations for young children to enter school prepared to achieve academically, and ongoing deliberations within the early childhood profession regarding its course to professionalism.

Changing Societal Context

Before the onset of preschool intervention programs during the mid-1960s, the availability of early childhood education prior to first grade was sporadic. Nursery education was primarily an optional, enrichment-oriented program mostly for children from middle-class families; "day care" was considered a social welfare program for low-income families; and kindergartens had yet to become a fixture of public school education.

By the close of the 1990s, a majority of America's children participated in early childhood programs before entering first grade. Most 5-year-olds attend kindergarten, and a majority of preschoolers with a nonemployed parent attended nursery school. The most dramatic transformation, however, occurred in the use of child care. Parents of two thirds of America's children under the age of 6 currently are in the workforce, and their children are attending child care.

Current interest in early childhood curriculum models emanates, in part, from faith in their ability to ensure that early childhood education will support child outcomes critical to school readiness. This aspiration, of course, mirrors expectations from the late 1960s and early 1970s that first spurred development of preschool intervention programs such as Head Start and the systematic development of early childhood curriculum models.

During the mid-1960s, preschool intervention programs, in general, and Head Start, in particular, emerged from national concern about alleviating poverty juxtaposed with changing assumptions regarding the malleability of intelligence during the early years of life. This combination of events exploded into an optimism regarding the inoculating power of early childhood education and initiated a search for curriculum models that could most effectively harness this potential. In the 1990s, ongoing concern for the unequal school success of poor children originated from economic anxieties regarding the availability of a skilled labor force and the social costs to society of an uneducated citizenry.

Thus, unlike the 1960s, when interest in early childhood education revolved primarily around promoting school readiness as a means for creating equal opportunity for economically disadvantaged children, current attention to early childhood education has coalesced around school reform as a means for increasing academic achievement and preparation to join the workforce. A larger group of young children are targeted, and interested stakeholders include public school officials, parents, policy makers, and corporate and civic leaders. As a result, early childhood education increasingly is seen as critical to deflecting the ill effects of poverty by promoting children's school readiness, undergirding the success of public school reform efforts, bolstering the global competitiveness of American businesses, and supporting parents as employees. These expectations, in turn, exert pressure on communities and the early childhood profession to provide high-quality early care and education programs.

Changing Professional Context

Early childhood experiences prior to kindergarten and first grade frequently are classified as children's first encounter with formal education. The presence of so many children in early childhood settings has heightened professional concern regarding what children experience when in these settings. Simultaneously, public interest in the contributions of early educational experiences to children's success with formal schooling places pressure on early childhood programs to fulfill society's mounting expectations for early childhood education.

Preparation of early childhood personnel, however, has not kept pace with increased demand or changing expectations. As demands for program availability and expectations for program quality that lead to specified child outcomes have swelled, competition for qualified early childhood personnel has intensified. Preparing and keeping qualified personnel, however, is undermined by the inferior compensation and benefits offered to early childhood educators, especially those who work outside the public school system. Building a cadre of professionally prepared early educators is further hampered by the profession's struggle to define the formal requirements associated with professionalism (see, for example, Bredekamp & Willer, 1993; Bownan, 1997). As a result, depending on whether early childhood education occurs within a family child care setting, public school, nursery school, Head Start, or child care program, expectations for teacher qualifications can range from no prerequisites to a high school diploma to a Child Development Associate credential to a 4-year degree.

Thus, at the time of this writing, the field of early childhood care and education lacks the capacity to respond to escalating demands for consistent program quality and accountability. Not surprisingly, the repercussions are disheartening. Across program types, too many children are in programs deemed inadequate to support their development in positive ways. The findings of the Cost, Quality, & Child Outcomes Study Team (1995) and of Galinsky et al. (1994) revealed that the majority of young children in child care centers and family child care homes were in less than optimum settings. Almost a third of children are in care considered harmful to their development. Similar concerns have been articulated for Head Start (Zigler & Muenchow, 1992).

◌ CURRICULUM MODELS AND EARLY CHILDHOOD EDUCATION: A DILEMMA

In the 1960s, curriculum models were developed specifically for disadvantaged child populations as alternative curricula to what was offered in traditional, "middle-class" nursery schools. They were intended to provide economically disadvantaged children with educational experiences that would prepare them to enter public schooling on an equal footing with their middle-class peers.

In response to the growing number of underachieving students from low-income families, the use of curriculum models, often expanded as schoolwide reform initiatives, can now also be found in elementary schools. Program designers of these models acknowledge the learning from Project Follow Through and Head Start Planned Variation of undertaking large-scale, multisite program implementation. The issue of "going to scale" or "scaling up"—of extending the benefits of proven programs to large numbers of children—is central to their work. "The best chance for real reform in the vast majority of schools," according to Pogrow (1996), "lies in adapting those few "precrafted" programs that work" (p. 40).

This challenge is not limited to program designers concerned with school reform. It extends, as well, to the replication of effective early childhood programs.

Curriculum models are being advanced for two distinct, yet interdependent and overlapping, ends: (a) as vehicles for improving the overall quality and predictability of early childhood education—as a framework for mainstream early education—and (b) as a critical component of comprehensive school reform efforts targeting children from low-income families.

Few would disagree that the consistent provision of high-quality early care and education programs is one of the most important tasks that confronts the early childhood profession. But, herein lies the dilemma.

The greater use of curriculum models might, in fact, improve programmatic quality by providing well-articulated curriculum frameworks that could be employed in place of existing, widely varying routines. Improved program quality, plus greater public accountability, could result from the replacement of existing practices with standard programming across settings. Hence, the dissemination and consistent application of curriculum models could change the *floor* of program quality in early childhood education. Children across programs would receive consistent educational experiences, and variability in the professional preparation of their teachers would be reduced by providing all teachers with similar training in the curriculum model and its implementation.

By momentarily disregarding our knowledge of the complexities involved in program implementation (see Chapter 6) and temporarily suspending the critical question of how one selects among available curriculum models (see Chapter 7), it is possible to argue that consistent implementation of curriculum models might provide a vehicle for raising the standard of care and education experienced by young children and improve their chances for school success.

But, as we now know, curriculum models affect not only the lives of children, but also the lives of their teachers. Thus, using curriculum models may improve the daily lives of children (up to a certain point), but does this achievement, regardless of the chosen curriculum model, occur at the expense of the profession's vision for itself and its teachers?

This consequence would occur because curriculum models also are vehicles for lowering expectations regarding the professional responsibilities and possibilities of early childhood teachers—regardless of the model's or approach's complexity. The premises that undergird curriculum models delegate teachers to the role of technicians who implement the educational ideas of others, a role in dramatic contrast with dynamic interpretations of learning and generative views of teaching (see Chapters 7 and 9). Reliance on curriculum models as a means for achieving consistent program quality restrains discussion about quality to issues of implementation—rather than to critical reflection on the vitality of learning and growth being experienced by children and teachers or to critical deliberations of the purposes of education.[1]

---

[1]Pogrow (1996) argues that this suggestion is "akin to asking an actor to perform a Shakespeare play after first writing it" (p. 40).

Current interest in curriculum models is fueled partly by the need to improve the quality of existing early care and education programs in the absence of a sufficiently educated early childhood workforce—both in the present and the foreseeable future. Interest also is fueled by the challenge of "going to scale"; that is, figuring out how to provide high-quality early childhood programs in a wide variety of settings that regularly and predictably prepare children to enter school prepared to succeed academically.

According to Pogrow (1996), a designer of Higher Order Thinking Skills, a program for Title I and students with learning disabilities in grades 4–8: "Given the complexity of figuring out how to implement theory or philosophy, it does not make sense as a large-scale strategy to expect practitioners to develop their own techniques for implementing a complex and vague reform idea" (p. 40). But the decision to use curriculum models as a solution to this dilemma promises to affect the field by shaping both public and professional perceptions of early childhood education as a technical enterprise. The dilemma confronting the early childhood profession is how to improve what a majority of today's children experience in early childhood settings and—at the same time—advocate for a view of professionalism that acknowledges the dynamic complexity of teaching young children.

This dilemma is not new to early childhood education. On reviewing her career, Carolyn Pratt (1948/1990), a pioneer in early childhood education and founder of the City and Country School, stated:

> All my life I have fought against formula. Once you have set down a formula, you are imprisoned by it as surely as the primitive tribesman is imprisoned by the witch doctor's magic circle. I would not be talked into making out any blueprints for education, outside the school or within it. [But] this refusal to formulate a "system" made me a problem to our teachers. (p. 56)

Schorr (1997), a prominent activist, suggests that Pratt's conclusion is equally applicable to large-scale change efforts:

> As a member of three different national commissions that sought during the past four years to come up with a single model that communities throughout the country could adopt to solve the child care and school readiness problem, I can testify that there probably is no such thing. The more we learned about the complex and varied needs around the country, and the impressive, if spotty and fragmented, efforts now under way to meet them, the less confident we became that we could come up with one model for nationwide local implementation. (p. 241)

Thus, we must ask: How, within the current context of contradictory expectations and demands, does the early childhood profession respond to the immediate and pragmatic needs of today's children and practitioners and still realize its enduring vision for future generations of children and early childhood educators?

Chapter Nine

Posing New Questions and Seeing Old Questions in New Ways
The Reggio Emilia Approach

Educators in Reggio Emilia have no intention of suggesting that their program should be looked at as a model to be copied in other countries; rather, their work should be considered as an educational experience that consists of reflection, practice, and further careful reflection in a program that is continuously renewed and readjusted. However, the Reggio Emilia schools and their approach to early childhood education are not considered "experimental." These schools are part of a public system that strives to serve both the child's welfare and the social needs of families, while also supporting the child's fundamental rights to grow and learn in a favorable environment, in the company of peers and with caring, professional adults.

Lella Gandini, *"Foundations of the Reggio Emilia Approach,"* 1997a

While there are many talented teachers who can come up with highly innovative techniques, it's too demanding and too hit-or-miss a process, especially for major changes. Most practitioners (or academicians) do not have the skill or time to develop new processes.

Stanley Pogrow, *Education Week*, 1996

U. S. educators have only recently learned of the publicly funded system of early childhood care and education in the northern Italian community of Reggio Emilia. A small group of early childhood scholars from the United States had been studying the programs in Reggio Emilia and the surrounding region since the early 1980s (see, for example, Corsaro & Emiliani, 1992; Edwards & Gandini, 1989; Forman, 1989; Gandini, 1984; New, 1988). But it was a traveling exhibit titled "The Hundred Languages of Children," created by the teachers and the community of Reggio Emilia, that brought the first glimpse of the infant-toddler centers and preprimary schools to the United States in 1987 (Gandini, 1997b). Soon thereafter, two prominent professional publications, *Child Care Information Exchange* and *Young Children,* began to include articles on the programs (Bredekamp, 1993; Gandini, 1991, 1993, 1994; Katz, 1990; Malaguzzi, 1993b, 1994a, 1994b; New, 1990; Neugebauer, 1994), and *Newsweek* (1991) pronounced the early childhood programs of Reggio Emilia to be one of the "ten best schools in the world."

Inspired by the accounts of the programs of Reggio Emilia, more than 50 delegations of early childhood practitioners from the United States traveled to Italy during the 1990s to see the infant-toddler and preprimary programs (Municipality of Reggio Emilia, 1996b). Readers will recall that 80 years earlier, travelers from the United States visited the Italian programs of Maria Montessori and waxed eloquently upon their return. Yet, in less than 5 years Montessori's ideas were discarded by early childhood educators as outdated (see Chapter 2). The initial response of visitors to Montessori's programs and to the programs in Reggio Emilia has been strikingly similar. Still to be determined is whether, as more U.S. educators learn about efforts to replicate the work of Reggio Emilian teachers, its history in the United States will follow a similar trajectory.

In less than a decade, the infant-toddler centers and preprimary schools of Reggio Emilia have captured the imaginations of educators in the United States and enlarged conversations about how teachers think about their practice. Acclaim for the programs has produced a Reggio Emilia track at the National Conference of the NAEYC; a quarterly journal devoted to articles by U.S. and Italian educators, *Innovations in Early Education: The International Reggio Exchange;* numerous web sites; and a growing number of publications, videos, and conferences devoted to articulating the philosophical framework and describing attempts to adapt the framework to early childhood programs in the United States.

The distinctive approach of Reggio Emilians to early education challenges U.S. practices, especially those associated with curriculum models. In particular, its images of children dramatically expand expectations regarding children's possibilities. Its conceptualization of teachers as collaborators with community, children, and other teachers in the construction of curriculum elevates the responsibility of teachers. And, its structure for supporting the dynamic, complex work of teaching recognizes the teaching–learning process as an intricate social exchange—from the perspectives of both teachers and children.

The programs of Reggio Emilia are reflective, in this regard, of U.S. trends toward reconceptualizing the teacher and her role as described in Chapter 7. These characteristics highlight the significance of the U.S. context as a platform from which this approach to early education will be assessed by U.S. educators and others.

The Reggio Emilia approach describes itself as a set of beliefs and values about children, families, and teaching. The approach has evolved (and continues to evolve) from particular (and changing) historical, cultural, and economic circumstances. The Reggio Emilia approach portrays an alternative conceptualization to teachers as curricular technicians. The approach also is embedded in an alternative conceptualization of children and the purpose for their early education. As a result, the Reggio Emilia approach illuminates in striking ways the issues raised throughout the text regarding the purpose, function, and impact of early childhood curriculum models.

As in earlier chapters, we draw heavily on quotes to express the philosophical as well as practical aspects of the programs in Reggio Emilia. However, unlike previous chapters on curriculum models, where references were limited to those written by primary architects of the model, this chapter incorporates the writings of Italian educators, as well as U.S. interpreters, who contribute to ongoing discussions and continuing development of the teaching practices in Reggio Emilia.

Readers will be introduced to a new vocabulary about teaching and learning, a vocabulary that introduces new images and practices to conceptualizations of early education.

✌ THE ITALIAN CONTEXT: CREATING A UNIVERSAL SYSTEM OF EARLY CHILDHOOD CARE AND EDUCATION

While educators in the United States have only recently become familiar with the infant-toddler centers and preprimary schools of Reggio Emilia, the history of the programs spans a period of more than 50 years. Appreciating the events that shaped its early years as well as the evolution of the work of the Italian educators is essential for understanding the philosophical and pedagogical ideas that influence their teaching practices.

The municipal system of early care and education in Reggio Emilia formally began with the establishment of government-sponsored *scuole dell'infanzia* (preprimary schools for children, ages 3–6) in 1968 and *asili nido* (infant-toddler centers for children, ages 4 months through 3 years) in 1971, hence the frequent reference to the 30-year history of the Reggio Emilia approach. However, Loris Malaguzzi, the guiding spirit of the programs until his death in 1994, traced the origins of the schools to the spring of 1945, when the townspeople and farmers from a small village outside Reggio Emilia salvaged bricks and beams from bombed houses, and used the revenue from the sale of a German tank to build a school for their young children (Malaguzzi, 1998). The "people's nursery school" at Villa Cella became a symbol for the renewal of the social and political fabric of the Italian community, and in the 20 years that followed, seven more schools were formed in neighborhoods of Reggio Emilia (Malaguzzi, 1998).

Many of the guiding principles of current educational practices were developed during the early years of parent-run schools. Parents organized and managed the schools; teachers therefore, learned to work closely with families. Malaguzzi (1998) explained, "[Parents] asked for nothing less than that this school, which they had built with their hands, be a different kind of school, a school that could educate their children in a different way from before" (p. 58).

Rejecting both the custodial model of the nursery school programs provided by the Catholic Church and the didactic model of the national schools, teachers also developed new ways to conceptualize their work with children. Inspired by a strong movement in the 1950s and 1960s of Italian educators who sought to develop teaching practices more congruent with the modern, democratic spirit of the country (Gandini, 1997b), teachers in Reggio Emilia became astute observers of children, developed an experimental approach to curriculum based on long-term projects, and valued learning that promoted both individual and social growth (Malaguzzi, 1998).

In the 1960s, the parent-run schools in Reggio Emilia joined in the national campaign to provide social services for families, including schools for young children. Twenty years of collaborative experiences prepared teachers and families to play a prominent role as advocates in the campaign for publicly funded schools for young children (Malaguzzi, 1998). The first city-run school for 60 children was opened in Reggio Emilia in 1963.

A group of teachers from the parent-run schools came to work at the new municipal school, and collaborated with families to raise public consciousness about the program's benefits. Their strategy was to "bring" the school once a week to the public squares, parks, and municipal theater of Reggio Emilia, where the community could observe, ask questions of the teachers, and become interested in young children's education (Malaguzzi, 1998). Efforts to pass national legislation for a system of municipally funded public preprimary schools were successful, and by 1968, the parent-run schools became part of the system of programs funded and managed by the city of Reggio Emilia.

Three years later, Reggio Emilia opened the first infant-toddler center for children under 3 years. Through years of collaborative efforts by teachers, families, and the community, the first school at Villa Cella grew to become a system of programs with 13 infant-toddler centers and 22 preprimary schools in the community-governed system.[1]

From this 50-year history of building a public system of early care and education has emerged a philosophy of teaching and learning that is deeply grounded in advocacy for programs that support both children and families. The infant-toddler centers and preprimary schools of Reggio Emilia were created to serve the dual purposes of providing care and education for children and permitting women to participate in the labor force. Women were prominent in the building of the early parent-run schools, and continue to play central roles in the program's management. They are active politically in assuring social services, child care, and schools that meet the needs of families (Edwards, Gandini, & Forman, 1998b).

Reggio Emilia is now a prosperous community with low rates of crime and unemployment, and effective local government and social services. Edwards et al. (1998b) describe traditions of participatory democracy, and economic and social cooperation across social class as a source of considerable community and regional pride. The creation of the Reggio Emilia programs is viewed as continuing evidence of the spirit of collaboration to ensure community well-being.

The history of the early childhood programs in Reggio Emilia has a distinctive legacy of (a) teachers and families acting as partners in providing high-quality programs for young children; (b) a pedagogical approach that views teaching as an evolving learning process; (c) an appreciation for the importance of developing support for early childhood programs by making what happens in schools engaging to the public; and (d) an expectation that schools should be informed by ongo-

---

[1]In Reggio Emilia, a city with a population of 130,000, approximately 93% of the children 3–6 years old attend school. In addition to the 22 preprimary schools run by the municipality of Reggio Emilia, there are 10 national schools for preschool-aged children; and 19 schools operated by religious orders. Thirty percent of the children under 3 years attend the municipal infant-toddler centers Children from all socioeconomic classes attend the municipal, programs and children with special needs are given priority in enrollment (Gandini, 1997a).

ing community discussions and debates about the relationship of services for children and families to the social, cultural, and political values of their society (Edwards et al., 1998b).

Organization of the Centers and Schools

Infant-toddler centers each have approximately 70 children who are grouped together by age (4–9 months; 10–18 months; 19–24 months; and 24–36 months). In each center, there are 11 teachers, 6 additional full-time and part-time staff, and a cook. (The infant-toddler centers are well-developed components of the educational system in Reggio Emilia; however, the focus of this chapter will be on the preprimary schools.) The preprimary schools typically have three classrooms for 75 children, with a 3-year-, 4-year-, and 5-year-old group. Each preprimary school also has an *atelierista* (a teacher with special training in the visual arts), 5 additional full-time and part-time staff, and a cook (Gandini, 1997b).

Unlike most early childhood programs in the United States, schools in Reggio Emilia are organized so that children, teachers, and families create stable, long-term relationships. Children and teachers remain together for 3-year cycles in both the infant-toddler and preprimary programs. These extended relationships are intentional, not only for the stability of relationships among children and their teachers, but so children experience a secure community of adults, as families and teachers learn to work together (New, 1990).

Individual schools are managed by the teachers, staff, cook, families, and a community advisory board (Gandini, 1997b). Their work is supported by a *pedagogista*, who supervises three to four schools, and follows the progression of children's projects, supports the continuing professional development of teachers, and serves as a liaison among teachers, families, and the municipal system (Gandini, 1997b).

Most children remain at the school from 8:30 a.m. to 4:00 p.m., with the option of coming at 7:30 a.m. and leaving at 6:20 p.m. All but two of the programs are open from September 1 through June 30, with a single infant-toddler center and preprimary school open in the summer (Gandini, 1997b). Teachers are with the children for 31 hours per week, and have another 5 hours for working with families, planning, documentation of children's learning and projects, and school management activities. The schedule of the day provides ample, unhurried time for children to enjoy meals, play, and engage in project work. Staffing throughout the day is flexible, so that teachers and children can plan for a variety of activities.

✐ THE PEDAGOGICAL APPROACH: GUIDING PRINCIPLES

Howard Gardner (1999) has characterized Loris Malaguzzi as a "charismatic genius" (p. 92) whose educational vision and leadership guided the programs of Reggio Emilia. However, unlike the single theorists or individuals who became the primary architects and/or interpreters associated with the curriculum models and approaches considered in this text, the evolving pedagogical principles in the programs of Reggio Emilia reflect the *continuing* contributions of many teachers, families, and the community.

The goal of the Reggio Emilia programs is to "promote children's education through the development of all their *languages:* expressive, communicative, symbolic, cognitive, ethical, metaphorical, logical, imaginative, and relational" (emphasis in the original; Municipality of Reggio Emilia, 1996a, p. 19). This expansive goal stands in stark contrast to the current, more specific goal in U.S. preschools of ensuring children's school readiness. The program's pedagogical principles are based on a view of:

- schools as "amiable" communities, built on a belief in the importance of social relationships and emotional well-being for all participants (Malaguzzi, 1993b, p. 9);
- families as partners in the education of their children;
- children as competent, capable, curious learners;
- in-depth project work, emerging from the interests of children and teachers, to organize learning as a co-constructed and evolving experience;
- the importance of cultivating children's ability to use many *symbolic languages* (music, drawing, painting, clay, wire, block construction, dramatic play, dance, and so forth) to represent and communicate their understandings, feelings, and memories;
- *documentation* of children's learning as a way for teachers to understand children, evaluate their own teaching practice, communicate to other adults the complexity and depth of project work at the school, and for children to see that their ideas are valued; and
- teachers as learners, researchers, and advocates for children and families.

Teachers and interpreters of the "Reggio Emilia approach" (Edwards, Gandini, & Forman, 1998a) or the "Reggio way" (Hendrick, 1997)—designations intended to emphasize the approach as a set of guiding principles rather than a curriculum model—speak of the complexity and interrelationship of ideas and practices. Summary of the principles only suggests the richness of ideas and implications for teaching practice. Readers are encouraged, therefore, to explore the list of readings at the end of the chapter.

The School: Creating Relationships and Provoking Investigation

> We place enormous value on the role of the environment as a motivating and animating force in creating spaces for relations, options, and emotional and cognitive situations that produce a sense of well-being and security. It has been said that the environment should act as a kind of aquarium which reflects the ideas, ethics, attitudes and culture of the people who live in it. This is what we are working toward. (Malaguzzi, 1966a, p. 40)

The schools of Reggio Emilia are viewed as social spaces, designed to invite exploration, interaction, reflection, and communication among all the participants. Unlike curriculum models or other approaches that define the curriculum as a set of interactions among teachers and children that occur within a classroom, the educators of Reggio Emilia envision the school, and all the experiences and relationships between the school and the community, as having pedagogical dimensions.

Each school is built around a central space or *piazza,* envisioned in the manner of an Italian city square, where children, teachers, families, and school staff come together to exchange ideas and share experiences (Gandini, 1998). Kitchens are open and inviting, so that the cooks and their daily work can be valued in the community of the school. Dining areas are gracious, comfortable spaces created for children and adults to enjoy the ritual of meals and conversations. Rooms are stocked with richly diverse collections of materials, including the block and dramatic play areas familiar to U.S. visitors. Carefully displayed photographs, artifacts, and narratives of project work communicate the intellectual life of the children and teachers to the school's visitors.

Large workshops, or *ateliers,* and *mini-ateliers* in the classrooms play a vital and unique role in the life of schools. *Ateliers* are envisioned as workshops or studios where children learn, with the assistance of the *atelierista,* to use a variety of tools and materials to explore and represent their ideas. *Ateliers* are also sites of "provocation" for teachers to develop their understandings of children by learning from children how they express their ideas in many symbolic "languages" including drawing, painting, clay, wire, and a wide array of other materials (Vecchi, 1998). Malaguzzi (1998) described the *atelier* as a pedagogical idea that contributes significantly to the continuing development of their approach by providing a "laboratory" for children and teachers to learn together. More recently, *ateliers* have become workshops where teachers and the *atelierista* prepare the documentation that supports teachers' professional development and communicates the richness of project work to families and community (Malaguzzi, 1998). (Documentation will be more fully explained shortly.)

Schools are situated in highly visible settings within the city to permit children and teachers to contribute to the daily activity of the community, and to allow the schools to be appreciated as vital, dynamic aspects of city life. The Diana School, for example, is in a public park in the central city, where people of all ages walk, bicycle, and eat lunch. Gandini (1991, 1998) has helped U.S. readers appreciate that each school is a unique and "particular" environment, reflecting the history of the school, the children and families, and the neighborhood. Teachers value the neighborhoods and activity surrounding the schools, and plan many opportunities for children to learn about their town, its daily life, and its history and culture.

Partnerships with Families

> The ideas and skills that the families bring to the school and, even more importantly, the exchange of ideas between parents and teachers, favors the development of a new way of educating, and helps teachers to view the participation of families not as a threat but as an intrinsic element of collegiality, and as the integration of different wisdoms (Spaggiari, 1998, p. 104)

Families play a unique and complex role in the pedagogical principles of the Reggio Emilia approach. From the early years of the parent-run schools, families defined the vision for their children, and, through their activism with teachers, helped to shift the issues of care and education of young children from a private familial issue to a collective, community responsibility (Edwards et al., 1998b).

The history of partnership and mutual accomplishments created a unique alliance between teachers and families—one that has endured through successive generations of families and teachers (Edwards et al., 1998b). Family involvement is grounded also in the democratic nature of institutions in Reggio Emilia. The citizens of the municipality have a strong tradition of working together to address problems, and as Edwards et al. (1998b) conclude, "ideas about participatory democracy and civic community are fundamental to what the educators in Reggio Emilia feel about their educational vision and mission" (p. 8).

Working closely with families is viewed as an essential teacher role. It is important to notice the value attributed to reciprocal relationships between teachers and families, not only in participating in program governance but in contributing valued perspectives to educational conversations. None of the curriculum models or other approaches examined in this text, in their reliance on developmental psychology (Developmental-Interaction, Kamii-DeVries, and High/Scope), instructional strategies (Direct Instruction), or didactic materials (Montessori method), envisions a curriculum that integrates the "different wisdoms" of families (Spaggiari, 1998, p. 104). Nor are the programs in Reggio Emilia, as so often in the United States, built on assumptions that families are unable to provide for the optimal development of their children. Rather, the schools of Reggio Emilia are seen as providing a valued service to the community and families by contributing to the education of the community's children.

Images of Children

> Our image of children no longer considers them as isolated and egocentric, does not see them only engaged in action with objects, does not emphasize only the cognitive aspects, does not belittle feelings or what is not logical, and does not consider with ambiguity the role of the affective domain. Instead our image of the child is rich in potential, strong, powerful, competent, and most of all, connected to adults and other children. (Malaguzzi, 1993b, p. 10)

Perhaps no aspect of the Reggio Emilia approach has challenged the thinking of educators in the United States as have the images of children. As a teacher in the United States explained about the U.S. view of children when compared to the approach of the Reggio Emilians: "[W]e are trained from early on to focus on the deficit, on what is wrong, and what needs to be fixed" (Haigh, 1997, p. 160). Children in the programs of Reggio Emilia are viewed as citizens of a community with the right to be taken seriously, respected for their intelligence and feelings, and valued for their lives in the here and now—not merely to be prepared for success with later schooling. Central to this image is the belief that children are contributing participants in the social and cultural activity of the community. Participation is broadly interpreted by the teachers in Reggio Emilia as providing opportunities for children to have multiple and varied occasions to explore, discuss, argue, and reflect on experiences with one another, and with adults.

This view of children contrasts with contemporary views of children in the United States, where the qualities of childhood are defined by children's distinctive developmental and individual "needs." As a result of their different viewpoints, teachers in Reggio Emilia envision their work with children as a shared venture, where adults and children partner in exploring, finding meaning, and understanding their world (Rinaldi, 1998).

Project Work. The teachers of Reggio Emilia place special importance on indepth project work to organize children's participation in collaborative inquiry with peers and adults. Notably, the curriculum is not planned in advance of this collaborative inquiry. Rather, a good project is one that emerges out of real questions and interests shared by a group of children and teachers (Malaguzzi, 1998).

Although each project develops in different ways, most projects begin as a result of a meeting of the teachers and *atelierista* to evaluate the possibilities of an idea. Gandini (1997a) describes the importance of these meetings as providing teachers opportunities to develop "hypotheses" or predictions about potentially fruitful areas of exploration for teachers and children, and for noticing the particular curiosities, explanations, and meaningful themes that children have recently identified. Teachers emphasize the emergent nature of planning that arises from listening to children, thinking and evaluating with other adults, and negotiating the project as it evolves (Rinaldi, 1998).

One such project, "The Wind Machine," arose from a conversation with children in a 4-year-old class (Rabitti, 1994). Children were talking about the frustrations of a balloon-blowing game, and one child exclaimed that he could invent a machine that would blow the balloons. The teachers noticed other children's interest in his idea.

After determining with the other teachers and the *atelierista* that the child's proposal for a wind machine might form an engaging topic for exploration with multiple opportunities for children and teachers to discover and pose problems about the construction of the machine, the teachers offered the idea back to interested children.

Projects usually are the work of small groups of children, rather than a whole-group experience. Four children, two boys and two girls, decided to work on planning and building a wind machine.

Discussing and Representing: Using Many Languages. In the next steps of the wind machine project, teachers and children had conversations to further explore children's thinking and plan the next steps. Discussions with children are valued by teachers as ways to stimulate children's thinking, pose challenges, share ideas with one another, and learn from children. Unlike the focused emphasis on language and literacy development in the United States, the educators of Reggio Emilia have created an appreciation for the many "languages" of children and encourage children's use of diverse materials and tools to pose questions and express understandings. Thus, teachers asked participating children to make graphic representations of their ideas for the wind machine. By representing their thinking through drawing, children had the opportunity to deepen their under-standing by translating ideas expressed through spoken language into the two-dimensional graphic language of pen and paper.

Forman (1994), whose work with teachers and children in Reggio Emilia pro-vides insights that can assist U.S. educators in understanding children's "hundred languages," explains that different media provide distinctive properties and con-straints for representing ideas. For example, by drawing their vision of a wind machine, children might be able to express complex ideas that could not be com-municated as effectively by words. At the same time, the two-dimensional nature of graphic representation poses new challenges for children as they attempt to communicate ideas about a three-dimensional object.

Learning with Adults. Learning to test, develop, and refine ideas through differ-ent media are valued as ways to encourage children's abilities to think, imagine, argue, and express feelings. Importantly, this process occurs within a context of experiences that are meaningful to children, with adults who share their curiosity and pleasure in the process. As the children evaluated their drawings of the wind machine, they decided to use the plan that provided the most details because, ac-cording to the children, it appeared to be the easiest to build (Rabitti, 1994).

As children began the work of building a model of the wind machine, they pro-ceeded by trial and error (Rabitti, 1994). When problems were encountered, the *atelierista* assisted by helping the children clarify their ideas. For example, when children encountered the problems of translating their two-dimensional drawing into a three-dimensional object, the atelierista asked children to draw the machine from different points of view in order to better understand the machine (Rabitti, 1994).

Educators from the United States have sometimes misinterpreted children's drawings, paintings, clay, and other constructive work as art products, instead of as tools for representing and communicating children's thinking. Educators have been astonished by the sophistication of children's representations. But Houk (1997), a former art teacher and coordinator of the "Hundred Languages of Chil-dren" exhibition, notes that children in the programs of Reggio Emilia have had visual training from their earliest experiences in the program—experiences com-parable to the heightened emphasis on print awareness in preschools in the United States. However, as Vea Vecchi (1998), the *atelierista* at the Diana School, explains, children's use of visual representation is far more than "aesthetic expres-sion and perceptual exploration" (p. 147). Instead, graphic representation (or chil-dren's use of other media)—similar to spoken and written language—serves as a way for children to recall, hypothesize, and communicate ideas to others.

On another occasion during the wind machine project, the *atelierista* assisted by helping children to connect pieces of the machine (Rabitti, 1994). U.S. visitors have struggled to understand the direct assistance children sometimes are given by adults when using materials and tools. Contrary to prescriptions often given teach-ers in the United States to allow children to explore the qualities and capacities of materials without adult intervention (derived primarily from Piagetian theory and promoted by an overly rigid distinction of "developmentally appropriate practice" versus "inappropriate practice"), teachers in Reggio Emilia provide direct assistance in learning how to use tools and materials. They do not want children to be limited as they attempt to represent their thinking by their experience or knowledge of the materials. As more experienced members of the community, teachers provide assistance when it allows a child's intentions, questions, and conclusions to be clearly expressed and more readily appreciated by other participants (Edwards, 1998).

Revisiting Experiences. Projects develop carefully and thoughtfully through the interaction of children, teachers, and the *atelierista* over an extended period of time. As a group of children works, the teachers observe, audiotape, videotape, and take photographs. When teachers meet with the children, teachers often bring to the group the ideas from the day before—acting as the memory for the group—so that children might "revisit" their experiences. Revisiting experiences is understood as a means for encouraging children to find patterns, unresolved questions, and new understandings that were not apparent when children were in the midst of an experience (Forman & Fyfe, 1998).

Documentation. Documentation through the gathering and analysis of audio- and videotapes of conversations, drawings, photographs, and other examples of children's work provides opportunities for teachers and children to consider emerging possibilities in a project. Gathering and interpreting evidence through a process of *documentation* is viewed as a powerful learning tool for teachers to use in theorizing about children and their learning, and in reflecting on their practice as teachers (Rinaldi, 1998). Documentation also provides a way to create "solidarity and friendship" with children (p. 95). When children observe teachers listening with great attentiveness and seeking to understand children's thinking, teachers communicate to children the value and significance of their ideas.

Teachers emphasize that documentation is not merely a record of the children's learning (Rinaldi, 1998). Rather, documentation is conceptualized as an interpretive process, allowing teachers to revisit experiences, find new meanings, develop hypotheses about children's thinking, and, as a group of teachers explained, "experience that wonderful excitement that arises when an interpretive spark provides a sliver of illumination about what has taken place, stimulating new theoretical definitions and directions for our work" (Castagnetti, Mori, Rubizzi, Strozzi, & Vecchi, 1997, p. 94).

Teachers bring transcriptions, photographs, and drawings to their daily meetings with the *atelierista* to interpret events, compare ideas, formulate new hypotheses about children's thinking, and generate new questions or provocations to challenge and extend children's understandings. The process of listening, analyzing, and planning is represented by the metaphor of the teachers catching and returning the ball thrown by the children (Edwards, 1998). Teachers attempt to identify children's hypotheses and provide responses or "provocations" that extend children's thinking, or "throw back to the children the most advanced points of their research" (Castagnetti et al., 1997, p. 95). Sustaining children's involvement, extending their abilities, and ensuring the experience is pleasurable and stimulating are essential elements of the teacher–child relationship in this delicate, dynamic, and complex process (Edwards, 1998).

One of the persistent qualities of the interplay between adults and children in project work is the deliberative and often questioning nature of teachers as they respond to children's thinking. Understandings derived from Vygotsky's zone of proximal development—the range between what a child or children can accomplish independently and what they can accomplish in the company of more experienced adults and peers—play a central role in thinking about this interplay between and among children and teachers (New, 1998). Appreciating the dynamic process of learning, teachers carefully consider how best to assist children in accomplishing more than they might on their own. This approach requires teachers to have knowledge not only of a child's (or group of children's) current developmental abilities, but to continually be aware of the child's (or children's) potential capabilities (New, 1998). Incorporating Rogoff's (1990) idea of *guided participation* in culturally valued activities, teachers view shared experiences in the company of skilled, interested adults as an important way for children to experience learning as a mutually constructed activity. Children are understood to be active participants in the process of learning; their decisions about how and with whom to learn are respected as central to the learning process (New, 1998).

As projects develop, families are kept appraised of their progress, and often contribute ideas and questions to further the project. The wind machine took several months to complete and, finally, the machine and the carefully documented process of its creation were displayed in the school for everyone to view (Rabitti, 1994). When a project is complete, teachers present the documentation in group meetings with families to share both children's and teachers' learning. Documentation is seen as a potent tool for providing families and community a detailed account of what happens in schools and a salient means for stimulating interest, dialogue, and support for young children's education (Rinaldi, 1998). In contrast to U.S. teaching practices, educational issues are not understood to be the private domain of professionals. Families and the public are valued participants in ongoing dialogue about education of the community's children.

Relationship of Theory to Practice

> The teacher ought to be intellectually curious, one who rebels against a consumeristic approach to knowledge and is willing to build upon knowledge rather than to consume it. (Rinaldi, 1994, p. 49)

When Malaguzzi (1998) was asked to name the theorists who contributed to the pedagogical philosophy of the Reggio Emilia approach, he included John Dewey, Jean Piaget, Lev Vygotsky, Erik Erikson, Urie Bronfenbrenner, Jerome Bruner, David Hawkins, and John Gardner.

From these, John Dewey provided philosophical roots for the teaching practices that evolved in Reggio Emilia (Gandini, 1997a). His view of education as both an individual and social process, where understandings are created through direct experiences that are meaningful to children, is the centerpiece of pedagogical practices. Teachers have a deep respect for children's understandings of the world, and value children as they develop and contribute to the richness of the social community.

Piaget's view of the child, who like a scientist, is engaged in serious inquiry about the world, further affirmed teachers, as they learned from their own teaching practices about children's capacities for "inquiring, ordering, and even transgressing the given schemes of meaning" (Malaguzzi, 1998, p. 81). However, the child envisioned by Piaget did not accommodate the highly valued social participation of children in the cultural and social life of the Reggio Emilian community (Malaguzzi, 1998).

The necessary social image of children was found in Vygotsky's sociocultural theory of learning and development, a perspective that attributes significance both to the social context, and to the social exchanges that occur within that context (New, 1998). Vygotsky's theory views children as learning within particular social, cultural, and historical settings; further, values and beliefs mediate how children make sense of experiences (see Chapter 7). It is a theory of learning and development that views children as members of a particular family, community, and society—each interacting with one another (Malaguzzi, 1998; New, 1998).

Malaguzzi (1998) stated, however, that the "task of theory is to help teachers understand better the nature of their problems" (p. 86) rather than organize and prescribe a view of learning and teaching or define a particular set of practices. Malaguzzi (1998) reminded U.S. educators accustomed to using theory to determine practice and define images of the child (see, for example, Kessen, 1979, 1983) that the teachers of Reggio Emilia use theoretical frameworks to shed light on educational problems, not as a determinant or prescription for practice. Instead of conceptualizing teaching as the application of theory, Malaguzzi (1998) described theories as opportunities to examine, debate, and expand on practices and values.

Unlike the U.S notion of curriculum models, developed to lessen the mistakes that teachers might make without a firm set of objectives, materials, procedures, and designated relations with children, the risks and mistakes of teachers in Reggio Emilia are viewed as part of being actively engaged with children's learning. Instead of providing assurances about the process and outcomes of teaching, Malaguzzi (1998) cautioned that certainties should be questioned, and reflection should always guide the work of the teacher. When an approach attempts to "pour ideas into teachers" so teachers can "shape the children according to prespecified objectives" (Rinaldi, 1994, p. 47), then teaching overlooks the most important element of education: the child.

It is important at this point to note the benefits attributed to discussion, debate, and conflict about children's learning. The image of teaching in Reggio Emilia is not one of the practitioner in isolation, or of teachers working within the confines of their profession, but, rather, one of reciprocal relationships with other teachers, children, families, and community. Education within a democratic society is understood to be a collective effort, wherein the most important ideas are produced by dialogue, a view that reflects the strong collective spirit of northern Italy (Edwards et al., 1998b). This collective effort differs from the use of curriculum models in the United States, where individual teachers are the primary instruments through which results are achieved (see Chapter 8).

℘ CHALLENGING U.S. BELIEFS AND PRACTICES

When educators from the United States discovered the early childhood programs of Reggio Emilia, they found many familiar beliefs, values, and teaching practices: the view of children as active learners; the contributions of materials and environment to stimulating learning; and the importance of family involvement in successful early childhood programs. As Rebecca New (1994b) so aptly observed, "many of us first became interested in Reggio Emilia because it provides such a compelling illustration of *our own* ideals of early education" (emphasis in original, p. 33).

Learning about teaching practices in the programs of Reggio Emilia has inspired U.S. teachers to reexamine the importance of carefully designed environments; rediscover project work as a means of organizing the curriculum; and experiment with documentation as a tool for teacher research (see, for example, Cadwell, 1997; Edwards et al., 1998a; Hendrick, 1997; McClow & Gillespie, 1998). However, teaching practices in the preprimary schools of Reggio Emilia have not only affirmed our ideals. The complex and evolving nature of the program, and images of the school, children, teachers, families, and community, have provoked fundamental questions about our vision for the early care and education profession and, more importantly, aspirations for our children.

Each of the enduring curriculum models or approaches considered in earlier chapters, with the exception of the Montessori method, were created in the United States. They developed to accommodate a particular set of expectations and assumptions about children, teachers, families, and the nature of early care and education. Their use has been promoted in particular social and political climates (see Chapter 1). The programs of Reggio Emilia developed from a different history, purposes, and expectations and are based on a set of pedagogical principles that provide a different context for thinking about teaching and learning.

The similarities and differences have provoked U.S. educators to learn about the Reggio Emilia approach. As so often happens with cross-cultural experiences, it has provoked self-examination of the distinctive U.S. context that created a different view of children, teachers, families, and early childhood programs.

From Curriculum Models to Flexible Approaches to a Focus on Teaching and Learning

Each of the curriculum models or approaches previously described has been derived from or closely associated with specific theories of child development and learning. Each is distinguished from another by differing theoretical frameworks, providing different guidelines and anticipated end points for informing curricular decisions.

Each operates from a predictable representation of teaching and learning—and relies on fixed interpretations of children and teachers. Each has been created and codified to be replicable in any setting and capable of reproducing its effectiveness.

In contrast, guided by a framework of pedagogical principles, the teachers of Reggio Emilia are viewed as creating theories of teaching and learning from their practice. Portraits of teachers meeting together to deliberate about teaching decisions, working closely with families and community to support children's learning, and communicating children's capabilities to stakeholders portray a much more active and complex role for teachers than the image of teaching created by early childhood curriculum models in the United States or by early childhood programs in general.

U.S. educators have been interested to learn that teachers in Reggio Emilia enter the program with little preservice education. In the early 1990s, Malaguzzi noted the program's preference for teachers who had not been formally trained for elementary classrooms (remarks to U.S. Visitors, June 7, 1991). Teachers with formal training as elementary teachers, it is believed, will be less open to the values, beliefs, and flexible practices of the Reggio Emilia approach. Recall, in contrast, program designers' preference for elementary teachers to implement the Bereiter-Engelmann model because of their greater philosophical rapport with the principles of direct instruction (see Chapter 4).

Rather than relying on preservice preparation, the Reggio Emilia approach has institutionalized opportunities for teachers to grow and develop as they work with other teachers through an elaborate system of professional development and support. Teachers work in pairs as equals, rather than the typical U.S. hierarchy of teacher and assistant, and both are viewed as continually developing teachers through study of children's learning and their teaching (much as described in Chapter 7). Expectations and opportunities for ongoing development contrast sharply with the Montessori method, where a 12-month training program provides all that teachers need to know (see Chapter 2), or the High/Scope Curriculum, where ongoing technical assistance in the model's implementation is provided by High/Scope consultants (see Chapter 5).

The documentation of project work in Reggio Emilia's programs and the resultant theorizing about children's learning are seen as essential tools for professional development. Support for this reflective aspect of teaching is provided through the unique pedagogical function of the *atelierista*, who works closely with teachers in planning projects, identifying educational "knots," or provocations that might stimulate children's thinking and exploration, and preparing documentation (Edwards, 1998). In addition to the *atelierista* located at each site, teachers are given further support from a *pedagogista*, who is responsible for supporting teachers as they question their practices and plan for their ongoing professional development. One of the important roles of the *pedagogista* is to create learning relationships with teachers, acting as the sensitive partner, listening, questioning, and responding (Filippini, 1998).

Just as there is no predetermined daily or annual agenda for children's learning, there is no set of techniques or pieces of knowledge that are pretransmitted to teachers. Instead, uncertainty, and openness to questioning and provocations caused by other points of view are valued as an essential dimension of teaching. Each week teachers are given time to work together in both small and large groups to explore their teaching. As U.S. teachers have begun to explore the Reggio Emilia approach in their own classrooms, the process of questioning and reexamining their teaching practices has been cited as the most fruitful aspect of the approach (Cadwell, 1997).

Teachers in Reggio Emilia are provided with a systematic, wide-ranging network of resources and support to create relationships with children and their families, and develop understandings about how children think and learn. And, as visitors from the United States have noticed, these supports make a difference for teachers and their work (Phillips & Bredekamp, 1998). This approach to teaching as an ongoing and collective enterprise challenges Pogrow's chapter-opening quote regarding teacher competence to develop new processes.

One of the primary questions that confronts interested U.S. educators is how resources and commitment might be directed to creating similar kinds of relationships, schedules, and expectations. Small, private programs have begun to develop the necessary structural supports to begin this approach to teaching (see, for example Cadwell, 1997; Haigh, 1997; Saltz, 1997). The question remains, however, whether larger publicly funded programs with less flexibility for substantive changes could respond to these requirements.

Teaching as Advocacy: Creating Positive Images of Children

U.S. educators are learning about the potential of publicly communicating teachers' thinking and children's learning as a tool for generating community support of the school and as advocacy for valued ways of working with young children (Forman & Fyfe, 1998). Through the persistent advocacy of teachers and parents, the infant-toddler centers and preprimary schools have become a source of great pride for the Reggio Emilia community, contributing to the city's social fabric and creating community engagement with the schools that, in turn, helps ensure the strength and effectiveness of the early childhood programs.

The programs of Reggio Emilia demonstrate the powerful nature of early childhood care and education when teachers respond to images of children that accent their strengths and competencies; invite families and communities into curriculum issues; and listen, explain, and pose problems for mutual investigation.

This dimension of teaching is viewed as central to the teacher's role as a professional, as an intellectual, and as a citizen (Rinaldi, 1998). In contrast, U.S. practitioners are socialized to rely on educational researchers and child advocates to publicize the benefits of early childhood programs. Educators in the United States are beginning to assume greater responsibility for defining the nature of quality in early childhood care and education (Bredekamp, 1987; Bredekamp & Copple, 1997). Programs in Reggio Emilia remind U.S. early childhood educators that involving the community in deliberations about the nature of programs and services for young children and their families on a regular basis over an extended period of time is essential to creating an enduring web of support (New, 1997).

Rebecca New (1998), one of the early scholars to visit Reggio Emilia, explains that the teachers of Reggio Emilia have an explicit political purpose in documenting children's strengths and competencies, and organizing the curriculum to reveal children's potential through projects that are engaging to adults. Teachers in Reggio Emilia believe the ethical responsibilities of their profession demand that children have rich, fulfilling childhoods. Their view of capable, curious children is not simply a pedagogical perspective: Its political component is intended to ensure that ample resources and high expectations are available for all children. As Bredekamp (1993) noted upon her return from visiting the early childhood programs in Reggio Emilia, "They believe viewing children as needy permits adults to do the very least for them, while recognizing children as competent requires that we provide them with the best environments and experiences possible" (p. 13). Viewing children as competent contrasts with the focus in the United States on low-income children and their perceived needs as the driving force behind increasing preschool programs and constructing curriculum based on adult determined objectives.

Gardner (1998) cautions U.S. readers, however, that it is a mistake to "romanticize" (p. xvii) the programs of Reggio Emilia, or to overlook the substantial and persistent challenges encountered in building its educational system, and the teaching practices associated with the programs. Reggio Emilians describe the decades of commitment to addressing problems, responding to changing social, political, and cultural conditions, and engaging the public in debating and creating the support necessary for building and maintaining the system of programs (Gandini, 1999; Malaguzzi, 1998). Harsh battles with the Catholic Church about who should provide for children's preschool education; political struggles at the local and national levels; and concerns that elementary schooling will undermine the early educational experiences of children have been enduring issues (Malaguzzi, 1998). Teachers and families have worked together to create support for public education for young children; viewed public debate as healthy and essential in a democratic society; created community understanding for teaching practices that are sharply distinct from the highly academic practices of Italian elementary schools; and promoted the value of expansive goals for children's education.

Early Childhood Education and the Public Schools

> If the school for young children has to be preparatory and provide continuity with the elementary school, then we as educators are already prisoners of a model that ends up a funnel. (Malaguzzi, 1998, p. 88)

The Reggio Emilia approach has evolved within programs that are distinctly separate from the highly academic Italian elementary schools. Teachers have developed and refined their approach to educating young children without the pressures of promoting economic equity or ensuring the future academic success of children as defined by the Italian school system. In a community with well-developed social services, economic prosperity, and cultural homogeneity, early education is not defined as the fulcrum for children's future academic and economic success. The approach of the teachers in Reggio Emilia, consequently, was not developed to target the deficits of particular children.

To the contrary, the approach evolved from a strong belief that the program should be based on a view of all children as having "rights" to an education (Malaguzzi, 1993a, 1998). Within this context, the approach to teaching and learning has continuously evolved, and through a vigorous system of support in each of the schools and centers, teachers are envisioned as researchers of their own teaching practice, and contributors to professional knowledge.

In contrast, curriculum models in the United States were developed to ensure that preschool programs prepared children from poor and low-income families for school success. The expansion of public prekindergarten programs and a growing emphasis on literacy in the 1990s has prompted further, more explicit linkages between preschool and elementary classrooms, creating additional pressures to view early education as formal preparation for school. Further, calls for public accountability link public funds to the use of research-based curriculum models with demonstrable results.

The endurance of the Montessori method is instructive in understanding the importance of timing, and the influence of the broader social, political, and economic contexts in relationship to the sustained popularity and usefulness of a particular curriculum model. When the Montessori method first arrived in the United States in the early 1900s, kindergarten teachers rejected the model because, in part, it did not align with the goals of progressive education, including the importance of children's curiosity, initiative, and social-emotional growth. Further, teachers were given a seemingly distant and passive role by Montessori's method, contrary to the growing appreciation for the teacher in creating the investigatory climate of the classroom. Perhaps more significant for understanding the contemporary U.S. context, when the Montessori method was imported to the United States, kindergarten experiences were not widespread nor were they invested with the economic and academic significance that preschools are today.

Yet, Montessori's method endured its initial dismissal by early childhood educators. The ability of her method to be packaged, replicated by using a set of materials, and, most important today, to provide curriculum content aligned with the academic goals of elementary schools, suggests that the life span of curriculum models may be tied less to acceptance by the profession than to the support provided by converging social, economic, and political forces.

It can be predicted that the approach taken by the teachers and community of Reggio Emilia faces a considerable challenge as an option for U.S. early educators, despite their positive response to the approach. The programs of Reggio Emilia, as well as their teachers, are expected to grow and change continuously. This approach promotes variability over time and among programs. The Reggio Emilia approach intentionally avoids production of a preset curriculum and teacher manual for the purposes of promoting uniformity—qualities that place it at odds with current U.S. trends toward academic achievement and program accountability.

The programs of Reggio Emilia may face similar challenges in Italy. International acclaim for the programs prompted a request from the Italian Ministry of

Education for Reggio Emilia's educators to create teacher development programs throughout the national education network (Municipality of Reggio Emilia, 1996b). "Going to scale" beyond the community of Reggio Emilia and introducing the philosophy of the programs in different educational contexts will test the ability of its educators to maintain their dynamic approach to teaching.

Herein lies a challenge. As more U.S. educators learn about the Reggio Emilia approach, can it retain its vitality? Or like the early history of the Developmental-Interaction approach, will prevailing forces demand compromise? And, critically, given the demands placed on very young children to succeed with the institutional expectations of public schools, is it reasonable to do otherwise?

ᴄ FOR FURTHER READING

Cadwell, L. B. (1997). *Bringing Reggio Emilia home: An innovative approach to early childhood education.* New York: Teachers College Press.

> Louise Cadwell spent a year as an intern in the schools of Reggio Emilia, and returned to the United States to become an *atelierista* in a private, independent school in St. Louis. Cadwell provides a detailed account of the challenges of implementing the approach in an U.S. program.

Edwards, C., Gandini, L., & Forman, G. (Eds.). (1998a). *The hundred languages of children: The Reggio Emilia approach—advanced reflections* (2nd ed.). Greenwich, CT: Ablex.

> An extensive collection of writings by Italian and U.S. interpreters provides the most comprehensive account of the history, philosophy, and practices of the Reggio Emilia approach.

Hendrick, J. (1997). *First steps toward teaching the Reggio way.* Upper Saddle River, NJ: Merrill/Prentice Hall.

> A book written for teachers explaining the basic elements of the approach, and describing the experiences of teachers in the United States as they have attempted to implement the teaching practices from Reggio Emilia.

Videotapes

The Amusement Park for Birds. (1994). By G. Forman & L. Gandini. Performance Press (19 The Hollow, Amherst, MA).

> This videotape provides an interesting glimpse of project work with fine examples of teachers talking about children's representations of ideas.

References

Almy, M. (1988). The early childhood educator revisited. In B. Spodek, O. N. Saracho, & D. L. Peters (Eds.), *Professionalism and the early childhood practitioner* (pp. 48–55). New York: Teachers College Press.

American Institutes for Research. (1999, November 1). *An educator's guide to schoolwide reform* [Online]. Available: http://www.aasa.org/.

American Montessori Society. (1999, December 12). [Online]. Available: http://www.amshq.org/.

Anderson, V., & Bereiter, C. (1972). Extending direct instruction to conceptual skills. In R. K. Parker (Ed.), *The preschool in action: Exploring early childhood programs* (pp. 339–350). Boston: Allyn & Bacon.

Antler, J. (1982). Progressive education and the scientific study of the child: An analysis of the Bureau of Educational Experiments. *Teachers College Record, 83,* 559–591.

Antler, J. (1987). *Lucy Sprague Mitchell: The making of a modern woman.* New Haven, CT: Yale University Press.

Apple, M. W., & Beyer, L. E. (1983). Social evaluation of curriculum. *Educational Evaluation and Policy Analysis, 5,* 425–434.

Baer, D. M. (1975). In the beginning, there was the response. In E. Ramp & G. Simb (Eds.), *Behavior analysis: Areas of research and application* (pp. 16–30). Upper Saddle River, NJ: Prentice Hall.

Barnett, W. S. (1986). Methodological issues in economic evaluation of early intervention programs. *Early Childhood Research Quarterly, 1,* 249–268.

Barnett, W. S. (1995). Long-term effects of early childhood programs on cognitive and school outcomes. *The Future of Children, 5,* 25–50.

Barnett, W. S. (1998). Long-term cognitive and academic effects of early childhood education on children in poverty. *Preventive Medicine, 27,* 204–207.

Barnett, W. S., Frede, E. C., Mobasher, H., & Mohr, P. (1987). The efficacy of public preschool programs and the relationship of program quality to program efficacy. *Educational Evaluation and Policy Analysis, 10,* 37–39.

Barone, T. E. (1992). On the demise of subjectivity in educational inquiry. *Curriculum Inquiry, 22,* 25–38.

Baxter, C. (1999, December 13). AMI/USA [Online]. Available e-mail: info@montessori-ami.org/.

Beatty, B. (1995). *Preschool education in America: The culture of young children from the Colonial era to the present.* New Haven, CT: Yale University Press.

Becker, W. C., Engelmann, S., Carnine, D. W., & Rhine, W. R. (1981). Direct instruction model. In W. R. Rhine (Ed.), *Making schools more effective: New directions from Follow Through* (pp. 95–154). New York: Academic Press.

Belsky, J. (1984). Two waves of day care research: Developmental effects and conditions of quality. In R. C. Ainslie (Ed.), *The child and the day care setting: Qualitative variations and development* (pp. 1–34). New York: Praeger.

Bentley, R. (1964). Publisher's foreword to the 1964 edition. *The Montessori method* (pp. xvii–xxii). Cambridge, MA: Robert Bentley.

Bereiter, C. (1968). A nonpsychological approach to early compensatory education. In M. Deutsch, I. Katz, & A. R. Jensen (Eds.), *Social class, race, and psychological development* (pp. 337–346). New York: Holt, Rinehart & Winston.

Bereiter, C. (1970). Designing programs for classroom use. In F. F. Karten, S. W. Cook, & J. I. Lacey (Eds.), *Psychology and the problems of society* (pp. 204–207). Washington, DC: American Psychological Society.

Bereiter, C. (1972). An academic preschool for disadvantaged children: Conclusions from evaluation studies. In J. C. Stanley (Ed.), *Preschool programs for the disadvantaged: Five experimental approaches to early childhood education* (pp. 1–21). Baltimore: The Johns Hopkins University Press.

Bereiter, C. (1986). Does direct instruction cause delinquency? *Early Childhood Research Quarterly, 1*, 289–292.

Bereiter, C. (1990). Aspects of an educational learning theory. *Review of Educational Research, 60*, 603–624.

Bereiter, C., & Engelmann, S. (1966a). Observations on the use of direct instruction with young disadvantaged children. *Journal of School Psychology, 4*(3), 55–62.

Bereiter, C., & Engelmann, S. (1966b). *Teaching disadvantaged children in the preschool.* Upper Saddle River, NJ: Prentice Hall.

Berk, L. E., & Winsler, A. (1995). *Scaffolding children's learning: Vygotsky and early childhood education.* Washington, DC: National Association for the Education of Young Children.

Berlak, A., & Berlak, H. (1981). *Dilemmas of schooling: Teaching and social change.* London: Methuen.

Berrueta-Clement, J. R., Schweinhart, L. J., Barnett, W. S., Epstein, A. S., & Weikart, D. P. (1984). *Changed lives: The effects of the Perry Preschool Program on youths through age 19.* Ypsilanti, MI: The High/Scope Press.

Biber, B. (1967a). The impact of deprivation on young children. *Childhood Education, 44*, 110–116.

Biber, B. (1967b). A learning–teaching paradigm integrating intellectual and affective processes. In E. M. Bower & W. G. Hollister (Eds.), *Behavioral science frontiers in education* (pp. 112–155). New York: John Wiley & Sons.

Biber, B. (1969). Challenges ahead for early childhood education. *Young Children, 24*, 196–205.

Biber, B. (1977a). Cognition in early childhood education: A historical perspective. In B. Spodek & H. Walberg (Eds.), *Early childhood education: Issues and insights* (pp. 41–64). Berkeley, CA: McCutchan.

Biber, B. (1977b). A developmental-interaction approach: Bank Street College of Education. In M. C. Day & R. K. Parker (Eds.), *The preschool in action: Exploring early childhood programs* (2nd ed., pp. 421–460). Boston: Allyn & Bacon.

Biber, B. (1979a). Introduction to section III: "The preschool education component of Head Start." In E. Zigler & J. Valentine (Eds.), *Project Head Start: A legacy of the War on Poverty* (pp. 155–161). New York: The Free Press.

Biber, B. (1979b). Thinking and feeling. *Young Children, 35*, 4–16.

Biber, B. (1981). The evolution of the developmental-interaction view. In E. K. Shapiro & E. Weber (Eds.), *Cognitive and affective growth: Developmental interaction* (pp. 9–30). Hillsdale, NJ: Lawrence Erlbaum.

Biber, B. (1984). *Early education and psychological development.* New Haven, CT: Yale University Press.

Biber, B. (1988). The challenge of professionalism: Integrating theory and practice. In B. Spodek, O. N. Saracho, & D. L. Peters (Eds.), *Professionalism and the early childhood practitioner* (pp. 29–47). New York: Teachers College Press.

Biber, B., & Franklin, M. B. (1967). The relevance of developmental and psychodynamic concepts to the education of the preschool child. *Journal of the American Academy of Child Psychiatry, 6,* 5–24.

Biber, B., Gilkeson, E., & Winsor, C. (1959, April). Teacher education at Bank Street College. *Personnel and Guidance Journal, 37,* 558–568.

Biber, B., Shapiro, E., & Wickens, D. (1977). *Promoting cognitive growth: A developmental interaction point of view* (2nd ed.). Washington, DC: National Association for the Education of Young Children.

Biber, B., & Snyder, A. (1948). How do we know a good teacher? *Childhood Education, 24,* 280–285.

Bissell, J. S. (1973). Planned variation in Head Start and Follow Through. In J. C. Stanley (Ed.), *Compensatory education for children ages two to eight: Recent studies of educational intervention* (pp. 63–107). Baltimore: The Johns Hopkins University Press.

Blackwell, F., & Hohmann, C. (1991). *High/Scope K-3 Curriculum Series, Science,* Ypsilanti, MI: High/Scope Press.

Blenkin, G., & Kelly, V. (1987). Education as development. In G. Blenkin & A. V. Kelly (Eds.), *Early childhood education: A developmental curriculum* (pp. 1–31). London: Paul Chapman.

Bloch, M. N. (1987). Becoming scientific and professional: An historical perspective on the aims and effects of early education. In T. S. Popkewitz (Ed.), *The formation of the school subjects: The struggle for creating an American institution* (pp. 25–62). New York: Falmer.

Bloch, M. N. (1991). Critical science and the history of child development's influence on early education research. *Early Education and Development, 2,* 95–108.

Bloch, M. N. (1992). Critical perspectives on the historical relationship between child development and early childhood education research. In S. A. Kessler & B. B. Swadener (Eds.), *Reconceptualizing the early childhood curriculum: Beginning the dialogue* (pp. 3–20). New York: Teachers College Press.

Bloom, B. S. (1964). *Stability and change in human characteristics,* New York: John Wiley & Sons.

Bodrova, E., & Leong, D. J. (1996). *Tools of the mind: The Vygotskian approach to early childhood education.* Upper Saddle River, NJ: Prentice Hall.

Bowman, B. T. (1997). New directions in higher education (pp. 107–110). In S. L. Kagan & B. T. Bowman. (Eds.), *Leadership in early care and education.* Washington, DC: National Association for the Education of Young Children.

Bowman, B. T., & Stott, F. M. (1994). Understanding development in a cultural context: The challenge for teachers. In B. L. Mallory & R. S. New (Eds.), *Diversity and developmentally appropriate practices: Challenges for early childhood education* (pp. 119–133). New York: Teachers College Press.

Bransford, J. D., Brown, A. L., & Cocking, R. R. (Eds.). (1999). *How people learn: Brain, mind, experience, and school.* Washington, DC: National Research Council.

Bredekamp, S. (Ed.). (1987). *Developmentally appropriate practice in early childhood programs serving children from birth through age 8.* Washington, DC: National Association for the Education of Young Children.

Bredekamp, S. (1991). Redeveloping early childhood education: A response to Kessler. *Early Childhood Research Quarterly, 6,* 199–209.

Bredekamp, S. (1993). Reflections on Reggio Emilia. *Young Children. 49,* 13–17.

Bredekamp, S., & Copple, C. (Eds.). (1997). *Developmentally appropriate practice in early childhood programs* (rev. ed.). Washington, DC: National Association for the Education of Young Children.

Bredekamp, S., & Willer, B. (1993). Professionalizing the field of early childhood education: Pros and cons. *Young Children, 84,* 82–84.

Bronfenbrenner, U. (1974). *A report on longitudinal evaluations of preschool programs. Is early intervention effective?* (Vol. 2). Washington, DC: U.S. Department of Health, Education and Welfare, Office of Child Development.

Bronfenbrenner, U. (1986). Ecology of the family as a context for human development: Research perspectives. *Developmental Psychology, 22,* 723–742.

Bronfenbrenner, U. (1989). Ecological systems theory. In R. Vasta (Ed.), *Six theories of child development: Revised formulations and current issues. Annals of child development: A research annual* (Vol. 6, pp. 187–249). Greenwich, CT: JAI Press.

Bronfenbrenner, U., Kessel, F., Kessen, W., & White, S. (1986). Toward a critical social history of developmental psychology: A propaedeutic discussion. *American Psychologist, 41,* 1218–1230.

Bronfenbrenner, U., & Weiss, H. R. (1983). Beyond policies without people: An ecological perspective on child and family policy. In E. F. Zigler, S. L. Kagan, & E. Klugman (Eds.), *Children, families, and government: Perspectives on American social policy* (pp. 393–414). Cambridge: Cambridge University Press.

Brophy, J. E. (1979). Teacher behavior and its effects. *Journal of Educational Psychology, 71,* 733–750.

Brophy, J. E. (1986). Teacher behavior and student achievement. In M. C. Wittrock (Ed.), *Handbook of research on teaching* (3rd ed., pp. 328–375). New York: Macmillan.

Bruer, J. T. (1999a). In search of . . . brain-based education. *Phi Delta Kappan, 80,* 648–657.

Bruer, J. T. (1999b). *The myth of the first three years: A new understanding of early brain development and lifelong learning.* New York: Free Press.

Bruner, J. (1990). *Acts of meaning.* Cambridge, MA: Harvard University Press.

Bruner, J. (1996). *The culture of education.* Cambridge, MA: Harvard University Press.

Bruner, J., & Haste, H. (1987). Introduction. In J. Bruner & H. Haste (Eds.), *Making sense: The child's construction of the world* (pp. 1–25). New York: Methuen.

Buchmann, M. (1984). The use of research knowledge in teacher education and teaching. *American Journal of Education, 92,* 421–439.

Buchmann, M. (1990). *Learning and action in research reporting* [Issue Paper 90-8]. East Lansing, MI: The National Center for Research on Teacher Education.

Bukowski, W. M., Newcomb, A. F., & Hartup, W. W. (Eds.). (1998). *The company they keep: Friendship in childhood and adolescence.* London: Cambridge University Press.

Burman, E. (1994). *Deconstructing developmental psychology.* New York: Routledge.

Burts, D. C., Hart, C. H., Charlesworth, R., & Kirk, L. (1990). A comparison of frequencies of stress behaviors observed in kindergarten children in classrooms with developmentally appropriate versus developmentally inappropriate instructional practices. *Early Childhood Research Quarterly, 5,* 407–423.

Bushell, D., Jr. (1973). The behavior analysis classroom. In B. Spodek (Ed.), *Early childhood education* (pp. 163–175). Upper Saddle River, NJ: Prentice Hall.

Bushell, D., Jr. (1982). The behavior analysis model for early education. In B. Spodek (Ed.), *Handbook of research in early childhood education* (pp. 107–184). New York: The Free Press.

Butler, A. L. (1976). Today's child—Tomorrow's world. *Young Children, 32,* 4–11.

Cadwell, L. B. (1997). *Bringing Reggio Emilia home: An innovative approach to early childhood education.* New York: Teachers College Press.

Cahan, E. D. (1989). *Past caring: A history of U.S. preschool care and education for the poor. 1820–1965.* National Center for Children in Poverty, School of Public Health, Columbia University (154 Haven Avenue, New York, NY, 10032).

Cahan, E., Mechling, J., Sutton-Smith, B., & White, S. (1993). The elusive historical child: Ways of knowing the child of history and psychology. In G. H. Elder, Jr., J. Modell, & R. D. Parke (Eds.), *Children in time and place: Developmental and historical insights* (pp. 192–223). London: Cambridge University Press.

Caldwell, B. M. (1984). From the president. *Young Children, 39,* 53–56.

Caldwell, B. M. (1989). Foreword: Prologue to the past. In E. D. Cahan, *Past caring: A history of U.S. preschool care and education for the poor, 1820–1965* (pp. vii–xi). National Center for Children in Poverty, School of Public Health, Columbia University (154 Haven Avenue, New York, NY, 10032).

Campbell, D. T. (1987). Problems for the experimenting society in the interface between evaluation and service providers. In S. L. Kagan, D. R. Powell, B. Weissbourd, & E. F. Zigler (Eds.), *America's family support programs* (pp. 345–351). New Haven, CT: Yale University Press.

Cannella, G. S. (1997). *Deconstructing early childhood education: Social justice and revolution.* New York: Peter Lang.

Carlton, E., & Weikart, P. (1994). *Foundations in elementary education: Music.* Ypsilanti, MI: High/Scope Press.

Carnegie Corporation of New York. (1994). *Starting points: Meeting the needs of our youngest children.* New York: Author.

Carnegie Corporation of New York. (1996). *Years of promise: A comprehensive strategy for America's children.* New York: Author.

Carnine, D., Carnine, L., Karp, J., & Weisberg, P. (1988). Kindergarten for economically disadvantaged children: The direct instruction component. In

C. Warger (Ed.), *A resource guide to public school early childhood programs* (pp. 73–98). Alexandria, VA: Association for Supervision and Curriculum Development.

Carnine, D., Grossen, B., & Silbert, J. (1995) Direct instruction to accelerate cognitive growth. In J. H. Block, S. T. Everson, & T. R. Guskey (Eds.), *School improvement programs: A handbook for educational leaders* (pp. 289–312). New York: Scholastic Leadership Policy Research.

Carolina Abecedarian Project. (2000, January 2). [Online]. Available: http://www.fpg.unc.edu/~abc/embargoed/executive summary.htm.

Case, R., & Bereiter, C. (1984). From behaviourism to cognitive behaviourism to cognitive development: Steps in the evolution of instructional design. *Instructional Science, 13,* 141–158.

Castagnetti, M., Mori, M., Rubizzi, L., Strozzi, P., & Vecchi, V. (1997). The adventure of learning. In Municipality of Reggio Emilia, Infant-Toddler Centers and Preschools. *Scarpa e metro [Shoe and meter: Children and measurement: First approaches to the discovery, function, and use of measurement]* (pp. 94–97). Reggio Emilia, Italy: REGGIO CHILDREN S.r.l.

Cazden, C. B., & Mehan, H. (1989). Principles from sociology and anthropology: Context, code, classroom, and culture. In M. C. Reynolds (Ed.), *Knowledge base for the beginning teacher* (pp. 47–57). New York: Pergamon Press.

Ceglowski, D. (1998). *Inside a Head Start Center: Developing policies from practice.* New York: Teachers College Press.

Center for the Child Care Workforce. (1998). *Worthy work, unlivable wages.* Washington, DC: Author.

Charlesworth, R. (1998). Developmentally appropriate practice is for everyone. *Childhood Education, 74,* 274–282.

Chase-Lansdale, P. L., & Gordon, R. A. (1996). Economic hardship and the development of five- and six-year-olds: Neighborhood and regional perspectives. *Child Development, 67,* 3338–3367.

Chattin-McNichols, J. (1992a). What does research say about Montessori? In M. H. Loeffler (Ed.), *Montessori in contemporary society* (pp. 69–100). Portsmouth, NH: Heinemann.

Chattin-McNichols, J. (1992b). *The Montessori controversy.* Albany, NY: Delmar.

Cicirelli, V. (1969). *The impact of Head Start: An evaluation of the effects of Head Start on children's cognitive and affective development.* Athens, OH: Westinghouse Learning Corporation.

Cicirelli, V. G. (1984). The misinterpretation of the Westinghouse Study: A reply to Zigler and Berman. *American Psychologist, 39,* 915–917.

Clandinin, D. J., & Connelly, F. M. (1995). *Teacher's professional knowledge landscapes.* New York: Teachers College Press.

Clarke, A. M. (1984). Early experience and cognitive development. In E. W. Gordon (Ed.), *Review of research in education* (Vol. 2, pp. 125–157). Washington, DC: American Educational Research Association.

Clarke, A. M., & Clarke, A. D. B. (Eds.). (1976). *Early experience: Myth and evidence.* New York: The Free Press.

Clarke, S. H., & Campbell, F. A. (1998). Can intervention early prevent crime later? The Abecedarian project compared with other programs. *Early Childhood Research Quarterly, 13,* 319–343.

Clarke-Stewart, K. A. (1987a). In search of consistencies in child care research. In D. A. Phillips (Ed.), *Quality in child care: What does research tell us?* (pp. 105–120). Washington, DC: National Association for the Education of Young Children.

Clarke-Stewart, K. A. (1987b). Predicting child development from child care forms and features: The Chicago Study. In D. A. Phillips (Ed.), *Quality in child care: What does research tell us?* (pp. 21–41). Washington, DC: National Association for the Education of Young Children.

Clarke-Stewart, K. A. (1988). Evolving issues in early childhood education: A personal perspective. *Early Childhood Research Quarterly, 3,* 139–149.

Clarke-Stewart, K. A., & Fein, G. G. (1983). Early childhood programs. In J. Campos & M. Haith (Vol. Eds.), *Infancy and developmental psychobiology* (Vol. 2, pp. 917–999). In P. Mussen (Series Ed.), *Manual of child psychology,* 4th ed. New York: John Wiley & Sons.

Clarke-Stewart, K. A., & Gruber, C. P. (1984). Day care form and features. In R. C. Ainslie (Ed.), *The child and the day care setting: Qualitative variations and development* (pp. 35–62). New York: Praeger.

Cleverley, J., & Phillips, D.C. (1986). *Visions of childhood: Influential models from Locke to Spock.* New York: Teachers College Press.

Cochran-Smith, M. (1991). Learning to teach against the grain. *Harvard Educational Review, 61,* 279–310.

Cochran-Smith, M., & Lytle, S. L. (1993). *Inside/outside: Teacher research and knowledge.* New York: Teachers College Press.

Cochran-Smith, M., & Lytle, S. L. (1999). The teacher research movement: A decade later. *Educational Researcher, 28,* 15–25.

Cohen, D. (1975). The value of social experiments. In A. M. Rivlin & P. M. Timpane (Eds.), *Planned variation in education: Should we give up or try harder?* (pp. 147–175). Washington, DC: The Brookings Institution.

Cohen, S. (1969). Maria Montessori: Priestess or pedagogue? *Teachers College Record, 71,* 313–326.

Cole, M. (1998). *Cultural psychology: A once and future discipline.* Cambridge, MA: Belknap Press.

Cole, M., & Cole, S. R. (1996). *The development of children.* (3rd ed.). New York: W. H. Freeman.

Committee for Economic Development. (1987). *Children in need: Investment strategies for the educationally disadvantaged.* New York: Author.

Committee for Economic Development. (1991). *The unfinished agenda: A new vision for child development and education.* New York: Author.

Committee for Economic Development. (1993). *Why child care matters: Preparing young children for a more productive America.* New York: Author.

Committee of Nineteen. (1913). *The kindergarten.* Boston: Houghton Mifflin.

Condry, S. (1983). History and background of preschool intervention programs and the Consortium for Longitudinal Studies. In The Consortium for Longitudinal Studies (Ed.), *As the twig is bent . . . Lasting effects of preschool programs* (pp. 1–31). Hillsdale, NJ: Lawrence Erlbaum.

Consortium for Longitudinal Studies. (1979). *Lasting effects after preschool.* Washington, DC: U.S. Department of Health, Education and Welfare.

Consortium for Longitudinal Studies. (1983). *As the twig is bent . . . Lasting effects of preschool programs.* Hillsdale, NJ: Lawrence Erlbaum.

Copple, C., Sigel, I., & Saunders, R. (1979). *Educating the young thinker: Classroom strategies for cognitive growth.* New York: D. Van Nostrand.

Corsaro, W. (1988). Peer culture in the preschool. *Theory into Practice, 27,* 19–24.

Corsaro, W. A. (1997). *The sociology of childhood.* Thousand Oaks, CA: Pine Forge Press.

Corsaro, W. A., & Emiliani, F. (1992). Child care, early education, and children's peer culture in Italy. In M. E. Lamb, K. J. Sternberg, C. P. Hwang, & A. G. Broberg (Eds.), *Child care in context* (pp. 81–115). Hillsdale, NJ: Erlbaum.

Cost, Quality, & Child Outcomes Study Team. (1995). *Cost, quality, and child outcomes in child care centers.* Denver, CO: Department of Economics University of Colorado at Denver.

Council of Chief State School Officers. (1988). *Early childhood and family education: Foundations for success. A Council Policy Statement.* Washington, DC: Author.

Council of Chief State School Officers. (1999). *Early childhood and family education: New realities, new opportunities. A Council Policy Statement.* Washington, DC: Author.

Cravens, H. (1993). *Before Head Start: The Iowa Station & America's children.* Chapel Hill: The University of North Carolina Press.

Cremin, L. (1964). *The transformation of the school: Progressivism in American education 1876–1957.* New York: Vintage. (Originally published in 1961 by Alfred A. Knopf)

Cuban, L. (1992). Managing dilemmas while building professional communities. *Educational Researcher, 21,* 4–11.

Cuffaro, H. K. (1977). The developmental-interaction approach. In B. D. Boegehold, H. K. Cuffaro, W. H. Hooks, & G. J. Klopf (Eds.), *Education before five: A handbook on preschool education* (pp. 45–52). New York: Bank Street College of Education.

Darling-Hammond, L. (1985). Valuing teachers: The making of a profession. *Teachers College Record, 87,* 205–218.

Darling-Hammond, L. (1999). Rethinking practice and policy. In G. A. Griffin (Ed.), *The education of teachers.* The Ninety-eighth Yearbook of the National Society for the Study of Education (pp. 221–256). Chicago: University of Chicago Press.

Day, D. E. (1983). *Early childhood education: A human ecological approach.* Glenview, IL: Scott, Foresman.

Day, M. C. (1977). A comparative analysis of center-based programs. In M. C. Day & R. K. Parker (Eds.), *The preschool in action* (2nd ed., pp. 461–487). Boston: Allyn & Bacon.

Delgado-Gaitan, C. (1994). Socializing young children in Mexican-American families: An intergenerational perspective. In P. M. Greenfield & R. R. Cocking

(Eds.), *Cross-cultural roots of minority child development* (pp. 55–86). Hillsdale, NJ: Erlbaum.

Delpit, L. D. (1988). The silenced dialogue: Power and pedagogy in educating other people's children. *Harvard Educational Review, 58,* 280–298.

Delpit, L. (1995). *Other people's children: Cultural conflict in the classroom.* New York: New Press.

DeVries, R. (1970). The development of role-taking in bright, average, and retarded children as reflected in social guessing game behavior. *Child Development, 41,* 759–770.

DeVries, R. (1978). Early education and Piagetian theory: Applications versus implications. In J. M. Gallagher & J. A. Easley, Jr. (Eds.), *Knowledge and development: Piaget and education* (Vol. 2, pp. 75–92). New York: Plenum.

DeVries, R. (1984). Developmental stages in Piagetian theory and educational practice. *Teacher Education Quarterly, 11,* 78–94.

DeVries, R. (1991). The eye beholding the eye of the beholder: Reply to Gersten. *Early Childhood Research Quarterly, 6,* 539–548.

DeVries, R. (1992). Development as the aim of constructivist education: How can it be recognized in children's activity? In D. G. Murphy & S. G. Goffin (Eds.), *Project Construct: A curriculum guide. Understanding the possibilities* (pp. 15–34). Jefferson City: Missouri Department of Elementary and Secondary Education.

DeVries, R. (1993, April). Using constructivist theory and research to design a framework for curriculum and assessment. Paper presented as part of a symposium on "Translating Constructivist Theory of Research into Educational Practice." American Educational Research Association, Atlanta.

DeVries, R. (1997). Piaget's social theory. *Educational Researcher, 26,* 4–17.

DeVries, R., & Fernie, D. (1990). Stages in children's play of Tic Tac Toe. *Journal of Research in Education, 4,* 98–111.

DeVries, R., & Goncu, A. (1987). Interpersonal relations in four-year dyads from constructivist and Montessori programs. *Journal of Applied Developmental Psychology, 8,* 481–501.

DeVries, R., Haney, J. P., & Zan, B. (1991). Sociomoral atmosphere in direct-instruction, eclectic, and constructivist kindergartens: A study of teachers' enacted interpersonal understanding. *Early Childhood Research Quarterly, 6,* 449–471.

DeVries, R., & Kohlberg, L. (1987). *Programs of early education: The constructivist view.* New York: Longman. (Published in 1990 as *Constructivist education: Overview and comparison with other programs* by the National Association for the Education of Young Children)

DeVries, R., Reese-Learned, H., & Morgan, P. (1991). Sociomoral development in direct-instruction, eclectic, and constructivist kindergartens: A study of children's enacted interpersonal understanding. *Early Childhood Research Quarterly, 6,* 473–517.

DeVries, R., & Zan, B. (1994). *Moral classrooms, moral children: Creating a constructivist atmosphere in early education.* New York: Teachers College Press.

DeVries, R., & Zan, B. (1995). Creating a constructivist classroom atmosphere. *Young Children, 51,* 4–13.

Dewey, J. (1938). *Experience and education.* New York: Collier.

Dodge, D. T. (1992). *The creative curriculum for early childhood.* Washington, DC: Teaching Strategies.

Dodge, D. T. (1993). *A guide for supervisors and trainers on implementing the creative curriculum for early childhood.* Washington, DC: Teaching Strategies.

Doll, W. E., Jr. (1988). Curriculum beyond stability: Schon, Prigogine, and Piaget. In W. F. Pinar (Ed.), *Contemporary curriculum discourse* (pp. 114–133). Scottsdale, AZ: Gorsuch, Scarisbrick.

Dowley, E. M. (1971). Perspectives on early childhood education. In R. H. Anderson & H. G. Shane (Eds.), *As the twig is bent: Readings in early childhood education* (pp. 12–21). Boston: Houghton Mifflin.

Durkin, D. (1987). Testing in the kindergarten. *The Reading Teacher, 40,* 766–770.

Edwards, C. (1998). Partner, nurturer, and guide: The role of the teacher. In C. Edwards, L. Gandini, & G. Forman (Eds.), *The hundred languages of children: The Reggio approach—advanced reflections* (2nd ed., pp. 179–198). Greenwich, CT: Ablex.

Edwards, C. P., & Gandini, L. (1989). Teachers' expectations about the timing of developmental skills: A cross-cultural study. *Young Children, 44,* 15–19.

Edwards, C., Gandini, L., & Forman, G. (Eds.). (1998a). *The hundred languages of children: The Reggio approach—advanced reflections* (2nd ed.) Greenwich, CT: Ablex.

Edwards, C., Gandini, L., & Forman, G. (1998b). Introduction: Background and starting points. In C. Edwards, L. Gandini, & G. Forman (Eds.), *The hundred languages of children: The Reggio approach—advanced reflections* (2nd ed., pp. 5–25). Greenwich, CT: Ablex.

Egan, K. (1983). *Education and psychology: Plato, Piaget, and scientific psychology.* New York: Teachers College Press.

Egan, K. (1988). Metaphors in collision: Objectives, assembly lines, and stories. *Curriculum Inquiry, 18,* 63–86.

Egertson, H. A. (1987). Recapturing kindergarten for 5-year-olds. *Education Week, 6,* 19–28.

Eisner, E. (1992). Objectivity in educational research. *Curriculum Inquiry, 22,* 9–15.

Elder, G. H., Jr., Modell, J., & Parke, R. D. (Eds.). (1993). *Children in time and place: Developmental and historical insights.* London: Cambridge University Press.

Elias, M. J. (1997). *Promoting social and emotional learning: Guidelines for educators.* Alexandria, VA: Association for Supervision & Curriculum Development.

Elkind, D. (1970). The case for the academic preschool: Fact or fiction? *Young Children, 25,* 132–140.

Elkind, D. (1986). Formal education and early childhood education: An essential difference. *Phi Delta Kappan, 67,* 631–636.

Elkind, D. (1987). Early childhood education on its own terms. In S. L. Kagan & E. F. Zigler (Eds.), *Early schooling: The national debate* (pp. 98–115). New Haven, CT: Yale University Press.

Elkind, D. (1989). Developmentally appropriate practice: Philosophical and practical implications. *Phi Delta Kappan, 71,* 113–117.

Elliott, J. (1989). Educational theory and the professional learning of teachers: An overview. *Cambridge Journal of Education, 19,* 81–101.

Ellsworth, J., & Ames, L. J. (1998). Hope and challenge: Head Start past, present, future. In J. Ellsworth & L. J. Ames (Eds.), *Critical perspectives on Project Head Start: Revisioning the hope and challenge* (pp. 334–341). Albany: State University of New York Press.

Engelmann, S. (1999). A response: How sound is High/Scope research? *Educational Leadership, 56,* 83–84.

Entwisle, D. R. (1995) The role of schools in sustaining early childhood program benefits. *The Future of Children, 5,* 133–144.

Epstein, A. S., Schweinhart, L. J., & McAdoo, L. (1996). *Models of early childhood education.* Ypsilanti, MI: High/Scope Press.

Evans, E. D. (1975). *Contemporary influences in early childhood education* (2nd ed.). New York: Holt, Rinehart & Winston.

Evans, E. D. (1982). Curriculum models. In B. Spodek (Ed.), *Handbook of research in early childhood education* (pp. 107–134). New York: The Free Press.

Evans, E. D. (1985). Longitudinal follow-up assessment of differential preschool experience for low-income minority group children. *Journal of Educational Research, 78,* 197–202.

Fashola, O. S., & Slavin, R. E. (1998). Schoolwide reform models: What works? *Phi Delta Kappan, 79,* 370–379.

Fein, G., & Schwartz, P. M. (1982). Developmental theories in early education. In B. Spodek (Ed.), *Handbook of research in early childhood education* (pp. 82–104). New York: The Free Press.

Fenstermacher, G. D. (1979). A philosophical consideration of recent research on teacher effectiveness. In L. S. Shulman (Ed.), *Review of research in education* (Vol. 6, pp. 157–185). Itasca, IL: American Educational Research Journal.

Ferreiro, E., & Teberosky, A. (1982). *Literacy before schooling.* Portsmouth, NH: Heinemann. (Original work published in 1979)

Filippini, T. in collaboration with Bonilauri, S. (1998). The role of the *pedagogista:* An interview with Lella Gandini. In C. Edwards, L. Gandini, & G. Forman (Eds.), *The hundred languages of children: The Reggio Emilia approach-advanced reflections* (2nd ed., pp. 127–137). Greenwich, CT: Ablex.

Flanagan, O. (1993). *The science of the mind* (2nd ed.). Cambridge, MA: The MIT Press.

Forman, G. (1989). Helping children ask good questions. In B. Neugebauer (Ed.), *The wonder of it: Exploring how the world works* (pp. 21–24). Redmond, WA: Exchange Press.

Forman, G. (1994). Different media, different languages. In L. G. Katz & B. Cesarone (Eds.), *Reflections on the Reggio Emilia approach* (pp. 37–46). Urbana, IL: ERIC Clearinghouse on Elementary and Early Childhood Education.

Forman, G. (1995). The amusement park for birds and the fountains. In Municipality of Reggio Emilia, Infant-Toddler Centers and Preschools, *The fountains: The unheard voice of children.* Reggio Emilia, Italy: Reggio Children S.r.l.

Forman, G., & Fyfe, B. (1998). Negotiated learning through design, documentation, and discourse. In C. Edwards, L. Gandini, & G. Forman (Eds.), *The hundred languages of children: The Reggio approach—advanced reflections* (2nd ed., pp. 239–260). Greenwich, CN: Ablex.

Forman, G., & Hill, F. (1980). *Constructive play: Applying Piaget in the preschool.* Monterey, CA: Brooks/Cole.

Forman, G., & Kuschner, D. (1977). *The child's construction of knowledge: Piaget for teaching children.* Monterey, CA: Brooks/Cole.

Franklin, M. B. (1981). Perspectives on theory: Another look at the developmental-interaction point of view. In E. K. Shapiro & E. Weber (Eds.), *Cognitive and affective growth: Developmental interaction* (pp. 65–84). Hillsdale, NJ: Lawrence Erlbaum.

Franklin, M. B., & Biber, B. (1977). Psychological perspectives and early childhood education: Some relations between theory and practice. In L. G. Katz, M. Z. Glockner, S. T. Goodman, & M. J. Spencer (Eds.), *Current issues in early childhood education* (Vol. 1, pp. 1–32). Norwood, NJ: Ablex.

Frede, E. C. (1995). The role of program quality in producing early childhood program benefits. *The Future of Children 5,* 115–132.

Frede, E., & Barnett, W. S. (1992). Developmentally appropriate public school preschool: A study of implementation of the High/Scope Curriculum and its effects on disadvantaged children's skills at first grade. *Early Childhood Research Quarterly, 7,* 483–499.

The Future of Children, 5. (1995). The long-term outcome of early childhood programs [Special issue].

Galinsky, E., Howes, C., & Kontos, S., & Shinn, M. (1994). *The study of children in family child care and relative care.* New York: Families and Work Institute.

Gallagher, J. J., & Ramey, C. T. (1987). *The malleability of children.* Baltimore: Paul H. Brookes.

Gallagher, J. M., & Sigel, I.E. (Eds.). (1987). Hothousing of young children [Special issue]. *Early Childhood Research Quarterly, 2*(3).

Gandini, L. (1984, Summer). Not just anywhere: Making child care centers into "particular" places. *Beginnings: The magazine for teachers of young children,* 17–20.

Gandini, L. (1991). Not just anywhere: Making child care centers into "particular" places. *Child Care Information Exchange, 78,* 5–9.

Gandini, L. (1993). Fundamentals of the Reggio Emilia approach to early childhood education. *Young Children, 49,* 4–8.

Gandini, L. (1994). What can we learn from Reggio Emilia: An Italian–American collaboration. An interview with Amelia Gambetti and Mary Beth Radke. *Child Care Information Exchange, 96,* 62–66.

Gandini, L. (1997a). Foundations of the Reggio Emilia approach. In J. Hendrick (Ed.), *First steps toward teaching the Reggio way* (pp. 14–25). Upper Saddle River, NJ: Merrill/Prentice Hall.

Gandini, L. (1997b). The Reggio Emilia Story. In J. Hendrick, (Ed.), *First steps toward teaching the Reggio way* (pp. 2–13). Upper Saddle River, NJ: Merrill/Prentice Hall.

Gandini, L. (1998). Educational and caring spaces. In C. Edwards, L. Gandini, & G. Forman (Eds.), *The hundred languages of children: The Reggio approach—advanced reflections* (2nd ed., pp. 161–178). Greenwich, CT: Ablex.

Gandini, L. (1999, November). Learning and working together to create meaningful experiences through observation, interpretation, documentation, and projects.

Seminar at the annual conference of the National Association for the Education of Young Children, New Orleans, Lousiana.

Garcia Coll, C., Lamberty, G., Jenkins, R., McAdoo, H. P., Crnic, K., Wasik, B. H., & Garcia, H. V. (1996). An integrative model for the study of developmental competencies in minority children. *Child Development, 67,* 1891–1914.

Gardner, H. (1983). *Frames of mind: The theory of multiple intelligences.* New York: Basic Books.

Gardner, H. (1991). *The unschooled mind: How children think and how schools should teach.* New York: Basic Books.

Gardner, H. (1998). Foreword: Complementary perspectives on Reggio Emilia. In C. Edwards, L. Gandini, & G. Forman (Eds.), *The hundred languages of children: The Reggio approach—advanced reflections* (2nd ed., pp. xv–xviii). Greenwich, CT: Ablex.

Gardner, H. (1999). *The disciplined mind: What all students should understand.* New York: Simon & Schuster.

Gersten, R. (1986). Response to "Consequences of Three Preschool Curriculum Models through Age 15." *Early Childhood Research Quarterly, 1,* 293–302.

Gersten, R. (1991). The eye of the beholder: A response to "Sociomoral atmosphere . . . A study of teachers' enacted interpersonal understanding." *Early Childhood Research Quarterly, 6,* 529–537.

Gersten, R., Carnine, D., Zoref, L., & Cronin, D. (1986). A multifaceted study of change in seven inner-city schools. *The Elementary School Journal, 86,* 257–276.

Gersten, R., Darch, C., & Gleason, M. (1988). Effectiveness of a direct instruction academic kindergarten for low-income students. *The Elementary School Journal, 89,* 227–240.

Gersten, R., & George, N. (1990). Teaching reading and mathematics to at-risk students in kindergarten: What we have learned from field research. In C. Seefeldt (Ed.), *Continuing issues in early childhood education* (pp. 245–259). New York: Merrill/Macmillan.

Gilkeson, E. C., Smithberg, L. M., Bowman, G. W., & Rhine, W. R. (1981). Bank Street model: A developmental-interaction approach. In W. R. Rhine (Ed.), *Making schools more effective: New directions from Follow Through* (pp. 249–288). New York: Academic Press.

Gilligan, C. (1977). In a different voice: Women's conceptions of self and of morality. *Harvard Educational Review, 47,* 481–517.

Gilligan, C. (1988). *The origins of morality in early childhood* [Working paper series 7]. Cambridge, MA: The Project on Interdependence at Radcliffe College.

Glaser, R. (1990). The reemergence of learning theory within instructional research. *American Psychologist, 45,* 29–39.

Goffin, S. G. (1983). A framework for conceptualizing children's services. *American Journal of Orthopsychiatry, 53,* 282–290.

Goffin, S. G. (1989). Developing a research agenda for early childhood education: What can be learned from the research on teaching? *Early Childhood Research Quarterly, 4,* 187–204.

Goffin, S. G. (1993). *Curriculum models and early childhood education: Appraising the relationship.* Upper Saddle River, NJ: Merrill/Prentice Hall.

Goffin, S. G. (1996). Child development knowledge and early childhood teacher preparation: Assessing the relationship—A special collection. *Early Childhood Research Quarterly, 11,* 117–133.

Goffin, S. G. (in press). Whither early childhood care and education in the next century? In L. Corno (Ed.), *Centennial volume. National Society for the Study of Education.* Chicago: University of Chicago Press.

Goffin, S. G., & Lombardi, J. (1988). *Speaking out: Early childhood advocacy.* Washington, DC: National Association for the Education of Young Children.

Goffin, S. G., Stegelin, D. A., & Walsh, D. J. (1992). Early childhood education and the public schools [Special issue]. *Early Education and Development, 3*(2).

Goleman, D. (1995). *Emotional intelligence.* New York: Bantam Books

Goncu, A. (Ed.). (1999). *Children's engagement in the world: Sociocultural perspectives.* London: Cambridge University Press.

Goodykoontz, B., Davis, M.D., & Gabbard, H. F. (1948). Recent history and present status of education for young children. In N. B. Henry (Ed.), *Early childhood education: The forty-sixth yearbook of The National Society for the Study of Education* (Part 2, pp. 44–69). Chicago: University of Chicago Press.

Graue, M. E. (1993). *Ready for what? Constructing meanings of readiness for kindergarten.* Albany, NY: State University of New York Press.

Gray, S. W., Ramsey, B. K., & Klaus, R. A. (1982). *From 3 to 20: The Early Training Project.* Baltimore: University Park Press.

Greenberg, P. (1987). Lucy Sprague Mitchell: A major missing link between early childhood education in the 1980s and progressive education in the 1890s–1930s. *Young Children, 42,* 70–84.

Greenberg, P. (1990a). Before the beginning: A participant's view. *Young Children, 45,* 41–52.

Greenberg, P. (1990b). *The devil has slippery shoes.* Youth Policy Institute, P.O. Box 40132, Washington, DC. (Originally published in 1969 by Macmillan)

Greenberg, P. (1992). Why not academic preschool? (Part 2). Autocracy or democracy in the classroom? *Young Children, 47,* 54–64.

Greene, M. (1978). *Landscapes of learning.* New York: Teachers College Press.

Greene, M. (1988). What happened to imagination? In K. Egan & D. Nadaner (Eds.), *Imagination and education* (pp. 45–56). New York: Teachers College Press.

Greene, M. (1989). Beyond the predictable: Possibilities and purposes. In L. R. Williams & D. P. Fromberg (Eds.), *Proceedings of defining the field of early childhood education: An invitational symposium* (pp. 153–179). Charlottesville, VA: W. Alton Foundation.

Greenfield, P. M., & Cocking, R. R. (Eds.). (1994). *Cross-cultural roots of minority child development.* Hillsdale, NJ: Lawrence Erlbaum.

Greeno, J. J. (1989). A perspective on thinking. *American Psychologist, 44,* 134–141.

Gregory, B.C., Merrill, J. B., Payne, B., & Giddings, M. (Eds). (1908). *The coordination of the kindergarten and the elementary school: Seventh yearbook of the National Society for the Scientific Study of Education* (Part 2). Chicago: University of Chicago Press.

Grubb, W. N. (1987). *Young children face the states: Issues and options for early childhood programs.* Paper prepared for the Center for Policy Research in Education, Rutgers University, New Brunswick, NJ.

Grubb, W. N., & Lazerson, M. (1988). *Broken promises: How Americans fail their children.* Chicago: The University of Chicago Press.

Haberman, M. (1988). What knowledge is of most worth to teachers of young children? *Early Child Development and Care, 38,* 33–41.

Haigh, K. (1997). How the Reggio approach has influenced an inner-city program: Exploring Reggio in Head Start and subsidized child care. In J. Hendrick (Ed.), *First steps toward teaching the Reggio way* (pp. 152–166). Upper Saddle River, NJ: Merrill/Prentice Hall.

Harris, A. V. S., Kirkpatrick, E. A., Kraus-Boelte, M., Hill, P. S. Mills, H. M., & Vandewalker (1907). *The kindergarten and its relations to elementary education.* The Sixth Yearbook of the National Society for the Study of Education, Part II. Bloomington, IL: Public School Publishing Company.

Harris, J. D., & Larsen, J. M. (1989). Parent education as a mandatory component of preschool: Effects on middle class, educationally advantaged parents and children. *Early Childhood Research Quarterly, 4,* 275–287.

Hartup, W. W. (1984). Commentary: Relationships and child development. In M. Perlmutter (Ed.), *Parent–child interaction and parent–child relations in child development. The Minnesota Symposia on child psychology* (Vol. 17, pp. 177–184). Hillsdale, NJ: Lawrence Erlbaum.

Hartup, W. W. (1989). Social relationships and their developmental significance. *American Psychologist, 44,* 120–126.

Haskins, R. (1989). Beyond metaphors: The efficacy of early childhood education. *American Psychologist, 44,* 274–282.

Hauser-Cram, P. (1990). Designing meaningful evaluations of early intervention services. In S. J. Meisels & J. P. Shonkoff (Eds.), *Handbook of early childhood intervention: Theory, practice, and analysis* (pp. 583–602). Cambridge, MA: Cambridge University Press.

Hauser-Cram, P., & Shonkoff, J. P. (1988). Rethinking the assessment of child-focused outcomes. In H. B. Weiss & F. H. Jacobs (Eds.), *Evaluating family programs* (pp. 73–94). New York: Aldine DeGruyter.

Hebbeler, K. (1985). An old and a new question on the effects of early education for children from low-income families. *Educational Evaluation and Policy Analysis, 7,* 207–216.

Hendrick, J. (Ed.). (1997). *First steps toward teaching the Reggio way.* Upper Saddle River, NJ: Merrill/Prentice Hall.

Henry, A. (1996). Five black women teachers critique child-centered pedagogy: Possibilities and limitations of oppositional standpoints. *Curriculum Inquiry,* 363–384.

Hewes, D. W. (1983). (Letter to the editor.) *Young Children, 38,* 3.

Hiebert, E. H. (Ed.). (1988). Early childhood programs in public schools [Special issue]. *The Elementary School Journal, 89*(2).

High/Scope Educational Research Foundation. (1999, June 8). [Online]. Available: *http://www.highscope.org.*

High/Scope Foundation. (1991). *The Child Observation Record.* Ypsilanti, MI: High/Scope Press.

Hilgard, E. R., & Bower, G. H. (1975). *Theories of learning* (4th ed.). Upper Saddle River, NJ: Prentice Hall.

Hodges, W., Branden, A., Feldman, R., Follins, J., Love, J., Sheehan, R., Lumbley, J., Osborn, J., Rentfrow, R. K., Houston, J., & Lee, C. (1980). *Follow Through: Forces for change in the primary schools.* Ypsilanti, MI: The High/Scope Press.

Hodges, W. L., & Sheehan, R. (1978). Follow Through as ten years of experimentation: What have we learned? *Young Children, 34,* 4–18.

Hofferth, S. L. (1989). What is the demand and supply of child care in the United States? *Young Children, 44,* 28–33.

Hofferth, S. L., & Phillips, D. A. (1987). Child care in the United States, 1970 to 1995. *Journal of Marriage and the Family, 49,* 559–571.

Hohmann, C. (1991). *High/Scope curriculum series. Mathematics.* Ypsilanti, MI: High/Scope Press.

Hohmann, C., & Buckleitner, W. (1992a). *High/Scope K–3 curriculum series. Learning environment.* Ypsilanti, MI: High/Scope Press.

Hohmann, C., & Buckleitner, W. (1992b, Fall). Getting started: Opening the doors to High/Scope's K–3 approach. *High/Scope ReSource, 11,* 1, 10–13.

Hohmann, M., Banet, B., & Weikart, D. (1979). *Young children in action: A manual for preschool educators.* Ypsilanti, MI: The High/Scope Press.

Hohmann, M., & Weikart, D. P. (1995). *Educating young children: Active learning practices for preschool and child care programs.* Ypsilanti, MI: High/Scope Press.

Horowitz, F. D., & O'Brien, M. (1989). In the interest of the nation: A reflective essay on the state of our knowledge and the challenges before us. *American Psychologist, 44,* 441–445.

Horowitz, F. D., & Paden, L. Y. (1973). The effectiveness of environmental early intervention programs. In B. M. Caldwell & H. N. Ricciuti (Eds.), *Review of child development research* (Vol. 3, pp. 331–402). Chicago: The University of Chicago Press.

Houk, P. (1997). Lessons from an exhibition: Reflections of an art educator. In J. Hendrick (Ed.), *First steps toward teaching the Reggio way* (pp. 26–40). Upper Saddle River, NJ: Merrill/Prentice Hall.

House, E. R. (1990). Trends in evaluation. *Educational Researcher, 19,* 24–28.

House, E. R. (1993). *Professional evaluation: Social impact and political consequences.* Newbury Park, CA: Sage Publications.

House, E. R., & Hutchins, E. J. (1979). Issues raised by the Follow Through evaluation. In L. G. Katz, M. Z. Glockner, C. Watkins, & M. Spencer (Eds.), *Current topics in early childhood education* (Vol. 2, pp. 1–11). Norwood, NJ: Ablex.

Humphryes, J. (1998). The developmental appropriateness of high-quality Montessori programs. *Young Children, 53,* 4–16.

Hunt, J. McV. (1961). *Intelligence and experience.* New York: Ronald.

Hunt, J. McV. (1964). Introduction: Revisiting Montessori. In M. Montessori, *The Montessori method* (pp. xi–xxxix). New York: Schocken Books.

Hunter, M. (1976). Teacher competency: Problem, theory, and practice. *Theory into Practice, 15,* 162–171.

Hunter, M. (1977). A tri-dimensional approach to individualization. *Educational Leadership, 34,* 351–355.

Hunter, M. (1979). Teaching is decision making. *Educational Leadership, 37,* 62–64.

Huston, A., McLoyd, V. C., & Garcia Coll, C. (1994) Children and poverty: Issues in contemporary research. *Child Development, 65,* 275–282.

Hymes, J. L., Jr. (1978). America's first nursery schools: An interview with Abigail A. Eliot. *Early childhood education living history interviews* (Book 1, pp. 7–25). Carmel, CA: Hacienda Press.

Hymes, J. L. (1985). Head Start: Hopes and disappointments. *Young Children, 40,* 16.

Inagaki, K. (1992). Piagetian and post-Piagetian conceptions of development and their implications for science education in early childhood. *Early Childhood Research Quarterly, 7,* 115–133.

Inoway-Ronnie, E. (1998). High/Scope in Head Start programs serving Southeast Asian immigrant and refugee children and their families: Lessons from an ethnographic study. In J. Ellsworth & L. J. Ames (Eds.), *Critical perspectives on Project Head Start: Revisioning the hope and challenge* (pp. 167–199). Albany, NY: State University of New York Press.

Iran-Nejad, A., McKeachie, W. J., & Berliner, D. C. (1990a). The multisource nature of learning: An introduction. *Review of Educational Research, 60,* 509–515.

Iran-Nejad, A., McKeachie, W. J., & Berliner, D. C. (Eds.). (1990b). Toward a unified approach to learning as a multisource phenomenon [Special issue]. *Review of Educational Research, 60* (4).

Irwin-DeVitis, L., & DeVitis, J. L. (1998). What is this work called teaching? *Educational Theory, 48,* 267–278.

Issacs, S. (1966). *Intellectual growth in young children.* New York: Schocken Books. (Originally published in 1930)

Jacobs, F. (1988). The five-tiered approach to evaluation: Context and implementation. In H. B. Weiss & F. H. Jacobs (Eds.), *Evaluating family programs* (pp. 37–68). New York: Aldine DeGruyter.

James, A., Jenks, C., & Prout, A. (1998). *Theorizing childhood.* New York: Teachers College Press.

Jordan, T. J., Grallo, R., Deutsch, M., & Deutsch, C. P. (1985). Long-term effects of early enrichment: A 20-year perspective on persistence and change. *American Journal of Community Psychology, 13,* 393–415.

Kagan, J. (1983). Classifications of the child. In P. H. Mussen (Vol. Ed.), *History, theory, and methods* (Vol. 1, pp. 527–560). In W. Kessen (Series Ed.), *Handbook of child psychology* (4th ed.) New York: John Wiley & Sons.

Kagan, J. (1984). *The nature of the child.* New York: Basic Books.

Kagan, J. (1998). *Three seductive ideas.* Cambridge, MA: Harvard University Press.

Kagan, S. L. (1987). Early schooling: On what grounds? In S. L. Kagan & E. F. Zigler (Eds.). *Early schooling: The national debate* (pp. 3–23). New Haven, CT: Yale University Press.

Kagan, S. L. (1989). Early care and education: Tackling the tough issues. *Phi Delta Kappan, 70,* 433–439.

Kagan, S. L. (1990). *Excellence in early childhood education: Defining characteristics and next-decade strategies.* Washington, DC: Office of Educational Research and Improvement, U.S. Department of Education.

Kagan, S. L. (Ed.). (1991). Editor's Preface. *The care and education of America's young children: Obstacles and opportunities.* The Ninetieth Yearbook of the National Society for the Study of Education, Part I (pp. ix–xiii). Chicago: University of Chicago Press.

Kagan, S. L., & Cohen, N.E. (1997). *Not by chance: Creating an early care and education system for America's children.* Full Report, The Quality 2000 Initiative. New Haven, CT: The Bush Center in Child Development and Social Policy.

Kagan, S. L., & Garcia, E. E. (Eds.). (1991). Educating linguistically and culturally diverse preschoolers [Special issue]. *Early Childhood Research Quarterly, 6*(3).

Kagan, S. L., Powell, D. R., Weissbourd, B., & Zigler, E. F. (Eds.). (1987). *America's family support programs.* New Haven, CT: Yale University Press.

Kagan, S. L., Rosenkoetter, S., & Cohen, N. (1997). *Considering child-based results for young children: Definitions, desirability, feasibility, and next steps.* New Haven, CT: The Bush Center in Child Development and Social Policy.

Kagan, S. L., & Zigler, E.F. (Eds.). (1987) *Early schooling: The national debate.* New Haven, CT: Yale University Press.

Kamii, C. K. (1971). Evaluation of learning in preschool education: Socio-emotional, perceptual-motor, and cognitive development. In B. S. Bloom, J. T. Hastings, & G. Madaus (Eds.), *Handbook on formative and summative evaluation of student learning* (pp. 281–398). New York: McGraw-Hill.

Kamii, C. (1972). A sketch of the Piaget-derived preschool curriculum developed by the Ypsilanti Early Education Program. In S. J. Braun & E. Edwards (Eds.), *History and theory of early childhood education* (pp. 295–312). Worthington, OH: Charles A. Jones.

Kamii, C. (1975). One intelligence indivisible. *Young Children, 30,* 228–237.

Kamii, C. (1981a). Application of Piaget's theory to education: The preoperational level. In I. E. Sigel, D. M. Brodzinsky, & R. M. Golinkoff (Eds.), *New directions in Piagetian theory and practice* (pp. 231–363). Hillsdale, NJ: Lawrence Erlbaum.

Kamii, C. (1981b). Teachers' autonomy and scientific training. *Young Children, 36,* 5–14.

Kamii, C. (1982). *Number in preschool and kindergarten: Educational implications of Piaget's theory.* Washington, DC: National Association for the Education of Young Children.

Kamii, C. (1984). Autonomy: The aim of education envisioned by Piaget. *Phi Delta Kappan, 65,* 410–415.

Kamii, C. (1985). Leading primary education toward excellence. *Young Children, 40,* 3–9.

Kamii, C. (1992). Autonomy as the aim of constructivist education: How can it be fostered? In D. G. Murphy & S. G. Goffin (Eds.), *Project Construct: A curriculum guide. Understanding the possibilities* (pp. 9–14). Jefferson City: Missouri Department of Elementary and Secondary Education.

Kamii, C. (1994). *Young children continue to reinvent arithmetic, 3rd grade.* New York: Teachers College Press.

Kamii, C. (1998). The importance of a scientific theory of knowledge. *The Constructivist, 13*, 5–11.

Kamii, C. K., with DeClark, G. (1985). *Young children reinvent arithmetic: Implications of Piaget's theory* New York: Teachers College Press.

Kamii, C., & DeVries, R. (1976). *Piaget, children, and number.* Washington, DC: National Association for the Education of Young Children.

Kamii, C., & DeVries, R. (1977). Piaget for early education. In M. C. Day & R. K. Parker (Eds.), *The preschool in action: Exploring early childhood programs* (2nd ed., pp. 365–420). Boston: Allyn & Bacon.

Kamii, C., & DeVries, R. (1980). *Group games in early education: Implications of Piaget's theory.* Washington, DC: National Association for the Education of Young Children.

Kamii, C. & DeVries, R. (1993). *Physical knowledge in preschool education: Implications of Piaget's theory* (Reissued with a new introduction). New York: Teachers College Press. (Original work published in 1978)

Kamii, C., with Housman, L. B. (2000). *Young children reinvent arithmetic: Implications of Piaget's theory* (2nd ed.). New York: Teachers College Press.

Kamii, C., & Joseph, L. (1989). *Young children continue to reinvent arithmetic, 2nd grade.* New York: Teachers College Press.

Kamii, C. K., & Radin, N. L. (1967). A framework for a preschool curriculum based on some Piagetian concepts. *Journal of Creative Behavior, 1*, 314–324.

Kamii, C. K., & Radin, N. L. (1970). A framework for a preschool curriculum based on some Piagetian concepts. In I. J. Athey & D. O. Rubadeau (Eds.), *Educational implications of Piaget's theory* (pp. 89–100). Waltham, MA: Gina-Blaisdell.

Kantor, R., Elgas, P. M., Fernie, D. E. (1989). First the look and then the sound: Creating conversations at circle time. *Early Childhood Research Quarterly, 4*, 433–448.

Karmiloff-Smith, A. (1992). *Beyond modularity: A developmental perspective on cognitive science.* Cambridge, MA: The MIT Press.

Karnes, M. B., Shwedel, A. M., & Williams, M. B. (1983). A comparison of five approaches for educating young children from low-income homes. In The Consortium for Longitudinal Studies (Ed.), *As the twig is bent . . . Lasting effects of preschool programs* (pp. 133–169). Hillsdale, NJ: Lawrence Erlbaum.

Karoly, L. A., Greenwood, P. W., Everingham, S. S., Hoube, J., Kilburn, M. R., Rydell, C. P., Sanders, M., & Chiesa, J. (1998). *Investing in our children: What we know and don't know about the costs and benefits of early childhood interventions.* Santa Monica, CA: Rand.

Karweit, N. (1988). Quality and quantity of learning time in preprimary programs. *The Elementary School Journal, 89*, 119–133.

Katz, L. G. (1990). Impressions of Reggio Emilia preschools. *Young Children, 45*, 10–11.

Katz, L. G. (1991). Pedagogical issues in early childhood education. In S. L. Kagan (Ed.), *The care and education of America's young children: Obstacles and opportunities.* The Ninetieth Yearbook of the National Society for the Study of Education, Part I (pp. 79–100). Chicago: University of Chicago Press.

Kennedy, M. M. (1978). Findings from the Follow Through Planned Variation Study. *Educational Researcher, 7*, 3–11.

Kerr, D. H. (1981). The structure of quality in teaching. In J. F. Soltis (Ed.), *Philosophy and education.* The Eightieth Yearbook of the National Society for the Study of Education, Part I (pp. 61–93). Chicago: University of Chicago Press.

Kessel, F. S., & Siegel, A. W. (Eds.). (1983). *The child and other cultural inventions.* New York: Praeger.

Kessen, W. (1979). The American child and other cultural inventions. *American Psychologist, 34,* 815–820.

Kessen, W. (1983). The child and other cultural inventions. In F. S. Kessel & A. W. Siegel (Eds.), *The child and other cultural inventions* (pp. 26–47). New York: Praeger.

Kessler, S. A. (1990, April). *Early childhood education as caring.* Paper presented at the annual meeting of the American Educational Research Association, Boston.

Kessler, S. A. (1991a). Alternative perspectives on early childhood education. *Early Childhood Research Quarterly, 6,* 183–197.

Kessler, S. A. (1991b). Early childhood education as development: Critique of the metaphor. *Early Education and Development, 2,* 137–152.

Kessler, S., & Swadener, B. B. (Eds.). (1992). *Reconceptualizing the early childhood curriculum: Beginning the dialogue.* New York: Teachers College Press.

Kilpatrick, W. H. (1914). *The Montessori system examined.* Boston: Houghton Mifflin.

Kliebard, H. M. (1986). *The struggle for the American curriculum 1893–1958.* New York: Routledge.

Kohlberg, L. (1981). From *is* to *ought:* How to commit the naturalistic fallacy and get away with it in the study of moral development. In L. Kohlberg, *The philosophy of moral development: Moral stages and the idea of justice* (pp. 101–189). San Francisco: Harper & Row.

Kohlberg, L. (1984). *The psychology of moral development.* New York: Harper & Row.

Kohlberg, L., & Lickona, T. (1987). Moral discussion and the class meeting. In R. DeVries & L. Kohlberg (Eds.), *Constructivist early education: An overview and comparison with other programs* (pp. 143–181). New York: Longman. (Published in 1990 as *Constructivist education: Overview and comparison with other programs* by the National Association for the education of Young Children)

Kohlberg, L., & Mayer, R. (1972). Development as the aim of education. *Harvard Educational Review, 42,* 449–496.

Kramer, R. (1988). *Maria Montessori: A biography.* Reading, MA: Addison-Wesley. (Originally published in 1976).

Labov, W. (1969). *The study of non-standard English.* Washington, DC: ERIC Clearinghouse for Linguistics.

Lally, J. R., Mangione, P. L., Honig, A., & Wittner, D. S. (1988). More pride, less delinquency: Findings from the 10-year follow-up study of the Syracuse University Family Development Research Program. *Zero to Three, 4,* 13–18.

Lampert, M. (1985). How do teachers manage to teach? Perspectives on problems in practice. *Harvard Educational Review, 55,* 178–194.

Lampert, M. (1999). Knowing teaching from the inside out. In In G. A. Griffin (Ed.), *The education of teachers.* The Ninety-eighth Yearbook of the National Society for the Study of Education (pp. 167–184). Chicago: University of Chicago Press.

Laosa, L. M. (1982). The sociocultural context of evaluation. In B. Spodek (Ed.), *Handbook of research in early childhood education* (pp. 501–520). New York: The Free Press.

Larsen, J. M., & Robinson, C. C. (1989). Later effects of preschool on low-risk children. *Early Childhood Research Quarterly, 4,* 133–144.

Lavatelli, C. (1970). *Piaget's theory applied to an early childhood curriculum.* Boston: American Science and Engineering.

Lavatelli, C. (1971). Introduction to early childhood education series. In E. D. Evans (Ed.), *Contemporary influences in early childhood education* (pp. vii–viii). New York: Holt, Rinehart & Winston.

Lawton, J. T., & Fowell, N. (1989). A description of teacher and child language in two preschool programs. *Early Childhood Research Quarterly, 4,* 407–432.

Lazar, I. (1980). Social research and social policy: Reflections on relationships. In R. Haskins & J. J. Gallagher (Eds.), *Care and education of young children in America* (pp. 59–71). Norwood, NJ: Ablex.

Lazar, I. (1983). Discussion and implications of the findings. In the Consortium for Longitudinal Studies (Ed.), *As the twig is bent . . . Lasting effects of preschool programs* (pp. 461–466). Hillsdale, NJ: Lawrence Erlbaum.

Lazar, I. (1988). Measuring the effects of early childhood programs. *Early Childhood Family Education, 15,* 8–11.

Lazerson, M. (1970). Social reform and early childhood education: Some historical perspectives. *Urban Education, 5,* 83–102.

Lazerson, M. (1972). The historical antecedents of early childhood education. In I. J. Gordon (Ed.), *Early childhood education.* The Seventy-First Yearbook of the National Society for the Study of Education, Part 2 (pp. 33–53). Chicago: University of Chicago Press.

Lee, P. C. (1989). Is the young child egocentric or sociocentric? *Teachers College Record, 90,* 375–391.

Lee, V. E., Brooks-Gunn, J., & Schnur, E. (1988). Does Head Start work? A 1-year follow-up comparison of disadvantaged children attending Head Start, no preschool, and other preschool programs. *Developmental Psychology, 24,* 210–222.

Lee, V. E., Brooks-Gunn, J., Schnur, E., & Liaw, F-R. (1990). Are Head Start effects sustained? A longitudinal follow-up comparison of disadvantaged children attending Head Start, no preschool, and other preschool programs. *Child Development, 61,* 495–507.

Lerner, R. M. (1987). The concept of plasticity in development. In J. J. Gallagher & C. T. Ramey (Eds.), *The malleability of children* (pp. 3–14). Baltimore: Paul H. Brookes.

Levin, H. M. (1988, June). *Cost-benefit and cost-effectiveness analysis of interventions for children in poverty.* Paper presented for a Working Conference on Poverty and Children, Lawrence, KS.

Liljestrom, R. (1983). The public child, the commercial child, and our child. In F. S. Kessel & A. W. Siegel (Eds.), *The child and other cultural inventions* (pp. 124–157). New York: Praeger.

Lubeck, S. (1985). *Sandbox society: Early education in black and white America.* London: The Falmer Press.

Lubeck, S. (1994). The politics of developmentally appropriate practice: Exploring issues of culture, class, and curriculum. In B. L Mallory & R. S. New (Eds.), *Diversity and developmentally appropriate practices: Challenges for early childhood education* (pp. 17–43). New York: Teachers College Press.

Lubeck, S. (1996). Deconstructing "child development knowledge" and "teacher preparation." *Early Childhood Research Quarterly, 11,* 147–167.

Lubeck, S. (1998). Is developmentally appropriate practice for everyone? *Childhood Education, 74,* 283–298.

Maccoby, E. E., & Zellner, M. (1970). *Experiments in primary education: Aspects of Project Follow-Through.* New York: Harcourt Brace Jovanovich.

Macmillan, C. J. B., & Garrison, J. W. (1984). Using the "new philosophy of science" in criticizing current research traditions in education. *Educational Researcher, 13,* 15–21.

Maehr, J. (1991). *High/Scope K–3 curriculum series. Language and literacy.* Ypsilanti, MI: High/Scope Press.

Malaguzzi, L. (1993a). A charter of rights. In Municipality of Reggio Emilia, Infant-Toddler centers and Preschools. *A journey into the rights of children: As seen by children themselves* (pp. 67–69). Reggio Emilia, Italy: REGGIO CHILDREN S.r.l.

Malaguzzi, L. (1993b). For an education based on relationships. *Young Children, 49,* 9–12.

Malaguzzi, L. (1994a). Listening to children. *Young Children, 49,* 55.

Malaguzzi, L. (1994b). Your image of the child: Where teaching begins. *Child Care Information Exchange, 96,* 52–61.

Malaguzzi, L. (1996). The right to an environment. In Municipality of Reggio Emilia, Infant-Toddler Centers and Preschools. *The municipal infant-toddler centers and preschools of Reggio Emilia: Historical notes and general information* (p. 40). Reggio Emilia, Italy: REGGIO CHILDREN S.r.l.

Malaguzzi, L. (1998). History, ideas, and basic philosophy: An interview with Lella Gandini. In C. Edwards, L. Gandini, & G. Forman (Eds.), *The hundred languages of children: The Reggio approach—advanced reflections* (2nd ed., pp. 49–97). Greenwich, CT: Ablex.

Mallory, B. L., & New, R. S. (Eds.). (1994). *Diversity and developmentally appropriate practices: Challenges for early childhood education.* New York: Teachers College Press.

Marcon, R. A. (1992). Differential effects of three preschool models on inner-city 4-year olds. *Early Childhood Research Ouarterly, 7,* 517–530.

Marcon, R. A. (1999). Differential impact of preschool models on development and early learning of inner-city children: A three cohort study. *Developmental Psychology, 35,* 358–375.

Matusov, E. (1998). When solo activity is not privileged: Participation and internalization models of development. *Human Development, 41,* 326–349.

Mayer, R. S. (1971). A comparative analysis of preschool curriculum models. In R. H. Anderson & H. G. Shane (Eds.), *As the twig is bent. Readings in early childhood education* (pp. 286–314). Boston: Houghton Mifflin.

McClow, C. S., & Gillespie, C. W. (1998). Parental reactions to the introduction of the Reggio Emilia approach in Head Start classrooms. *Early Childhood Education Journal, 26,* 131–136.

McDermott, J. J. (1965). Introduction. In M. Montessori, *The advanced Montessori method: Spontaneous activity in education* (pp. xi–xxviii). New York: Schocken Books.

McDonald, J.P. (1992). *Teaching: Making sense of an uncertain craft.* New York: Teachers College Press.

Melton, G. B. (1987). The clashing of symbols: Prelude to child and family policy. *American Psychologist, 42,* 345–354.

Michel, S. (1999). *Children's interests/mothers' rights: The shaping of America's child care policy.* New Haven, CT: Yale University Press.

Miller, L. B. (1979). Development of curriculum models in Head Start. In E. Zigler & J. Valentine (Eds.), *Project Head Start: A legacy of the War on Poverty* (pp. 195–220). New York: The Free Press.

Miller, L. B., & Bizzell, L. P. (1983a). Long-term effects of four preschool programs: Sixth, seventh, and eighth grades. *Child Development, 54,* 727–741.

Miller, L. B., & Bizzell, L. P. (1983b). The Louisville experiment: A comparison of four programs. In The Consortium for Longitudinal Studies (Ed.), *As the twig is bent . . . Lasting effects of preschool programs* (pp. 171–199). Hillsdale, NJ: Lawrence Erlbaum.

Miller, L. B., Bugbee, M. R., & Hybertson, D. W. (1985). Dimensions of preschool: The effects of individual experience. In I. E. Siegel (Ed.), *Advances in applied developmental psychology* (Vol. 1, pp. 25–90). Norwood, NJ: Ablex.

Miller, L. B., & Dyer, J. L. (1975). Four preschool programs: Their dimensions and effects. *Monographs of the Society for Research in Child Development, 40* (5–6, Serial No. 162).

Mitchell, A., & David, J. (Eds.). (1992). *Explorations with young children: A curriculum guide from the Bank Street College of Education.* Mt. Ranier, MD: Gryphon.

Mitchell, A., with Ripple, C., & Chanana, N. (1998) *Prekindergarten programs funded by the states: Essential elements for policy makers.* New York: Families and Work Institute.

Mitchell, A., Seligson, M., & Marx, F. (1989). *Early childhood programs and the public schools: Between promise and practice.* Dover, MA: Auburn Publishing.

Moll, L., Amanti, C., Neff, D., & Gonzalez, N. (1992). Funds of knowledge for teaching: Using a qualitative approach to connect households and classrooms. *Theory into Practice, 31,* 132–141.

Montessori, M. (1913). *Pedagogical anthropology* (F. T. Cooper, Trans.). New York: Frederick A. Stokes.

Montessori, M. (1948). *The discovery of the child* (M. A. Johnstone, Trans.). Adyar, Madras, India: Kalakshetra Publications.

Montessori, M. (1963). *The absorbent mind* (C. A. Claremont, Trans.). Adyar, Madras, India: The Theosophical Publishing House. (Original work published 1949)

Montessori, M. (1964). *The advanced Montessori method: The Montessori elementary material* (A. Livingston, Trans.). New York: Schocken Books. (Original work published in English in 1917)

Montessori, M. (1964). *Dr. Montessori's own handbook.* Cambridge, MA: Robert Bentley. (Original work published 1914)

Montessori, M. (1964). *The Montessori method* (A. E. George, Trans.). New York: Schocken Books. (Original work published in English in 1912)

Montessori, M. (1965). *The advanced Montessori method: Spontaneous activity in education* (F. Simmonds, Trans.). New York: Schocken Books. (Original work published in English in 1917)

Montessori, M. (1966). *The secret of childhood* (M. Joseph Costelloe, Trans.). Notre Dame, IN: Fides (Original work published 1937)

Montessori, M. (1970). *The child in the family* (N. R. Cirillo, Trans.). Chicago: Henry Regnery. (Original work published in English in 1936)

Moore, S. G. (1977). Research in review. Old and new approaches to preschool education. *Young Children, 33,* 69–72.

Moore, S. G. (1983). Comments on Weikart's chapter. In M. Perlmutter (Ed.), *Development and policy concerning children with special needs, The Minnesota Symposia on child psychology* (Vol. 16, pp. 197–205). Hillsdale, NJ: Lawrence Erlbaum.

Morss, J. R. (1996). *Growing critical: Alternatives to developmental psychology.* New York: Routledge.

Moskovitz, S. T. (1968). Some assumptions underlying the Bereiter approach. *Young Children, 24,* 24–31.

Municipality of Reggio Emilia, Infant-Toddler Centers and Preschools. (1996a). *I centro linguaggi dei bambini [The hundred languages of children: Narrative of the possible].* Exhibit Catalog. Reggio Emilia, Italy: REGGIO CHILDREN S.r.l.

Municipality of Reggio Emilia, Infant-Toddler Centers and Preschools. (1996b). *The municipal infant-toddler centers and preschools of Reggio Emilia: Historical notes and general information.* Reggio Emilia, Italy: REGGIO CHILDREN S.r.l.

Murray, F. (1979). The generation of educational practice from developmental theory. *Educational Psychology, 14,* 30–43.

NAEYC Organizational History and Archives Committee. (1976). NAEYC's first half century, 1926–1976. *Young Children, 31,* 462–476.

National Association for the Education of Young Children and National Association of Early Childhood Specialists in State Departments of Education. (1991). Position statement: Guidelines for appropriate curriculum content and assessment in programs serving children ages 3 through 8. *Young Children, 46,* 21–38.

National Association of Elementary School Principals. (1990). *Early childhood education and the elementary school principal: Standards for quality programs for young children.* Alexandria, VA: Author.

National Association of State Boards of Education. (1988). *Right from the start.* Alexandria, VA: Author.

National Association of State Boards of Education. (1991). *Caring communities.* Alexandria, VA: Author.

National Center for Education Statistics. (1996, October). *ECE program participation for infants, toddlers and preschoolers.* Washington, DC: Author.

National Commission on Children. (1991). *Beyond rhetoric: A new American agenda for children and families.* Final report of the National Commission on Children. Washington, DC: Author.

National Research Council. (1999). *Starting out right: A guide to promoting children's reading success.* Washington, DC: National Academy Press.

Nelson, C. A., & Bloom, F. E. (1997). Child development and neuroscience. *Child Development, 68,* 970–987.

Neugebauer, B. (1994). Unpacking my questions and images: Personal reflections on Reggio Emilia. *Child Care Information Exchange, 96,* 67–70.

New, R. (1988). Parental goals and Italian infant care. In R. A. LeVine, P.M. Miller, & M. M. West (Eds.), *Parental behavior in diverse societies. New Directions for Child Development, 40,* 51–64.

New, R. (1990). Excellent early education: A city in Italy has it! *Young Children, 45,* 4–10.

New, R. S. (1994a). Culture, child development, and developmentally appropriate practices: Teachers as collaborative researchers. In B. L. Mallory & R. S. New (Eds.), *Diversity and developmentally appropriate practices: Challenges for early childhood education* (pp. 65–83). New York: Teachers College Press.

New, R. (1994b). Reggio Emilia: Its visions and its challenges for educators in the United States. In L. G. Katz & B. Cesarone (Eds.), *Reflections on the Reggio Emilia approach* (pp. 31–36). Urbana, IL: ERIC Clearinghouse on Elementary and Early Childhood Education.

New, R. S. (1997). Reggio Emilia's commitment to children and community: A reconceptualization of quality and DAP. *Canadian Children,* 7–12.

New, R. S. (1988). Theory and praxis in Reggio Emilia: They know what they are doing, and why. In C. Edwards, L. Gandini, & G. Forman (Eds.), *The hundred languages of children: The Reggio Emilia approach-advanced reflections* (2nd ed., pp. 261–284). Greenwich, CT: Ablex.

Noddings, N. (1992). *The challenge to care in schools.* New York: Teachers College Press.

Noddings, N. (1999). Caring and competence. In G. A. Griffin (Ed.), *The education of teachers.* The Ninety-eighth Yearbook of the National Society for the Study of Education (pp. 205–220). Chicago: University of Chicago Press.

North American Montessori Teacher Association. (2000, January 11). [Online]. Available: e-mail: *staff@montessori-namta.org.*

Nuthall, G., & Snook, I. (1973). Contemporary models of teaching. In R. M. W. Travers (Ed.), *The second handbook of research on teaching* (pp. 47–76). Chicago: Rand McNally.

O'Brien, L. M. (1993). Teacher values and classroom culture: Teaching and learning in a rural, Appalachian Head Start program. *Early Education and Development, 4,* 5–19.

Ogbu, J. U. (1987). Cultural influences on plasticity in human development. In J. J. Gallagher & C. T. Ramey (Eds.), *The malleability of children* (pp. 155–169). Baltimore: Paul H. Brookes.

Ogbu, J. U. (1994). From cultural differences to differences in cultural frame of reference. In P. M. Greenfield & R. R. Cocking (Eds.), *Cross-cultural roots of minority child development* (pp. 365–391). Hillsdale, NJ: Lawrence Erlbaum.

Ogbu, J. U., & Simons, H. D. (1998). Voluntary and involuntary minorities: A cultural-ecological theory of school performance with some implications for education. *Anthropology & Education Quarterly, 29,* 155–188.

Olson, L. (1998). Models for reform. *American Educator, 22,* 18–19.

Osborn, D. K. (1980). *Early childhood education in historical perspective.* Athens, GA: Education Associates.

Osborne, D., & Gaebler, D. (1993). *Reinventing government: How the entrepreneurial spirit is transforming the public sector.* New York: Plume.

Peisner-Feinberg, E., Burchinal, M. R., Clifford, R., Yazejian, N., Culkin, M. L., Zelazo, J., Howes, C., Byler, P., Kagan, S. L., & Rustici, J. (1999). *The children of the Cost, Quality and Child Outcomes Study go to school.* Chapel Hill: Frank Porter Graham National Center for Early Development and Learning, University of North Carolina at Chapel Hill.

Peters, D. L. (1977). Early childhood education: An overview and evaluation. In H. L. Hom, Jr., & P. A. Robinson (Eds.), *Psychological processes in early education* (pp. 1–21). New York: Academic Press.

Peters, D. L., Neisworth, J. T., & Yawkey, T. D. (1985). *Early childhood education: From theory to practice.* Monterey, CA: Brooks/Cole.

Phillips, C.B. (1994). The movement of African-American children through socio-cultural contexts: A case of conflict resolution. In B. L. Mallory & R. S. New (Eds.), *Diversity and developmentally appropriate practices: Challenges for early childhood education* (pp. 137–154). New York: Teachers College Press.

Phillips, C. B., & Bredekamp, S. (1998). Reconsidering early childhood education in the United States: Reflections from our encounters with Reggio Emilia. In C. Edwards, L. Gandini, & G. Forman (Eds.), *The hundred languages of children: The Reggio approach—advanced reflections* (2nd ed., pp. 439–454). Greenwich, CT: Ablex.

Phillips, D. A. (1987). Epilogue. In D. A. Phillips (Ed.), *Quality in child care: What does research tell us?* (pp. 122–126). Washington, DC: National Association for the Education of Young Children.

Pinar, W. F. (Ed.). (1988). Introduction. *Contemporary curriculum discourses* (pp. 1–13). Scottsdale, AZ: Gorsuch Scarisbrick.

Pinar, W. (1999). *Contemporary curriculum discourses: Twenty years of JCT.* New York:Peter Lang.

Pitcher, E. (1966). An evaluation of the Montessori method in schools for young children. *Childhood Education, 42,* 489–492.

Pizzo, P. (1983). Slouching toward Bethlehem: American federal policy perspectives on children and their families. In E. F. Zigler, S. L. Kagan, & E. Klugman (Eds.), *Children, families, and government. Perspectives on American social policy* (pp. 10–32). Cambridge, MA: Cambridge University Press.

Plomin, R. (1989). Environment and genes: Determinants of behavior. *American Psychologist, 44,* 105–111.

Plomin, R. (Ed.) (1997). *Behaviorial genetics.* New York: W. H. Freeman & Co.

Pogrow, S. (1996, September 25). On scripting the classroom. *Education Week,* pp. 52, 20.

Pogrow, S. (1998). What is an exemplary program, and why should anyone care? A reaction to Slavin and Klein. *Educational Researcher, 27,* 22–29.

Polakow, V. (1986). Some reflections on the landscape of childhood and the politics of care. *Journal of Education, 168,* 7–12.

Polakow, V. (1989). Deconstructing development. *Journal of Education, 171,* 75–87.

Polakow, V. (1993). *Lives on the edge: Single mothers and their children in the other America.* Chicago: University of Chicago Press.

Postman, N. (1994). *The disappearance of childhood.* New York: Vintage. (Originally published in 1982 by Delacorte)

Powell, D. R. (1987a). Comparing preschool curricula and practices: The state of research. In S. L. Kagan & E. F. Zigler (Eds.), *Early schooling: The national debate* (pp. 190–211). New Haven, CT: Yale University Press.

Powell, D. R. (1987b). Methodological and conceptual issues in research. In S. L. Kagan, D. R. Powell, B. Weissbourd, & E. F. Zigler (Eds.), *America's family support programs* (pp. 311–328). New Haven, CT: Yale University Press.

Pratt, C. (1990). *I learn from children.* New York: Perennial Library. (Originally published in 1948)

Quintero, E. (1999). The new faces of Head Start: Learning from culturally diverse families. *Early Education and Development, 10,* 475–497.

Rabitti, G. (1994). An integrated art approach in preschool. In L. G. Katz & B. Cesarone (Eds.), *Reflections on the Reggio Emilia approach* (pp. 51–67). Urbana, IL: ERIC Clearinghouse on Elementary and Early Childhood Education.

Ramey, C. T., Bryant, D. M., & Suarez, T. M. (1985). Preschool compensatory education and the modifiability of intelligence: A critical review. In D. Ditterman (Ed.), *Current topics in intelligence* (pp. 247–298). Norwood, NJ: Ablex.

Ramey, C. T., & Ramey, S. L. (1998). Early intervention and early experience. *American Psychologist, 53,* 109–120.

Ramey, C. T., & Suarez, T. M. (1984). Early intervention and the early experience paradigm: Toward a better framework for social policy. *Journal of Children in Contemporary Society, 17,* 3–13.

Ramey, S. L., & Ramey, C. T. (in press). Early childhood experiences and developmental competence. *Investing in Children Conference volume.* New York: Sage Publishing.

Ramp, E. A., & Rhine, W. R. (1981). Behavior analysis model. In W. R. Rhine (Ed.), *Making schools more effective: New directions from Follow Through* (pp. 155–200). New York: Academic Press.

Random House. (1988). *The Random House College Dictionary* (rev. ed.). New York: Author.

Rashid, H. M. (1984). The role of case studies in the longitudinal evaluation of preschool effects: Some make it, some don't. *Dimensions, 12,* 11–14.

Read, K. (1966). *The nursery school: A human relations laboratory.* Philadelphia: W. B. Saunders.

Reese, H. W., & Overton, W. R. (1970). Models of development and theories of development. In L. R. Goulet & P. B. Bales (Eds.), *Life span developmental psychology: Research and theory* (pp. 116–145). New York: Academic Press.

Rescorla, L., Hyson, M. C., Hirsh-Pasek, K. (Eds.). (1991a). Editors' notes. Academic instruction in early childhood: Challenge or pressure? *New directions for child development* (No. 53, pp. 1–4). San Francisco: Jossey-Bass.

Rescorla, L., Hyson, M. C., Hirsh-Pasek, K. (Eds.). (1991b). Academic instruction in early childhood: Challenge or pressure? *New directions for child development* (No. 53). San Francisco: Jossey-Bass.

Reynolds, A. J. (1992). Mediated effects of preschool intervention. *Early Education and Development, 3,* 139–164.

Reynolds, A. J. (1994). Effects of a preschool plus follow-on intervention for children at risk. *Developmental Psychology, 30,* 787–804.

Reynolds, A. J. (1997). *The Chicago Child-Parent Centers: A longitudinal study of extended early childhood intervention* [Discussion Paper No. 1126-97 Online]. Madison, WI: Institute for Research on Poverty. Available: http://www.ssc.wisc.edu/irp/.

Reynolds, A. J., Mann, E., Miedel, W., & Smokowski, P. (1997). The state of early childhood intervention: Effectiveness, myths and realities, new directions. *Focus, 19,* 5–11.

Rhine, W. R. (Ed.). (1981). *Making schools more effective: New directions from Follow Through.* New York: Academic Press.

Rickover, H. G. (1959). *Education and freedom.* New York: E. P. Dutton.

Rinaldi, C. (1998). Projected curriculum constructed through documentation—progettazione: An interview with Lella Gandini. In C. Edwards, L. Gandini, & G. Forman (Eds.), *The hundred languages of children: The Reggio approach—advanced reflections* (2nd ed., pp. 113–125). Greenwich, CT: Ablex.

Rinaldi, C. (1994). Staff development in Reggio Emilia. In L. G. Katz & B. Cesarone (Eds.), *Reflections on the Reggio Emilia approach* (pp. 47–50). Urbana, IL: ERIC Clearinghouse on Elementary and Early Childhood Education.

Ripple, C. H., Gilliam, W. S., Chanana, N., & Zigler, E. (1999). Will fifty cooks spoil the broth? The debate over entrusting Head Start to the states. *American Psychologist, 54,* 327–343.

Rivlin, A. M., & Timpane, P. M. (1975). Planned variation in education: An assessment. In A. M. Rivlin & P. M. Timpane (Eds.), *Planned variation in education: Should we give up or try harder?* (pp. 1–21). Washington, DC: The Brookings Institution.

Rogers, V. R. (1970). *Teaching in the British primary school.* New York: Macmillan.

Rogoff, B. (1990). *Apprenticeship in thinking: Cognitive development in social context.* New York: Oxford University Press.

Rogoff, B., & Moreilli, G. (1989). Perspectives on children's development in cultural psychology. *American Psychologist, 44,* 343–348.

Roopnarine, J. L., & Johnson, J. E. (1999). *Approaches to early childhood education* (3rd ed.). Upper Saddle River, NJ: Merrill/Prentice Hall.

Royce, J. M., Murray, H. W., Lazar, I., & Darlington, R. B. (1982). Methods of evaluating program outcomes. In B. Spodek (Ed.), *Handbook of research in early childhood education* (pp. 618–652). New York: The Free Press.

Rutter, M. (1985). Family and school influences on cognitive development. *Journal of Child Psychology and Psychiatry, 26,* 683–704.

Rutter, M., & Rutter, M. (1993). *Developing minds: Challenge and continuity across the life span.* New York: Basic Books.

St. Pierre, R. G., & Layzer, J. I. (1998). *Improving the life chances of children in poverty: Assumptions and what we have learned* [Social Policy Report]. Society for Research in Child Development. (Available from SRCD Executive Office, University of Michigan, 505 East Huron, Suite 301, Ann Arbor, MI 48104-1522.)

Saltz, R. (1997). The Reggio Emilia influence at the University of Michigan-Dearborn Child Development Center: Challenges and change. In J. Hendrick (Ed.), *First steps toward teaching the Reggio way* (pp. 167–180). Upper Saddle River, NJ: Merrill/Prentice Hall.

Schweinhart, L. J., Barnes, H. V., & Weikart, D. P., with Barnett, W. S., & Epstein, A. S. (1993). *Significant benefits: The High/Scope Perry preschool study through age 27* (Monographs of the High/Scope Educational Research Foundation, 10). Ypsilanti, MI: High/Scope Press.

Scheffler, I. (1991). Four languages of education. *In praise of the cognitive emotions and other essays in the philosophy of education* (pp. 118–125). New York: Routledge.

Schon, D. A. (1983). *The reflective practitioner: How professionals think in practice.* New York: Basic Books.

Schon, D. A. (1987). *Educating the reflective practitioner.* San Francisco: Jossey-Bass.

Schorr, L. B. (1997). *Common purpose: Strengthening families and neighborhoods to rebuild America.* New York: Doubleday.

Schubert, W. H. (1986). *Curriculum: Perspective, paradigm, and possibility.* New York: Macmillan.

Schulman, K., Blank, H., & Ewen, D. (1999). *Seeds of success: State prekindergarten initiatives 1998–1999.* Washington, DC: The Children's Defense Fund.

Schwandt, T. A. (1989). Recapturing the moral discourse in evaluation. *Educational Researcher, 18,* 11–16, 35.

Schweinhart, L. J. (1987, Spring–Summer). Child-initiated activity: How important is it in early childhood education? *High/Scope ReSource, 6,* 1, 6–10.

Schweinhart, L. J., & McNair, S. (1991). New Child Observation Record (COR) for ages 2 1/2–6. *High/Scope ReSource. 10,* 4–7.

Schweinhart, L. J., & Weikart, D. P. (1985). Evidence that good early childhood programs work. *Phi Delta Kappan, 66,* 545–553.

Schweinhart, L. J., & Weikart, D. P. (1993). Changed lives, significant benefits: The High/Scope Perry Preschool project to date. *High/Scope ReSource, 12,* 1, 10–14.

Schweinhart, L. J., & Weikart, L. J. (1997a). The High/Scope preschool curriculum comparison study through age 23. *Early Childhood Research Quarterly, 7,* 117–143.

Schweinhart, L. J., & Weikart, L. J. (1997b). *Lasting differences: The High/Scope preschool curriculum comparison study through age 23.* Ypsilanti, MI: High/Scope Foundation.

Schweinhart, L. J., & Weikart, L. J. (1998). Why curriculum matters in early childhood education. *Educational Leadership, 55,* 57–60.

Schweinhart, L. J., Weikart, D. P., & Larner, M. B. (1986). Consequences of three preschool curriculum models through age 15. *Early Childhood Research Quarterly, 1,* 15–45.

Seitz, V. (1987). Outcome evaluation of family support programs: Research design alternatives to true experiments. In S. L. Kagan, D. R. Powell, B. Weissbourd, & E. F. Zigler (Eds.), *America's family support programs* (pp. 329–344). New Haven, CT: Yale University Press.

Selman, R. (1980). *The growth of interpersonal understanding.* New York: Academic Press.

Selman, R., & Kohlberg, L. (1972a). *First things: Values.* White Plains, NY: Guidance Associates.

Selman, R., & Kohlberg, L. (1972b). *A strategy for teaching values.* Pleasantville, NY: Guidance Associates.

Selman, R., Kohlberg, L., & Byrne, D. (1974a). *A strategy for teaching social reasoning.* Pleasantville, NY: Guidance Associates.

Selman, R., Kohlberg, L., & Byrne, D. (1974b). *First things: Social reasoning.* White Plains, NY: Guidance Associates.

Senge, P. M. (1990). *The fifth discipline: The art and practice of the learning organization.* New York: Doubleday.

Shapiro, E., & Biber, B. (1972). The education of young children: A developmental-interaction approach. *Teachers College Record, 74,* 55–79.

Shapiro, E., & Mitchell, A. (1992). Principles of the Bank Street approach. In A. Mitchell & J. David (Eds.), *Explorations with young children: A curriculum guide from the Bank Street College of Education.* Mt. Ranier, MD: Gryphon.

Shapiro, E. K., & Nager, N. (2000). The developmental-interaction approach to education: Retrospect and prospect. In N. Nager & E. K. Shapiro (Eds.), *Revisiting a progressive pedagogy: The developmental-interaction approach* (pp. 11–46). Albany, NY: State University of New York Press.

Shapiro, E. K., & Wallace, D. B. (1981). Developmental stage theory and the individual reconsidered. In E. K. Shapiro & E. Weber (Eds.), *Cognitive and affective growth: Developmental interaction* (pp. 111–130). Hillsdale, NJ: Lawrence Erlbaum.

Shapiro, E. K., & Weber, E. (Eds.). (1981). *Cognitive and affective growth: Developmental interaction.* Hillsdale, NJ: Lawrence Erlbaum.

Shore, R. (1997). *Rethinking the brain: New insights into early development.* New York: Families and Work Institute.

Shulman, K., Blank, H., & Ewen, D. (1999). *Seeds of success: State kindergarten initiatives 1998–1999.* Washington, DC: The Children's Defense Fund.

Shulman, L. S. (1987). Knowledge and teaching: Foundations of the new reform. *Harvard Educational Review, 57,* 1–22.

Sigel, A. W., & White, S. H. (1982). The child study movement: Early growth and development of the symbolized child. In H. R. Reese (Ed.), *Advances in child development and behavior* (Vol. 17, pp. 233–285). New York: Academic Press.

Sigel, I. (1972). Developmental theory and preschool education: Issues, problems and implication. In I. J. Gordon (Ed.), *Early childhood education.* The Seventy-first Yearbook of the National Society for the Study of Education, Part II (pp. 13–31). Chicago: The University of Chicago Press.

Sigel, I. E. (1990). Psychoeducational intervention: Future directions. *Merrill-Palmer Quarterly, 36,* 159–172.

Sigel, I. E. (1991). Preschool education: For whom and why? In L. Rescorla, M. C. Hyson, & K. Hirsh-Pasek (Eds.), *Academic instruction in early childhood: Challenge or pressure? New directions for child development* (No. 53, pp. 83–91). San Francisco: Jossey-Bass.

Silin, J. G. (1985). Authority as knowledge: A problem of professionalization. *Young Children, 40,* 41–46.

Silin, J. G. (1986). Psychology, politics, and the discourse of early childhood educators. *Teachers College Record, 87,* 611–617.

Silin, J. G. (1987). The early childhood educator's knowledge base: A reconsideration. In L. G. Katz & K. Steiner (Eds.), *Current topics in early childhood education* (Vol. 7, pp. 17–31). Norwood, NJ: Ablex.

Silin, J. G. (1988). On becoming knowledgeable professionals. In B. Spodek, O. N. Saracho, & D. L. Peters (Eds.), *Professionalism and the early childhood practitioner* (pp. 117–134). New York: Teachers College Press.

Silin, J. G. (1995). *Sex, death and the education of children: Our passion for ignorance in the age of AIDS.* New York: Teachers College Press.

Silver Ribbon Panel. (1990). *Head Start: The nation's pride, a nation's challenge.* Alexandria, VA: National Head Start Association.

Simons, J. A., & Simons, F. A. (1986). Montessori and regular preschools: A comparison. In L. G. Katz & K. Steiner (Eds.), *Current topics in early childhood education* (Vol. 6, pp. 195–223). Norwood, NJ: Ablex.

Skeels, H. M. (1966). Adult status of children with contrasting early life experiences. *Monographs of the Society for Research in Child Development, 31* (3, Serial No. 105).

Skeels, H. M., & Dye, H. B. (1939). A study of the effects of differential stimulation on mentally retarded children. *Proceedings and Addresses of the American Association on Mental Deficiency, 44,* 114–136.

Skrtic, T. (1991). The crisis in modern knowledge. *Behind special education: A critical analysis of professional and school organization* (pp. 1–24). Denver: Love.

Slavin, R. E., Madden, N. A., Dolan, L. J., Wasik, B. A. (1996). *Every child/every school: Success for All.* Thousand Oaks, CA: Corwin Press.

Smilansky, S. (1968). *The effects of sociodramatic play on disadvantaged preschool children.* New York: John Wiley & Sons.

Smylie, M. A., Bay, M., & Tozer, S. E. (1999). Preparing teachers as agents of change. In G. A. Griffin (Ed.), *The education of teachers.* The Ninety-eighth Yearbook of the National Society for the Study of Education (pp. 29–62). Chicago: University of Chicago Press.

Sonquist, H. D., & Kamii, C. K. (1967). Applying some Piagetian concepts in the classroom for the disadvantaged. *Young Children, 22,* 231–246.

Spaggiari, S. (1998). The community-teacher partnership in the governance of the schools: An interview with Lella Gandini. In C. Edwards, L. Gandini, & G. Forman (Eds.), *The hundred languages of children: The Reggio approach—advanced reflections* (2nd ed., pp. 99–112). Greenwich, CT: Ablex.

Spodek, B. (1973). *Early childhood education.* Upper Saddle River, NJ: Prentice Hall.

Spodek, B. (1977). What constitutes worthwhile educational experiences for young children? In B. Spodek (Ed.), *Teaching practices: Reexamining assumptions* (pp. 5–20). Washington, DC: National Association for the Education of Young Children.

Spodek, B. (1986). Development, values, and knowledge in the kindergarten curriculum. In B. Spodek (Ed.), *Today's kindergarten: Exploring the knowledge base. Expanding the curriculum* (pp. 32–47). New York: Teachers College Press.

Spodek, B. (1988). Conceptualizing today's kindergarten. *The Elementary School Journal, 89,* 203–211.

Spodek, B., & Walberg, H. J. (1977). Introduction: From a time of plenty. In B. Spodek & H. J. Walberg (Eds.), *Early childhood education: Issues and insights* (pp. 1–7). Berkeley, CA: McCutchan.

Stallings, J. A. (1975). Implementations and child effects of teaching practices in Follow Through classrooms. *Monograph of the Society for Research in Child Development, 40,* 7–8.

Stallings, J. A., & Stipek, D. (1986). Research on early childhood and elementary school programs. In M. C. Wittrock (Ed.), *Handbook of research on teaching* (pp. 727–753). New York: Macmillan.

Steiner, G. Y. (1981). *The futility of family policy.* Washington, DC: The Brookings Institution.

Stodolsky, S. S. (1984). Teacher evaluation: The limits of looking. *Educational Researcher, 13,* 11–18.

Stott, F., & Bowman, B. (1996). Child development knowledge: A slippery base for practice. *Early Childhood Research Quarterly, 11,* 169–183.

Suransky, V. P. (1982). *The erosion of childhood.* Chicago: University of Chicago Press.

Sutton-Smith, B. (1989). Radicalizing childhood. In L. R. Williams & D. P. Fromberg (Eds.), *Proceedings of defining the field of early childhood education: An invitational symposium* (pp. 77–151). Charlottesville, VA: W. Alton Jones Foundation.

Swadener, B. B., & Kessler, S. (Eds.). (1991a). Introduction to the special issue. *Early Education and Development, 2,* 85–94.

Swadener, B. B., & Kessler, S. (Eds.). (1991b). Reconceptualizing early childhood education [Special issue]. *Early Education and Development, 2* (2).

Takanishi, R. (1977). Federal involvement in early education (1933–1973): The need for historical perspective. In L. G. Katz (Ed.), *Current topics in early childhood education* (Vol. 1, pp. 139–163). Norwood, NJ: Ablex.

Takanishi, R. (1979). Evaluation of early childhood programs: Toward a developmental perspective. In L. G. Katz, M. Z. Glockner, C. Watkins, & M. J. Spencer (Eds.), *Current topics in early childhood education,* (Vol. 2, pp. 141–168). Norwood, NJ: Ablex.

Takanishi, R. (1981). Early childhood education and research: The changing relationship. *Theory into Practice, 20,* 86–92.

The 10 best schools in the world, and what we can learn from them. (1991, December 2). *Newsweek,* 50–59.

Tharp, R. G. (1989). Psychocultural variables and constants: Effects on teaching and learning in schools. *American Psychologist, 44,* 349–359.

Tobin, J. J., Wu, D. Y. H., & Davidson, D. H. (1989). *Preschool in three cultures.* New Haven, CT: Yale University Press.

Travers, J. R., & Light, R. J. (Eds.). (1982). *Learning from experience.* Washington, DC: National Academy Press.

U.S. Department of Education. (1986). *What works: Research about teaching and learning.* Washington, DC: Author.

U.S. Department of Education. (1991). *America 2000: An education strategy.* Washington, DC: Author.

U.S. Department of Labor, Bureau of Labor Statistics. (1999). Unpublished data.

Vandenberg, B. (1993, March). *Is development an anachronism?* Paper presented at the Society for Research in Child Development, New Orleans.

Vecchi, V. (1998). The role of the *atelierista:* An interview with Lella Gandini. In C. Edwards, L. Gandini, & G. Forman (Eds.), *The hundred languages of children: The Reggio approach—advanced reflections* (2nd ed., pp. 139–147). Greenwich, CT: Ablex.

Vinovskis, M. A. (1993). Early childhood education: Then and now. *Daedalus, 122,* 151–176.

Vygotsky, L. S. (1978). *Mind in society: The development of higher psychological processes.* Cambridge, MA: Harvard University Press.

Wallgren, C. (1990, Spring/Summer). Introducing a developmentally appropriate curriculum in the primary grades. *High/Scope ReSource, 9,* 4–10.

Walsh, D. J. (1987). Changes in kindergarten: Why here? Why now? *Early Childhood Research Quarterly, 4,* 377–391.

Walsh, D. J., Smith, M. E., Alexander, M., & Ellwein, M. C. (1993). The curriculum as mysterious and constraining: Teachers' negotiations of the first year of a pilot programme for at-risk 4-year-olds. *Journal of Curriculum Studies, 25,* 317–332.

Warger, C. (Ed.). (1988). *A resource guide to public school early childhood programs.* Alexandria, VA: Association for Supervision and Curriculum Development.

Washington, V., & Andrews, J.D. (Eds.). (1998). *Children of 2010.* Washington, DC: The National Association for the Education of Young Children.

Waters, G. A. (1998). Critical evaluation for education reform. *Education Policy Analysis Archives, 6* (20), 1–40.

Weber, E. (1969). *The kindergarten: Its encounter with educational thought in America.* New York: Teachers College Press.

Weber, E. (1970). *Early childhood education: Perspectives on change.* Worthington, OH: Charles A. Jones.

Weber, E. (1984). *Ideas influencing early childhood education: A theoretical analysis.* New York: Teachers College Press.

Weikart, D. P. (1981). Effects of different curricula in early childhood intervention. *Educational Evaluation and Policy Analysis, 3,* 25–35.

Weikart, D. P. (1983). A longitudinal view of a preschool research effort. In M. Perlmutter (Ed.), *Development and policy concerning children with special needs, The Minnesota Symposia on child psychology* (Vol. 16, pp. 175–196). Hillsdale, NJ: Lawrence Erlbaum.

Weikart, D. P. (1984). Preface. In J. R. Berrueta-Clement, L. J. Schweinhart, W. S. Barnett, A. S. Epstein, & D. P. Weikart (Eds.), *Changed lives: The effects of the Perry Preschool Program on youths through age 19.* Ypsilanti, MI: High/Scope Press.

Weikart, D. P. (1987). Curriculum quality in early education. In S. L. Kagan & E. F. Zigler (Eds.), *Early schooling: The national debate* (pp. 168–189). New Haven, CT: Yale University Press.

Weikart, D. P. (1988). Quality in early childhood education. In C. Warger (Ed.), *A resource guide to public school early childhood programs.* Alexandria, VA: Association for Supervision and Curriculum Development.

Weikart, D. P. (1989). *Quality preschool programs: A long-term social investment.* New York: Ford Foundation.

Weikart, D. P. (1990, Fall). Celebrating 20 years. *High/Scope ReSource, 9,* 11–16, 22–23.

Weikart, D. P. (1992, Winter). "The right stuff": Early childhood programs with lasting impact. *High/Scope ReSource, 11,* 1, 10–13.

Weikart, D. P. (1995). Early childhood education. In J. H. Block, S. T. Everson, & T. R. Guskey (Eds.), *School improvement programs: A handbook for educational leaders* (pp. 289–312). New York: Scholastic Leadership Policy Research.

Weikart, P., & Carlton, E. (1995). *Foundations in elementary education: Movement.* Ypsilanti, MI: High/Scope Press.

Weikart, D. P., Hohmann, C. F., & Rhine, W. R. (1981). High/Scope Cognitively Oriented Curriculum model. In W. R. Rhine (Ed.), *Making schools more effective: New directions from Follow Through* (pp. 201–247). New York: Academic Press.

Weikart, D. P., Rogers, L., Adcock, C., & McClelland, D. (1971). *The cognitively oriented curriculum: A framework for preschool teachers.* Urbana: University of Illinois.

Weikart, D. P., & Schweinhart, L. J. (1987). The High/Scope Cognitively Oriented Curriculum in early education. In J. L. Roopnarine & J. E. Johnson (Eds.), *Approaches to early childhood education* (pp. 253–268). Upper Saddle River, NJ: Merrill/Prentice Hall.

Weikart, D. P., & Schweinhart, L. (1993). The High/Scope Curriculum for early childhood care and education. In J. L. Roopnarine & J. E. Johnson (Eds.), *Approaches to early childhood education* (2nd ed., pp. 195–208). Upper Saddle River, NJ: Merrill/Prentice Hall.

Weinberg, R. A. (1979). Early childhood education and intervention: Establishing an American tradition. *American Psychologist, 34,* 912–916.

Weiss, B. (1992). Foreword. In J. Chattin-McNichols (Ed.), *The Montessori controversy* (p. iv). Albany, NY: Delmar.

Weiss, C. H. (1983). Ideology, interests, and information: The basis of policy decisions. In D. Callahan & B. Jennings (Eds.), *Ethics, the social sciences, and policy analysis* (pp. 213–245). New York: Plenum.

Weiss, H. B. (1988). Family support and educational programs: Working through ecological theories of human development. In H. B. Weiss & F. H. Jacobs (Eds.), *Evaluating family programs* (pp. 3–36). New York: Aldine DeGruyter.

Welker, R. (1991). Expertise and the teacher as expert: Rethinking a questionable metaphor. *American Educational Research Journal, 28,* 19–35.

White, K. R. (1988). Cost analysis in family support programs. In H. B. Weiss & F. H. Jacobs (Eds.), *Evaluating family programs* (pp. 429–433). New York: Aldine DeGruyter.

White, S. H. (1970). The learning theory tradition and child psychology. In P. H. Mussen (Ed.), *Carmichael's manual of child psychology* (Vol. 1, pp. 657–701). New York: John Wiley & Sons.

White, S. H. (1983a). The idea of development in developmental psychology. In R. M. Lerner (Ed.), *Developmental psychology: Historical and philosophical perspectives* (pp. 55–77). Hillsdale, NJ: Lawrence Erlbaum.

White, S. H. (1983b). Psychology as a moral science. In F. S. Kessel & A. W. Siegel (Eds.), *The child and other cultural inventions* (pp. 1–25). New York: Praeger.

White, S. H., & Buka, S. L. (1987). Early education: Programs, traditions, and policies. In E. Z. Rothkopf (Ed.), *Review of research in education* (Vol. 14, pp. 43–91). Washington, DC: American Educational Research Association.

Willer, B. (1987). *The growing crisis in child care: Quality, compensation, and affordability in early childhood programs.* Washington, DC: The National Association for the Education of Young Children.

Williams, L. R. (1977). The behavioral approach. In B. D. Boegehold, H. K. Cuffaro, W. H. Hooks, & G. J. Klopf (Eds.), *Education before five: A handbook on preschool education* (pp. 53–67). New York: Bank Street College of Education.

Williams, L. R. (1994). Developmentally appropriate practice and cultural values: A case in point. In B. L Mallory & R. S. New (Eds.), *Diversity and developmentally appropriate practices: Challenges for early childhood education* (pp. 155–165). New York: Teachers College Press.

Wilson, C. (1999). *Telling a different story: Teaching and literacy in a urban preschool.* New York: Teachers College Press.

Winsor, C. (1973). *Experimental schools revisited: Bulletins of the Bureau of Educational Experiments.* New York: Agathon Press.

Wittrock, M. C., & Lumsdaine, A. A. (1977). Instructional psychology. In M. R. Rosenzweig & L. W. Porter (Eds.), *Annual Review of Psychology* (Vol. 28, pp. 417–459). Palo Alto, CA: Annual Reviews.

Woodhead, M. (1988). When psychology informs public policy: The case of early childhood intervention. *American Psychologist, 43,* 443–454.

Woodhead, M. (1997). Psychology and the cultural construction of children's need. In A. James & A. Prout (Eds.), *Constructing and reconstructing childhood: Contemporary issues in the sociological study of childhood* (2nd ed., pp. 63–84). London: Falmer.

Yoshikawa, H. (1995). Long-term effects of early childhood programs on social outcomes and delinquency. *The Future of Children, 5,* 51–75.

Zeichner, K. M., & Liston, D. P. (1996). *Reflective teaching: An introduction.* Mahwah, NJ: Lawrence Erlbaum.

Zelizer, V. A. (1985). *Pricing the priceless child: The changing social value of children.* New York: Basic Books.

Zervignon-Hakes, A. M. (1995). Translating research findings into large-scale public programs and policy. *The Future of Children, 5,* 175–191.

Zigler, E. (1984a). Foreword. In B. Biber (Ed.), *Early education and psychological development* (pp. ix–xi). New Haven, CT: Yale University Press.

Zigler, E. (1984b). Meeting the critics on their own terms. *American Psychologist, 39,* 916–917.

Zigler, E. F. (1987). Formal schooling for four-year-olds? No. In S. L. Kagan & E. F. Zigler (Eds.), *Early schooling: The national debate* (pp. 27–44). New Haven, CT: Yale University Press.

Zigler, E., & Anderson, K. (1979). An idea whose time had come: The intellectual and political climate. In E. Zigler & J. Valentine (Eds.), *Project Head Start: A legacy of the War on Poverty* (pp. 3–19). New York: The Free Press.

Zigler, E. F., & Freedman, J. (1987). Evaluating family support programs. In S. L. Kagan, D. R. Powell, B. Weissbourd, & E. F. Zigler (Eds.), *America's family support programs* (pp. 352–361). New Haven, CT: Yale University Press.

Zigler, E. F., Kagan, S. L., & Klugman, E. (Eds.). (1983). *Children, families and government: Perspectives on American social policy* (pp. 10–32). Cambridge: Cambridge University Press.

Zigler, E., & Muenchow, S. (1992). *Head Start: The inside story of America's most successful educational experiment.* New York: Basic Books.

Zigler, E., & Styfco, S. J. (1994). Is the Perry Preschool better than Head Start? Yes and no. *Early Childhood Research Quarterly, 9,* 269–287.

Zimiles, H. (1977). A radical and regressive solution to the problem of evaluation. In L. G. Katz, M. I. Glockner, S. T. Goodman, & M. J. Spencer (Eds.), *Current topics in early childhood education* (Vol. 1, pp. 63–70). Norwood, NJ: Ablex.

Zimiles, H. (1986). Rethinking the role of research: New issues and lingering doubts in an era of expanding preschool education. *Early Childhood Research Quarterly, 1,* 189–206.

Zimiles, H. (1987). The Bank Street Approach. In J. L. Roopnarine & J. E. Johnson (Eds.), *Approaches to early childhood education* (pp. 163–178). Upper Saddle River, NJ: Merrill/Prentice Hall.

Zumwalt, K. K. (1982). Research on teaching: Policy implications for teacher education. In A. Lieberman & M. W. McLaughlin (Eds.), *Policy making in education. Eighty-first yearbook of the National Society for the Study of Education, Part I* (pp. 215–248). Chicago: University of Chicago Press.

Zumwalt, K. K. (1986). Working together to improve education. In K. K. Zumwalt (Ed.), *Improving teaching.* Alexandria: VA: Association for Supervision and Curriculum Development.

Zumwalt, K. (1989). Beginning professional teachers: The need for a curricular vision of teaching. In M. C. Reynolds (Ed.), *Knowledge base for the beginning teacher* (pp. 173–184). New York: Pergamon Press.

Index